Descartes to Derrida

For Siân and Nia Elin

Descartes to Derrida

An Introduction to European Philosophy

Peter Sedgwick

BLACKWELL
Publishers

Copyright © Peter R. Sedgwick 2001

The right of Peter R. Sedgwick to be identified as author of this work has been asserted in accordance with the Copyright, Designs and Patents Act 1988.

First published 2001

2 4 6 8 10 9 7 5 3 1

Blackwell Publishers Ltd
108 Cowley Road
Oxford OX4 1JF
UK

Blackwell Publishers Inc.
350 Main Street
Malden, Massachusetts 02148
USA

British Library Cataloguing in Publication Data
A CIP catalogue record for this book is available from the British Library.

Library of Congress Cataloging-in-Publication Data has been applied for

ISBN 0-631-20142-4 (hardback); 0-631-20143-2 (paperback)

Typeset in 10.5/12.5pt Ehrhardt
by Graphicraft Limited, Hong Kong

This book is printed on acid-free paper.

Contents

Preface

This book explores some of the central themes in European philosophy. Knowledge, metaphysics and ontology, ethics and politics are of course all interrelated. However, each theme is given particular emphasis in individual chapters. This allows the reader to perceive the distinct but connected nature of philosophical themes. Underlying and holding together this structure is the theme of the subject, or self. Thus, chapter 1 begins with Descartes's subject-centred theory of knowledge and considers the ensuing debate in the writings of Locke, Hume and Kant. The second chapter discusses the turn toward a more social and historical conception of knowledge offered by Hegel, Nietzsche, Adorno, and Horkheimer. The significance of this for our understanding of the self is also analysed. Chapter 3 provides an account of the ontological approaches of Heidegger and Deleuze and Guattari, situating their work in relation to problems raised in chapter 2. Chapter 4 explores the question of ethics in the work of the later Heidegger, Levinas and Derrida. These thinkers share an anti-humanist stance that informs their approach to the issue of subjectivity. The fifth chapter offers a consideration of some central issues in political theory as they present themselves in classical liberal thought, Althusserian Marxism, Nietzschean power theory, and the writings of Foucault and Lyotard. This chapter also includes brief considerations of Habermas's and Apel's response to Lyotard's work, and the feminist approaches to philosophy of Irigaray and Le Doeuff. Of key interest in this chapter is the political significance of views of the self. The afterword offers some comments about the nature of philosophical enquiry. If there is a tendency that is traced in this volume it is to be found in the fact that many of the thinkers discussed favour the movement away from a timeless conception of subjectivity. Most of them have in common at least one thing – that which they seek to displace.

The great majority of writers mentioned here would usually be termed 'continental' philosophers. Continental philosophers are generally contrasted with 'analytic' philosophers. Analytic philosophy can be characterized by its concern with providing a conceptual analysis of language. Such an analysis aims to show how language refers to the natural world, and hence how our beliefs about the world are justified. To this extent, it is often held that many analytic philosophers can be said to be primarily interested in formulating theories about language which concentrate upon the problems of meaning and reference. However, even from the outset no single theory of meaning or reference could be said to be characteristic of the analytic approach.[1] Additionally, we should also consider that both the later Wittgenstein and some more recent analytic philosophers have come to reject the view that language is to be understood by way of its purportedly referential function.[2] This being the case, we should rest content with the view that the analytic tradition is *loosely* characterized by way of a particular concern with language, rather than by any single thesis with regard to how to address this concern.

In contrast to the analytic approach, with its emphasis on conceptual analysis, continental thinkers could in general be said to take a more social and historical view of philosophical issues. Also, many of what, for the sake of brevity, one might call 'post-Nietzschean' continentals tend to spurn attempts to provide a 'theory' of knowledge and are suspicious of compartmentalizing philosophy. For example, to speak of studying the 'philosophy of language' as if it were a philosophical sub-discipline that was sealed from ethical, political or cultural issues would not be a view that many of these thinkers would endorse. The stylistic components of philosophical discourse, such as commonly used philosophical metaphors, may likewise be of central interest to some of these philosophers. Generally, the philosophers discussed in this book display one or more of these features. As with analytic philosophy, however, to talk in such terms is to talk in the manner of broad generalization. No matter how many definitions of continental philosophy one could offer there will always be exceptions to the rule. Perhaps this is because there is no *one* determining feature that makes a philosopher a philosopher – whether 'analytic' or 'continental'. In any case, it is unhelpful to talk about philosophy in this divisive way. This is not the place to go into detail, but it is possible that the differences that separate analytic philosophers from their continental counterparts may be as much *institutional* in nature as they are 'purely' philosophical. However, even if the two camps could be characterized as adopting radically different approaches it does not follow that they have nothing to say to each other. Necessarily, this book is situated within the context of the division just mentioned in so far as it concentrates upon the ideas of a range of continental thinkers. However, it is not so much the fact that they are 'continental' that links the majority of these philosophers as the fact that they are suspicious of an uncritical acceptance of the view that philosophical enquiry *begins* with subjectivity.

Notes

1   Thus, on the one hand, analytic thinkers like Bertrand Russell (1872–1970) and, in the early part of his career, Ludwig Wittgenstein (1889–1951) developed 'atomistic' theories of meaning. Such theories argue that sentences can be broken down into smaller parts, the meaning of which springs from their directly referring to a non-linguistic reality. In contrast, another key analytic thinker, Gottlob Frege (1848–1925), argued for a theory which holds that it is only possible to refer to objects in the world in so far as they can already be attributed a meaning, in other words that sense *precedes* reference. Although

Russell, for one, sought to negotiate between these two positions, it is clear that they imply a difference in approach that is not easily reconciled. See Bertrand Russell, 'Logical Atomism' (1924), in R. C. Marsh (ed.), *Logic and Knowledge* (London: Hyman, 1988); Ludwig Wittgenstein, *Tractatus Logico-Philosophicus* (1921), tr. D. F. Pears and B. F. McGuinnes (London: Routledge & Kegan Paul, 1961); and Gottlob Frege, 'On Sense and Reference' (1892), tr. Max Black, in A. W. Moore (ed.), *Meaning and Reference* (Oxford: Blackwell, 1993).

2   For some discussion of the later Wittgenstein see chapter 5, below. Amongst contemporary analytic philosophers, the work of Donald Davidson furnishes a good example of an approach that differs from earlier analytic accounts of meaning and reference. Indeed, Davidson reaches the point of actually abandoning the idea of reference – see, for example, his *Inquiries into Truth and Interpretation* (Oxford: Clarendon Press, 1984).

Acknowledgements

Sincere thanks are due to all my colleagues in the Philosophy Section at Cardiff for the help they have given in the writing of this book. In particular, I must single out Andrew Edgar and Christopher Norris in this regard. Over the years, discussions with Andrew and Chris have enriched my understanding of philosophy and their suggestions concerning this volume have been invaluable. Special thanks are also due to Michael Durrant, from whom I have learned a great deal (his knowledge of Aristotle has been of enormous assistance in aiding my attempts at understanding Heidegger's philosophy). Additionally, a word of thanks is due to David Skilton, Head of English, Communication and Philosophy at Cardiff, for offering some invaluable assistance when it was needed. Finally, especial thanks to my wife Siân for her enormous patience and her assistance with portions of the text.

The author and publishers gratefully acknowledge permission to reproduce extracts from the following:

Althusser, Louis, 'Ideology and Ideological State Apparatuses' from *Lenin and Philosophy and other essays* (tr. Ben Brewster). NLB, London, 1971;

Deleuze, Gilles, *The Logic of Sense* (tr. Mark Lester, with Charles Stivale). The Athlone Press, London and Columbia University Press, New York, 1990;

Heidegger, Martin, *Being and Time* (tr. John Macquarrie and Edward Robinson). Copyright © 1962 by SCM Press Ltd. Reprinted by permission of HarperCollins Publishers Inc., and Blackwell Publishers, Oxford;

Heidegger, Martin, 'Letter on Humanism' from *Martin Heidegger: Basic Writings* (ed. David Farrell Krell). Routledge, London, 1993; HarperCollins Publishers Inc., New York, 1993;

Hume, David, *A Treatise of Human Nature*, (ed. L. A. Selby-Bigge). Clarendon Press, Oxford, 1990;

Kant, Immanuel, *Critique of Pure Reason* (tr. Norman Kemp Smith). Macmillan Ltd., London and St. Martin's Press, New York, 1990;

that I have already rejected: René Descartes (1596–1650). Although much of what Descartes argued is open to question, there are nevertheless some good reasons for beginning with a cursory account of his theory of knowledge. The arguments that Descartes put forward set an important agenda for the philosophical debates about knowledge and metaphysics that occurred after him. Descartes stands as a key figure in the definition of what is called 'modern' philosophy. In order to understand much about modern philosophy, therefore, some appreciation of Descartes's thinking is essential.

As will become clear, in his *Discourse on Method* and *Meditations on First Philosophy*[3] Descartes offers a view of knowledge that has a number of important features. Foremost amongst these features are: Descartes's foundational metaphor of knowledge (his drawing of an analogy between our knowledge and the *structure* of a building) and his stress on the role that the human individual conceived as a *rational self* must play in securing the foundations of this structure. These two features imply something very specific concerning what is necessary in order for us to be in possession of something that counts as 'knowledge'. Namely that, like a building, our knowledge must rest upon secure foundations given to it by first principles and that these principles are to be found within the individual human mind.

1 Descartes, Knowledge and Certainty

In offering his theory of knowledge Descartes seeks to refute scepticism. To put it simply, a sceptic is someone who holds that nothing can be known. This is not by any means a modern view, for the ideas of sceptical philosophers have a pedigree that can be traced back as far as the third century BC to the teachings of the ancient philosopher Pyrrho of Elis.[4] Among those in closer proximity to Descartes's time, Michel de Montaigne, drawing inspiration from the writings of another sceptic, Sextus Empiricus, forcefully argued that it is impossible to know anything for certain. Arguing against this, Descartes sets himself the task of showing that there is at least one certain piece of knowledge we are safely in possession of and cannot doubt. Significantly, Descartes attempts to construct his own theory of what we know from the starting point of scepticism. Arriving at certain knowledge can be achieved, Descartes holds, by employing a 'sceptical method', which is a shorthand way of saying that one starts by doubting everything that it is possible to doubt. What Descartes therefore begins with is the kind of ground–clearing exercise that is beloved of many philosophers of various persuasions. Through subjecting all of his beliefs to doubt Descartes aims to uncover the basic, foundational principles that underlie all our knowledge. This is the starting point for the Cartesian system.[5]

Descartes begins the *Meditations* by noting that he has been struck by the large number of false beliefs he has accepted since he was a child. Following the example of sceptical thinking, he resolves to begin by demolishing all his uncritically held beliefs. Only when this has been done will it be possible, Descartes argues, to elucidate the foundations of knowledge, and thereby secure a structure upon which to build a stable and lasting science. Of course, it would in reality be rather impractical to go through all of one's beliefs and show each of them to be false. In the first place, such a course of action would, at the very least, make for a book that would be a lot longer than, and about as entertaining to read as, a telephone directory. In order for Descartes to begin his argument, however, it is, he tells us, sufficient only to bring into question *some* of his accepted beliefs. These are those beliefs that form the 'foundation' for all the rest. In other words, it is enough for Descartes to assert that his most fundamental beliefs are *not certain and can be doubted*, rather than to demonstrate that all of them are false: 'because undermining the foundations will cause what has been built upon them to crumble of its own accord, I will attack straightaway those principles which supported everything that I once believed' (Meditation 1, 60). One such foundational belief is that the evidence given to us by way of our senses is reliable. But the senses can, on occasion, deceive us, so their veracity can be doubted. Hence, Descartes dismisses the knowledge that we may gain through our senses as being a reliable basis for what we know.

Of course, there are some beliefs even of this kind that it may be very difficult to doubt: 'for example, that I am sitting here next to the fire, wearing my winter dressing gown, that I am holding this sheet of paper in my hands, and the like' (p. 60). However, even this kind of belief, says Descartes, can be questioned. For instance, how can we distinguish with certainty between being awake and asleep? Having sensations could, after all, be a product of the imagination. Descartes might be *dreaming* that he is sitting in his room in his dressing gown. Nevertheless, even if the sensation of having a body is merely a dream, perhaps there are some things that are real. Although he might be dreaming, is it not the case that the images that are seen during sleep 'could only have been produced in the likeness of true things . . . eyes, head, hands, and the whole body' (p. 61)? However, by the same token we can surely doubt the existence of these things, too: it does not follow from the fact that I have an image of something that this thing exists. Is there anything left? Perhaps, Descartes muses, there are 'certain other things', which are 'even more simple and universal' than the images presented to us in our dreams. These would be the basic 'components' out of which the dream images we have are made. These components would 'include corporeal nature in general': notions of extension, quantity, shape, size, time, place, number, etc. The dream image of a hand or a limb may be regarded as being assembled from these basic components. A hand has a shape, it occupies space (i.e. is extended), it is thought of as existing somewhere at some particular time, etc. Although the composite image may be doubted, surely the building blocks out of which it is composed may not be. If we were to accept this then we might be tempted to draw a distinction between the physical sciences (physics, astronomy, etc.) which depend upon these composite notions (they conceive of objects as having specific sizes, shapes, etc.), and other forms of knowledge (geometry, mathematics, etc.) which do not. The propositions of the mathematician, for example, are less easy to doubt than the claims of the astronomer, for the astronomer deals with composite notions (e.g. planets, which have diverse properties) whereas the mathematician does not. Whether asleep or awake these mathematical or geometrical forms of knowledge, we could argue, hold true: if we add two and three together, we get the number five, and a square always has four sides.

Levinas, Emmanuel, *Totality and Infinity* (tr. Alphonso Lingis). Duquesne University Press, Pittsburgh, 1998.

The publishers apologize for any errors or omissions in the above list and would be grateful to be notified of any corrections that should be incorporated in the next edition or reprint of this book.

1

Knowledge, Reason and Experience: Descartes, Locke, Hume and Kant

I take this from the street. I heard one of the common people say, 'he knew me right away.' Then I asked myself: What is it that the common people take for knowledge? What do they want when they want 'knowledge'? Nothing more than this: Something strange is to be reduced to something *familiar*. And we philosophers – have we really *meant* more than this when we have spoken of knowledge? What is familiar means what we are used to so that we no longer marvel at it, our everyday, some rule in which we are stuck, anything at all in which we feel at home.[1]

These are the words of the German philosopher, Friedrich Nietzsche (1844–1900), writing in 1887. On the view put forward here, the word 'knowledge' is commonly used by people to render something that is strange to them into something comfortingly familiar. In other words, when we talk of 'knowledge' we are all too often interpreting our experiences in such a way as to allow them to be placed firmly within the domain of our common, everyday understanding. Two things are striking about Nietzsche's approach here. The first is his contention that 'familiarity' can be taken as a defining characteristic of what people mean when they use the word 'knowledge'. For, he is implying, the meaning of the word can be understood from noting its role in everyday life (its use). How people use a word, it follows, is important when it comes to analysing what it means. Second, Nietzsche claims that philosophers, too, are not exempt from this condition. When philosophers speak of 'knowledge' (and thus use that word) they, too, seek to articulate what is unfamiliar to them in familiar terms. What Nietzsche is therefore inviting us to consider is the possibility that philosophers, like everyone else as he sees it, are really more interested in feeling 'at home' in the world than in attaining 'knowledge' concerning it.

Nietzsche's claim is, of course, a very sweeping and contentious one. It is, in fact, a claim that is perfectly in keeping with Nietzsche's generally provocative approach to philosophy. For Nietzsche is a thinker who is at least as much concerned with making us think again about how defensible the beliefs we may hold are as with offering us the 'right' answers to philosophical questions. This is not the place to get involved in a detailed discussion of Nietzsche (to whom I will return in due course).

Suffice it to say that whatever the merits of Nietzsche's view, it raises the question of what we mean when we talk about 'knowledge'. When philosophers talk about 'knowledge' are they, as Nietzsche seems to be suggesting, simply providing an unwitting rationalization of their own everyday beliefs? Or does philosophical talk about knowledge offer something more than this? Indeed, does Nietzsche himself perhaps offer more than this, as the above quotation implies? Surely, by alluding to the predominance of everyday rules 'in which we are stuck' is not Nietzsche himself in effect speaking in a manner that suggests we need not always be stuck in them? As a preamble to addressing such questions it is worth considering the issues philosophers concern themselves with when they talk about knowledge. Equally, such a consideration requires that some important terms and distinctions within philosophical talk about knowledge are also made clear.

As must by now be apparent, 'theory of knowledge', or 'epistemology' as it is often called,[2] is a domain of philosophical enquiry which concerns itself with a number of issues relating to (1) how we know things and (2) how reliable our knowledge is. Most obviously, then, to engage in epistemological enquiry means both raising questions and offering possible explanations about what the word 'knowledge' means. This, in turn, involves offering some definitions of knowledge. Further to this, providing such definitions requires that some related issues also be addressed, for example: What are the sources of our knowledge? Does a commitment to one kind of theory of knowledge commit us to any other beliefs (for instance, does accepting a particular theory mean that we must also hold other beliefs about the nature of existence)? Are there different *kinds* of knowledge? What is the role of perception and experience in knowledge? These are all, to some degree or other, complex issues. But just because these issues are complex does not mean that they cannot be addressed with clarity and in a manner that is understandable, even if the more difficult writings of some philosophers might on occasion give us reason to think otherwise.

An immediate question to be encountered in developing any account of these issues is: where does one start? There are two possible routes. First, one could go straight to the problems themselves and unpack them in a more or less systematic manner. In doing this, one would effectively be compiling a kind of 'philosophical dictionary'. But if, as Nietzsche seems to be suggesting, the use of a word is as important as its formal definition, it might be a better strategy to begin with a fairly detailed analysis of how some individual philosophers have discussed the nature of knowledge. A second option, therefore, is to consider the work of some individual philosophers. This can be done with a view to looking at some of the epistemological problems they address, at the suggestions they make for overcoming those problems, and some of the problems that their thinking on these issues raises in its own turn. The second of these approaches offers at least three distinct advantages. First, it allows us to discover what some thinkers have argued to be the important features of any account of knowledge. Second, we can take the opportunity to see *how* these thinkers argue their case, and thereby gain some further insight into the nature of philosophical argument. Third, examining some of the ideas of particular thinkers can provide us with a *context* from which it is then possible to approach the writings of other philosophers.

Let us start, then, with a philosopher who locked himself up in a room and sought to derive an account of knowledge in a manner akin to the first of the two options

Whatever one may make of this, says Descartes, imagine a scenario in which there is an omnipotent God 'who is able to do anything'. How could we tell if such a God has not deceived us into believing that the evidence of our senses is true? Likewise, might we not be being deceived when we count the sides of a square and arrive at the number four each time? One might be tempted to argue that the existence of an omnipotent God guarantees that these beliefs are true, since 'God has not willed that I be deceived in this way, for he is said to be supremely good', and if God is supremely good he will not be deceitful. But suppose that 'I am so imperfect that I am always deceived.' Then, even these purportedly certain beliefs are doubtful. Moreover, imagine there is 'not a supremely good God . . . but rather an evil genius, supremely powerful and clever, who has directed his entire effort at deceiving me'. Descartes thus envisages a situation in which he might think that two plus three equals five, but really he is being fooled. What then? One thing remains *certain*, Descartes argues. Even if he is being deceived, he is still thinking: 'Thus, after everything has been most carefully weighed, it must finally be established that this pronouncement "I am, I exist" is necessarily true every time I utter it or conceive it in my mind' (Meditation 2, 64).

Descartes has reached the point at which he can now safely hold that however much he may be deceived by this evil genius he has envisaged, it is nevertheless always true that he must exist in order to be subject to this genius's will. But this of itself does not really say enough. For, it is not especially helpful to say that 'I exist' unless I can also say what I am. 'Here I make my discovery: thought exists; it alone cannot be separated from me . . . But what then am I? A thing that thinks. What is that? A thing that doubts, understands, affirms, denies, wills, refuses, and that also imagines and senses' (Meditation 2, 65–6). Descartes has therefore formulated the view that he is in possession of one certain piece of knowledge: he exists, and his existence is defined by thought. This is most famously expressed in a phrase that is found in part IV of the *Discourse on Method*: 'I think, therefore I am' (*cogito, ergo sum*) (IV, 19).[6]

1.1 *Mind and body*

What, though, is this 'I' that thinks? First, there is the mechanical structure of the human body, which is a matter concerning the senses. Second, there is a matter concerning the activities which humans pursue: they walk about, eat, have perceptions from their senses, they assert, they doubt. These activities are, according to Descartes, the actions of a soul or *mind*. The properties of a body are physical: it can be seen, touched, occupies a particular space, can be moved, etc. The ability to think, however, is not a property we can attribute to a merely physical body, for given the presence of the malicious demon, the body can be doubted. But the self that thinks cannot be doubted, for it is what is doing the doubting. 'At this time I admit nothing that is not necessarily true. I am therefore precisely nothing but a thinking thing; that is, a mind, or intellect, or understanding, or reason.' Descartes thus holds that he is a mind, 'not that concatenation of members we call the human body' (Meditation 2, 65). Note, then, that what is usually referred to as Descartes's 'mind-body dualism' (or 'Cartesian dualism') is thereby set firmly in place. He is, he claims, a mind, not a body. In other words, what is essential about him is that he is a thinking thing, and *mind is a substance that is essentially different from body*. This forms the basis for Descartes's view of knowledge. Certain knowledge derives from the 'I think', that is, from a conception of the self as a mental substance that is different in kind from that other substance we call 'matter'.

One thing worth noting at this juncture is that if we were to follow Descartes, then we would thereby be committed to a position that has *metaphysical* ramifications. 'Metaphysics' is a word that has had many different meanings for different philosophers, but I will mention just two of these meanings. 'Metaphysics' can be regarded as a branch of philosophical enquiry which is concerned with either (1) the fundamental nature of reality, and hence with those first principles which can serve as a ground for all our knowledge; or (2) an exploration of the necessary conditions of our having any sensory experiences at all. Descartes's position is metaphysical in the first of these senses, whereas a philosopher such as Immanuel Kant (see below) conceives of metaphysics primarily in terms of the second sense. As will become increasingly apparent, if one accepts either of these views of metaphysics, then metaphysical issues and questions of knowledge can be taken as being inextricably entangled with one another. For the moment, though, it is worth turning at this point to some of the comments that preface Descartes's formulation of the *cogito* as a means of further elucidating his views.

1.2   Foundations

A reader who glanced randomly at one or two pages of the *Discourse on Method* might be forgiven for thinking that they were perusing a work that is a cross between a reflection on the aesthetic merits of different forms of architecture and a practical guide for builders. Here are some examples:

> often there is less perfection in works made of several pieces and in works made by the hands of several masters than in those works upon which but one master has worked. Thus one sees that buildings undertaken and completed by a single architect are commonly more beautiful and better ordered than those that several architects have tried to patch up . . .

> one does not see people pulling down all the houses in a city simply to rebuild them some other way and to make the streets more attractive; but one does see that several people tear down their houses in order to rebuild them, and that even in some cases they are forced to do so when their houses are in danger of collapsing and the foundations are not very steadfast.

> Now just as it is not enough, before beginning to rebuild the house where one lives, to pull it down, to make provision for materials and architects, or to take a try at architecture for oneself, and also to have carefully worked out the floorplan; one must provide for something else in addition, namely where one can be conveniently sheltered while working on the other building . . .

> (*Discourse on Method*, II, 7, 8; III, 13)

The metaphor of a *building* is a key element within Descartes's account of knowledge in both the *Discourse* and the *Meditations*. For knowledge, he tells us, is an edifice, and like any edifice, our knowledge must be built upon a secure foundation. The *cogito*, it must by now be apparent, is that foundation, since although we can in principle doubt all sorts of things, Descartes is sure that we cannot doubt that we are thinking even as we doubt. We are therefore presented with an important *metaphor* for knowledge: knowledge as a kind of edifice constructed according to principles that will ensure it won't fall down in the face of the mildest gust of wind. In this sense, Descartes is like a builder, for he is *constructing* his account of knowledge by starting with the foundation and working up from there. Moreover, in keeping with the general principle enshrined within the *cogito*, which in effect states that what is to count as certain, and hence true, must be what is certain for an individual mind engaged in self-reflection, Descartes's enterprise takes on a very personal character: 'My plan has never been more than to . . . build upon a foundation which is completely my own' (*Discourse on Method*, II, 9). Likewise, it is perhaps also significant in this connection that much of the *Discourse on Method* takes the form of a personal memoir concerning how and why Descartes has ended up thinking about both what he is doing and how he is doing it. He is constructing an account of human knowledge, and he is doing this by way of reflection on his own ability to *think*. But thinking itself, which describes what is essential about having a mind, is no merely arbitrary activity. If the *cogito* (the 'I think') forms the foundation of Descartes's epistemology, then we are entitled to expect him to tell us a bit more concerning what this thinking thing is. It is not really sufficient to rest content with the claim that the *cogito* is made of a substance (mind) that ought not to be confused with anything else (namely, material substance). What, in short, is special about the mind such that we can derive a model of knowledge exclusively from it?

1.3 Reason

Descartes's answer to this question is an interesting one. What is special about the mind is that it can act spontaneously, rather than simply respond to external phenomena, as is the case with animals. To recall Descartes's claim in the second Meditation, humans have understanding, entertain doubts, affirm and deny things, etc. We are therefore beings who are endowed with independent will and reflective ability. To put it another way: 'reason or good sense . . . alone makes us men and distinguishes us from animals, [and] I prefer to believe that it exists whole and entire in each one of us' (*Discourse on Method*, I, 2). We are first and foremost *rational beings* in that we reflect upon our own thoughts through the use of our reason. If we can use reason, then it is because we have 'intellect'. In turn, it is the intellect that reveals even the external, physical world to us: 'even bodies are not, properly speaking, perceived by the senses or by the faculty of imagination, but by the intellect alone, and . . . they are not perceived through their being touched or seen, but *only through their being understood*' (Meditation 2, 69, italics added). It is because human beings have rational understanding that they are able to grasp the world about them in a meaningful way. Moreover, as rational beings who have intellect we also must have *representations* of things, or 'ideas', and the truest ideas will be those which are presented to us 'with such clarity and distinctness' that we cannot find good cause to doubt them (*Discourse on Method*, II, 11). Human reason, according to Descartes, provides us with the *yardstick* with which to evaluate what counts as 'knowledge'. And it can do this because 'reason is a universal instrument that can be of help in all sorts of circumstances' (*Discourse on Method*, V, 32). Hence, Descartes has formulated the view that not only are we rational beings made of a substance called 'mind', but what is also distinctive about us is that we *use* our reason to gain knowledge. Reason is the essential tool or 'instrument' that can serve us in our search for certain knowledge. It is because of this commitment to the view that it is possible to establish certain knowledge on the basis of reason alone that Descartes is allocated a place within the canon of 'rationalist' philosophers.[7] Equally significant, in this regard, is the fact that Descartes attempts to establish his theory solely on the basis of introspection. This amounts to holding that by contemplating what he is, in isolation from the world he inhabits, Descartes believes he can uncover a secure foundation for what can be known.

Of course, even if we were to agree with Descartes thus far, it does not follow that he has got himself out of a further quandary. He may have convinced us that, at the very least, we are rational beings who are made of a substance called 'mind' and are certain that we are thinking, even if all else can be doubted. But there is now the problem of the external world to consider. Even if I am sure that I am thinking, how is it possible for me to know for certain that there is a world outside my mind? Descartes's answer to this question is not entirely convincing, for he ends up by invoking the existence of God as the sole guarantor of an external reality. His argument for the existence of God takes the form of what is generally termed his 'ontological argument'. Descartes has, he argues, within his mind a clear and distinct conception of God, that is, of a supreme and perfect being. Since Descartes himself is finite, he cannot of himself be the origin of this idea, so it must have come from somewhere else (see Meditation 3). Moreover, he argues, existence is an attribute of God's perfection, since it is more perfect to exist than not to exist (see Meditation 5). Therefore, God must exist. In turn, the existence of God allows Descartes to argue for knowledge of an external world, since, he holds, an essential component in God's perfection is the fact that he is truthful. Since God is truthful, it follows that he would not allow us to be deceived with regard to the perceptions that we have by way of our senses. The existence of God thereby serves to ensure that our perceptions of the external world are accurate. There are, of course, a number of possible objections to Descartes's arguments. For instance, does it really make sense to hold that existence itself is a perfection? It may be the case that in order for something to be perfect it must necessarily exist, but it does not follow from this that there is something that exists which is perfect.[8] Equally, if we are not inclined to believe in God, or we can find convincing reasons for doubting that God's existence can be proven by rational argument, then we are not going to be convinced that he can serve as the foundational principle for our knowledge of the external world. But I propose to leave this issue to one side in favour of considering in more detail two important and related features of Descartes's theory of knowledge that I have already mentioned. The first of these is the *cogito*. The second concerns his view of reason.

1.4 The self and reason

One thing is clear about Descartes's position: he has placed the self (i.e. the 'I' that thinks, or what I shall henceforth refer to as the 'subject') at the centre of his epistemology. A subject can be succinctly defined as a kind of being that, in virtue of its self-consciousness, has an immediate sense of what it is to be itself. A subject has, in short, *subjectivity*. What counts as 'knowledge', on this view, always springs from the certainty that a subject can attain first and foremost through an act of pure introspection. If we are to accept this view, then what are we really committing ourselves to? First, and most evidently, what Descartes's view implies is a form of *individualism* with regard to knowledge. 'Individualism' is a word that has a number of important meanings, not least for anyone interested in political theory where it plays, for example, an important role within the political philosophy of classical liberalism.[9] In Descartes's case, the individual is taken as something that is unproblematically *given*. Speaking like Descartes, we would say that the sense of individual identity and what accompanies this sense (rationality, will, the ability to have clear and distinct ideas of things, etc.) are so self-evident that we can have no grounds for doubting the veracity of our own intuitions concerning what we ourselves are. So, Descartes is presupposing that our immediate sense of what and who we are is of itself a kind of complete and certain knowledge. In effect, he is stating that the self is essentially 'transparent'. In other words, our thought is always rational and conscious, it does not have an unconscious or hidden dimension (e.g. thinking is not governed in any way by instincts, etc.). Everything important by way of knowledge that can be said about what a subject is can be said solely by way of reference to that subject's own conscious understanding of itself. Descartes's theory of knowledge rests upon the assumed primacy of conscious thought; his philosophy is a 'philosophy of consciousness'.

It is on the basis of this presupposition that Descartes offers an account of what a subject is, and hence what knowledge is, that begins by excluding all reference to the material and social conditions that might make some contribution to human identity. According to this view, a subject can be essentially defined as a rational being made of a particular kind of 'stuff' (i.e. mental substance) that need not itself be defined by way of recourse to any other kind of 'stuff' (in Descartes's terms, material substance). It is evident that Descartes's theory of knowledge rests upon the belief that the mind does not need to be situated within a particular context in order to be what it is, because the question of contexts is an issue which concerns physical bodies alone, not the attributes of minds. In part, at least, Descartes's justification for this view rests upon the contention that the mind is 'utterly indivisible', since it cannot be divided into parts in the way that a body can: 'Although the entire mind seems to be united to the entire body, nevertheless, were a foot or an arm or any other bodily part to be amputated, I know that nothing has been taken away from the mind on that account' (Meditation 6, 102). It is significant, in this connection, that when he tries to elucidate how it is that humans have bodies (which are made of material stuff), Descartes appears to be obliged to formulate a rather unconvincing hypothesis: that the mind is linked to the body by way of the pineal gland, which is situated in the brain. This, of course, does not really solve the problem, for the pineal gland is itself a physical body just like an amputated limb would be, and so Descartes is open to the objection that he has still not solved the problem of how mind and body interact. Equally, Descartes cannot give us a convincing reason as to why he has selected *this* particular gland, rather than another, to carry the burden of performing such an important function. But, to return to the main point, ought we really to be convinced by Descartes's claim that there is a mental substance (self-consciousness) that can be defined on its own terms and, following this fact, that it is because we are made of this substance that we are what we are? Is it not equally possible that subjectivity, thought and knowledge might depend upon other (material and social) conditions which render them possible?

As we have seen, if we construct a theory of knowledge on the basis of individual introspection, then what we are in effect committing ourselves to is the view that subjectivity itself is something that is universally given. According to Descartes's theory, this in turn involves a commitment to a particular view of reality. This view is a metaphysical one: the world is made up of two substances – mind and body. What we are presented with is a model in which the assumed priority of a transparent and unified self-consciousness (the primacy of 'mind' as opposed to 'body') forms the basic foundation for knowledge. We are, for Descartes, first and foremost conscious beings; but, most significant of all, the defining feature of our consciousness is our rationality. As he states in the *Discourse on Method*, 'our reason makes us act' (V, 32). Equally, reason, Descartes tells us, also assures the validity of his chosen philosophical method: 'what pleased me most about this method was that by means of it I was assured of using my reason in everything, if not perfectly, then at least as best I can' (III, 12). That we are rational, therefore, is the cause of our being the kinds of creatures that we are; and it is because we are rational that we can have certainty since, to recall a passage cited earlier, 'reason is a universal instrument' (V, 32). We can infer that it is the very universality of its application that makes reason such an essential tool in our attempts to discover true knowledge. However, if rationality is essentially a feature of a substance called 'mind', then what would happen to our conception of reason if we were to arrive at the opinion that mind itself is not a substance that is independent of material substance? What, in short, would happen if we were to reject Descartes's metaphysics? Surely, 'reason' would cease to have the kind of universality that Descartes attributes to it as soon as the concept of 'mental substance' was dissolved. This fact alone should cause us to question at least those aspects of Descartes's theory which seek to ground knowledge in what is at best a questionable metaphysics. Moreover, the view of the subject that Descartes favours is not especially compelling. We may have good reason to doubt more than the mind–body dualism that Descartes favours in order to develop his account of the self. One might also wonder if it is really the case that one can arrive at an adequate conception of subjectivity without paying attention to the fact that human beings are social creatures. Is it not, after all, possible that subjectivity is itself constituted and thereby constructed out of the broader fabric of human life that goes to make up what we might call 'social reality'? In short, there may be persuasive reasons for thinking of individual subjectivity as being essentially dependent upon a web of social relations (economic, personal, etc.) that extend far beyond it. If this is the case, then knowledge cannot be adequately understood in terms of mere individual subjectivity, as Descartes would have us believe, for what we call 'knowledge' would, first and foremost, have a social basis.

But let us put Descartes to one side by returning to Nietzsche. As I noted at the beginning of this chapter, Nietzsche is a thinker who might well be taken as advocating a version of the kind of view I have just mentioned. But he also had something to say concerning the *cogito* and doubt that is pertinent to the present discussion.

> There are still harmless self-observers who believe that there are 'immediate certainties'; for example, 'I think' . . . When I analyze the process that is expressed in the sentence, 'I think,' I find a whole series of daring assertions that would be difficult, perhaps impossible, to prove; for example, that it is *I* who think, that there must necessarily be something that thinks, that thinking is an activity and an operation on the part of a being who is thought of as a cause, that there is an 'ego,' and, finally, that it is already determined what is to be designated by thinking – that I *know* what thinking is . . . In place of the 'immediate certainty' which the people may believe in the case at hand, the philosopher thus finds a series of metaphysical questions presented to him . . .[10]

One might be tempted to think that Nietzsche is perhaps overstating his case here. But his observations relate to a point made earlier: Descartes's conception of the subject presupposes a model of consciousness which holds that an individual mind has an awareness of itself that is *transparent*, and that being in possession of such an awareness is thereby certain and so counts as 'knowledge'. Only if this is the case is the 'immediate certainty' of the *cogito* possible. But this contention in its own turn, as Nietzsche remarks, presupposes more than Descartes's account could possibly prove. Above all, of course, it presupposes that thinking is an activity that is *caused* by somebody who is thinking – that the individual is a being who is the 'cause' of their own thoughts. Nietzsche's view also implies that any attempt to talk about the self as that which first and foremost *thinks* involves the danger of getting stuck in a metaphysical mire of doubtful assertions. In turn, the 'certainty' which was meant to spring from Descartes's embracing a method of introspective doubt perhaps raises more questions than it answers. Rather than looking 'inward' to the self as a means of grounding our knowledge might it not, therefore, be a better option to look elsewhere, to the world that we experience?

2   Empiricism: Locke and the Role of Experience in Knowledge

Descartes rejects the senses as forming a reliable basis for knowledge. Instead, he turns to an analysis of thinking as a means of securing a foundation for certain knowledge. This move, as we have seen, brings with it its own distinctive problems and presuppositions. One alternative approach that may be less prone to some of these problems is that of *empiricism*. In its modern form, empiricism is most famously associated with the writings of the English philosopher John Locke (1632–1704) and the Scottish philosopher David Hume (1711–76).[11] In contrast to the emphasis placed by Descartes on certain innate, rational principles in the mind, empiricists stress the primary role of *experience* in all human understanding and knowledge. Thus Locke, in *An Essay Concerning Human Understanding* (1690)[12] argues for the view that all of our ideas derive ultimately from our experiences.[13] An 'idea', according to Locke, is 'whatsoever is the Object of the Understanding when a Man thinks' (*Essay*, 47, section 8). On this account, whenever we think we have in our minds ideas, and it is these ideas that we think about. The ideas we have are the result of the *qualities* bodies have. And a quality 'is the Power to produce any *Idea* in our mind' (p. 134, section 8). Locke then draws a distinction between 'original' or *primary* qualities, and *secondary* qualities. Primary qualities include things like '*Solidity*, *Extension*, *Figure*, and *Mobility*', and are inseparable from the existence of bodies: for example, one cannot think of any body without thinking of it as being extended, as occupying space. Secondary qualities are, in contrast, 'nothing in the Objects themselves, but Powers to produce various Sensations in us by their *primary Qualities*' – things like colours, sounds, tastes, temperature (p. 135, section 10). Thus, our ideas of primary qualities *resemble* the objects that give rise to them; whereas our ideas of secondary qualities need not resemble what gives rise to them. The latter are 'in truth nothing in the Objects themselves, but Powers to produce various Sensations is us' (p. 137, section 14); they are, in other words, merely *subjective*.

Of course, there are problems with Locke's distinction between primary and secondary qualities. For instance, that the surface of a body has a certain temperature that can be measured and established by way of contrast to other bodies of different temperatures is hardly a subjective matter. Be that as it may, the important point to note is that Locke's central claim about our ideas concerns their *origin*: ideas cannot be claimed to derive from any universal and innate principles which lie ready made within the human mind. Locke then presents a number of good reasons for doubting the view that there are such innate ideas. First, he says, even if there were ideas that are shared by all human beings, this fact of itself would in no way prove that they are innate. Second, Locke adds to this the stronger claim 'that there are none such: Because there are none to which all Mankind give an Universal Assent' (*Essay*, 49, sections 3–4). In other words, it can be doubted that there are innate ideas which all humans demonstrably share simply because there is no way of showing in a convincing manner that all human beings really do share common ideas.

On the basis of his rejection of innate principles of knowledge, Locke presents us with a model that offers a strikingly different account of the sources of knowledge and rationality from that offered by Descartes. In terms of their respective presentation of the issues, the difference between the two thinkers can be seen in their respective choices of metaphor in describing knowledge. Descartes, recall, likened knowledge to a building that needs solid, rational foundations. The cornerstone, so to speak, of this structure is the *cogito*. In contrast, Locke offers two striking metaphors of the human mind which show how his approach is different. Here is the first of them:

> The Senses at first let in particular *Ideas*, and furnish the yet empty Cabinet: And the Mind by degrees growing familiar with some of them, they are lodged in the Memory, and Names got to them. Afterwards, the Mind proceeding farther, abstracts them, and

by Degrees learns the use of general Names. In this manner the Mind comes to be furnish'd with Ideas and Language, the Materials about which it exercises its discursive Faculty: And the use of Reason becomes daily more visible, as these Materials, that give it employment, increase. (*Essay*, 55, section 15)

It is worth spending some time unpacking this passage in detail. The first thing to note is the likening of the human mind to an 'empty Cabinet'. From this, we can infer that humans are not born with any ideas or knowledge already present within their minds. Rather, humans are like empty vessels that must in their own turn be 'filled' with ideas, in the same manner in which a filing cabinet can be filled with files. Ideas, moreover, have a particular *origin*; they come from the senses, from experience. Hence, for Locke, humans are first and foremost to be regarded as *sentient* beings. This is another way of saying that we are bodily creatures endowed with the ability to see, hear, touch, taste, and smell the world around us. We are, above all, beings that are endowed with senses and our ideas derive from this fact. In turn, the individual mind grows accustomed to some of these ideas, and hence it learns to *remember* them by baptising them with names. Next, by way of a process of 'abstraction', the mind learns to apply these names in a general fashion. For Locke, our general notions of things are the consequence of our encountering particular instances of them *first*. Only subsequently do we apply these particular notions to a broader range of like (or 'general') instances. Whereas a thinker like Descartes constructs a model of thinking on the basis of which we proceed from general principles to particular knowledge claims, Locke argues the contrary case. Finally, reason, on Locke's view, is not something already given to us at birth. Rather, our rationality is derived from the 'exercise' of our minds as they use the materials presented to them by experience. Where Descartes might be tempted to see universal and innate principles at work in things like mathematics (recall that he *knows* that two plus three equals five merely through the activity of rational introspection), Locke can argue that 'A Child knows not that Three and Four are equal to Seven, till he comes to be able to count to seven, and has got the Name and *Idea* of Equality' (*Essay*, 55, section 16). It is only when humans have 'acquired' the ability to think in certain ways that they are able to do so.

The second of Locke's metaphors is presented at the beginning of Book II of the *Essay*: 'Let us then suppose the Mind to be, as we say, white Paper, void of all characters, without any *Ideas*; How comes it to be furnished? Whence comes it by that vast store, which the busy and boundless Fancy of Man has painted on it, with an almost endless variety? Whence has it all the materials of Reason and Knowledge?' (p. 104, section 2). As with the empty cabinet metaphor, the mind is again presented as something that is to start with empty, or in this case 'blank'. Only subsequently, through the influence of experience, does this blank sheet become filled with characters. Here, though, Locke has also reiterated the question about where our knowledge comes from (that is, its *source*), the answer to which he will now supply in more detail.

It is apparent that Locke is committed to two things. On the one hand, there are no innate ideas that can serve as the basis for our knowledge of the world. On the other hand, humans must nevertheless have the innate *ability* to respond to the world around them so as to be able to acquire these ideas, and thereby knowledge. There are, he tells us at the beginning of Book II of the *Essay*, only two *sources* or 'Fountains of Knowledge'. It is from these sources that 'all the *Ideas* we have, or can naturally have, do spring'. First, there are the senses, which produce in the mind, in the form of '*Perceptions*', our ideas of such qualities as hardness, softness, heat, cold, etc. This source Locke calls 'sensation' (p. 105, section 3). The second source 'is the *Perception of the Operations of our own Minds* within us'. Our understanding is, on Locke's account, also furnished 'with another set of *Ideas*, which could not be had from things without', such as our abilities to perceive, to doubt, to believe, to reason, to know, and to will. This second source Locke gives the name 'reflection' (p. 105, section 4). Between them, sensation and reflection give us all we need to have in order for ideas, and hence knowledge, to be possible: sensation is the external source of our experience of the world, and reflection (or the 'internal sense', as Locke also calls it) is the source of our sense of individual subjectivity.

In turn, ideas can be either 'simple' or 'complex'. Simple ideas are given to us only by way of sensation or reflection and include such qualities as motion, a particular colour, a particular taste, whether they are hard or soft, etc. (p. 119, sections 1–2). The combination of these simple ideas produces complex ideas: 'When the Understanding is once stored with these simple *Ideas*, it has the Power to repeat, compare, and unite them even to an almost infinite Variety, and so can make at Pleasure new complex *Ideas*' (section 2). In turn, this implies that the acquisition of simple ideas is something that is passive, whereas complex ideas are actively produced by thinking (since uniting or combining are acts) (p. 163, section 1). The production of complex ideas thus implies an act of combination on the part of the mind. The concept of *substance* is derived from this act of combination:

> The Mind being . . . furnished with a great number of simple *Ideas*, conveyed in by the *Senses* . . . takes notice also, that a certain number of these simple *Ideas* go constantly together; which being presumed to belong to one thing . . . are called so united in one subject, by one name . . . not imagining how these simple *Ideas* can subsist by themselves, we accustom our selves, to suppose some *Substratum*, wherein they do subsist, and from which they do result, which therefore we call *Substance*. (*Essay*, 294, section 1)

We receive simple ideas from the senses, and notice that these ideas often occur together in various combinations. These regular conjunctions of ideas we attribute as being caused by something else that unites them, namely, substances. It is for this reason, Locke argues, that if we attempt to elucidate what is meant by a phrase like '*pure Substance in general*' we will discover that all we are presented with is a presupposition that can in no way be proven. What is meant by the term 'substance' amounts to no more than the collection of particular combinations of ideas ('Man, Horse, Gold, Water, *etc.*'). Locke claims that it is no more nonsensical to talk of 'material' substance than to talk of 'spiritual' substance, for both are arrived at by combining ideas wherein 'we represent particular sorts of *Substances* to our selves', and neither can be shown to be better understood than the other (p. 298, section 6; p. 308, section 23; p. 313, section 30). From this Locke concludes that in the same manner as we derive the complex ideas we have of material substances from simple ideas, so we likewise arrive at '*the complex* Idea of *an immaterial Spirit*' by combining simple ideas of thought, perception, freedom of will, etc. (p. 305, section 15).[14]

2.1 The Lockean self

Locke's emphasis on the role of experience as the source of our ideas means that, for him, we only think so long as we exist as perceivers: 'To ask, *at what time a Man has first any* Ideas, is to ask, when he begins to perceive; having *Ideas* and Perception being the same thing' (*Essay*, 108, section 9). Equally, on this view an individual's identity could not be understood in any meaningful way if we were to remove from it the sensations that that individual can have (p. 110, section 11). Thus,

> *Self* is that conscious thinking thing, (whatever Substance, made up of, whether Spiritual, or Material, Simple, or Compounded, it matters not) which is sensible, or conscious of Pleasure and Pain, capable of Happiness or Misery, and is so concerned for it *self*, as far as that consciousness extends. Thus every one finds, that whilst comprehended under that consciousness, the little Finger is as much a part of it *self*, as what is most so. (*Essay*, 341, section 17)

As with Descartes, then, *consciousness* is for Locke the defining characteristic of being a subject. However, for Locke, the discussion of consciousness should not be concerned with notions of *substance*, as Descartes's theory is. This is because, in the first place, Locke rejects talk of 'substances' as being inadequate for the purpose of defining what a self is. The idea of substance can only be derived indirectly from sensation or reflection (which are the only two sources of our knowledge). Consequently, the notion of substance is a vague one: 'We have no such *clear Idea* at all, and therefore signify nothing by the word *Substance*, but only an uncertain supposition of we know not what' (p. 95, section 18). In the second place, Locke argues, there is no demonstrable connection between a sense of self and a particular substance such that the former can be shown to rely upon the latter in order to be what it is. To put it another way, 'consciousness removed, that Substance is no more it *self*, or makes no more part of it, than any other Substance, as is evident in the instance, we have already given, of a Limb cut off' (p. 345, section 24). It is on the basis of this that Locke contends that 'self is not determined by Identity or Diversity of Substance . . . but only by Identity of consciousness' (p. 345, section 23; see also section 25).

By now it should be clear that on Locke's account our knowledge will always be *knowledge about our experiences as conscious beings*, since experience (in the form of sensation and reflection) is the only source from which we derive our ideas, and we are defined *only* by way of the identity we have in virtue of the fact that we are conscious. The subject therefore remains as central to Locke's account of knowledge as it does to Descartes's. Likewise, there is for Locke an indubitable certainty with regard to the existence of the subject: 'As for *our own Existence*, we perceive it so plainly, and so certainly, that it neither needs, nor is capable of any proof . . . If I doubt of all other Things, that very doubt makes me perceive my own *Existence*, and will not suffer me to doubt of that.' And this is a fact taught to us by *experience*, since in having sensations, thinking or using our ability to reason 'we are conscious to ourselves of our own Being' (*Essay*, 618–19, section 3). As with Descartes, therefore, conscious thought is for Locke a *given* and hence certain kind of knowledge, in so far as we have an unmediated (i.e. a direct) intuition of ourselves as thinking creatures.

Likewise, on Locke's view, our *reason* tells us that we have knowledge of the existence of God. This is because 'it is impossible that Things wholly void of Knowledge, and operating blindly, and without any Perception, should produce a knowing Being . . . For it is . . . repugnant to the *Idea* of senseless Matter, that it should put into itself Sense, Perception, and Knowledge' (pp. 621–2, section 5). In other words, although he holds that all our knowledge of the external world can only come from the senses, Locke finds it unthinkable to conclude from this that thinking itself could be a consequence of the interaction of brute matter. Reason tells us that there is a God because physical bodies and thought are different in kind. In short, Locke is claiming that it is impossible for something that is *opposed* to mind (namely, body) to give rise to what is essential about it (namely, thinking). Reason, in turn, can be defined as the faculty (or ability) to draw inferences concerning the relationship between our different ideas and thereby connect them together so as 'to discover what connexion there is in each link of the Chain' (p. 668, section 2). Knowledge and opinion both derive from this activity. If we see a 'certain Agreement or Disagreement of any two *Ideas*' we have knowledge. If we see a probable connection between any two ideas we have opinion. Reasoning, therefore, is the activity wherein we assess our different ideas so as to find out which are certain or, if they do not appear to be immediately certain, which are the more probable. The ability to do this is universal (p. 670, section 4). Given its universality, and the claim that it is through reasoning that we can have knowledge of God, it perhaps comes as no surprise that, in the last analysis, the ability to reason is, according to Locke, God-given (p. 671, section 4).

Locke's empiricism, then, does not really take us very far from some of the central tenets that Descartes already propounded. The origins of reason are still divine ones, and consciousness still occupies a central role in defining what can be known. Equally, the ability of the mind to have *representations* still remains a key feature of Locke's theory – in that both simple and complex ideas are, in the last analysis, always representations of sense perceptions.

3   Hume's Empiricism

David Hume follows Locke's empiricist approach in stressing the importance of the senses in our acquisition of knowledge. Hume's *A Treatise of Human Nature* (1739) (later recast in 1748 as the *Enquiries Concerning Human Understanding and Concerning the Principles of Morals*)[15] sets out to elucidate nothing less than a 'science of MAN' whereby it will become possible to arrive at a firm understanding of all other forms of human knowledge (*Treatise*, Introduction, xv). Hume's account of human understanding aims to construct a theory of human nature. This theory is in turn envisaged as providing the basis for other disciplines, such as those of mathematics and the physical sciences. To this end, Hume attempts to construct a model of human understanding that elucidates the central role that sense perception must play in our ideas, and hence knowledge. As will become clear, Hume's emphasis on the role that experience must play in our knowledge implies two things. First, certain knowledge, in the form that Descartes seeks, is not a viable option. Second, the empiricist model has particular implications for the nature of the subject that Hume extrapolates to the point where he abandons the view that subjectivity alone must be the foundation of our knowledge. However, it is not simply because of these two points that Hume's views are important. In addition, it is Hume's thought which paves the way for the German philosopher Immanuel Kant's attempt to achieve a synthesis of the rationalist and empiricist approaches to knowledge. Hume's influence does not stop there. In spite of his self avowed individualism with regard to such matters, Nietzsche's attack on Kantian metaphysics and epistemology is in many ways inspired by the thought of Hume. Equally, many of Hume's insights (principally into the social dimension of thought and therefore subjectivity) are equally pertinent to an understanding of the writings of more recent philosophers, such as T. W. Adorno (one of the founding figures of the Frankfurt School) and Gilles Deleuze (a figure associated with contemporary movements within French philosophy).

3.1   Impressions and ideas

Hume's Lockean approach is clear from the outset of the *Treatise*: 'All the perceptions of the human mind resolve themselves into two distinct kinds, which I shall call IMPRESSIONS and IDEAS' (p. 1). 'Impressions' include all those perceptions that are the direct consequence of sense experience; and 'ideas' are 'the faint images of these in thinking and reasoning'. Hume castigates Locke for having 'perverted' the usual meaning of the word 'idea' by using it to stand for all our sense perceptions. On Hume's view, 'ideas' are always to be understood only as being mental 'copies' of the impressions we receive from our sense perceptions. Again, following Locke, he then proceeds to distinguish between 'simple' and 'complex' perceptions and their analogues in our impressions and ideas. Simple perceptions cannot be divided into any parts, whereas complex perceptions can be divided up in this way. For example, an apple is a complex perception which is composed of simple ones (such as colour, taste and smell) (*Treatise*, 2). The most significant feature of Hume's account, however, concerns his claim that all of our impressions and ideas *resemble* one another. The only difference between them concerns the respective 'force or vivacity' with which they strike the mind, in so far as ideas are the fainter copies of our impressions: 'The one seem to be in a manner the reflexion of the other; so that all the perceptions of the mind are double, and appear as both impressions and ideas'. To put it more directly, 'Ideas and impressions appear always to correspond to each another' (p. 3).

   However, having said this, Hume then decides that he has perhaps gone a bit too far. This is because it is obvious some of our *complex ideas* do *not* have corresponding impressions. Nor, for that matter, could all of our *complex impressions* be said to have their exact copies in our ideas. At the level of complex ideas and impressions 'the rule is not universally true, that they are exact copies of each other' (*Treatise*, 3).[16] Although Hume offers us an account of human understanding that stresses the *representational* aspect of thinking, he nevertheless bumps up against the fact that there are limitations with this model. Nevertheless, this problem can perhaps be resolved: even if complex impressions and ideas are not always the exact copies of one another, Hume affirms that this will be the case with all of our *simple* impressions and ideas. He can, in turn, propound a *rule* for thinking that states that 'every simple idea has an impression, which resembles it.' Moreover, since it is true that all our simple ideas correspond to their impressions, and that all 'the complex are formed from them, we may affirm in general that these two species of perception are exactly correspondent' (*Treatise*, 4). From this it follows that all thinking is derived from our basic ability to have perceptions from our senses, which are then rendered in the form of impressions as suitable material from which to manufacture all of our ideas.

From the above, Hume concludes that we can construct an order of causality with regard to our simple impressions and ideas: simple impressions must come first. Only when we have an impression can we then derive some idea on the basis of that impression. Equally, an impression will always give rise to an idea (*Treatise*, 5). That said, however, there is another problem with the representational account Hume has offered us, for certain simple ideas *can* be derived *independently* of their corresponding impressions. Take, says Hume, a person who has 'enjoyed his sight for thirty years'. During this time, he has seen all of the shades of a particular colour *except for one*. If all the shades he has seen are placed before him in order 'descending gradually from the deepest to the lightest', he will obviously be able to 'perceive a blank' in the series where the missing shade should be and then supply it 'from his own imagination' (*Treatise*, 6). If this is true (and Hume affirms that it is), then not even all our simple ideas necessarily have their origin in simple impressions. There is, therefore, an 'exception' to the rule that Hume has formulated concerning our simple ideas. Hume, however, concludes that this example is 'so singular' that it need not deter him from sticking to his 'general maxim' that simple ideas have their origins in our impressions and so correspond to them. But this is not the only possible objection. It is equally the case that we can generate 'secondary' ideas from the 'primary' ideas that we already have.[17] If we can do this, then we must be able to do so *independently* of our experiencing any impressions that correspond to these secondary ideas (p. 6). Again, Hume seeks to overcome this by arguing that such combinations of primary ideas nevertheless presuppose their existence, and these, he has already shown, are the consequences of our impressions. For this reason, 'it still remains true, that all our simple ideas proceed mediately or immediately, from their correspondent impressions' in sense experience (p. 7).

3.2   Sensation and reflection

In spite of the possible objections to his thesis, then, Hume finally comes to the conclusion that the correspondence theory of impressions and ideas he has offered remains a valid one. He then proceeds to follow the Lockean paradigm by dividing our impressions into two categories: those of 'sensation' and those of 'reflexion'

(*Treatise*, 7ff). We can feel sensations of pain, pleasure, hunger, heat, cold, etc. Such sensations give rise to impressions of them (which is why they are called 'impressions of sensation'). This ability derives from 'unknown causes'; which is another way of saying that we are simply the kind of beings who can have sensations and impressions derived from them, and little more can be said concerning this matter. Of impressions of sensation 'there is a copy taken by the mind, which remains after the impression ceases; and this we call an idea' (p. 8). Impressions of sensation thus form the source of our ideas. 'Impressions of reflexion' are rather different. 'Secondary, or reflective impressions' arise from our impressions of sensation 'either immediately or by the interposition of an idea' (p. 275). Whereas impressions of sensation entail that one *feels* such things as cold, pain, or hunger, impressions of reflexion involve making judgements concerning what we feel. Impressions of reflexion, therefore, concern 'the passions, and other emotions resembling them' in that, by way of these impressions, we reflect upon what we have felt. Thus, 'A fit of gout produces a long train of passions, as grief, hope fear' (p. 276). Impressions of reflexion are, it follows, to do with the attitudes we have toward things like pain or pleasure.[18] From this we can also note that impressions of sensation and the ideas we construct out of them always come with associated aversions, attractions, etc.: we are never indifferent with regard to them. Thus, our ideas concern our attitudes toward our impressions.

Ideas preserve impressions. We recall our ideas by way of 'memory and imagination'. The function of memory, it follows, is to preserve 'the original form' in which ideas are presented to the mind in terms of 'their order and position'. Imagination allows us to combine these ideas in new ways (thus we can create ideas of 'winged horses, fiery dragons, and monstrous giants'). But does it follow from this that our ideas can be put together in any way that we choose? Hume thinks not.

3.3   Resemblance, contiguity and cause and effect

Although all our ideas are the consequence of representations, there are, according to Hume, three rules or 'universal principles' that govern the way in which we link our ideas together. In Hume's parlance, this issue concerns the way in which our ideas are 'associated' or 'connected'. These are 'RESEMBLANCE, CONTIGUITY in time or place, and CAUSE and EFFECT' (*Treatise*, 11). In the cases of resemblance and contiguity, our imagination links ideas by noting an association between them: either they are similar, or they occur together at a particular time and place. Cause and effect, in contrast, link our ideas in a manner such that 'there is no relation, which produces a stronger connexion in the fancy' (i.e. in the imagination). It is the imagination, therefore, that supplies us with the notion of cause and effect, *not* any of our impressions. There are no impressions derived from our sensations that *correspond* to causality. Hume is arguing that through cause and effect we arrive at our most compelling beliefs about the world, and it is his analysis of cause and effect that has exerted greatest influence upon the thought of subsequent philosophers.

All our complex ideas are derived from the act of combining simple ideas. And all our complex ideas may be divided into three kinds: those concerning '*Relations,*

Modes, and *Substances*' (*Treatise*, 13). With regard to substances and modes, Hume argues that we can have no idea of either apart from them being combinations of simple ideas, united together by way of the imagination. Thus, both are complex ideas produced by association. For instance, all talk of substance involves the attribution of 'an unknown *something*', a 'fiction' which is supposed to unite certain combinations of ideas together. This kind of talk Hume has little time for. As for 'relations', Hume locates seven philosophically important ones: '*resemblance, identity, relations of time and place, proportion in quantity or number, degrees in any quality, contrariety, and causation*' (p. 69; cf. 13–15).[19] As we have seen, through resemblance, we compare ideas – although it does not always follow that resemblance 'always produces a connexion or association of ideas'. Equally, the other six relations allow us to link and compare our ideas. Identity is the 'most universal' of relations, in so far as any being that exists for any period must have an identity which makes it what it is; identity allows us to posit and compare different beings (p. 14). Space and time allows us to situate ideas in terms of where and when they occurred; while we also can think in terms of their quantity and number, where applicable. Contrariety concerns our ideas of 'existence or non-existence', i.e. whether something exists or does not exist. Finally, cause and effect is that relation whereby we infer that an idea has either been caused by, or is the cause of, another idea. As already noted, this latter notion Hume takes to be of central importance to human understanding.

Hume's analysis of cause and effect is developed in some detail in the *Treatise*, in the context of his discussion of knowledge. He develops his account on the basis of the following principle:

> 'Tis impossible to reason justly, without understanding perfectly, the idea concerning which we reason; and 'tis impossible perfectly to understand any idea, without tracing it up to its origin, and examining that primary impression, from which it arises. (pp. 74–5)

Hume is telling us that in order to arrive at a clear analysis of the notion of 'causation' we must first understand what we mean by it. Achieving such an understanding involves examining the *source* of this idea. It is only when we are in a position to say from where the concept of causality originates that we will be able to present an adequate account of it. On Hume's terms, such an enterprise involves finding the *impression* that gives rise to our concept of causation. Hume therefore starts by envisaging two objects, call them x and y: one is a cause and the other an effect of that cause. Wherein do we find the impression 'which produces an idea of such prodigious consequence'? First, the concept of causality cannot be derived from the 'particular *qualities* of the objects; since, which-ever of these qualities I pitch on, I find some object, that is not possest of it, and yet falls under the denomination of cause and effect'. In other words, there is no quality that *all* objects have in common. This being the case, it is useless to look to the notion of quality as a means of identifying what causality is. What, then, about the relation between objects? Certainly, the relations of time and place (of '*contiguity* and *succession*') seem to be essential to the concept of causation. If we take our objects, x and y, then we can say that x appears always to have some relation to y in terms of time and place. In order to be a cause, then, *x* must exist *prior* to *y* and also exist in some spatial relation to it. But this, of itself, does not furnish us with a proper elucidation of what causality is; it merely states that there is a particular temporal and spatial relation between the objects *x* and *y*. What would this mean, though, if we put it by way of an example, for instance, the proposition '*x* is the cause of motion in *y*'? 'When we consider these objects with the utmost attention, we find only that the one body approaches the other; and that the motion of it precedes that of the other, but without any sensible interval. 'Tis vain to rack ourselves with *farther* thought and reflexion upon this subject. We can go no *farther* in considering this particular instance' (*Treatise*, 77). In other words, all we have here is the knowledge that *x* preceded *y*, not that *x* was the *cause* of *y* being set in motion. Likewise, says Hume, if we consider the possibility that there is a 'necessary connexion' between the two objects we will also run up against a dead-end: 'When I cast my eye on the *known qualities* of objects, I immediately discover that the relation of cause and effect depends not in the least on them' (p. 77). This amounts to saying that we cannot have *knowledge* of the relation of cause and effect.

Why, then, do we always think that it is *necessary* for anything that comes into existence to have a cause (*Treatise*, 78)? With regard to this question, Hume argues that if we carefully examine this belief, we will find that it is a presupposition that cannot be demonstrated, for there is 'in it no mark of any . . . intuitive certainty' (p. 79). One might be tempted to argue that everything must have a cause, because if it did not, then it would have to be the cause of itself before it existed, which is absurd. Or, one may claim that whatever comes into existence without a cause would have to be caused by nothing, which is impossible. In such cases, says Hume, all one is doing is presupposing the concept of causality in order to argue for it. If something were to come into being without a cause then it would certainly not be the cause of itself, and claiming that it was would be begging the question. In the same way, it will not do to claim that someone who envisages a being that is caused by nothing takes 'nothing' to be a cause – since they manifestly are not doing so. What one is *not* doing with such arguments is demonstrating that we have an intuitive concept of cause. The important thing to note about Hume's argument here is that he is denying that we possess any notion of causality that can be derived from 'knowledge or any scientific reasoning' (p. 82).

When we engage in the activity of inferring effects from causes 'we must establish the existence of these causes' (*Treatise*, 82–3). This is only possible in two ways: via our impressions and ideas, or by drawing an inference on the basis of 'other causes'. The second option will not work, because if we try to demonstrate the notion of cause in this manner, then we will find ourselves in an infinite regress. Take any chain of causes and effects in history, and try to trace that chain back to its origin in order to ground the concept of causality. For example, Julius Caesar was killed on the Ides of March, and this is a matter of historical fact that can, in principle, be traced back to the testimony of those who witnessed the event. Tracing the event back in this way shows that our knowledge of the event is based upon the senses and memories of the witnesses who saw the event, which were subsequently written down in the form of historical documents. So, Hume concludes, 'without the authority of either the memory or the senses our whole reasoning wou'd be chimerical and without foundation.' This is because if we subtract the senses and memory from our account of this, each 'link of the chain' would necessarily rest upon another link, and no notion of causality can be inferred on such a basis. Belief or evidence thus rests upon testimony that is itself derived from the senses and memory. Hume then extrapolates this example so as to conclude that 'all reasonings concerning causes and effects are originally derived from some impression', and hence from experience (p. 84).

Hume's most famous discussion of this matter occurs in *An Enquiry Concerning Human Understanding* (sections 24ff). We imagine, says Hume, that when we see one billiard ball hit another, and the second ball in turn move, that there is a relation of causality which determines the first billiard ball to be the cause of the second billiard ball's movement. However, since for Hume all knowledge of the world around us is the result of our experiences, it is by no means clear that there exists a direct causal relation between the first ball coming to rest after hitting the second, and the second ball starting to move. We infer that the first ball causes the second to move on the basis of our previous experiences of similar events, not on the basis of some knowledge derived independently from our experiences. For Hume the 'ultimate springs and principles [which govern the behaviour of these phenomena] are totally shut up from human curiosity and enquiry' (section 26). We have seen it happen before, and so we believe it will happen again. What Hume has hit upon here is the central problem of *inductive reasoning*, i.e. reasoning which depends upon the existence of previous experiences and upon their ability to set a precedent for future experience. Induction, however, does not offer us *certainty* in the domain of knowledge. All we can get from induction is a tolerable degree of *probability* that rests upon prior experiences. Experience, in turn, presents us with ideas in relations that cannot be inferred from the ideas themselves, since our ideas are heterogeneous with regard to one another. That is, no single idea is deducible from any other idea on the basis of that idea alone. For instance, if you envisage a 'blue chair', the idea of 'blueness' cannot be inferred from the idea of 'chair' or vice versa, since there is no intrinsic link between the two concepts. The point for Hume is that other, more commonly held ideas that go together (like 'fire' and 'heat') might likewise have this heterogeneity with regard to one another: we experience the two as being conjoined, but there is no way of inferring from the ideas themselves that fire is the cause of heat.

When we reason on the basis of causality, then, what we do is conjoin a series of heterogeneous (i.e. incompatible) elements that are 'essentially different from one another'. On Hume's account, this involves our first getting impressions from our senses. We should recall here that this is an ability which, he notes, is ultimately unanalysable: one cannot offer a convincing account of how it is that humans can do this (*Treatise*, 84). It is on the basis of *memory* that we then draw inferences from the ideas caused by these impressions. Our beliefs, therefore, are those ideas that strike us with the greatest force or 'vivacity', such that it would be perverse to deny them.[20] Thus, ''Tis merely the force and liveliness of the perception, which constitutes the first act of judgment, and lays the foundation of that reasoning, which we build upon, when we trace the relation of cause and effect' (p. 86). It is for this reason, Hume claims, that it is impossible to infer the existence of any object on the basis of the existence of another object. *Experience*, therefore, sets the bounds of our reasoning in this regard: ''Tis therefore by EXPERIENCE only, that we infer the existence of one object from that of another' (p. 87). Thus, *memory* is what serves as the foundation for all our talk about causes and effects. From this we can note that causality is grounded in an 'impression of reflection'.[21] It is because of this that the concept of causality is meaningful to us, not because it has a validity that is independent of our experiences. In turn, all talk about cause and effect is governed by one rule: it is undertaken only 'in conformity to our past experience'.

3.4 Habit or custom

This is not to say that the concept of causality is therefore to be unceremoniously dumped in the waste bin, since it is unable to fulfil our demands for certainty with regard to knowledge. On the contrary, for Hume, cause and effect is the 'only connexion . . . which can lead us beyond the immediate impressions of our memory and senses' (*Treatise*, 89). The point is that our reason, and hence our knowledge of objects, has limits beyond which we cannot pass. Reason cannot ever show us the causal connections between objects, even if it is aided by experience. This is because the principles on the basis of which we conjoin ideas are not of themselves rational ones. Rather, 'the mind is determin'd by custom to pass from any cause to its effect . . . Their constant conjunction in past instances has produc'd such a habit in the mind, that it always conjoins them in its thought, and infers the existence of the one from that of its usual attendant' (p. 128). Or, in the words of the *Enquiry* (section 31):

> From causes which appear *similar* we expect similar effects. That is the sum of our experimental conclusions. Now it seems evident that, if this conclusion were formed by reason, it would be as perfect at first, and upon one instance, as after ever so long a course of experience. But the case is far otherwise. Nothing so like as eggs; yet no one, on account of this appearing similarity, expects the same taste and relish in all of them.

What Hume is arguing is that all our judgements concerning matters of fact (i.e. those events and the facts we infer from them concerning the world around us) are founded upon the relation of cause and effect. This, in turn, is grounded in experience, and hence *custom* or *habit*. As we have seen, for Hume it is only through understanding the world in terms of causes and effects as they relate to our ideas that we are able to pass beyond the evidence given to us by the senses and, in turn, make judgements about experience. However, Hume has then gone on to assert that it is not in fact possible to draw a necessary connection between our act of inferring causes and effects and the world about which such judgements are made. It is because of this that '*causes and effects are discoverable, not by reason but by experience*' (*Enquiry*, section 24). But what does Hume mean by 'custom'. Moreover, what is the role of the subject in all of this?

We only infer causality on the basis of custom. But, custom, Hume notes in the *Enquiry*, 'where it is strongest . . . not only covers our natural ignorance, but even conceals itself, and seems not to take place, merely because it is found in the highest degree' (section 24). So, for Hume, the influence of custom is a subterranean phenomenon; it is something which, necessarily, we are unaware of even as we use it in the course of making judgements. This fact is of the greatest significance when you consider that, in turn, our reasoning abilities cannot, on Hume's view, function as the source of our knowledge about experience: 'All inferences from experience . . . are effects of custom, not of reasoning' (*Enquiry*, section 36; see also *Treatise*, 97). On this conception, we are not, therefore, primarily *rational* beings, since most of our lives are played out according to the dictates of custom, which is 'the great guide of human life'. And it is this fact that allows Hume to draw some conclusions concerning our relationship to other kinds of being. A dog, for example, is no different from a human in so far as both draw inferences on the basis of experience. As you treat a dog, so 'he varies his reasoning' accordingly, so that, for instance, he will come to know when to expect a beating. Like us, 'beasts', says Hume, are equally subject to the dictates of custom. For this reason, 'habit is nothing but one of the principles of nature, and derives all its force from that origin' (*Treatise*, 178–9; see also *Enquiry*, section 84). Humans, it follows, are not in this important respect essentially different from animals.[22] In turn, the distinction between reason and experience beloved of some philosophers is, on Hume's view, at best a superficial one, at worst an error (*Enquiry*, section 36, footnote).

3.5   The Humean self

Hume's emphasis on custom implies that humans are in one essential respect directly connected with 'nature'. Like animals, they are 'natural' beings in so far as their knowledge derives from the influence of custom or habit and this, we have already seen, is a 'principle of nature'. But who is the knower within Hume's model? The short answer to this question is that for Hume, whenever I speak of *myself* I always do so in the context of some particular thought or feeling. In other words, as with his discussion of causality, Hume's approach to this issue stresses the role that *experience* must play in formulating an understanding of what the self is. Thus, he asks, 'from what impression cou'd this idea be derived?' (Treatise, 251). The first thing to note is that the notion of self cannot be reduced to a single impression. Certainly, it is true that when we think we have impressions, for Hume has based his entire philosophy on this principle. However, he then poses the question as to whether having impressions entitles us to assume that there is a kind of being (a self) that is the bearer of these impressions and unites them together in one consciousness:

> For my part, when I enter most intimately into what I call *myself*, I always stumble on some particular perception or other, of heat or cold, light or shade, love or hatred, pleasure or pain. I never can catch *myself* at any time without a perception, and never can observe anything but the perception. When my perceptions are remov'd for any time, as by sound sleep; so long am I insensible of *myself*, and may truly be said not to exist. And were all my perceptions to be remov'd by death, and cou'd I neither think, nor feel, nor see, nor love, nor hate after the dissolution of my body, I shou'd be entirely annihilated, nor do I conceive what is farther requisite to make me a non-entity. (*Treatise*, 252)

Hume is claiming that there is no sense to the word 'self' that is meaningful over and above the sensations and thoughts that accompany our bodily existence. What 'I' am, therefore, is a bundle of sensations. The self is a product of a body's ability to have sensations, experiences, etc. For Hume, nothing about the self can be said to exist independently of such sensations: the self is mortal. Moreover, the self is therefore something *added* to experiences; and as such it is a fiction or an illusion: 'The identity which we ascribe to the mind of man, is only a fictitious one, and of a like kind with that which we ascribe to vegetables and animal bodies' (p. 259). We ascribe a fictitious 'identity' to objects, which are in reality mere collections of impressions and ideas that are subsequently called by a name which unites these properties, and so, too, our own identity is produced in this manner. Put another way, the self is a kind of *interpretation* of these sensations. In turn, Hume is content to cast the problem of identity to the realm of language, as a 'grammatical' rather than 'philosophical' difficulty (p. 262). Of course, such a 'self' can never be the foundational principle of our knowledge, for there is no stable subject lying behind the physiological processes that go to make up the production of the impressions and ideas called 'experience'.[23]

It is clear from this that the implications of Hume's account of knowledge lead us well beyond the terrain marked out by Descartes's sceptical method. Indeed, adopting a stance of Cartesian doubt, Hume says, would lead to a scepticism that 'would be entirely incurable; and no reasoning could ever bring us to a state of assurance and conviction upon any subject' (*Enquiry*, section 116). With regard to our knowledge, we must remain content with probabilities that rest upon the authority of experience, rather than seeking to attain indubitable certainty. 'Reason' becomes at best a means whereby we can limit the possibility of our beliefs straying too far from the bounds of good sense: 'Our reason must be consider'd as a kind of cause, of which truth is the natural effect; but such-a-one as by the irruption of other causes, and by the inconstancy of our mental powers, may frequently be prevented. By this means all knowledge degenerates into probability . . .' (*Treatise*, 180).

Hume thereby articulates a strong case for our understanding questions of knowledge in a less systematic and formal sense than Descartes does. Equally, although Hume does not always make it explicit, it is nevertheless the case that there is an inexorably *social* dimension implicit in his account of human understanding. Such an approach is, perhaps, most evidenced in the discussions presented in the later parts of the *Enquiry*, where Hume stresses the role played by social convention in establishing values. For example, Hume claims that 'Particular customs and manners alter the usefulness of qualities: they also alter their merit. Particular situations and accidents have, in some degree, the same influence'. In the same vein, he argues that conduct that promotes the general good of the community will be valued by the community, and that the good fortune or misery of others provokes, in each case, a like response in us (section 199). According to this view, humans are fundamentally social beings whose good manners are the result of their need to live together: 'I hate a drinking companion, says the Greek proverb, who never forgets. The follies of the last debauch should be buried in eternal oblivion, in order to give full scope to the follies of the next' (section 170). Such comments pay testimony to the importance Hume places on the role of conventions and shared norms in social intercourse.

Likewise, given his sceptical attitude toward any attempt at defining the self in isolation from the realm of experience, it is perhaps a short step toward defining subjectivity principally in terms of its social dimension. So, one might argue that for Hume, when it comes to understanding what one is, how one affects others is a far more important issue than how one introspectively 'understands' oneself (and attempting the latter, as we have seen, he would find absurd, in any case). To this extent, one might say that on a Humean view 'my' *precedes* 'I' in the sense that it is the extent to which 'my' actions affect others that gives rise to my sense of self (the 'I'). To put it another way, one could say that there is no 'I' that exists independently of, or prior to, 'you' and 'we'. Knowledge, too, could in this way become susceptible to being re-articulated in terms of its *role* within a web of social relations. Following this line of reasoning, we would then end up arriving at the view that shared social structures exert a determining effect with regard to our conceptual abilities.

4   Kant

When the German philosopher Immanuel Kant (1724–1804) read Hume he experienced a kind of philosophical revelation. It was Hume's empiricist approach, coupled with his scepticism about causality that, Kant said, awakened him from his dogmatic (rationalist) slumbers. Kant, however, rejects Hume's conclusions about knowledge. Instead, he responds to Hume by reaffirming the role that objectivity plays in our acquisition of knowledge. This he seeks to do by way of attempting to provide an account of the necessary conditions of our knowledge. Contrary to Hume, such conditions, Kant contends, are not reducible to 'mere experience'. Rather, these conditions are what make any form of experience possible for us as thinking beings. Kant's thought might justly be described as the working through of this one central idea, which is then applied to a number of different areas of philosophical concern. The essentials of Kant's approach are to be found in the *Critique of Pure Reason*[24] (1781, with a revised second edition published in 1787). This work, usually referred to as the first *Critique*, could not in all fairness be described as an 'easy read'. Nevertheless, it has exerted an extensive influence upon many of Kant's successors, both in the nineteenth and twentieth centuries. The first *Critique*, when conjoined with the second and third *critiques* – the *Critique of Practical Reason* (1788) and the *Critique of Judgement* (1790) – amounts to a systematic examination of the scope and limits of human rational powers in the theoretical, practical and aesthetic realms. However, it is the first *Critique* that offers the fundamentals of Kant's thought, and it is this text that I shall discuss in some detail here.

4.1   A priori *and* a posteriori *judgements*

Kant seeks to elucidate an account of knowledge that avoids falling into scepticism (a position exemplified for him by Hume's sceptical version of empiricism). For

Kant, such a project involves rejuvenating metaphysics, which, he notes early in the first *Critique*, is an area of enquiry that has been much maligned by some of his more recent predecessors: 'Time was when metaphysics was entitled the Queen of the sciences . . . Now, however, the changed fashion of the time brings her only scorn' (Aviii). In Kant's view, metaphysics is that area of enquiry that is concerned with the possibility of formulating true judgements about experience. And our knowledge of experience turns on the metaphysical conditions that render it possible. Kant's appreciation of the achievement of Locke and Hume is evident from the outset of the *Critique*. The empiricist emphasis on the role experience plays in our knowledge is thereby affirmed by him. However, this affirmation is a qualified one: 'There can be no doubt that all our knowledge begins with experience . . . But though all our knowledge begins with experience, it does not follow that it all arises out of experience' (B1). In other words, although we might be committed to the view that all our knowledge is concerned with experience, this does not of itself entitle us to endorse the further claim that experience is the sole *source* of all our knowledge. According to Kant, there are, in fact, two kinds of knowledge, which come from different sources. First, there is the knowledge that we derive from making judgements on the basis of our empirical experiences. Judgements of this kind Kant calls *a posteriori* judgements; in other words, such judgements are made 'after the fact' on the basis of experience. There is, however, another species of judgements, which Kant calls *a priori* judgements. The essential thing about *a priori* judgements is that they can be arrived at, and have validity, independently of experience: '*a priori* knowledge . . . [is] . . . knowledge absolutely independent of all experience. Opposed to it is empirical knowledge, which is knowledge possible only *a posteriori*, that is, through experience' (B2–3).

How, then, ought we to characterize *a priori* judgements? This can be done, says Kant, by way of analysing the necessity and universality involved in judgements that are *a priori*. In order for a proposition that expresses a judgement to be *a priori* two factors must come into play. First, it must, in being thought, be thought of as being necessary. Second, it must be thought of as being universal. In Kant's own words, 'Necessity and strict universality are . . . sure criteria of *a priori* knowledge, and are inseparable from one another' (*Critique*, B4). Necessity involves thinking about something in such a way that one could not think about it differently. Universality involves thinking about something in such a way that it would be always and everywhere the case. As long as any proposition accords with these two conditions, then it can safely be said to encapsulate an *a priori* judgement.

There are two types of *a priori* judgement: analytic and synthetic. With an analytic judgement, if we take a subject, *A*, and a predicate, *B*, the predicate is contained within *A* as part of its definition. By way of example, one can say that the judgement expressed in the proposition 'All bachelors are unmarried' is an analytic judgement, since the predicate ('unmarried') is contained within the subject ('bachelors'): a bachelor is, by definition, unmarried. Kant's own example sounds rather more complex, but the same principle applies. He tells us that the proposition 'All bodies are extended' is an analytic judgement because the notion of extension (the predicate) is implicitly contained within the concept of a body (the subject): we cannot think of any body that is not extended. It is worth noting the role that necessity and universality play here. If I think of a body, I must also think of it as having extension (hence, there is *necessity* involved in the judgement); equally, I am unable to think of any body whatsoever without always thinking of it as having extension (hence, there is also *universality* involved in the judgement). Analytic judgements can be contrasted with 'synthetic judgements'. In synthetic judgements, a predicate, *B*, is external to the subject, *A* (*Critique*, A7/B11). Synthetic judgements, it follows, involve an act of *inference* which takes us beyond the scope of the concepts one has at one's disposal independently of experience. For example, the proposition 'All bodies are heavy' involves a synthetic judgement, since the predicate 'heavy' is not implicit within the concept of a body as we think it in general. All judgements based on experience are synthetic: one cannot derive from the concept of 'body' alone the concept of 'weight'; and we only think of bodies as being heavy or light because we encounter ones that possess these characteristics in the world around us.

Kant's central concern, however, is to show that not all our synthetic judgements are derived from experience. In other words, he wishes to argue that we make at least some judgements about experience that do not rely solely upon experience (and therefore inductive reasoning) for their justification. If we recall Hume's account of causality and rephrase it in Kantian terms, it is clear that Hume's contention is that when we think in terms of causes and effects we think 'synthetically'. We do so because we infer a causal relation between two objects, neither of which have the concept of causality contained within them. Kant, likewise, regards all judgements that are concerned with experience as synthetic. However, he thinks that Hume makes a mistake when he characterizes causality as resting purely upon experience, and hence inductive reasoning. Kant argues that if we take

> the proposition, 'every alteration must have a cause' . . . [we find that] . . . the very concept of a cause so manifestly contains the concept of a necessary connection with an effect and of the strict universality of the rule, that the concept would be altogether lost if we attempted to derive it, as Hume has done, from a repeated association of that which happens with that which precedes, and from a custom of connecting representations, a custom originating in this repeated association, and therefore a merely subjective necessity.   (*Critique*, B5)

So, Kant is arguing, if we analyse what is contained within the concept of causality, we will find that it has implicit within it the very notion of necessary connection that Hume sought to deny to it. In other words, a cause, by definition, necessarily presupposes an effect. Moreover, when we think of this, we do so in a manner that is always and everywhere applicable. Nevertheless, it is equally the case that the proposition 'every alteration must have a cause' embodies a *synthetic judgement*. So, what kind of synthetic judgement is it? It is, says Kant, both synthetic and *a priori*. Such judgements as these, which cannot be reduced to experience but which are nevertheless *about* experience, Kant calls '*a priori* synthetic judgements'. It is the central project of the first *Critique* to show how such judgements are possible, and in this way to establish the validity of a form of reasoning that has objectivity because it is independent of empirical, and hence merely subjective, experience. Thus, *a priori* synthetic judgements are judgements that are made concerning experience, but whose significance cannot be reduced to it. Kant attempts to show that this claim is true by pointing out that in order to possess any knowledge of the world at all we must already have within our minds concepts whose *source* is not simply reducible to experience or, in Humean terms, habit or custom.

In one sense, it is a quite simple point that Kant is making here. It is true that we are beings who are capable of having experiences, and it is true that all our knowledge rests upon this fact. But is it convincing to argue that we are, like Lockean empty cabinets, the passive receivers of sense impressions? One problem with the empiricist view is that in order to have any experiences at all humans must surely already possess the ability to recognize an experience as such. An ability of this kind cannot be derived from experience itself, for experience presupposes it. But if that is the case, how is it that we can do this? Hume rests content with the conclusion that we simply have this ability, and cannot explain it. Kant's answer to this question, in contrast, is that the possession of such an ability implies that we must already have an understanding of what it means to have experiences that is both *independent* of and *prior* to our actually having any. Both (1) our ability to receive impressions from the senses and (2) our understanding are therefore structured according to principles which, taken together, constitute the preconditions of the possibility of experience. These preconditions serve as the basis of our knowledge.

I have already noted that Kant sets out to answer one key question: 'How are *a priori* synthetic judgements possible?' (*Critique*, B19). It is for this reason that the notion of the *a priori* is fundamental to his theory of knowledge. In analysing such knowledge, Kant needs to address two key problems. On the one hand, he must tell us how it is that a subject can have any experiences at all. On the other hand, he must also provide convincing arguments that will avoid the position he has castigated Hume for adopting, namely, the view that our knowledge of experience is the result of 'a merely subjective necessity'. This is another way of saying that our knowledge of experience must be derived from objective principles, i.e. principles that are not merely the result of individual, subjective experience. These principles guarantee that our knowledge has objectivity. Kant's task can thus be broken into two parts. First, he needs to show how our ability to have sense impressions is structured in an *a priori* fashion. Second, he must then show how our understanding is governed by *a priori* rules.[25]

4.2 The matter and form of appearances

The first of these requirements needs to be addressed. So, Kant turns his attention to an analysis of our ability to be affected by the impressions of our senses. We 'relate to objects', Kant holds, in one way only: by means of '*intuition*' (*Critique*, B33/A19). We always exist in some determinate relation to objects in the world around us, and Kant clearly thinks this is an 'immediate relation': all external objects of experience directly affect us by giving rise, via the senses, to intuitions. Intuitions, however, are only possible because the human mind has the ability to be 'affected in a certain way' by external objects such that it can have representations of them. In order to have an intuition of an object I must always have an accompanying representation of that object. The ability to be affected in this way Kant entitles 'sensibility'. Sensibility, it follows, gives rise to intuitions. In turn, these intuitions are '*thought* through the understanding, and through the understanding arise *concepts*'. As with the empiricist model, therefore, all knowledge must ultimately relate to our intuitions. This is because it is only through intuitions that we can have any experiences and, to recall the quotation from the beginning of Kant's text, 'all our knowledge begins with experience'.

Any intuition that is derived from sensation Kant calls an 'empirical intuition'. The object of any such intuition is called its '*appearance*' (*Critique*, B34/A20). Any appearance can be divided into two components. First, there is that part of the appearance 'which corresponds to sensation'. This is the '*matter*' of the appearance. Second, there is the component of any appearance that orders it 'in certain relations'. This is the '*form* of appearance'. Therefore, Kant draws a distinction between the *content* of what we encounter in any experience, and the *form* in which we encounter it. All appearances, it follows, involve a substantive, empirical component. But, if taken on its own,[26] the empirical world would appear to us as a mere chaotic mass of sensations (what he calls the 'manifold' of appearance). In order for these sensations to be presented to us in a meaningful way, they must be *ordered*. The matter and form distinction is an important one because 'while the matter of all appearance is given to us *a posteriori* only, its form must lie ready for the sensations *a priori* in the mind, and so must allow of being considered apart from all sensation' (B34/A20). In other words, while all our representations are always representations concerning experience, their form involves 'nothing that belongs to sensation'. From this Kant concludes that there is a special kind of representation; one that is not empirical but '*pure*'. Such pure representations indicate that there is a 'pure form of sensibility' or 'pure *intuition*' in the human mind. The study of these principles is a 'science', and Kant entitles this science '*transcendental aesthetic*' (B35/A21). It is '*transcendental*' since it concerns principles that are *independent of experience*.[27] It concerns the '*aesthetic*' since it is about our 'sensibility', i.e. our ability to be affected by objects by way of our senses.

4.3   *The transcendental aesthetic*

The science of transcendental aesthetic involves analysing our *sensibility*, not our concepts. This is because, as we have seen, concepts arise from intuitions; and intuitions are only possible because we have sensibility. Two things are required. First, Kant must '*isolate* sensibility, by taking away from it everything which the understanding thinks through its concepts'. Second, sensibility itself must then be shorn of 'everything that belongs to sensation'. In this way, Kant argues, he will provide an analysis of '*pure intuition*'. This amounts to saying that what he is going to tell us about concerns only the *form* that our representations of objects must take, not the content of such representations. The science of transcendental aesthetic, therefore, involves isolating and analysing the form in which we must think of objects in order for them to be represented to our minds. There are two such forms: space and time. Kant proceeds to offer what he terms a 'metaphysical *exposition*' of these two forms.

4.4   What is a 'metaphysical exposition'?

Strangely enough, given that the isolation of sensibility requires he remove all that the understanding thinks by way of concepts, Kant's exposition of space and time starts with an analysis of their *concepts*. There is, however, a good reason for this: the analysis of these concepts will reveal that space and time are not in fact mere concepts. However, before we get to this stage in the argument, it is worth noting what Kant means by a 'metaphysical exposition'. If we provide an 'exposition' of a concept, says Kant, then what we are doing is constructing a 'not necessarily exhaustive' but 'clear' account of what belongs to that concept. An exposition will serve to tell us what goes to make a concept the kind of concept it is. In addition, Kant calls any exposition 'metaphysical' when that exposition entitles us to make the further claim that the concept it is an analysis of is *'given a priori'* (*Critique*, B38/ A23). The purpose of providing any metaphysical exposition is to tell us whether the concept we are studying is given to us independently of experience. Kant wishes to affirm this point with regard to space and time.

4.5   The metaphysical exposition of space

Whenever we think of objects 'we represent to ourselves [the] objects as outside us, and all without exception in space' (*Critique*, B37/A22). However, if we analyse the concept of space we will discover that it 'is not an empirical concept which has been derived from outer experiences' (B38/A23). Rather, space is the *form* of representation that we must always presuppose whenever we think of objects. This is shown, Kant argues, by the fact that we can never think of any object without thinking of it as being situated in space. True, he adds, we can think of the absence of all objects, but even when we do so we can never think of the absence of space itself. Space 'must therefore be regarded as the condition of the possibility of appearances, and not as a determination dependent upon them' (B39/A24). If this is the case, then space cannot be regarded as 'a discursive . . . or general concept of relations of things in general'. In other words, Kant's analysis of the concept of space leads him to the conclusion that space itself is not a concept, but a *pure intuition*: 'the original representation of space is an *a priori* intuition, not a concept' (B40/A25). If space were only a concept, then it would be something that we could *choose* to apply or not to apply to objects when we think of them. But we make no such choice in this regard: we *must always* think of objects as occupying space. There is necessity ('must') and universality ('always') involved with regard to space. For these reasons 'an *a priori*, not an empirical, intuition underlies all concepts of space' (B39/A25). The pure intuition of space, in turn, is a unity (i.e. it is 'essentially one'), since we cannot, through any form of analysis, break it into any parts. We can, indeed, talk of 'spaces', but all such talk presupposes the unity of the transcendental intuition of space (I cannot think of 'spaces' unless I already have a concept of 'space', and this concept is derived from the pure intuition of it).

4.6   The transcendental exposition of space

Having offered a 'metaphysical exposition', Kant then offers a 'transcendental exposition' of the concept of space. This is an important move, for it allows him to progress to the next stage in his argument. This next stage is needed because it is not enough for him to show that underlying the concept of space is a pure intuition that can in turn yield us synthetic knowledge of objects (i.e. the knowledge that all objects, whatever they are, must exist in space). What must additionally be shown is that we are also able to demonstrate that it is possible to arrive at an understanding of other synthetic *a priori* knowledge by way of analysing a given concept (in this case the concept of space). A transcendental exposition involves 'the explanation of a concept, as a *principle* from which the possibility of other *a priori* synthetic knowledge can be understood' (*Critique*, B40/A25, italics added). In other words, if we provide a transcendental exposition of a concept, what we are doing is showing that the concept in question can then be used to provide us with a 'principle' for the acquisition of further knowledge. On the basis of such a principle we can infer that synthetic *a priori* knowledge is attainable. For this to be possible two conditions must be fulfilled. Kant needs to show us (1) that other synthetic *a priori* knowledge can be generated from the concept, and (2) that this knowledge follows only when we explain the concept in a certain manner or 'mode'.[28]

Take the case of geometry. Geometry, Kant says, is a science that gives us knowledge of space that is synthetic and *a priori*. In order for this to be possible our representation of space must have its 'origin' in pure intuition and not be a mere concept. If space were only a concept, then we could not construct any propositions from it that would take us beyond the meanings contained within the concept itself, but in geometry we can do this. Since this is the case, space cannot only be a concept. Rather, space is a pure intuition. And the science of geometry generates further knowledge on the basis of the fact that we have an original representation of space by way of this intuition. Thus, condition (1) is fulfilled.

Equally, all geometrical propositions give us knowledge that has a compelling necessity, for example, the proposition 'space has only three dimensions'. The certainty of my knowledge that space has three dimensions indicates that such knowledge is not derived from experience, for I am always conscious of the fact that this is necessarily and universally the case with regard to space. The intuition upon which such knowledge rests must be 'found in us prior to any perception of an object and must therefore be pure, not empirical, intuition' (*Critique*, B41/A25). If this is so, then the manner in which I acquire synthetic *a priori* knowledge when I construct geometrical propositions concerning space must be derived from the fact that space itself is a pure intuition for me. This intuition 'has its seat in the subject only', not in experience. Thus, condition (2) is fulfilled.

From his analysis, Kant draws two conclusions. First, space cannot represent to us any particular properties or relations that we might attribute to the objects we perceive. It is merely the formal precondition whereby we are able to perceive any objects at all. Second, since space is 'the form of all appearances', it follows that it is 'the subjective condition of sensibility' (*Critique*, B42/A26). Therefore, the subject must be equipped with a form of 'receptivity' that is prior to the intuition of any particular objects. This is another way of saying that it is 'solely from the human standpoint that we can speak of space'. If we were to remove our subjectivity from the equation, then it would not be possible to talk in any meaningful sense about space. In the following sense only, space has '*reality*': as long as we think of objects, we must do so by conforming to the formal condition that they must exist for us in space, and this condition is what confers 'objective validity' on the concept of space. On this basis, Kant thinks he can have the best of both worlds:

> We assert, then, the *empirical reality* of space, as regards all possible outer experience; and yet at the same time, we assert its *transcendental ideality* – in other words, that it is nothing at all, immediately we withdraw the above condition, namely its limitation to possible experience, and so look upon it as something that lies in things in themselves. (B44/A28)

Space has empirical reality, since without it no cognition of external objects would be possible for us. At the same time, however, its transcendental 'ideality' tells us that no objects we perceive are in themselves 'in space'. This implies that it is not possible to have knowledge that concerns anything other than the *appearances* of objects, for 'space is not a form inhering in things in themselves as their intrinsic property . . . objects in themselves are quite unknown to us' (B45/A30). This last claim is very important. For, it amounts to holding that the objectivity of our knowledge is a matter that solely concerns the manner in which objects can appear to us. Although we might be tempted to think about the issue, any speculation about how things might be 'in themselves' can never count as 'knowledge'. In this way, Kant is asserting a metaphysically determined limit to our possible knowledge.

4.7   The metaphysical and transcendental expositions of time

Having offered the metaphysical and transcendental expositions of space, Kant then provides analogous expositions of the concept of time. Time, likewise, is 'not an empirical concept' (*Critique*, B46/A30). Rather, it is the *a priori* condition of the possibility of our having any representations of things as existing simultaneously or successively. We can think of objects either as existing together at one and the same time, or in succession (one after the other), only because we presuppose that they all occur in time. Time is a necessary condition of our thinking of any object whatsoever. Likewise, time is a unity that cannot be analysed out into component parts. Moreover, since time is not derived from experience, it is also a 'pure form of sensible intuition'. From the transcendental exposition of time, Kant then seeks to show how it can serve as a means of our acquiring other synthetic *a priori* knowledge. For example, he argues that the knowledge that we can derive from the concepts of alteration and motion presupposes the representation of time as a pure intuition that is independent of experience.

As with space, time is not to be taken as something that exists either in itself or as a property inhering in objects. It is, rather, 'nothing but the form of inner sense, that is, of the intuition of ourselves and of our inner state' (*Critique*, B49/A33). Where space performs the task of ordering the form our experiences must take with regard to the outer world, time orders our *inner* experiences in a like manner. However, in addition, time, Kant argues, 'is the *a priori* condition of all appearances whatsoever' (B50/A33). There is a good reason for this claim. For, whereas all our representations derived from space concern only what is external to us, no representations would be possible at all unless there were minds (i.e. us) that had them. Since time is the formal condition of our having an inner state, it is therefore the condition of the possibility of our having *any* representations at all. Time, then, is a *given* in so far as it is immediately presupposed in all of our experiences: 'It is the immediate condition of inner appearance (of our souls), and thereby the mediate condition of outer appearances' (B50/A34). No human being could think any representations of objects unless he or she already did so in virtue of existing in an immediate relation to time. I, as a thinking subject, can only have representations because they are ordered by way of my inner sense. I, therefore, exist in an unmediated relationship with this inner sense: time quite simply is *given* as the necessary precondition of my having any thoughts at all. In turn, I only have representations of the outer world of objects because I already have the ability to order these representations as they occur in relation to me.

As with Descartes, Locke and Hume, Kant therefore places the subject at the centre of his theory of knowledge. All our representations occur in virtue of the fact that we think them according to the principle that states that they must always conform to the determination of inner sense or time. And time is 'a purely subjective condition of our (human) intuition . . . and, in itself, apart from the subject, is nothing' (*Critique*, B51/A35). As with space, time therefore has both empirical reality and transcendental ideality. On the one hand, time is the objective condition of our having any representations at all. On the other hand, it is nevertheless dependent upon our existence, in so far as 'if we abstract from the subjective conditions of sensible intuition, time is nothing, and cannot be ascribed to objects in themselves' (B52/A36). The universal and necessary conditions of our intuitions are therefore essentially linked to the form of our subjectivity. But Kant's account has added one important qualification to the notion of subjectivity: in order to have intuitions we must always exist in conformity with the principle that time is the condition of the possibility of our having any representations at all. Subjects, therefore, need not be primarily defined on this view as being made of mental substance (Descartes), nor are they to be regarded as beings that have unmediated representations of external sensory impressions (Lockean 'ideas'). Nor is our knowledge of objects dependent upon the merely 'subjective' determinations of our individual experiences (as with Hume), for the mode in which objects are given is objectively determined. What the Kantian view of subjectivity entails is an issue to which I shall return in due course. Beforehand, it is perhaps a good idea to provide a recapitulation of Kant's position as it has been outlined thus far.

4.8   Summary

For Kant, we are beings who have representations of our sensory experiences, and what we can call 'knowledge' only counts as such if it concerns our experiences. However, just because all knowledge concerns experience, it does not follow that its origin is to be sought only in experience. Not all of our concepts come from experience: some are *a priori* (i.e. independent of experience). An analysis of the concepts of space and time shows them to be *a priori*. The analysis of these concepts shows that space and time are not 'mere concepts'. Rather, these concepts themselves rest upon the pure intuitions of space and time. These pure intuitions are *a priori* first because they cannot be shown to be derived from experience, and second because they satisfy the conditions of universality and necessity that serve to define all *a priori* knowledge. The intuitions of space and time yield us synthetic knowledge that is *a priori*, in so far as (1) they determine the *form* that all our experiences must take, and (2) other *a priori* synthetic knowledge can be derived from them. Taken together, they are 'the pure forms of all sensible intuition', and as such are the 'sources' of all our *a priori* synthetic knowledge (*Critique*, B55–6/A38–9). By this point in his argument Kant has, in part, answered his question: how is synthetic *a priori* knowledge possible? It is possible because all our empirical intuitions must conform to the conditions given by the pure forms of sensible intuition of space and time. These pure intuitions ground all our knowledge of the external and inner worlds of experience. On the basis of them we make all our judgements concerning any possible experience. These judgements are synthetic (since they concern experience), but they are also at the same time *a priori*, since their source and therefore their validity is derived independently of experience. Because these preconditions concern only our sensibility (i.e. our ability to receive impressions from our senses), our knowledge is, for Kant, always and only knowledge of appearances: 'intuition is nothing but the representation of appearance. . . . We know nothing but our mode of perceiving [objects]. . . . With this alone have we any concern' (B59/A42).

4.9   Why we can only know 'appearances', and why they are real, not illusions

A posteriori knowledge, which is always inductive in nature, rests upon the necessity of appearances conforming to the conditions given *a priori* by the pure intuitions of space and time. It is for this reason that questions concerning the relationship between our representations and the objects they are representations of is always a 'transcendental' issue. What we call 'drops of rain', says Kant, 'are mere appearances' and 'even their round shape, nay even the space in which they fall, are nothing in themselves, but merely modifications or fundamental forms of our sensible intuition'. It is for this reason that we can only *know* appearances. Because we can only know appearances, things in themselves remain illusive and shadowy entities that must remain forever closed off from the possibility of our asserting propositions that would count as knowledge concerning them: 'the transcendental object remains unknown to us' (*Critique*, B63/A46). Kant's claim, then, is that we can *think* about things in themselves (Bxxvii), but we cannot *know* anything about them, apart from in the negative sense of knowing that we cannot know them.

Appearances, in their own turn, are not however mere shadows or illusions (*Critique*, B69/A70). When we perceive any object as an appearance, this does not mean that the object merely *seems* to be outside of us: the object *is* outside of us, and this knowledge is not an illusion. Given that time, too, is only a form of appearance, this is an important point. For, if the word 'appearance' was synonymous with 'illusion', then our inner sense (which is derived from the pure intuition of time) would also be a mere illusion, and our subjectivity would thereby evaporate.

4.10   Pure understanding and transcendental knowledge

For Kant, we are beings who are capable (1) of receiving impressions and thereby generating representations from our senses, and (2) of having knowledge of objects by way of these representations. The objective validity of this knowledge is secured by the *a priori* conditions that we must accede to whenever we think any object in general.[29] With regard to the question of *a priori* synthetic knowledge, the analysis of our sensibility is, however, only half of the story. To this something else must be added, namely, an account of *how we think*. Our ability to receive impressions and generate representations from the senses Kant has already given the name 'sensibility'. Our ability to generate knowledge by *thinking* about our sense impressions he calls 'understanding'. An important division of labour is thereby asserted concerning sensibility and understanding. *Sensibility* is the mode in which we are affected by objects through our sense impressions. *Understanding*, in contrast, is the mode in which we *think* these objects and their relations. Both are necessary for *a priori* synthetic knowledge. Without sensibility we could have no objects to think about (there would be no content to our thought). Without understanding we could not think about any objects (for we would have no concepts with which to think): 'Thoughts without content are empty, intuitions without concepts are blind . . . The understanding can intuit nothing, the senses can think nothing. Only through their union can knowledge arise' (*Critique*, B75/A51). An essential precondition of knowledge is the fusion between intuitions and concepts, between sensibility and conceptual ability. Kant must, however, tell us more about the nature of the understanding as a prelude to formulating the grounds of this union. In order to do this, Kant now turns to an analysis of 'the science of the rules of the understanding in general, that is, logic' (B76/A52).[30]

4.11   General logic and transcendental knowledge

Kant's discussion of logic (*Critique*, B78/A52ff) is a complex one, and I do not propose to elaborate it in detail here. However, a number of points may be made concerning it. Logic, on Kant's view, is the study of the rules that operate in the understanding. Of principal interest to him is what he calls 'pure general logic'. This logic offers an account of the 'form of thought in general', and thereby elaborates the rules whereby the understanding connects different representations to one another (B80/A55). The elucidation of what Kant calls 'transcendental knowledge' is derived from the analysis of these rules. Transcendental knowledge is a special kind of knowledge. It is the kind of knowledge 'by which we know that – and how – certain representations (intuitions or concepts) can be employed or are possible purely *a priori*' (B80/A56). Transcendental knowledge thus tells us about the kind of *a priori* knowledge that we can have in two ways. First, it tells us *that* we can have *a priori* knowledge. Second, it also tells us *how* our *a priori* knowledge can (and indeed does) relate to the world of empirical experience. Transcendental knowledge belongs only to 'the pure understanding and reason, whereby we think objects entirely *a priori*' (B81/A57). The analysis of transcendental knowledge is the task of 'transcendental logic', and Kant spends some space telling us about this. To be brief, however, the point of all this is to elaborate the *rules of thought* that allow us to have concepts of objects independently of experience by laying bare 'that part of thought which has its origin solely in the understanding' (B87/A62). The understanding is thereby taken by Kant to be amenable to being analysed in its pure form. Such an analysis of 'pure understanding' contains nothing empirical.

Pure general logic, according to Kant, has as its principal aim the elucidation of *criteria* of truth. There are, he argues, no sufficient and universal criteria of truth with regard to the *content* of any particular proposition that we might construct. Logic, however, can provide an account of the '*form* of thought in general' (*Critique*, B80/A55, italics added). General logic 'only considers representations', whether *a priori* or empirical in origin, 'according to the laws which the understanding employs when, in thinking, it relates them to one another' (B80/A55). In other words, general logic is the analysis of the rules of thinking that govern how our representations are connected.

What Kant calls 'transcendental knowledge' is derived from the analysis of these rules. Importantly, the term 'transcendental knowledge' is not synonymous with the phrase 'all *a priori* knowledge'. We may have an *a priori* representation of space, for instance, but such a representation does not of itself count as a transcendental one, even though it is *a priori*. We can note, then, that Kant is drawing a further distinction concerning our knowledge. On the one hand, we can have both knowledge that is either independent of, or derived from, experience. On the other hand, however, we can also have *transcendental knowledge*. Such knowledge is a kind of 'knowledge about knowledge': it tells us that we can know about the kind of knowledge that we are capable of having. It is important here to be clear about what transcendental knowledge is concerned with. For transcendental knowledge ('knowledge about knowledge') is *not* therefore a matter of the relationship between what we know and the objects of our knowledge: 'The distinction between the transcendental and the empirical belongs . . . only to the critique of knowledge; it does not concern the relation of that knowledge to its objects' (*Critique*, B81/A57). The kind of knowledge that is involved here concerns neither our empirical experiences nor our sensibility. Hence, Kant argues, what is required is 'a science of the knowledge which belongs to the pure understanding and reason, whereby we think objects entirely *a priori*'. The purpose of such a science would be to tell us (a) what the origin of this knowledge is, (b) what things such knowledge is concerned with, i.e.

its 'scope', and (c) whether this kind of knowledge is objectively valid. The science in question is called '*transcendental logic*'. In effect, this is a science which has as its purpose the elucidation of the fundamental nature of thought as it relates to objects, for transcendental logic contains 'solely the rules of the pure thought of an object' (B80/A55).

In short, then, Kant believes that an outline of the rules of thinking can be given by way of transcendental logic. This is done through isolating the understanding in the same manner in which sensibility was isolated earlier by way of the transcendental aesthetic. What is required here, though, is the 'separating out from our knowledge [of] that part of thought which has its origin solely in the understanding' (*Critique*, B87/A62). So, Kant is now embarking upon an analysis of the principles of thought that allow us to think of objects. True to form, this aspect of transcendental logic is itself given a name: 'transcendental analytic'.

4.12   The transcendental analytic: the analytic of concepts

The transcendental analytic has as its purpose the exhibition of those concepts that are given by the understanding alone (and hence are derived from what Kant calls 'pure understanding'). The concepts included in the transcendental analytic must be (1) shown to be pure, not empirical; (2) demonstrated to have their source in thought and understanding alone, not in sensibility; (3) shown to be fundamental and unified, and not therefore be derivable from something else or capable of being broken into component parts; and (4) complete, i.e. the list must include *all* the concepts used by pure understanding. It is important to recall here that, on Kant's view, pure understanding contains nothing that is empiricial. Equally, it is completely distinct from sensibility since, as we have already seen, Kant asserts a fundamental distinction between having sense impressions and thinking about these impressions through the understanding in the form of concepts.

The transcendental analytic is itself broken up into two related parts. First, there is that part that analyses the concepts employed by the pure understanding (the 'analytic of concepts'). Second, there is that part which presents an analysis of the 'principles' or rules on the basis of which the pure understanding operates (the 'analytic of principles'). Of these two parts, the second is concerned primarily with how we make judgements about appearances on the basis of our possession of *a priori* rules. I do not propose to discuss this here. Rather, I will concentrate on Kant's account of human understanding as a 'faculty of rules' as it is presented in the analytic of concepts. There are some good reasons for taking this approach. First, it is in the analytic of concepts that Kant makes some important claims about the nature of human understanding, and this ties in with the earlier discussions of Descartes, Locke and Hume. Second, it is here, too, that he outlines his view of the thinking subject. Third, the question of judgement is also discussed here, as the defining characteristic of all understanding.

So far, Kant tells us at the beginning of the analytic of concepts, he has discussed the understanding in purely negative terms: he has said what it is not (i.e. that it is not to be confused with sensibility), but he has not said what it is. Now, Kant addresses this issue by first reminding us that we can only have knowledge in two ways: either via our intuitions, or via concepts. Sensibility is responsible for the first of these. Understanding is responsible for the second. Since we derive our concepts from our understanding, the understanding is, therefore, another source of our knowledge. There is a fundamental difference between these two sources. Whereas all intuitions presuppose our ability to be affected by the senses (our sensibility), 'concepts rest on functions' (*Critique*, B93/A68). What Kant is arguing is that concepts are functionally dependent on a kind of ability that is different in kind from sensibility. The ability to be affected by intuitions is, ultimately, a passive affair (we 'receive' impressions via our senses). In contrast, the *ability to think concepts* is a spontaneous and active matter. Moreover, when we think concepts we bring all of our 'various representations under one common representation'. The concept 'rose' takes a variety of representations and unites them in the one concept. All of our representations, it follows, are identified and ordered by concepts. At the same time, all of our concepts require that thinking orders *them* by bringing them together in a certain kind of arrangement. To make this last point clear we can say that the concept 'rose' unites a variety of representations, but concepts also need to be ordered in certain ways in relation to one another. For example, the proposition 'This rose is red' asserts that a relation exists between two specific concepts ('rose' and 'red').

How, then, are concepts brought together? This can happen in two ways: concepts are either thought in relation to (a) intuitions or (b) other concepts. In order for either (a) or (b) to be the case, some kind of judgement is required. The act of judgement is, it follows, a very special kind of activity, for in judging we actively mediate between different concepts. Every judgement involves using a concept that itself contains within it the assertion of a determinate relationship between other concepts. Such concepts in their own turn are ultimately linked to our intuitions and therefore to the objects of those intuitions (i.e. experience). 'Thus', for example, 'in the judgment, "all bodies are divisible", the concept of the divisible applies to various other concepts, but is here applied in particular to the concept of body, and this concept again to certain appearances that present themselves to us' (*Critique*, B93/A68). All acts of judgement, Kant is claiming, serve to unify different concepts in another '*higher* representation' (B94/A69). Judgements impose unity on diversity. Any act of understanding, says Kant, involves making judgements. And for this reason he can take the liberty of giving the understanding a name: it is 'a *faculty of judgment*'.

In this way, Kant characterizes the understanding as a spontaneous ability to link different representations together by subsuming them under higher order concepts. Let us, however, ignore all the particular judgements that might be made by the understanding and, instead, turn our attention to 'the mere form of understanding' that is involved in judgements in general. In what manner would it be appropriate to characterize the *form* that the understanding must always conform to whenever we make judgements, irrespective of the *content* involved in any individual judgement? (*Critique*, B94/A70). Kant answers this question by arguing that there are four kinds of judgement: quantity, quality, relation, and modality. Each of these he divides into four 'moments'.[31] We need not be detained by an analysis of the nature of these four kinds of judgement, or their respective moments. The essential point to grasp is that judgement occurs in these four ways only.

The above analysis tells us that when we engage in the act of understanding we make judgements. But there is something important that it does not tell us. It does not tell us how it comes about that acts of judgement are able to unify different representations by subsuming them under a 'higher representation'. It is one thing to show us what rules the understanding must abide by in order to judge; but it is a quite different matter to show us how the act of combining representations in an act of judgement actually happens. Kant now turns his attention to this issue.

4.13   Synthesis

The analysis of the transcendental aesthetic, Kant reminds us, showed us that there are pure forms of intuition (space and time). These pure forms make the representation of objects of experience possible for us. What they do *not* do is stipulate what the *content* (or, in Kant's terminology, the 'matter') of any of these intuitions must be. In other words, the pure intuitions of space and time do not of themselves give us a concrete (i.e. 'real') world. At best what we get from these pure intuitions is a world of pure appearances ('Such and such *looks* red to me'), not an objective knowledge of the world ('Such and such *is* red').

We can have many *different* representations, but they all abide by the same formal conditions. Within the pure intuitions of space and time, therefore, we find 'a manifold of pure *a priori* intuition' (*Critique*, B102/A77). However, knowledge of the diversity of those representations that go to make up this manifold can only be possible if it is organized in a specific manner. The activity of organizing this manifold of intuitions Kant entitles '*synthesis*'. The act of synthesis involves 'putting different representations together, and . . . grasping what is manifold in them in one [act of] knowledge . . . Synthesis of a manifold (be it given empirically or *a priori*) is what first gives rise to knowledge' (B103/A77). What Kant terms a '*pure*' act of synthesis happens when it occurs in relation to a manifold that is given *a priori*, as space and time are. It follows from this that if we can uncover the inner workings of the act of synthesis in its pure form, then we will discover nothing less than 'the first origin of our knowledge' (B104/A78).

Synthesis, taken in its broadest sense, is something human beings just do. It is an unconscious act, 'a blind but indispensable function of the soul' that springs from the spontaneity of human imagination (*Critique*, B104/A79). Even so, Kant holds that the *synthesis of concepts* is 'a function of the understanding'; and if we take care to examine the act of pure synthesis (i.e. the bringing together of a manifold that is given *a priori*) then what we will get from this examination is 'the pure concept of the understanding'. Kant thus wishes to show us what the understanding is like in its purest form, cleansed of any empirical aspects. This pure concept will reveal that there is an '*a priori* synthetic unity' underlying all acts of synthesis that are made in relation to concepts. To put it rather more clearly, Kant is going to argue that the act of synthesis rests upon something else. This 'something else' is in fact the 'transcendental subject', the fundamental structure of subjectivity itself.[32]

Analysing the pure concept of understanding shows us that there are four 'original pure concepts of synthesis' (*Critique*, B106/A80). These Kant calls the 'categories',[33] and they are strangely familiar. We have quantity (unity, plurality, totality); quality (reality, negation, limitation); relation (substance, causality, community); and modality (possibility, existence, necessity).[34] It is by way of reference to the categories, which are given *a priori* within the understanding, that *all* human beings perform the act of synthesizing the manifold of experience. The central function of the categories is to bestow unanimity upon the world of our experience because they apply to all conscious thought. It is only by way of the categories that we can 'think an object of intuition' at all. For example, we *must* be able to think of the relation between objects of intuition in terms of causality (i.e. in that one follows another).

As with Kant's account of judgement, it is not so much necessary to grasp what each of the categories does as to appreciate the importance of his claim that the ways of combining exemplified by the categories are given *prior* to experience from within the understanding itself.[35] Whenever we combine a manifold of representations, we must do so according to the dictates of the categories. By way of a final example, in performing an act of combination we must think in terms of quantity. Either there is unity, plurality or totality (the third of these being a plurality thought of as a unity) involved in our representations; or we must think in terms of modality: something is possible or impossible, exists or does not exist, is either necessary or contingent. We simply cannot perform any act of combination without thinking in the manner dictated by the categories. The existence of this fact is, for Kant, fundamental, for it tells us how we must think when we make synthetic judgements. However, he is obliged to address a further question. We may have arrived at the point at which the understanding is now shown to comply with *a priori* conditions in order to arrive at judgements concerning its representations, but these conditions are not the same as the objective *a priori* conditions of sensibility that were outlined in the transcendental aesthetic. This is because the *a priori* conditions of understanding are *subjective*: they are the rules that must be observed by us when we think, not the rules that govern our sensibility. What, then, is the relation between the two? This question is addressed in the Transcendental Deduction.

4.14   *The Transcendental Deduction*

A 'deduction', Kant tells us at the beginning of the Transcendental Deduction, is a manner of reasoning that can offer us a proof that has the status of a 'right'. As such, a deduction concerns the establishment of entitlement to something. As in matters of law, Kant argues, issues of right (*quid juris*) should not be confused with issues of fact (*quid facti*). Kant's use of the juridical metaphor here is no mere accident, for he has offered us an account of human understanding and knowledge that rests upon the importance of *a priori* rules and, for him, rules are to be understood in a primarily juridical sense. In the very following of rules we implicitly acknowledge that we are bound by them. Being bound by a rule is akin, in this sense at least, to being bound by legality: the latter only exists in virtue of its being observed by somebody (a thinking subject). When it comes to the question of human knowledge, the legal distinction between matters of fact and matters of right is equally pertinent. For, as we have seen already, on a Kantian view, we cannot justify *a priori* knowledge by mere title of fact (i.e. experience). Rather, in order for the claim that we are in possession of such knowledge to be justified it must also be shown that we possess it by title of right. *The possession of such title is what confers objectivity upon our knowledge.* Establishing this title of right is the task of the deduction: 'among the manifold concepts which form the highly complex web of human knowledge, there are some which are marked out for pure *a priori* employment . . . and their right to be so employed always demands a deduction' (*Critique*, B117/A85). However, not just any old (empirical) deduction is required for this purpose, but a *transcendental deduction*. An empirical deduction would tell us only one thing about our *a priori* concepts: it would explain their origin in terms of experience. A transcendental deduction, in contrast, concerns the 'legitimacy' of *applying these concepts to experience*, and such legitimacy must be established independently of experience. The function of a transcendental deduction is to provide a kind of certificate of 'legal' entitlement that justifies our use of *a priori* concepts independently of any reference to the empirical domain: 'they must be in a position to show a certificate of birth quite other than that of descent from experiences' (B119/A86-7). However, this requirement itself involves negotiating a further, and very tricky, problem relating to the link between understanding and sensibility.

In the forms of space and time Kant has already elucidated the two fundamental *a priori* preconditions of experience. These two forms 'relate to their objects without having borrowed from experience' by *ordering* the content that is given by it (*Critique*, B118/A86). Most important, this ordering of experience is something that has its origin in pure intuition and therefore thought. Space and time are, in this way, 'modes of knowledge' that 'make possible a synthetic knowledge of objects' (B121/A89). It is because the act of combination takes place within these modes of knowledge that 'the synthesis . . . has objective validity'.[36] This is all well and good so far as sensibility is concerned. But the understanding, as Kant has outlined it, does not allow of being treated in exactly the same fashion. This is because the categories (i.e. the rules) that determine how the understanding must think in order to combine its representations in an act of synthesis do not relate directly to the forms of our pure intuition (space and time). It is, in other words, one thing to say what *form* our intuitions must take, but it is quite another to say *how* the representations derived from these forms are combined when they are thought as pure concepts by the understanding. What Kant has done, therefore, is to create a model which accounts for our sensibility (that is, our ability to form representations out of intuitions) and our understanding (that is, our ability to combine these representations together) in two distinct, and possibly incompatible, ways. Both function according to *a priori* conditions that are independent of experience (the forms of space and time on the one hand, and the categories on the other), but it is not immediately obvious how the objective conditions of space and time connect with the subjective conditions of understanding. This, therefore, leaves open the question of how human understanding (which is subjective) can relate to its intuitions in such a way as to have objective knowledge concerning them. This is how Kant phrases the matter: 'The categories of understanding . . . do not represent the conditions under which objects are given in intuition. Objects may, therefore, appear to us without their being under the necessity of being related to the functions of understanding; and the understanding need not, therefore, contain their *a priori* conditions.' But if this should be the case, then 'Appearances might very well be so constituted that the understanding should not find them to be in accordance with the conditions of its unity' (*Critique*, B122–3/A89–90). To put it another way, the problem is one of 'how [the] *subjective conditions of thought* can have *objective validity*, that is, can furnish conditions of the possibility of all knowledge of objects' (B122/A89). We may think in terms of causality, for example, but it is by no means certain that 'appearances should contain anything of this kind'. There must, therefore, be a kind of 'meeting' of these two apparently incompatible realms. But where is one to look for the meeting place?

Since we can only know objects on the basis of our ability to have representations of them, it follows that our knowledge must be possible in virtue of *either* our intuitions *or* our concepts. We have already seen that *a priori* pure intuitions are the necessary preconditions of our empirical experiences; are *a priori* concepts, Kant wonders, also able to function in this way? Well, the answer to this question is a guarded 'yes', in so far as one cannot think of any object of experience without first presupposing the concept of an 'object in general'. If this is true, then 'Concepts of objects in general . . . underlie all empirical knowledge as its *a priori* conditions. The objective validity of the categories as *a priori* concepts rests, therefore, on the fact that, so far as the form of thought is concerned, through them alone does experience become possible' (*Critique*, B126/A93). To this extent, certain general concepts, too, are necessary for experience to be possible merely in virtue of the form they impose upon it. But such an observation does not amount to a 'deduction' of the objective validity of such concepts; it is 'only their illustration' (B126/A94). In other words, pointing out that concepts of this 'general' kind are necessary does not amount to establishing the certificate of birth required to prove their objective validity, it merely shows that they are necessary to the understanding. How does one now show that such concepts also have objectivity?

The act of combining representations in another 'higher representation', we should recall, Kant has already entitled 'synthesis'. He now proceeds to elaborate this claim. A synthesis indicates (1) 'that we cannot represent to ourselves anything as combined in the object [in question] which we have not ourselves previously combined', and (2) 'that of all representations *combination* is the only one which cannot be given through objects' (*Critique*, B130). This is another way of saying that the act of synthesis is something that cannot be derived from any empirical source. Equally, synthesis is a *spontaneous* act. From these two points two more follow. First, if synthesis does not have an empirical source, then its origin must be something that is *a priori* independent of experience. Second, if it is a spontaneous act, then it must be executed by a certain kind of 'somebody' simply in virtue of their being the kind of being that they are. This 'somebody' is, in fact, the thinking subject, for synthesis is 'an act of the self-activity of the subject, [and] it cannot be executed save by the subject itself'. The subject, then, can combine its representations in other, 'higher' representations, and *it is this ability that defines what a subject is*. Moreover, if we analyse the concept of combination that is involved here, then what we find is that 'Combination is representation of the *synthetic* unity of the manifold' (B131).

Combination, in other words, presupposes a *higher order representation* that underlies the possibility of all other 'higher representations'. The concept of combination tells us that the manifold of experience is always already combined in a manner that cannot be derived from experience, since the 'representation of this unity . . . is what, by adding itself to the representation of the manifold, first makes possible the concept of the combination [of the manifold]'. What, then, is this representation of unity that *adds itself* to all our other representations and thereby unifies them? It is, Kant says, none other than the 'I think' (the thinking subject).

The 'I think', therefore, is the higher order representation of the unity of all other representations. All of my representations are continually accompanied by the 'I think' as their necessary precondition, since without it none of those representations could be thought of as belonging to me. Moreover, 'this representation is an act of *spontaneity*, that is, it cannot be regarded as belonging to sensibility' (*Critique*, B132). Kant thus argues that the representation of the 'I think' cannot be derived from empirical experience since it is what makes my experience possible for me, and what is a condition of possibility for experience cannot be reduced to experience:

> I call it *pure apperception*, to distinguish it from empirical *apperception* . . . because it is that self-consciousness which, while generating the representation 'I think' . . . cannot itself be accompanied by any further representation. The unity of this apperception I likewise entitle the *transcendental* unity of self-consciousness, in order to indicate the possibility of *a priori* knowledge arising from it. For the manifold of representations, which are given in an intuition, would not be one and all *my* representations, if they did not all belong to one self-consciousness.   (*Critique*, B132)

Pure self-consciousness, therefore, generates the representation 'I think' independently of experience. Such pure self-consciousness is not itself a representation; and the 'I' that is generated by it cannot be divided into any component parts, for it is a unity: 'through the "I", as simple representation, nothing manifold is given; only in intuition, which is distinct from the "I", can a manifold be given; and only through *combination* in one consciousness can it be thought' (B135). So, Kant is committed to the view that there is a kind of self-consciousness that exists independently of experience, and without which no experience is possible. This pure self-consciousness is a transcendental unity since it is the sole origin of all possible *a priori* knowledge. And if it is a transcendental unity, then we do not need to look any further for the fundamental source of our knowledge, for we have found it. In the transcendental subject the *a priori* forms of experience and the pure concepts of the understanding are unified by the pure self-consciousness that manifests itself in the representation 'I think'. Most important of all, though, this transcendental self-consciousness is also the source of our objectivity because, like pure intuitions and pure concepts of understanding, it too is given *a priori*, and is therefore the condition of the possibility of *all* knowledge of experience. At the same time, though, the transcendental subject is not a 'self' in the sense that we might attribute the word to an individual person. It is a formal structure, a collection of rules that serve to make the existence of the individual person thinkable.

5   From Descartes to Kant: The Terrain of Themes in European Philosophy

We began with Descartes and his attempt to secure certain knowledge on the basis of rational introspection. Locke and Hume effectively question the validity of such an enterprise by recasting the nature of reason in experiential terms. In turn, Kant's work aims at negotiating a kind of 'middle way' between these approaches. These thinkers offer us an overview of the terrain upon which central themes in European philosophy are articulated. For, each of them is struggling with a common set of problems. These problems concern the nature of reason, of experience and of subjectivity. The issue of what it is that goes to make up human knowledge is articulated within the framework of these three problems. For this reason we can argue that the context of European philosophy as we are considering it in this volume is to be understood in terms of an ongoing debate concerning what the words 'reason', 'experience' and 'subjectivity' mean. As we will see, the precise status of these words is something that is subject to a process of reinterpretation that will take us out of the sphere of epistemology and into the domains of history, society, ontology, ethics, and politics. Above all, this process of reinterpretation concentrates upon the nature of the subject. With Hume and Kant alike, such a reinterpretation has already begun since neither of these thinkers agrees with Descartes's contention that our subjectivity, or indeed our rationality, can be assumed to exist in an unmediated fashion. For Hume, who we are is a matter that is mediated by our experiences. Kant, in contrast, affirms the view that we have an objectively determined rationality. But for him our rational abilities are objective only in so far as they are held in common by all human beings, not in so far as these abilities reflect the structure of an independently existing external world. And such an account implies that the content of our reasoning is mediated by the rules that govern the understanding. In turn, although subjectivity remains essential to Kant's account of knowledge, it is nevertheless also true that subjectivity itself is for him structured in a manner that is essentially *impersonal*. The transcendental subject is not a 'someone', but merely the formal structure that each individual subject must conform to in order to be a subject at all.

This is not the end of Kant's journey in the *Critique*. Our discussion has looked at the first 130 or so pages, and there are many left! The later parts of the first *Critique* contain much that is rich and rewarding, including an extensive analysis of the nature and limits of reason, which Kant regards as the highest faculty to be found for the unification of thought: 'All our knowledge starts with the senses, proceeds from thence to understanding, and ends with reason' (B355/A298). But let us leave Kant to his journey, and instead consider some important issues in theory of knowledge that arise from a consideration both of his work, and that of Descartes, Locke and Hume. We can do this in the next chapter by looking at the work of Hegel, Nietzsche, Horkheimer and Adorno.

Notes

1   Friedrich Nietzsche, *The Gay Science*, tr. Walter Kaufmann (New York: Vintage Books, 1974), section 355.
2   From the Greek word *èpisteme*: to know.
3   René Descartes, *Discourse on Method* and *Meditations on First Philosophy*, tr. Donald A. Cress (Indianapolis: Hackett, 1999). All further references to the *Discourse on Method* are given in the text.
4   We get the word 'pyrrhonism' from his name: to burn, or consume, everything in the flame of doubt.
5   In the same way that the term 'Nietzschean' refers to Nietzsche's thought, so the term 'Cartesian' is frequently used by philosophers to characterize Descartes's thought (when you notice that a thinker such as Hume refers to him as 'Des Cartes' the reason for the coinage becomes fairly obvious).
6   It is useful to bear in mind here that philosophers usually use the Latin word '*cogito*' as a shorthand way of expressing the Cartesian 'I think'.
7   The two other famous rationalist thinkers of the modern era are Gottfried Wilhelm Leibnitz (1646–1716) and Baruch Spinoza (1632–77). I do not propose to burden the reader with an account here of the work of these philosophers. For a discussion of rationalism see, for example, John Cottingham, *Rationalism* (London: Paladin, 1984).
8   This objection was put forward by one of Descartes's contemporaries, Pierre Gassendi.
9   For a more detailed discussion of this see chapter 5.
10 Friedrich Nietzsche, *Beyond Good and Evil*, in *Basic Writings of Nietzsche*, tr. Walter Kaufmann (New York: Modern Library, 1968), section 16.
11 One should also add to these two the name of the Irish thinker George Berkeley (1685–1753). For reasons of space, however, I do not propose to discuss his theories here.
12 John Locke, *An Essay Concerning Human Understanding*, ed. P. H. Nidditch (Oxford: Clarendon Press, 1990). All further references are given in the text with page and section number.
13 It is worth noting in this connection that Locke's work prompted the reply of another famous rationalist, Gottfried Leibniz (1646–1716). Leibniz attacked Locke's theories, and defended the view that there are innate principles in the mind, although he acknowledged the importance of the senses in playing a role in our knowledge (i.e. that we must acquire knowledge by way of them).
14 By way of an aside, one might be tempted to argue that the point of much of Locke's argumentation, as presented in this context, is to prevent us from assuming that the stress on experience and the senses in his theory necessarily implies a simple rejection of concepts of spirit, or indeed God.
15 David Hume, *A Treatise of Human Nature*, ed. L. A. Selby-Bigge (Oxford: Clarendon Press, 1990) and *Enquiries Concerning Human Understanding and Concerning the Principles of Morals*, ed. L. A. Selby-Bigge (Oxford: Clarendon Press, 1988). All further references to the *Treatise* are given in the text with page number; all references to the *Enquiries* are to the section numbers in the margins of the text.
16 Here is Hume's own example: 'I can imagine to myself such a city as the *New Jerusalem*, whose pavement is gold and whose walls are rubies, tho' I never saw such [a place]. I have seen *Paris*; but shall I affirm that I can form such an idea of that city, as will perfectly represent all its streets and houses in all their real and just proportions?' (*Treatise*, 3). In neither case, it follows, does an idea correspond exactly to an impression, or vice versa.

17 Primary ideas are 'images of our impressions', and secondary ideas are 'images of the primary' (*Treatise*, 6). In other words, they are secondary precisely because they are representational images that are derived from the images we generate by way of having impressions.

18 Hume offers a memorable example later in the *Treatise*: 'Were I present at any of the more terrible operations of surgery, 'tis certain, that even before it begun, the preparation of the instruments, the laying of the bandages in order, the heating of the irons, with all the signs of anxiety and concerns in the patient and assistants, wou'd have a great effect upon my mind, and excite the strongest sentiments of pity and terror' (p. 576).

19 Hume, we should note here, distinguishes between natural relations and philosophical ones. Either ideas are linked together by way of qualities such that 'the one naturally induces the other' (natural association of ideas). Or there is 'that particular circumstance, in which, even upon the arbitrary union of two ideas in the fancy, we may think proper to compare them' (philosophical association). Thus, Hume says, 'distance' is taken by philosophers to be a 'true relation, because we acquire an idea of it by the comparing of objects'. In everyday talk, however, to say one thing is distant from something else implies there is no relation between them (*Treatise*, pp. 13–14).

20 Nevertheless, Hume does not rule out the fact that such ideas are not merely a matter of memory. Memories can 'degenerate' to the point where it would be possible to mistake them for ideas constructed by the imagination. Equally, ideas of the imagination can acquire such force as to be taken for memories; as in the case of habitual liars, 'who by frequent repetition of their lies, come at last to believe and remember them, as realities' (*Treatise*, 86).

21 See section 3.2 above.

22 Recall, also, that Hume has already expressed his objections to notions of substance; now it is apparent that we are not made of some kind of substance, like 'mind', that is different in kind from the kind of 'stuff' that makes an animal a being, too.

23 What does underlie how we have perceptions (and hence impressions and ideas), recall, is for Hume a matter of indifference, for we cannot expose such principles.

24 Immanuel Kant, *Critique of Pure Reason*, tr. Norman Kemp Smith (New York: St. Martins Press, 1965; London: Macmillan, 1990). All further references are given in the text, citing A and B numbers given in the margin.

25 Such a reading of the implications of Hume's theory as Kant is offering here is perhaps questionable. As was noted at the end of the discussion of Hume, the predominance of 'custom' or 'habit' need not necessarily imply a merely subjective disposition to behave in certain ways according to the dictates of one's previous experiences. This is because Hume's thought can also be said to offer us the possibility of adopting a broader, social perspective on the nature of custom, in so far as subjective experience is, for him, something that is always negotiated in the broader context of other persons. Moreover, the Humean self is, after all, a mere bundle of sense impressions, so it would seem strange to root *any* kind of 'necessity' in such an account of subjective experience in the way Kant does when he criticizes Hume. Kant's understanding of the implications of Hume's achievement might, therefore, be a limited one in this regard.

26 It is worth mentioning that, in Kantian terms, such 'taking' would of course be impossible for humans.

27 The term 'transcendental' does *not* concern what is 'transcendent', since what is transcendent would transcend all possible experience, whereas the transcendental remains essentially connected with experience as its condition of possibility.

28 Namely, as arising from the fact that space is a pure intuition that cannot be generated from experience.

29   An analysis of what it means to think an object in general is one that is concerned with the conditions necessary for us to think of any object at all, rather than any particular object with determinate properties, e.g. 'this table', 'that chair', etc. On this account, thinking of any particular object presupposes an ability to think of an object in the capacity of its being an object.

30   Logic, to put the matter very schematically, is that branch of philosophy that studies the structures and rules that govern arguments. Arguments can be inductive (i.e. based upon experience). And, as we have seen in relation to Hume, such arguments yield only probability. Arguments, though, can also be deductive. For example, '1. Socrates is a person. 2. All people are mortal. 3. Therefore, Socrates is mortal' is a classic instance of a deductive argument. The point to note is that the third proposition (the conclusion) follows necessarily from the first two propositions (the premises). Arguments of this kind have *validity*, but this does not mean that all such arguments are 'sound'. The argument 'All presidents are good people. Mr X is a president. Therefore, Mr X is a good person' is valid in form; but it does not follow that the argument is sound, since not all presidents are, by definition (or indeed, experience) 'good'.

31   For example, judgements of quantity will be either (a) *universal*: '*all* Xs are such and such'; (b) *particular*: '*some* Xs are such and such'; or (c) *singular*: '*this* X is such and such'. It is worth mentioning here that Kant derives this account from Aristotelian logic (see Aristotle's *Categories* and *De Interpretatione*, tr. J. L. Ackrill (Oxford: Clarendon, 1963). It is the fact that we must adhere to this kind of logical structure that underpins the role of reason within Kant's epistemology.

32   A variant on this approach is developed by Edmund Husserl, and forms the basis for his conception of phenomenology. See chapter 3 for a brief discussion of Husserl.

33   Again, it should be noted that this model has an Aristotelian origin. The importance of the categories is that they allow Kant to argue that these 'original pure concepts of synthesis' are applicable to *all* (not just some part of) our experiences.

34   These are also discussed by Kant in the *Prolegomena to Any Future Metaphysics Which Will Be Able to Come forth as a Science*, sections 21ff. See, *Kant: Selections*, ed. Lewis White Beck (London: Collier Macmillan Publishers, 1988), p. 188. In this work Kant seeks to refine (and simplify) the account he offered earlier in the first edition of the *Critique*.

35   Indeed, Kant himself declines to provide us with a detailed account of the categories: 'In this treatise, I purposely omit the definitions of the categories, although I may be in possession of them' (*Critique*, B108/A82). This is because Kant himself is more interested in the implications that the categories may have, rather than in offering a detailed analysis of them.

36   It has objectivity, recall, because space and time exhibit both necessity and universality.

2

Knowledge, History and Society: Hegel, Nietzsche, Horkheimer and Adorno

In their respective discussions of knowledge, Descartes, Locke, Hume, and Kant are concerned first and foremost with articulating the possible links between *metaphysical issues* and *epistemological issues*. Theory of knowledge (epistemology), as we have seen, concerns itself with questions about the nature and necessary conditions of knowledge. On the other hand, and keeping to the limited definition I offered of it earlier, the word 'metaphysics' can be used to denote two things. First, metaphysics concerns itself with the fundamental nature of reality, and hence those fundamental principles that can serve as a foundation for our knowledge of that reality. Second, it can be taken in a Kantian sense to be an exploration of what constitutes the necessary conditions of our having any experiences at all.

These two conceptions of metaphysics have very different implications for how we are to understand knowledge, should we choose to accept either of them. The first definition implies that there is an essential and unmediated connection between reality and our knowledge: the nature of reality dictates the nature of our knowledge. Thus, when Descartes offers us his account, he develops the view that human beings only know what they do in virtue of the fact that they think. The very fact of thinking implies for him a substance (mind) that exists independently of material substance. Both thinking and the possibility of knowledge rest upon the fact that reality is arranged in a certain manner (taken as a whole, reality is composed of mind and body). It follows that Descartes's view of metaphysics is decisive with regard to his understanding of the nature of knowledge. In turn, his account of subjectivity itself rests upon this metaphysical foundation. Subjectivity, for him, is the pure self-consciousness of mind, and it can be exhaustively elaborated in a manner that is independent of any considerations concerning the material world. If I were Descartes, then I would tell you that in order to arrive at a definition of what thinking is, all that is needed is an act of self-conscious introspection on the part of the subject. Because of this, Descartes's metaphysical account of knowledge has an additional implication. The conditions of our knowledge might be *objective* (in so far as they are dependent upon the fact that reality is arranged in a certain manner), but this objectivity finds expression only in and through *subjectivity*. It is only because Descartes holds that he is first and foremost a 'thinking thing' that certain, and hence true, knowledge is possible. It is because of this that the certainty of all knowledge rests upon the foundation of the *cogito*. Descartes, as we have said already, is a kind of 'individualist' about knowledge. For him, knowledge is only possible because the subject is completely *given* to itself in the very activity of thought. Descartes's account of our subjectivity is a metaphysical one, since although our knowledge is likened to a building that requires strong foundations, these foundations themselves rest upon the metaphysical structure of the self. Of Locke, Hume and Kant, only Hume really moves decisively away from this view, by embracing an outright empiricism even with regard to human identity. Kant, in contrast, retains the subject at the centre of his theory of knowledge. But he does so only at the cost of formalizing it. The subject becomes 'transcendental', but in becoming such it ceases to have content (the transcendental subject is not a concrete self, like Descartes's *cogito*, but a structure of rules that stipulate conditions necessary for thinking to be possible). Kant's own view is open to numerous possible criticisms. We can encounter such criticisms by way of looking at the writings of other thinkers, principally Hegel and Nietzsche. So it is to them that we now turn.

1   Hegel's Dialectical Account of Knowledge

Georg Wilhelm Friedrich Hegel (1770–1831) was the most important German thinker of the generation that immediately followed Kant. Hegel's philosophical thought constitutes a complex but highly rewarding body of work. It is ambitious in its scope: Hegel's concerns include the areas of aesthetics, knowledge, metaphysics, political theory, and the nature of religion. Although his early writings exhibit an interest principally in Kantian ethics and theology, the mature Hegel came to appreciate the importance of the metaphysical preconditions of knowledge offered by Kant in the first *Critique*. One might say that Kant's epistemology forms the historical moment from which Hegel's mature thought emerges, especially as it is expressed in two of his key works: the *Phenomenology of Spirit* (1807) and part one of the *Encyclopaedia* (1817, with the final version published in 1830). In fact, Hegel regarded his own thought as taking Kant's achievement one stage further. In Hegelian terms, one might say that a fruitful encounter with Kant necessarily means going beyond him.

If there is one important contrast between Kant and Hegel, it lies in their respective conceptions of the metaphysical structure that underlies our cognition of physical objects. For Kant, as we have seen, metaphysics essentially involves the elucidation of the *a priori* forms of thought that make synthetic knowledge of objects and their relations possible. The key thing about this structure is that it is *fixed*. One might say that on a Kantian view what is essential for knowledge to be possible can be spelled out in terms of the formal conditions that govern our sensibility and understanding, and then finalized by way of their unification through the structure of the transcendental subject. Once they are correctly determined, these conditions cannot be susceptible to change, for they constitute the necessary and universal conditions that make human knowledge possible. Kant himself regards this model as performing what can be termed a 'Copernican Revolution' in metaphysics:

We must . . . make trial whether we may not have more success in the tasks of meta-physics, if we suppose that objects must conform to our knowledge . . . We should then be proceeding precisely on the lines of Copernicus' primary hypothesis. Failing of satisfactory progress in explaining the movements of the heavenly bodies on the supposition that they all revolved around the spectator, he tried whether he might not have better success if he made the spectator to revolve and the stars to remain at rest. A similar experiment can be tried in metaphysics, as regards the intuition of objects. (*Critique*, Bxvi)

Where Copernicus's experiment with the hypothesis that the earth orbits the sun, and not vice versa, yielded important results,[1] so Kant aims to achieve something similar in metaphysics. Doubtless, that there is a certain irony in all of this should not be missed. Where Copernicus, by Kant's own admission, holds that it is the spectator who is in a state of motion (it is we on earth who are moving, not the sun), Kant's model does precisely the opposite. For Kant, it is objects that must conform to the demands of our understanding, not the other way around. In the last instance, the transcendental subject is, for this reason, the fixed point of reference within the Kantian system of knowledge. Nevertheless, Kant's account can with some justice be called 'scientific' in spirit. By taking the achievement of Copernicus as his paradigm, Kant is effectively stating that philosophers, too, need to place their understanding of the nature of knowledge on a foundation that in its own way is as solid as the principles that ground the physical sciences. It is this commitment, however, that serves to indicate the difference between Kant and Hegel. Where Kant's juridical notion of the rules that govern the understanding has its inspiration in the fixed, and hence timeless, physical laws that govern the behaviour of bodies, Hegel looked to the dynamic (or in his terms 'dialectical') structure of thought as being fundamental to our knowledge. According to Hegel's conception, thinking is inherently *historical*, and it is this insight that decisively separates him from Kant.

From the time even of his earliest writings, Hegel's approach, in contrast to Kant's, embraces the view that *change* is an essential element in thought and, indeed, reality. A key feature of all of Hegel's thinking, as we have said, is an emphasis on the historical nature of existence. This is most famously expressed in the Hegelian *dialectic*. Where Kant believes that the categories of the understanding, and by implication all forms of rational and logical argument, must conform to the dictates of a fixed logical structure, Hegel regards even logic itself to be a manifestation of human history and culture. In other words, for Hegel, even logic cannot be regarded as an isolated or timeless formal structure that allows us to articulate the a-historical relations between different representations or propositions. Instead, logical thought is a kind of cultural achievement, just as religious thought, political life, or legal and govermental forms are all also manifestations of human activity. Logic is only what it is because it is also part of a greater web of human social existence, and human social existence is mapped out in terms of its relationship to the material world of nature. When we talk of such matters as 'logic' what we are considering is a kind of human achievement that is the direct result of the interaction between humans and their environment. This relationship is not static. It is a *dynamic* one. This is because humans, as conscious beings, respond to the world around them with understand-ing, and understanding the world is an *active engagement with it*. We can, and do, understand the world around us in different ways. When we do this, we can also move from one mode of understanding that is limited in some manner to another mode of understanding that illustrates or overcomes the limitations inherent in the first mode. It is in this dynamic movement of human thinking in relation to the world that Hegel locates what is essential not only about conscious thought but about reality itself. For, when we think in terms of logic we do so in the context of an understanding that operates in terms of a historically unfolding relationship between consciousness and the world. When Hegel talks of matters such as 'logic', he is always doing so in the context of change, since all human achievements are the product of historical development. This process of development is articulated through what Hegel calls the 'dialectic'. The dialectic, which is discussed most famously in the *Logic* (see below), is Hegel's attempt to deal with a number of problems that arise from his analysis of consciousness in the *Phenomenology of Spirit*. It is best, therefore, to approach the dialectic by considering some important aspects of the *Phenomenology* first.

1.1   The critique of 'immediacy'

Amongst other things, Hegel's account of the development of consciousness in the *Phenomenology of Spirit*[2] demonstrates how he departs from the kind of approach to subjectivity adhered to by Descartes, Locke, Hume, and Kant. The subject matter of philosophy, Hegel notes in section 73, is 'the actual cognition of what truly is'. But such cognition is not to be derived directly from the immediate certainty of subjective experience. Hegel is happy to agree with the empiricists that subjective sense-experience is the starting point of thinking. But, he argues, this beginning posits a dichotomy between thinking and what is known that must be overcome if we are to attain absolute (or true) knowledge. Indeed, the notion of a 'phenomenology' is itself only a starting point. This is because Hegel is attempting to present an account of how the phenomenon of 'natural consciousness' arises from the realm of nature and in turn becomes self-conscious. A phenomenology is therefore only a kind of prelude to philosophy proper, and it is the latter that aims to elucidate how absolute knowledge is possible for self-consciousness.

The aim of a phenomenological account of consciousness is to examine what it is that the self-consciousness of mind or spirit (*Geist*) regards itself to be. The next task is to show that it is in the very nature of spirit to transcend its own limitations dialectically, and thereby yield true knowledge: 'It is this coming-to-be of *Science as such* or of *knowledge*, that is described in this *Phenomenology* of Spirit. Knowledge in its first phase, or *immediate Spirit*, is the non-spiritual, i.e. *sense-consciousness*. In order to become genuine knowledge . . . it must travel a long way and work its passage' (*Phenomenology*, para. 27). The phenomenon of 'natural consciousness' contains within itself the germ of true knowledge but can never be equated with it; rather, it must strive to attain such knowledge by arriving at 'a completed experience of itself, the awareness of what it really is in itself' (para. 77). In following this path, natural consciousness starts with the purportedly 'simple' *immediacy* of sense certainty: it is immediately receptive to objects of sense-experience, in so far as such objects are regarded first and foremost by it as simply existing. However, 'in the event, this very *certainty* proves itself to be the most abstract and poorest *truth*. All that it says about what it knows is that it *is*' (para. 90). Stating that something merely *is*, that it has being, does not really say very much about it. Hence, we might say that the claims of immediate sense-certainty are only trivially true.

Hegel adds that such certainty also yields the 'I' of thinking; but again, this 'I' remains limited: 'consciousness is "I", nothing more, a pure "This"'. A further examination of immediate certainty tells us something more. Any moment of such certainty is really only an '*instance*' of a relationship between the 'I' and what is sensed. What we have, in fact, are two 'Thises': the 'I' and what is apprehended by it through sense-experience. In this way, what seemed to be immediately given shows itself to be already *mediated* by the relationship that exists between thought and its object. This mediation is then found to exist in *all* thought determinations of immediacy. For example, we can think of an object given by immediate sense certainty as existing *here* and *now*. But what is 'now'? If we answer 'Now is Night', we can, says Hegel, test its veracity by writing it down: 'We write down this truth; a truth cannot lose anything by being written down, any more than it can lose anything through our preserving it. If *now, this noon*, we look again at the written truth we shall have to say that it has become stale' (*Phenomenology*, para. 95). 'Now' is no longer night but day, and so the 'now' that was true in virtue of the fact that it existed is no longer; hence, it is no longer true. Even when we seek to allude to something in this mode of immediacy the truth that we aim to express by way of it slips away in the very act: 'The Now is pointed to, *this* Now. "Now" has already ceased to be in the act of pointing to it' (para. 106). Likewise, we can say the same for any other claim to immediate certainty. All involve a 'here', a 'this', etc., and all show themselves to become no longer true through the fact that they are always already mediated by conditions that transform the simple immediacy of a given moment into something mediated by other moments. In this way, the purportedly '*pure being*' of immediacy shows itself to be 'something to which negation and mediation are essential' (para. 99). Any claim of universality that might be attributed to immediate certainty shows itself to be flawed. Equally, the essential requirement that thought has an object which exists, whether or not it is being thought about, is overturned. This is because all sense-certainty depends upon the existence of thinking, not the object that is being thought about: 'Its truth is in the object as *my* object, or in its being *mine* [*Meinen*]; it is, because *I* know it' (para. 100).

Hegel has already pointed out that the 'I' is a limited notion. However, we might still be tempted by these reflections to regard the relation of immediacy as residing *not* in the object of thought, but in the 'I' that thinks. It is, after all, 'the immediacy of my *seeing, hearing*, and so on' that appears to remain the constant condition of the determination of objects as existing (*Phenomenology*, para. 101). But the same problem arises for the 'I' that thinks: 'in this relationship sense-certainty experiences the same dialectic acting upon itself . . . I, *this* "I", see the tree and assert that "Here" is a tree; but another "I" sees the house and maintains that "Here" is not a tree but a house instead.' This is another way of saying that whenever we speak of 'I' we in fact necessarily invoke 'all "Is"', not one particular 'I'. What is essential about sense-certainty, it follows, is to be found neither in the object that is thought, nor in the particular 'I' that thinks about an object. What is essential with regard to sense-certainty is to be located in the *totality of moments that go to make it what it is*: 'it is only sense-certainty as a *whole* which stands firm within itself as *immediacy*' (para. 103). However, if it is the 'whole' that is immediate, then what seems to be immediately given in any particular sense-experience is always mediated by this totality. To put it another way: the particular is always mediated by the universal.

1.2   Self-consciousness and subjectivity

An essential component in this totality is self-consciousness. But self-consciousness is not to be understood as the consciousness of a particular 'I' that thinks, for such an 'I' is not of itself a completed unity. Instead, Hegel argues, this totality is to be interpreted in terms of the *universal* conditions that underlie all self-consciousness. These conditions are themselves the consequence of mediation, for self-consciousness is no mere given. It is the outcome of processes of organic life. Self-consciousness, in other words, emerges from conditions that are antecedent to it: it springs from life, from the existence of organisms that initially are not conscious of themselves as existent beings. Such beings, we can infer, have a determinate relation to the material world they inhabit: they consume it, they live in it, they are themselves consumed by other beings. Self-consciousness emerges from these conditions. Beings equipped with the ability to have sensory impressions ultimately encounter themselves in terms of the external world, which is seen as a resource for the purpose of survival. Thus, self-consciousness only becomes what it is in virtue of its relation with the realm of sense-experience. It follows that self-consciousness is a kind of unity that is nevertheless at the same time only possible through the fact that it understands itself in terms of the dichotomy between subject and object. 'Consciousness, as self-consciousness . . . has a double object: one is the immediate object, that of sense-certainty and perception . . . and the second . . . [is] . . . *itself*' (*Phenomenology*, para. 167). Self-consciousness is not something that arrives in the world fully formed. It is the result of an engagement with that world.

Self-consciousness experiences itself first and foremost by encountering what is other than it: its existence is mediated[3] by the existence of this other. In turn, this other is understood in terms of its suitability for appropriation. At the most basic level, this concerns whether or not something can be eaten: 'as *being for itself* . . . it comes forward in antithesis to the universal substance . . . and . . . preserves itself by separating itself from its inorganic nature, and by consuming it' (*Phenomenology*, para. 171). Self-consciousness thereby regards the objects of its sense-experience in terms of its own needs; it cannot at first understand them apart from itself. But such objects do have an independent existence, and this too is discovered by encountering them: 'Self-consciousness which is simply *for itself* . . . will . . . learn through experience that the object is independent' (para. 168). To put it bluntly, objects in the world do not always yield to our needs and desires but can frustrate them.

As something which exists '*for itself*', self-consciousness can be characterized as 'desire' (para. 174). It wishes to seize hold of the other and subordinate it to itself and thereby to discover itself in the other through using it as a means of self-preservation. The consumption of something as food is the most obvious example of this. But this is only one manifestation of desire. The desire of self-consciousness to see itself preserved in the world is a desire for a kind of universality. In other words, Hegel is claiming that any self-conscious being regards the world in terms of itself and itself alone. Yet, at the same time, every self-conscious being is finite and knows that it is, since it understands that there are objects in the world that are not it. Such a being must nevertheless preserve itself, and one other way of doing so is by reproduction. Elsewhere, Hegel refers to this kind of relation as 'the Genus-process': it is the 'entering into relationship with an other which is itself a living individual, so that in the other it is in relationship with itself'.[4] So, in the other, self-consciousness finds itself: the kind of life that it is an instance of reproduces itself by encountering another self-conscious being and uniting with it.

The essence (i.e. the true significance) of desire and 'being *for itself*' is not to be found in immediate self-awareness because desire and the gratification that accompanies it are 'conditioned by the object' that is desired (be it food, or another being as means of reproduction). Ultimately, however, '*Self-consciousness achieves its satisfaction only in another self-consciousness*' (*Phenomenology*, para. 175). To put the matter more plainly: a self-conscious being discovers what it is neither by way of pure introspection, nor by means of appropriating the world around it. What is essential to self-consciousness can only be discovered by it when it enters into a relationship with another individual self-conscious being. Self-consciousness, in short, discovers itself in and through an 'I–Thou' relation. This is because all self-consciousness 'exists only in being acknowledged' (para. 178). The 'I' needs, therefore, to be *recognized* by another 'I' in order for it to understand what it truly is; any 'I' that thinks is always a 'Thou' for another. What any 'I' turns out to be is an 'I' that is also and at the same time a 'We' (para. 177). Hence, the purportedly 'simple immediacy' of the 'I' is only possible because 'I' is mediated by its relationship with 'We'.

Hegel's analysis of self-consciousness leads him to conclude that individual subjectivity is itself continually mediated by conditions that extend beyond the boundaries of simple sense-certainty and individuated consciousness. What is purportedly given as the immediately certain knowledge of sense-experience rests upon the fact that such experience is mediated by its object. In turn, individual self-consciousness discovers that it, too, is not simply present to itself in an unmediated relation of certainty. Any self-conscious being requires the acknowledgement of other self-conscious beings in order for it to truly be what it is. The outcome of Hegel's account of the dialectical unfolding of spirit, therefore, is to show that individuated subjective experience cannot serve as a satisfactory foundation for knowledge. Elucidating the conditions of knowledge involves not merely telling us what an individual subject must be like in order to possess knowledge (the rational subject of Descartes's '*cogito*'). Nor is it simply a matter of discussing the important roles that experience and subjectivity must play in our knowledge (issues which the empiricists and, following them, Kant sought to clarify). According to Hegel, such an account must show that subjective conditions are themselves, and in their very nature, *objective* conditions. Subjectivity emerges from these objective conditions and the analysis of this emergence tells us that there is no pure, individuated

'I think', and no unmediated empirical relation to the domain of sense-experience. Each particular 'I' finds itself grounded in the requirement that it be recognized by other 'Is', other selves. Equally, self-consciousness is not something that is independent of its world: it is part of it, and discovers what it truly is through the fact that it engages with that world.

1.3   Hegel's criticisms of empiricism and Kantian subjective idealism

As should by now be evident, Hegel's account of the nature of knowledge follows the pattern set by his analysis in the *Phenomenology* of the emergence of self-consciousness. Our knowledge is generated as the historical manifestation of an ongoing engagement between human beings and the world. Hegel has a number of things to say about the attitudes of the empiricists or a thinker such as Kant in this connection. Let us look at his comments about them as they are presented in the *Logic*.[5]

With regard to empiricism, Hegel contends that this philosophy can be interpreted as a consequence of addressing the requirement that human knowledge should aspire to a '*concrete* content' (*Logic*, section 37). Instead of seeking to ground human knowledge in thought, the empiricists sought to derive all knowledge from experience as a means of preserving this concreteness: 'In Empiricism there lies this great principle, that what is true must be in actuality and must be there for our perception' (section 38). The empiricist position, according to Hegel, ultimately rests upon the view that what is to count as true knowledge is derivable from the '*immediate presence*' of subjectivity in the world. A subject that thinks is located in the world. It is the supposedly immediate certainty that springs from the subject being situated in this way that the empiricist holds to justify their contention that all knowledge is derived from the embodied presence of thought in experience. So, 'In Humean scepticism, the *truth* of the empirical, the truth of feeling and intuition is taken as basic; and, on that basis, he attacks all universal determinations and laws, precisely because they have no justification by way of sense perception' (section 39).

There is, it follows, a good and bad side to empiricism (*Logic*, section 38). On the one hand, an 'important principle of freedom' is voiced from the empiricist perspective: what counts as 'knowledge' must rest upon our ability to recognize it for ourselves in our own experiences. For this reason, subjectivity must also recognize its own active role in knowledge. On the other hand, the empiricist approach restricts itself to what is finite (i.e. to given experiences, as Hume does when developing his sceptical position). The problem is that in seeking to interpret reality in this way empiricism at the same time *presupposes* metaphysical categories that cannot themselves be derived from any given experience. What Hegel terms 'the fundamental illusion of scientific empiricism' exhibits this latter tendency. Scientific empiricism always uses the 'metaphysical categories of matter, force, . . . of one, many, universality, and the infinite, etc.', and then proceeds in the most 'uncritical and unconscious manner' to derive conclusions from them without addressing the fact that these cannot themselves be derived directly from experience. Empiricism, it follows, remains a valuable but limited philosophy.

In Hegel's view, it is to Kant's credit that he highlights these problems. But Kant himself still maintains the empiricist approach in so far as the concepts of universality and necessity (which, as we have seen, define *a priori* knowledge) are for him still *disclosed* to us through experience, even if their source lies elsewhere (in that they cannot be derived from experience and are thus independent of it). In effect, says Hegel, Kant constructs an account that renders *all* experience a matter of subjectivity, since all possible experience, and so what is to count as 'knowledge', ends up by being understood solely in terms of our subjective abilities. In consequence, Kant collapses the empiricist distinction between our thought and our knowledge of experience by arguing that the subjective conditions of our sensibility and understanding are also the objective conditions of all possible knowledge (*Logic*, section 41). As a result of Kant's synthesis of the rationalist and empiricist approaches all that is left of a mind-independent realm is the 'thing in-itself' (the noumenon). In turn, Hegel argues,

> Kant's investigation of the thought-determinations suffers essentially from the defect that he did not consider them in and for themselves, but only to see whether they were *subjective* or *objective*. In ordinary language, to be 'objective' is to be present outside us and to come to us from outside through perception. Kant denied that the thought-determinations (cause and effect, for instance) were 'objective' in this sense, i.e., that they were given in perception; instead he regarded them as pertaining to our thinking itself or the spontaneity of thinking, and so in *this* sense as subjective.   (section 41, addition 2)

So, Kant's analysis of the *a priori* conditions of experience falls short in so far as he does not provide an immanent analysis of these conditions by considering them in themselves. Instead, Kant merely provides an account of these conditions in their relation to subjectivity and objectivity such that the distinction between the objective and subjective poles ends up by being dissolved. What, on a Kantian view, counts as 'objectivity' in fact remains essentially 'subjective', since the pure forms of intuition are determined by *us* in a purely subjective manner that is cut off from the world. That is why, for Kant, all knowledge is necessarily only knowledge of appearances: the 'thing in-itself' must remain forever closed off to us because it is our shared subjective abilities that confer objectivity on our knowledge of experience.

Hegel's response to this is to outline an approach in which objectivity is once again given its due, since 'the true objectivity of thinking consists in this: that thoughts are not merely our thoughts, but at the same time the *In-itself* of things and of whatever else is ob-jective.'[6] Such a claim may initially appear to be woefully opaque, so it is worth considering briefly. Thoughts, Hegel is claiming, are never merely subjective. In line with his contention later on in the *Logic* that reality and thinking pertain to the same logical structure, Hegel is arguing that thinking is itself something that is in its very nature objective. At this point in the *Logic*, Hegel says that his discussion entitles him to claim that the word 'objectivity' in fact has a tripartite significance. First, what is objective concerns what is 'externally present' to us when we think (the objects of our sense perceptions). Second, Hegel believes that Kant is right in claiming that objectivity is also a matter of the universal and necessary conditions that govern how thought must conceive of its objects. Third, however, objectivity also concerns 'the *In-itself* as thought-product, [that is,] the significance of what is there, as distinct from what is only thought by us'. In other words, it is true that the activity of thinking is what produces the concept of an independently existing 'object', of something that is understood as existing 'in-itself'. But the notion of something as existing 'in-itself' is not limited in its significance to the status of a mere projection of individual consciousness. The objects of thought also concern what *exists in-itself as it is posited by thinking*. This is because 'the things of which we have immediate knowledge are mere appearances, not only *for us*, but also *in-themselves*' (*Logic*, section 45, addition). There is, in other words, no need to posit a gulf separating appearances from a mind-independent reality. This is because appearances *are* reality in the process of coming to be. Hegel therefore rejects Kant's account of the metaphysical conditions of our knowledge because Kant ultimately understands these conditions as being wholly subjective in their determination. We can understand Hegel's criticism of Kant in the following manner. Kant is a transcendental idealist, but he remains an empirical realist. Kant's commitment to empirical realism implies that metaphysical issues are always to be addressed in relation to subjectivity alone, for it is our subjectivity that is taken by him as the necessary condition of experience. For Hegel, in contrast, metaphysics must be shown to be *objective* in the sense that it applies equally as the necessary condition of both what exists *and* how it is thought.

We have seen that Kant ultimately turns to the *form* of subjectivity (the transcendental subject) as providing the ground upon which the concepts of the understanding rest. For Kant, the categories, which confer objectivity upon all our knowledge, are ultimately derived from the transcendental unity of self-consciousness. In turn, the objectivity of our knowledge resides in the fact that certain universal and necessary conditions must be fulfilled whenever a subject thinks about objects (and so has representations of them). For Hegel this fact implies that Kant's conception of thinking remains essentially *subjective*. This is its limitation. Kant ignores the possibility of thought transcending its own particularity, since the possible knowledge that we can have remains, for him, ultimately subordinate to the conditions that govern the nature of our subjectivity: our knowledge of objects must always conform to the subjective conditions that *we impose upon them*. In Hegel's view, Kant is right in so far as he argues that questions of objectivity must be conjoined to the *a priori* conditions of our sensibility and understanding, and hence our subjectivity. However, as we have already noted, Hegel claims that the dynamic movement of thought itself is not to be regarded as a matter of arbitrariness or mere subjective contingency. Rather, thought shares a common logical structure with the world. It is because of this fact, Hegel argues, that objectivity is possible for thought.

Likewise, the claim that knowledge can be grounded in the immediate self-awareness of the transcendental subject remains, for Hegel, problematic. Kant subordinates our possible knowledge of experience to the rules that govern our sensibility and understanding. Because of this it is true to say that, for Kant, all possible sense experience, and likewise knowledge of such experience, is mediated by these rules. Kantian philosophy 'points to the *original identity* of the "I" within thinking (the transcendental unity of self-consciousness) as the determinate *ground* of the concepts of the understanding' (*Logic*, section 42). The categories rest upon this ground, in so far as they are derived from the pure spontaneity of thought that characterizes the transcendental self. But in arguing this Kant's philosophy 'took the easy way in its *finding* of the categories' (section 42, remark). Grounding the categories in the transcendental subject, as Kant does, is an easy way out of the problem of addressing the issue as to where the categories find their foundation because any appeal to such a conception of the subject ultimately rests upon nothing more than mere self-evidence. But, says Hegel, when understood as a purely self-evident and *given* unity, the transcendental subject is, in the last analysis, 'totally abstract and completely undetermined'. Kant's account of the subject, in short, remains bereft of any real content. As such, the Kantian transcendental subject cannot itself pertain to the kind of objective status that it must have in order for it to bequeath objectivity on experience. To put the matter in slightly different terms, one might say that Kant's conception of the unity of the transcendental subject is devoid of real content because it is in fact a kind of 'thing in-itself', not an object of possible experience. We cannot know ourselves (the 'I' that thinks) as an object of experience, since it is the 'I' that is the necessary condition of all possible experience. This problem is, once again, a consequence of Kant's drawing a distinction between subjective conditions and objective conditions. In the transcendental subject this distinction collapses, for the transcendental subject is the foundation for these conditions. Since, for Kant, we can only *know* appearances, not things in-themselves, it follows that subjectivity must remain for him essentially unknowable, and its rationality is thereby rendered empty and without content.

1.4 Representation

Hegel's discussion of the nature of subjectivity also has implications for the notion of 'representation'. We have seen that thinkers such as Descartes, Locke and Hume all start with the view that representations are fundamental to knowledge. For Descartes, the central issue concerns how the mind (as a thinking substance) can have true representations of the world (material substance). In the last analysis, this possibility rests upon the foundation of the *cogito* as the primary representation of consciousness. One might say that, for Descartes, the 'I think' in effect expresses the fact that pure self-consciousness is capable of representing itself to itself: in the 'I think' what is affirmed is a correspondence between thinking and self. This correspondence is, in its own turn, the foundation of human knowledge, but suffers from the fact that it remains trapped in the simple immediacy of itself: only God can get Descartes out of the problem of how thinking actually engages with the world of sensory experience. For empiricism, our ideas are representations that we derive directly from experience, and they are all representations of particular experiences. The Kantian move is to argue that such representations as we may have ultimately rest upon non-experiential conditions (i.e. upon rules that exist independently of experience and which govern our abilities both to have sense-experience and to think the relations between concepts). Representations remain fundamental to Kant's account of knowledge, but the issue of *how* we derive our representations is no longer for him a merely 'representational' matter.

Hegel takes this insight one step further. Our ability to have representations, on the Hegelian view, is of course linked to the question of how we have sense-experience. But representations do not of themselves pertain to a relation of pure immediacy to objects that we perceive through intuition. Our representations are *mediated* by the dialectical movement of thought itself and are produced by this movement. For Hegel, representations are not therefore given by the subjective conditions of our understanding (the Kantian transcendental subject), but are instead to be regarded as the mediated products of thought processes. Thus, philosophy, on Hegel's view, must begin by first doubting that any objects of experience can be given directly through representation: 'Philosophy lacks the advantage, which the other sciences enjoy, of being able to *presuppose* its *ob-jects*[7] as given immediately in representation' (*Logic*, section 1). No 'method' can be presupposed whereby we can claim the right, as philosophers, to construct an account of knowledge on the basis of an empirical model of how we have experience. True, says Hegel, philosophers, like everyone else, are familiar with objects as they are given in this way and must, to some degree, presuppose this. Hegel is happy to admit two things here. First, he affirms that our representations of objects are produced *prior* to our concepts of them 'in the order of time' (i.e. temporally). We cannot, in other words, have concepts of objects unless we already possess representations of them. Second, Hegel also claims that all thinking can only become knowledge by 'going *through* representation and by converting itself *to* it'. But representation itself falls short of what thinking can do. The reason for this is that mere representations can never yield the *content* of what is being thought through them. We start, therefore, with representation because it is most familiar to us, but this presupposition exists only in order to be overcome in the dialectical engagement between thinking and its own limitations. The purpose of starting with representations only shows itself *subsequently*: 'philosophy puts . . . *concepts*, in the place of representations. Representations in general [or "notions"] can be regarded as *metaphors* of thoughts and concepts' (section 3). Although thoughts and concepts *follow* representations in a temporal sense in so far as concepts, in the order of time, come after representations, it is thoughts and concepts that have *logical priority* over representations. The true significance of our ability to have representations only shows up when we think about this issue by way of concepts. Through conceptual thought we do not merely 'understand' our representations, we engage in an attempt to conceive or grasp them in a manner that endows them with significance. One might say that only when we think what it *means* to have representations (which implies the *concept* of 'representation'), will the true significance of the fact that we do have them come to light.

1.5   The Hegelian dialectic

We are now in a position to grasp the precise significance of Hegel's conception of dialectic. On the one hand, the dialectic represents the logical process of the unfolding of conscious thought as it engages with the material world through sense experience. On the other hand, however, this process is also reflected in the material world itself, in so far as brute physical reality also conforms to the dictates of the logical structure of the dialectic. This amounts to the *metaphysical* claim that reality is itself governed by the rules which constitute logic. Following the analysis of self-consciousness outlined in the *Phenomenology*, logic, as a human achievement, is nevertheless a direct consequence of thought encountering the world and, indeed, arises out of that encounter. In this way, Hegel seeks to close the gulf that Kant drew between noumena ('things in-themselves') and phenomena (the objects of our experience – 'appearances'). He is, it follows, staking an ambitious claim. Where Kant urges us to rest content with knowledge of appearances only, Hegel argues that it is possible for us to have knowledge of the world as it really is, since how it appears to us is essentially connected with how it is. In other words, for Hegel it is possible for the subjective conditions of thought to correspond to the objective conditions of reality.

Hegel is therefore interested in the kinds of epistemological question that Locke, Hume and Kant address, but wishes to overcome the limitations of their respective approaches. Here are two examples of the kind of question that Hegel is interested in: (1) is the judgement expressed in a proposition true because what it states corresponds to the way things are or because it satisfies conditions of understanding given by *a priori* structures in the mind (e.g. that it is not contradictory and is consistent with other judgements of this kind, etc.)? (2) is it possible for us to have knowledge that would be everywhere and unconditionally true, or is our knowledge relative to the perspectives we might have at any given moment? We can put this last question in more Hegelian terms: can we have absolute knowledge, or is our knowledge always condemned to particularity? Hegel's response to questions like these is to argue that both of the possibilities contained within them (*either* correspondence *or* non-correspondence, *either* universality *or* particularity) form part of a larger scheme. In short, he is arguing that each possibility can be synthesized into a larger unity by transcending the 'either–or' relation contained within it. So, for Hegel, our knowledge can correspond to reality, because both consciousness and the world share the same logical structure. Equally, all knowledge claims are relative in so far as they are articulated from specific standpoints, but again, these standpoints themselves comprise a larger, and hence unified, structure. This structure is given by way of the *dialectic*. We can clarify these points by way of a brief examination of sections 79 to 83 of the *Logic*.

According to Hegel, the formal structure of logic is comprised of three 'sides' or 'moments'. Hegel is thereby contending that logic itself is a unity comprised of these three moments. These moments are not, therefore, separate 'parts', but together make up this unity. The first moment is '*understanding*' (*Logic*, section 80). This is not pure empirical sensation (which animals also have and which is, in one sense, concrete, since it concerns actual experience). Rather, understanding is a conceptual moment in thought through which objects are *identified*. This allows for (1) the particular (that is, specific objects, and hence also the purposes that relate to one's dealings with such objects) to be known by way of being conceptualized; and (2) the universal to be postulated by way of abstracting concepts from the concrete experiential particulars to which they refer. Understanding is essential to thought in both its theoretical and practical domains. For example, in the realm of nature, it is through understanding that we posit 'distinctions . . . between matters, forces, kinds, etc, and they are marked off, each on its own account, in isolation from one another'.

Likewise, in the realm of practical conduct, it is because someone possesses understanding that they are able to determine what in particular interests them, to have purposes and to pursue those purposes to the exclusion of other interests.[8] However, what is always posited through understanding is abstract because the understanding works by way of individuating and isolating particulars. The act of understanding always involves *abstraction*. We encounter particulars in the world around us, and on the basis of these particulars we formulate universal (i.e. general) judgements – in Hegelian terms, we posit the universal or 'Absolute' on the basis of particulars. Every act of individual understanding, therefore, always seeks to go beyond itself. Thought for Hegel, we might say, by its very nature craves universality. When, through understanding, the universal is posited, a necessary consequence of this is that the concepts employed are split off from their connection with empirical reality as a precondition of their being abstracted in the first place. The moment of understanding is, it follows, a limited one, in so far as the universal as it is posited within this moment is incapable of satisfying the need for truth that the very notion of 'universality' presupposes. Realization of this factor leads to the next moment in logical thought.

The second moment is called '*dialectic*' (*Logic*, section 81). This is a negative and self-conscious stage, in which conceptual abstraction (which, as we have already noted, represents the tendency of thought toward the universal) is realized to be limited and self-contradictory. Every universal abstraction is sundered by its particularity.[9] This leads to the realization that the universal notion contained within it is not concrete and therefore not real. Again, Hegel makes it clear that the dialectical moment is not to be undervalued: 'It is in general the principle of all motion, of all life, and of all activation in the actual world. Equally, the dialectical is also the soul of all genuinely scientific cognition.' Life itself is dialectical to the extent that all life involves change. And all scientific thought, likewise, is dialectical to the extent that its critical possibility rests upon the ability of thought to transcend its own limitations. To put it another way, for Hegel, life and hence thought both contain the possibility of an '*immanent*' transcendence of their own limits. The notion of the 'immanent' is fundamental here, for what Hegel is in effect contending is that existence is a kind of process which is continually overcoming itself. On such a conception one does not need to look 'outside' the world, or outside thought, in order to find the basis of universality and truth. The universal is always already present within them both. The universal is that which drives what is particular, and thus finite, to transcend its own finitude: 'the finite is not restricted merely from the outside; rather it sublates itself by virtue of its own nature, and passes over, of itself, into its opposite'.[10] Absolute knowledge, or truth, is therefore possible for thought, since true knowledge is not to be understood as a relation between an inwardly oriented Cartesian self and an external world, but instead as the coming together of the two. This coming together is to be found in every moment of thought. So, for example, when we say of all humans that they are alive and yet also mortal, we might be tempted to regard death as being something that arises from 'external circumstances', i.e. as being unconnected with life. 'But the proper interpretation is that life as such bears the germ of death within itself, and that the finite sublates itself because it contradicts itself inwardly.' In this way Hegel can argue that life itself is dialectical in that it contains within it its own opposite (death). If taken no further, the second 'dialectical moment' corresponds to the sceptical position endorsed by Hume, i.e. the view that absolute knowledge of the world is impossible. The reason for this is that the dialectical moment will always reveal the inherent contradiction between the universal and the particular contained within thought. Just as life contains the germ of death within itself, so every universal claim will end up by being shown to contain its opposite (finitude), and so to fall short of the truth. However, reason allows the process to be taken one step further in the final moment.

The third moment is called the *'speculative or positively rational'* stage (*Logic*, section 83). The collapse of conceptual fixity arrived at in the second moment can now be overcome by way of reason. Reason posits new hypotheses which escape the contradictions thrown up by (and inherent in) the understanding, and does so *on the basis of them*. The third moment is *immanent*, since it occurs within thought itself and is not related to anything outside it. In Hegel's terms, this represents a movement away from the domain of mere concepts (the domain of the understanding) to the *Idea*, which is for him genuinely and concretely universal. It is universal because through the Idea reason is capable of perceiving the truly universal. Through reason it is realized that what is universally true about reality is the process of *change*. This process involves a movement from the comprehension of finite objects in the world to a comprehension and knowledge of the underlying and universal conditions in which their existence is grounded, i.e. what is usually termed *'becoming'*. In Hegel's view, it follows, reality is not to be understood in terms of static foundations, rules or principles upon which our empirical knowledge of the world of sense experience rests. Rather, reality is a self-driven and immanent process of change or becoming in which particulars come together in an ever more comprehensive rational synthesis.

From this it should be clear that Hegel's account of the nature of our knowledge rests upon a metaphysical account of the nature of reality, or what is more often referred to as an 'ontology'. What needs to be grasped concerning Hegel's view is that he is claiming that true knowledge is possible because the conditions that govern our knowledge are also the conditions of reality itself. In so far as thought has objectivity it does so because the world of nature shares this feature in common with conscious thinking. This is not to say that nature is 'conscious' and therefore thinks. On the contrary, 'man is distinguished from what is merely natural by virtue of thinking' (*Logic*, section 24). But nature can be understood as 'a system of thought without consciousness . . . an intelligence which . . . is petrified'. The world is not pure thought but 'a system of thought-determinations' in that 'there is reason in the world, by which we mean that reason is the soul of the world, inhabits it, and is immanent in it, as its own, innermost nature, its universal' (section 24).

The third moment of the dialectic represents a stage that is nearer to truth than the second moment of understanding because it can accommodate the fact of change and transience within a more unified view. The third moment is not a final moment, however. New contradictions will emerge and the process will reassert itself all over again:

> Each of the parts of philosophy is a philosophical whole, a circle that closes upon itself;
> but in each of them the philosophical Idea is in a particular determinacy of element.
> Every single circle also breaks the restrictions of its element as well, precisely because
> it is inwardly [the] totality, and it grounds a further sphere. The whole presents itself
> therefore as a circle of circles, each of which is a necessary moment . . . the whole
> Idea . . . appears in each single one of them.   (*Logic*, section 15)

Only when truth is arrived at (i.e. when reason has reached the stage of complete
self-knowledge, when the 'circle of circles' has been produced) may the process stop.
This final stage Hegel calls the moment of Absolute Spirit or Mind (*Geist*). It is
because the unfolding of the dialectic is to be understood as being grounded in the
Idea of the Absolute that Hegel's thought is generally characterized as a form of
'idealism'. In his own terms, his approach embodies an 'absolute idealism', as opposed
to the 'subjective idealism' expounded by Kant in the first *Critique*, since the conditions which determine and govern thought are also the conditions which determine
the nature of reality.

1.6   The Absolute and self-consciousness

Hegel argues for the view that knowledge can only be understood in terms of
the dialectical unfolding of thought. The *aim* of knowledge is to attain pure self-
consciousness by reaching the end of this process. It is this moment (the third
moment of the dialectic) which is called the 'Absolute'. Here, consciousness would
become truly transparent to itself: it would know itself for what it is absolutely, and
so the dialectical process of mediation would cease. Effectively, then, the Hegelian
system embodies not only a metaphysics of becoming, but a theological account of
the nature of existence, for the universal is, in fact, the 'divine Idea' (i.e. God) (*Logic*,
section 45, addition). It is clear from this that Hegel's metaphysics is *purposive*.
He regards history as embodying the development of consciousness toward self-
knowledge, and that is its purpose. To this extent, Hegel's philosophy shares a
common feature with that of Descartes, Locke, Hume, and Kant. All of these
thinkers approach questions of knowledge from the standpoint of *consciousness*, and
in turn take self-consciousness to be an essential and defining component of what
it is that constitutes knowledge. There are, in fact, some good reasons for believing
this. Surely the term 'knowledge' is an attribution made by conscious beings such
as ourselves, and all talk of 'knowledge' itself presupposes self-consciousness at
some level. However, this view might itself be regarded as a metaphysical one. Just
because the world of material relations has produced conscious beings in the form
of humans it does not necessarily follow that humans are the *necessary consequence* of
these material processes. We might be contingent beings: creatures who are a kind
of 'accident'. One might therefore ask: is it really the case the material world 'needs'
consciousness in order to fulfil itself, as the Hegelian account implies? Equally, is it
really adequate to offer an account of the meaning of consciousness in its own terms,
or do we need to think in terms of 'unconscious' forces governing our supposedly
transparent sense of self? Questions like these are Nietzschean questions.

2   Nietzsche, Knowledge and the Demands of Life

We have already seen, at the beginning of chapter 1, that Nietzsche is a thinker who expresses doubts about the validity of 'immediate' certainties (such as the Cartesian 'I think'). In doubting their value in this way he also questions their value for our understanding of the nature of human knowledge. Likewise, we have seen that one Nietzschean contention is that what we call 'knowledge' might come down to nothing more than a matter of 'familiarity'. What people *mean* when they make a knowledge claim ('I know X') is really no more than that they are already familiar with it in some manner or other, or can render it in familiar terms. However, this is by no means all there is to Nietzsche's view of knowledge. Although he ultimately contends that what we 'know' is to be understood in terms of the influence of the kinds of practices and habits we adopt in everyday life, the manner in which Nietzsche develops this approach is both interesting and, at times, complex. To put it another way: Nietzsche is a very difficult thinker to tackle. The difficulty is something that springs from two factors. On the one hand, he often cannot resist the temptation to develop his ideas in ironic and sometimes caustic terms.[11] Equally, Nietzsche is a philosopher whose thinking is frequently marked by a restless urge for development. He is happy for a while with one perspective, but soon regards it as falling short in some way. Or sometimes an insight is given a turn that produces conclusions that are the opposite of what one might expect from it. To this extent, Nietzsche never offers what one could call a 'theory of knowledge' in the sense in which thinkers like Kant do. Indeed, he tells us 'Philosophy reduced to "theory of knowledge", in fact no more than a timid epochism and doctrine of abstinence – a philosophy that never gets beyond the threshold and takes pains to *deny* itself the right to enter – that is philosophy in its last throes, an end, an agony, something inspiring pity' (*Beyond Good and Evil*, section 204).[12] Nietzsche, therefore, regards philosophizing as an activity wherein one ought to try to offer more than mere 'theories' about knowledge. In the last analysis, for him, philosophy is a form of 'legislation': it does not say how reality is, but seeks to control it by interpreting it.[13]

Because of the very diversity of his approaches, some interpreters have come to see Nietzsche's writings as embodying an overall incoherence, as being 'unsystematic'. Sometimes he will say one thing; another time he will say something that appears to contradict that earlier claim. It is true that Nietzsche is frequently scathing about other philosophers whose work embodies a theoretical 'system' (as those of Kant and Hegel do). A will to construct systems is, for him, a sign that something rather questionable is in the offing. Intellectual honesty, on a Nietzschean view, one might say, means accepting the fact that life is never 'systematic': it never adds up to a coherent Hegelian whole. At the same time, there is much in Nietzsche's thought which, in spite of what is often taken to be his dismissal of Hegel, has a 'dialectical' turn to it. Nietzsche loves contradictions, for they show us things that are interesting about the way in which we think, and also the limitations of our thinking. Likewise, he develops an account of metaphysics which has something in common with Hegel's. For Nietzsche and Hegel alike, reality is essentially a process of 'becoming': 'We Germans are Hegelians even if there never had been any Hegel, insofar as we (unlike all Latins) instinctively attribute a deeper meaning and greater value to becoming and development than to what is; we hardly believe in the justification of the concept of "being" ' (*The Gay Science*, section 357).[14] Leaving aside the question of what 'Germans' (or indeed 'Latins') in general may or may not think, it is clear that Nietzsche regards development and change as fundamental to the nature of existence. To the extent that reality needs to be understood in terms of development Hegel's insight is accepted by him, even if he is then equally happy to deny to Hegel any special privileges with regard to being the actual source of 'Hegelianism'!

This commitment on Nietzsche's part to the notion of becoming is, in fact, fundamental to his discussion of knowledge. On a Nietzschean view, since existence is always in a state of continual change, it can in fact be contrasted with the way in which human beings have been tempted to understand the world in which they live. In other words, he draws a distinction between what we experience and how we interpret those experiences. Existence may be in a state of becoming, but our interpretations of it – and above all, the 'metaphysical' interpretation of it that philosophers have taken as the paradigm instance of 'knowledge' – usually fail to express this. This view can, in fact, be traced back as far as 1873, to an early fragment entitled 'On Truth and Lie in an Extra-Moral Sense':

> In some remote corner of the universe, poured out and glittering with innumerable solar systems, there was once a star on which clever animals invented knowledge. That was the haughtiest and most mendacious moment of 'world history' – and yet only a minute. After nature had drawn a few breaths the star grew cold and the clever animals had to die.[15]

Let us refrain from emitting a sigh at this rather sad story, and instead note two things about it. First, knowledge is set in a specific context: it is earth-bound. If we were speaking like Hegel, we might say that human knowledge is doomed to remain particularized and is thereby unable to aspire to universality. What we call 'knowledge' is a product of our all-too-human physical existence and will vanish as soon as the material conditions rendering it possible cease. Second, knowledge is an 'invention': it is something that humans have *created* and is solely dependent upon their dispositions and needs. Any attempt to demonstrate a necessary connection between knowledge and an ultimate reality becomes, on this view, *a priori* doubtful. This is not least because we will simply not last long enough for our knowledge ever to be tested in such a manner as would demonstrate its universality: 'clever animals', like all other animals, have to die sooner or later. Moreover, and contrary to Hegel, reality (i.e. becoming) and consciousness are not one and the same; they do not share a common grounding and destination in the 'Absolute Idea'. Consciousness is simply one kind of becoming amongst others, and certainly not a 'fundamental' one.

One might say Nietzsche initiates a criticism of the manner in which the nature of knowledge has been understood by questioning the significance that consciousness has in relation to existence, and hence its adequacy as a means of grasping it. But he does not stop here. Even if we stick with the more limited Kantian question as to what the term 'knowledge' signifies from a purely human perspective, the issue of what we mean by 'consciousness' will again arise. According to Nietzsche, what defines us as living beings is not merely our consciousness. There are, for him, no 'facts' of consciousness upon which it would be possible to erect an epistemology. An account of knowledge that begins with the nature of self-consciousness adopts a method insufficient for explaining what self-consciousness or, for that matter, 'reality' is:

> by far the greater part of conscious thinking must still be included among instinctive activities, and that goes even for philosophical thinking. We have to relearn here, as one has had to relearn about heredity and what is 'innate'. As the act of birth deserves no consideration in the whole process and procedure of heredity, so 'being conscious' is not in any decisive sense the opposite of what is instinctive. (*Beyond Good and Evil*, section 3)

The lesson, then, is that we need to learn how to draw distinctions. The act of giving birth does not, of itself, confer heredity upon the one who is born; obviously, other important social and genetic factors do this. So, too, with conscious thinking: consciousness is not born of consciousness and nothing else. The genealogy of consciousness must also be understood in terms of its unconscious preconditions, for consciousness is something that emerges from unconscious conditions of thought. As Nietzsche puts it in a notebook entry dating from 1887–8, ' "Thinking", as epistemologists conceive it, simply does not exist: it is a quite arbitrary fiction, arrived at by selecting one element from the process and eliminating all the rest, an artificial arrangement for the purpose of intelligibility' (*The Will to Power*, section 477).[16] With regard to subjectivity, it is not adequate to speak in terms of 'inner' and 'outer sense', as Kant does. It is worth recalling here that, for Kant, it is our inner sense that ultimately grounds our ability to have representations of experiences. This inner sense is structured in *a priori* fashion, and is derived from the spontaneous ability to think possessed by the transcendental subject. Nietzsche's response to such a claim is to argue that, with regard to consciousness, no mental 'facts' exist that correspond to the term 'inner sense'. The 'inner' is as much a matter of 'phenomenality' as the purportedly 'outer' world of empirical experience. The Kantian approach begins by thinking of the subject as a kind of 'cause' (i.e. as that which spontaneously 'thinks'), but if consciousness is a kind of phenomenon, then the attribution even of causality to it may well be questionable. If thinking is not 'causal' in this sense, then, Nietzsche can ask, in what sense can we talk of the purportedly *a priori* preconditions of experience that Kant places so much store by as emerging from (i.e. as being 'caused' by) 'subjectivity'? His short way with the question is to argue that we simply cannot do so (section 478).

Likewise, where the Hegelian might be tempted to see material existence as leading necessarily to consciousness, and then consciousness unfolding into self-consciousness, Nietzsche would be keen to point out that self-consciousness rests upon both material and physiological (instinctive) preconditions that remain immanent to it: there is no 'pure' self-consciousness that exists independently of unconscious and non-conscious conditions. By the same token, there is no necessity involved in the development of one into the other, for 'instinct' cannot be distinguished absolutely from consciousness as being different in kind. Thus, one of Nietzsche's strategies is to mount an attack on the notion that self-consciousness can provide us with an adequate criterion for the assessment of what is to count as 'true knowledge'. Nietzsche doubts that oppositions (such as 'consciousness versus instinct') are very useful for the purpose of analysing what thinking, and hence knowledge, is. There is simply no epistemologically certain starting point from which an analysis of the nature of knowledge could be developed. To phrase the matter slightly differently: there are no 'first principles' on which our knowledge rests. This kind of approach is evident in the writings of Nietzsche's early maturity, starting with *Human, All-Too-Human* (1878).[17]

2.1   *Metaphysical versus historical philosophy*

Human, All-Too-Human in fact begins by making a relatively trivial, but very general, observation: 'Almost all the problems of philosophy once again pose the same form of question as they did two thousand years ago: how can something originate in its opposite, for example rationality in irrationality, . . . logic in unlogic, . . . truth in error?' (section 1).[18] Nietzsche's approach here to is to begin by asking a simple question about the *origins* of important concepts. His response to this question is twofold. On the one hand, he highlights the role of what he calls 'metaphysical philosophy' in the traditional understanding of these questions. This is an important move, since it initiates a discussion of the nature of metaphysics that Nietzsche follows through right up until 1888.[19] Metaphysical philosophy has, he says, always been committed to the view that such oppositions are fixed in place. Reason, metaphysics tells us, cannot be derived from unreason, logic cannot have an illogical source, and truth cannot be derived from error. This view has been held because reason, truth, etc., have generally been attributed a 'miraculous source' underlying experience 'in the very kernel and being of the "thing in itself"'. Metaphysical philosophy, in short, is 'metaphysical' precisely because it invokes what cannot be demonstrated by way of *experience* in order to justify its claims. But such philosophizing is also metaphysical because in invoking what lies beyond experience it makes the claim to have a supra-historical perspective. Metaphysics, therefore, is the invocation of the eternally true as the standard of measurement for determining 'reality'. According to metaphysical philosophy, Nietzsche argues, the word 'true' is taken to signify what does not change.

Nietzsche's other response to his question is to oppose metaphysical thinking to what he calls 'historical philosophy'. One might be tempted to see a kind of 'Hegelianism' implicit here, in so far as the historical is highlighted. But, to repeat the point, Nietzsche offers an account of historical philosophy that is distinctly *un*-Hegelian in so far as the self-conscious present cannot, for him, be read as emerging *necessarily* out of the development of the non-conscious or unconscious past of organic life. To put it another way, life is not intrinsically purposive. Nor can it be taken as gaining its justification from concepts of the divine essence (as Hegel's does).[20] In turn, for Nietzsche, how humans think is always also a physiological issue: we think because we are material and organic beings, and how (and indeed what) we think is therefore a matter that primarily concerns our status as beings located in the context of a physical environment.

On a Nietzschean view, it follows, one can and must conceive of human knowledge in terms of a process of development in which self-consciousness arose from material conditions of life. However, one important consequence of this process was to put in place assumptions that we are now unable to shake off, even if we wanted to. In other words, the manner in which we conceptualize our everyday experiences necessarily involves presuppositions that facilitate thought, and these presuppositions have their origin in the distant past of human development. Any account that would ignore this fails to address the fact that the present is rooted in the past and is thereby in part determined by it. Metaphysical philosophy is the uncritical inheritor of this kind of assumption, taking the thought conditions that govern present everyday human life and misreading them as timeless structures upon which our knowledge of 'reality' rests. What metaphysical philosophers have hitherto done, Nietzsche says, is taken these presuppositions to be a kind of unproblematic starting point from which one then is able to depart on the journey of inquiring into reality:

> All philosophers have the common failing of starting out from man as he is now and thinking that they can reach their goal through an analysis of him. They involuntarily think of 'man' as an *aeterna veritas* . . . as a sure measure of things . . . Everything that the philosopher has declared about man is, however, at bottom no more than a testimony as to the man of a *very limited* period of time. Lack of historical sense is the family failing of all philosophers . . . But everything has become: there are *no eternal facts*, just as there are no absolute truths. Consequently what is needed from now on is *historical philosophizing*, and with it the virtue of modesty. (*Human, All-Too-Human*, section 2)

Historical philosophy, it follows, rejects the belief that we can take humans as they are now as the foundation upon which to formulate judgements about metaphysical reality, for such judgements would be mere projections of 'a very limited period of time' recast in the form of a metaphysical Absolute.

Nevertheless, it is equally apparent here that Nietzsche explicitly makes a claim about reality; namely, that it is to be comprehended in terms of change, that 'everything has become'. This might be regarded as itself embodying a metaphysical commitment, but Nietzsche would argue that it does not. It is not a metaphysical claim to the extent that it merely states that we can only have knowledge of empirical experience, that is, of so-called 'appearances'. Appearances are, to this extent, 'everything', and everything, in this sense, 'has become'. Moreover, if we do away with the metaphysical notion of 'eternal facts', including the Kantian realm of 'things in-themselves', then, Nietzsche argues, one might just as well also dispense with the notion even of 'appearances': 'The real world – we have done away with it: what world was left? the apparent one, perhaps? . . . But no! *with the real world we have also done away with the apparent one!*' (*Twilight of the Idols*, 'How the "Real World" Finally became a Fable', section 6).[21] Understanding the world in terms of becoming, in short, means abandoning all the categories that tempt us to conceive of it metaphysically; and thinking in terms of 'appearances' is itself an example of a metaphysical way of thinking.

Nietzsche argues, therefore, that what philosophers have mistaken for reality is in fact unreality, and in making this mistake they have inverted the relationship between cause and effect by interpreting 'being' into 'becoming'. Thinking is thereby taken to be primary by metaphysical philosophy, and the prior conditions that culminated in thinking are taken by it to be merely secondary and derivative. But it is in fact the other way around; for life is possible without thought, but thought is not possible without life. When we talk of 'knowledge', and therefore also of things like 'truth', 'reason', or 'logic', we must, it follows, develop an account that gives its due to the life conditions under which such concepts have arisen. These conditions are not themselves inherently rational or logical, as metaphysics would have us believe. What Nietzsche's argument amounts to is the contention that we cannot justifiably make metaphysical claims about the ultimate nature of reality that attribute 'being' (the property of permanence) to it.[22]

Nietzsche's criticism of what Theodor Adorno has called the 'metaphysics of the persisting' amounts to a revitalization of aspects of Hume's sceptical form of empiricism.[23] Nietzsche's is a 'Humean' critique to the extent that it effectively denies the idea that we can derive any metaphysical claim asserting that being and reality are the same from the fact that we encounter experiential particulars. Likewise, this in turn involves the assertion that our rational abilities are not intrinsically 'rational', in so far as they are not 'representational' in function. 'Reason' does not facilitate the representation of an objective reality. Rather, as Nietzsche argues in *Twilight of the Idols* (1888), ' "Reason" is what causes us to falsify the evidence of the senses. If the senses show becoming, passing away, change, they do not lie . . .' (*Twilight of the Idols*, ' "Reason" in Philosophy', section 2). So, Nietzsche's attack on metaphysics springs from his adherence to a form of empiricism: we start with the senses, and what the senses tell us about experience is true if taken on their own terms. To this extent, sensory impressions are direct representations of the world of experience: they 'correspond' to reality, if only to the degree that it continually passes away. But Nietzsche differs from Hume in that, for him, our *concepts* or 'ideas' do not correspond to our sensory impressions. For concepts or ideas are not representations (as empiricism would have it); nor are they rules (as Kantianism would have it). Concepts are *interpretations* of sensory experience that render it in terms of predictability. So, in the activity of thinking (which means using concepts) what humans do is make experience familiar to them, and they do so in order to render it calculable. In so far as concepts regulate experience and make it calculable, one can say they are, for Nietzsche, *instruments*.

Nietzsche's attack on metaphysics springs from the fact that philosophers cannot, it seems, resist the temptation to interpret concepts in a manner that undercuts their true instrumental value. They ignore the utility of concepts (their predictive value) and instead take them to signify something about the nature of reality and thereby assert their purportedly 'ontological' value. In this way, Nietzsche argues in a manner reminiscent of the opening of *Human, All-Too-Human*, philosophers betray 'their lack of historical sense, their hatred of the very idea of becoming . . . All that philosophers have been handling for thousands of years is conceptual mummies; nothing real has ever left their hands alive. They kill things and stuff them, these servants of conceptual idols, when they worship – they become a mortal danger to everything when they worship' (*Twilight of the Idols*, ' "Reason" in Philosophy', section 1). Metaphysical philosophy is nothing more than the worshipping of false idols: the attribution of 'reality' to what lies at the furthest remove from it: the concept.

2.2   Language and metaphysics

In addressing the issue of how we construct a view of reality that is 'metaphysical', then, Nietzsche stresses something analogous to Hume's notion of 'habit'. But such habits are, for Nietzsche, not merely subjective in nature. On the contrary, they are the collective habits and customs of humankind. We do not think the way we do because we are individuals; we think the way we do because we are, in Nietzschean terms, 'herd animals'. To put it another way, our most important habits are shared habits. With regard to tracing the origins of metaphysical thinking, such habits are inseparable from the way in which humans use language:

> To the extent that man has for long ages believed in the concepts and names of things as in *aeternae veritates* he has appropriated to himself that pride by which he raised himself above the animal: he really thought that in language he possessed knowledge of the world. The sculptor of language was not so modest as to believe that he was only giving things designations, he conceived rather that with words he was expressing supreme knowledge of things . . . Happily, it is too late for the evolution of reason, which depends on this belief, to be again put back. (*Human, All-Too-Human*, section 11)

Because language works by means of referring to our experiences, we 'naturally' believe that words refer to things that exist independently of our language. But, Nietzsche is arguing, words do not of themselves entail the expression of some essential properties that exist independently of them.[24] Even as we name 'things' (and even the notion of a 'thing' is, after all, a kind of name), we are actively interpreting our experiences by presupposing that there must be entities that *correspond* to the names we utter. We are, it follows, *habitually* open to understanding words as representing in an unmediated manner the purportedly 'essential properties' of objects. This belief is perhaps an essential condition of language use, and to that extent it is necessary. But it does not follow from this that the belief is objectively true. Indeed, Nietzsche argues, this is not the case: names do not represent things (as metaphysical philosophy would assert). Like our concepts, names express something essential about the *relationship* between humans and their environment. Language is one of the ways in which we cope with our environment.

In a sense that is only loosely analogous to Kant's account of the subjective preconditions of knowledge, Nietzsche is arguing that it is 'subjective' conditions that determine language use. But these subjective conditions are not, for Nietzsche, worthy of the further designation 'objective' simply in virtue of the fact that we must all, as human beings, abide by them. Nietzsche is, like Kant, a kind of empirical realist. He would agree that the question of what is to count as 'knowledge' is one that starts with experience. But he is not a transcendental idealist, as Kant is. In other words, we do not, as Kant would have it, begin with experience, proceed to the understanding, and from there arrive at the transcendental source of all knowledge (the spontaneous and unconditioned transcendental subject). On the contrary, Nietzsche does not think there is anything about the sources or forms of our thought that ought to count as 'transcendental' at all. One reason for this, as we have already seen, is that Nietzsche argues that consciousness is a *phenomenon*. As a phenomenon consciousness cannot be said to possess in an unproblematic fashion the causal properties that metaphysics has generally attributed to it. This claim can now be spelled out in terms of language. It is *language* that 'sees doer and deed everywhere: it believes in the will as cause in general; it believes in the I, in the I as Being, in the I as substance, and *projects* the belief in the I-substance onto all things – only then does it create the concept "thing"' (*Twilight of the Idols*, '"Reason" in Philosophy', section 5). Strikingly, the implication here is that language is not so much 'used' by humans as it is something that 'manipulates' and determines human thought. Beliefs do not reside in subjects who are equipped with thoughts and utter those thoughts 'through' language. Beliefs are linguistic properties, and it is these properties which define what a subject is, not the other way around.

A further implication of this view is that consciousness and language are intrinsically linked to one another, that 'the development of language and the development of consciousness . . . go hand in hand' (*The Gay Science*, section 354). And, additionally, since it is in language that we must think, our reason, too, is derived from linguistic preconditions. Rationality springs from linguistic norms and practices, that is, from human beings reacting in certain ways in relation to their environment, producing instrumental interpretations of that environment *in* (rather than by means of) words and concepts. In turn, language is not implicitly 'rational' in the sense in which metaphysical philosophy would take it to be, i.e. as legitimizing the inference that concepts or words correspond to an 'order of things'. On the contrary, it is language that underlies the metaphysical interpretation of the significance of reason and consciousness alike: 'we become involved in a crude fetishism when we make ourselves conscious of the basic premises of the metaphysics of language, in plain words: of *reason* . . . "Reason" in language: oh what a deceitful old woman! I am afraid we are not getting rid of God because we still believe in grammar . . .' (*Twilight of the Idols*, '"Reason" in Philosophy', section 5). Language, in short, sows the seeds of our tendency to interpret experience metaphysically. The most metaphysical of concepts, such as 'Being' and 'God' (which, for Nietzsche, signify something uncannily similar), are rooted in our grammatical conventions. The power of language amounts to no more than the weight of tradition, our cherished belief in 'grammar', so that 'with every piece of knowledge one has to stumble over dead, petrified words, and one would sooner break a leg than a word'.[25] Metaphysics, too, is a matter of linguistic habit; and it is from this that it derives its traditional authority.

It is in our collective linguistic nature, not subjective experience, therefore, that we find a prime example of habit or custom. We 'use' language conventionally (and to that extent 'unconsciously'), and it is in language and the conventions that comprise it that our 'rationality' resides. We *have* to think rationally to the extent that we have to think linguistically: *'We cease to think when we refuse to do so under the constraint of language*; we barely reach the doubt that sees this limitation as a limitation. *Rational thought is interpretation according to a scheme that we cannot throw off'* (*The Will to Power*, section 522). What we do when we think rationally is interpret the world of sense-experience by way of linguistic conventions. When it comes to the matter of metaphysical issues, the mistake is to read anything more significant than this fact into our language. Language about reality does not actually represent the world. Such language merely expresses our need to think of our environment as something that can be 'represented' in order that we may survive in it.

Nevertheless, Nietzsche contends, this kind of metaphysical error is a necessary precondition for humans being able to conceptualize, and so engage with, their environment at all. Questions concerning the nature of knowledge, and of truth, arise only because, in the first place, erroneous metaphysical beliefs were held. If, on this basis, we were to answer the question posed at the beginning of *Human-All-Too-Human*, then we would be obliged to affirm that knowledge does indeed arise out of error. It is important to note that the word 'error' as Nietzsche uses it in this context denotes the *belief* that words correspond to 'things', the belief that there are 'things in-themselves' independent of language. It is important to bear this fact in mind, because when Nietzsche talks about 'errors' in this sense he is referring therefore to specific metaphysical beliefs. He is not claiming that our words somehow 'fail' to refer successfully to things – that there are things in the world to which words *could* correspond but somehow do not manage to do so. Words, on Nietzsche's view, cannot 'fail' to refer to things since there is nothing in this sense for them to refer to in the first place. This is because the meaning of words is derived from their role within a structure of linguistic conventions. Although Nietzsche is a kind of realist in that he holds that there is a world that exists independently of our conscious mental activity and linguistic abilities (a world of becoming), such a world is not composed of things, substances and the like. The founding 'errors' of our knowledge, it follows, are rooted in certain beliefs that have been held concerning the nature of reality; and these beliefs are false to the extent that they are ungrounded.

2.3   The 'origin of knowledge'

'We set up a word at the point at which our ignorance begins, at which we can see no further, e.g., the word "I", the word "do", the word "suffer": – these are perhaps the horizon of our knowledge, but not "truths"' (*The Will to Power*, section 482). On Nietzsche's view, linguistic terms are markers signifying the limits of our knowledge. They do not, it follows, guarantee that what we know is a true representation of what we encounter in experience, for language is not really concerned with this question. But, this all being said, why is it that Nietzsche himself so obviously regards questions about the nature of knowledge as being so important? In point of fact, the claim that something can arise out of its opposite is central to Nietzsche's ideas here. Knowledge can, and does, arise out of metaphysical errors; but just because we are able to trace its source to these conditions does not entitle us to the further belief that knowledge is thereby condemned to endless error and falsehood. A certain kind of 'objectivity' is possible for thinking, but this objectivity will *not* be the kind of objectivity that metaphysical philosophy equated with the truth of being.

One way of elucidating this is to begin with section 110 of *The Gay Science*, entitled the '*Origin of knowledge*'. There was a time, Nietzsche argues here, when 'the intellect produced nothing but errors'. Some of these, however, served a positive function: they helped to preserve human life, and were henceforth passed on to future generations as 'erroneous articles of faith'. These errors are none other than the 'metaphysics of language [or], in plain talk, the presuppositions of reason' that we have already encountered above. Such presuppositions include the beliefs 'that there are equal things; that there are things, substances, bodies; that a thing is what it appears to be; that what is good for me is also good in itself'. True to form, these erroneous metaphysical beliefs, Nietzsche then argues, formed a conceptual framework that allowed human life to flourish. To this extent, metaphysical thinking is a source of human survival. Given their utility, these beliefs entered into human nature and became 'almost part of the basic endowment of the species'. Indeed, so essential did these beliefs become that they eventually came to constitute the structure of unquestioned habits and customs upon which human society relies in order to function. In other words, such errors became norms for regulating human behaviour and thought alike because they facilitated survival.

The activity of placing these assumptions in question, of doubting them, only occurred much later: 'it was only very late that truth emerged – as the weakest form of knowledge.' It is therefore apparent that, for Nietzsche, talk about 'knowledge' means talking about those habitual beliefs we have inherited, and which allow us to survive irrespective of whether or not they truly 'represent' reality (which, as we have noted, becomes an altogether redundant question). But we may nevertheless talk about the possibility of questioning these beliefs, of raising the question of their truth. This possibility is 'knowledge' in the weakest of senses because of the predominance of the conceptual assumptions ('metaphysical errors') upon which humans relied as a means of helping them get about the world successfully. It is a weak form of knowledge because in order to question those errors one must inevitably resort to using the language that enshrines them. And yet the question of truth, Nietzsche then adds, nevertheless became a threat to those founding errors upon which knowledge rested. How did this happen?

Nietzsche answers this question by arguing that 'truth', understood as the contradiction of erroneous belief, first made its appearance in the form of philosophies of denial, in the guise of asceticism. The Eleatics[26] postulated truth as the opposite of those errors that go to make up our customary beliefs. In doing so they produced what Nietzsche terms an 'inverted knowledge'. The Eleatics were equally blind to the metaphysical falsehoods that beset their own thinking. This was because 'truth', as the Eleatics understood it, was in fact little more than an extension of the errors upon which human society rested. What they regarded as the truth was itself a mere inversion of customary beliefs: truth regarded as the supposed 'opposite' of common sense and custom. The development of a 'subtler honesty and skepticism' only arrived at the moment when it was realized that two contrary propositions can be equally 'applicable to life because both were compatible with the basic errors' that ground custom. As a consequence of this, such propositions, Nietzsche says, became ranked in accordance with their utility: they could be (1) beneficial, (2) harmful, or (3) neither beneficial nor harmful. In the space opened up by this third possibility 'there was room for the expression of an intellectual play impulse.' A person could say what they liked without fear of normative censure. This impulse to engage in intellectual debate finally took its place in human life alongside custom, so that 'the human brain became full of such judgements and convictions, and a ferment, struggle, and lust for power developed in this tangle.' The outcome of this process was that 'knowledge and the striving for the true found their place among other [human] needs.'

In this way Nietzsche envisages the need for truth becoming part of human nature. Since the need for true knowledge became a part of us, it follows that 'knowledge became a piece of life itself', growing in power until it inevitably collided with those earlier errors which grounded the social domain (for example, the most cherished metaphysical beliefs – those of religion). In the light of this, a battleground has been marked out upon which two seemingly incompatible urges struggle for power. On the one hand, there is the need for custom and stability, which facilitates the preservation of human social life. On the other, there is the philosophical need to question the assumptions upon which society rests – in other words, to discover the truth about these assumptions by subjecting them to doubt. This state of existence defines, for Nietzsche, the central dilemma of being a philosopher:

> two lives, two powers, both in the same human being. A thinker is now that being in whom the impulse for truth and those life preserving errors clash for their first fight, after the impulse for truth has also proved to be a life-preserving power. Compared with the significance of this fight, everything else is a matter of indifference: the ultimate question about the conditions of life has been posed here, and we confront the first attempt to answer this question by experiment. To what extent can truth endure incorporation? That is the question; that is the experiment.   (*The Gay Science*, section 110)

In other words, Nietzsche is asking here about the possibility and extent to which it is possible for human beings to stand apart from and criticize their beliefs, even though such beliefs constitute the necessary conditions of their existence.

The 'need' for truth thus springs from 'error'. This need (the philosophical need) is now nevertheless a form of life. We want truth, but wanting truth is not a matter of mere utility, as 'metaphysical knowledge' is. Equally, then, out of the usefulness of certain beliefs in preserving the species, there has arisen a need that is not useful but precisely its opposite to the degree that it involves questioning metaphysics. The central question, then, is: to what extent is it possible for us to aspire to truth and objectivity in our beliefs, given that this aspiration may entail sacrificing the erroneous metaphysical conditions upon which our very lives rest? Pursuing 'truth', in this sense, involves criticizing metaphysics, even as one finds oneself trapped within it. It means allowing 'convictions . . . no rights of citizenship' in the domain of knowledge: 'Only when they decide to descend to the modesty of hypotheses, of a provisional experimental point of view, of a regulative fiction, they may be granted admission and even a certain value in the realm of knowledge – though always with the restriction that they remain under police supervision, under the police of mistrust' (*The Gay Science*, section 344). But even this, Nietzsche then notes, entails 'some prior conviction . . . a faith'. In fact, this faith, too, is a *'metaphysical faith'*: the belief of Plato that truth is divine, 'our most enduring lie'. In the end, it is a moral demand. The demand for truth at any price, the ' "will to truth" does *not* mean "I will not allow myself to be deceived" but – there is no alternative – "I will not deceive, not even myself"; *and with that we stand on moral ground'*.

Given that such a moral demand as this is unconditional, it follows that it is also a metaphysical demand: it affirms the universality of an ethical principle with regard to thinking in that those who seek knowledge ought to aspire *not to deceive*. Moreover, it becomes apparent why Nietzsche, as we noted near the beginning of this discussion of him, regards any philosophy that aspires to being a mere 'theory of knowledge' as a timid and rather pathetic thing. The pursuit of nothing more than 'theory of knowledge' is an empty pursuit: putting flesh on the body of a philosophy means situating it in the world of history, arguing for its 'legislative' and moral importance. But, if an ethical demand is to be found in the philosopher's desire to know, then it is also the case that we therefore always remain, on Nietzsche's view, situated within metaphysics whenever we attempt to discuss what is of value in the realm of knowledge. The only answer to this kind of problem, it seems, is a special kind of self-consciousness: self-reflexivity. Self-reflexivity means understanding that all our knowledge claims rest upon presuppositions that cannot be demonstrated. Likewise, it means accepting that all thinking is, at bottom, metaphysical in the sense that it craves a certain degree of 'objectivity' and timelessness even as it remains bereft of both. Finally, it means accepting that questions of knowledge are also moral questions. But the ethical demand for truthfulness also points to the fact that there is a kind of 'objectivity' in knowledge that is worth aspiring to. Being truthful, after all, means acknowledging that we might be deceived, that our current view of a problem is not the only possible one. How, then, are we to police our hypotheses? One possible answer to this question is by fostering an attitude that Nietzsche calls 'perspectivism'.

2.4   Perspectivism

It is a necessary condition of our making any claims to knowledge that we must speak from somewhere. 'Insofar as the word "knowledge" has any meaning, the world is knowable; but it is *interpretable* otherwise, it has no meaning behind it, but countless meanings. – "Perspectivism" ' (*The Will to Power*, section 481). The will to truth demands perspectivism, for perspectivism preserves the desire for objectivity in knowledge, and yet at the same time allows for the rethinking of objectivity in terms of interests. No single viewpoint will serve this purpose, since metaphysical philosophy has shown the questionable nature of any such enterprise: there is no disinterested knowledge because all knowledge expresses an instrumental relation between humans and their environment. Metaphysical philosophy, recall, aims at providing a unified understanding of the nature of reality from a single viewpoint outside of historical experience. But, says Nietzsche, 'I should think that today we are far from the ridiculous immodesty that would be involved in decreeing from our corner that perspectives are permitted only from this corner' (*The Gay Science*, section 374). Every perspective that claims the status of the timeless and the universal condemns itself, for the world can always be interpreted differently. The supposed 'objectivity' of this kind of thinking reveals its partiality as soon as it speaks. It is not this kind of objectivity that should be aspired to. Rather, Nietzsche argues, the number of viewpoints we have access to must be multiplied if we are to arrive at an understanding that retains the spirit of 'objectivity', and which therefore aims at reliable knowledge:

> From now on, my philosophical colleagues, let us be more wary of the dangerous old conceptual fairy-tale which has set up a 'pure, will-less, painless, timeless, subject of knowledge' . . . here we are asked to think an eye that cannot be thought at all, an eye turned in no direction at all, an eye where the active and interpretative powers are to be suppressed, absent, but through which seeing still becomes a seeing-something, so it is an absurdity and a non-concept of an eye that is demanded. There is *only* a perspective seeing, *only* a perspective 'knowing'; the *more* affects we allow to speak about a thing, the *more* eyes, various eyes we are able to use for the same thing, the more complete will be our 'concept' of the thing, our 'objectivity'.[27]

The more varied and rich our understanding, the better our knowledge. We may remain trapped within metaphysics, and only a woeful lack of self-reflexivity would allow us to think otherwise. But metaphysics can, it turns out, be turned against itself: truth can emerge out of error in the guise of the demand for the true (the will to truth).

But what, one might ask, does the will to truth represent for Nietzsche? Certainly, it is nothing 'disinterested', since all claims to knowledge are perspectival in nature – and a perspective implies a standpoint, and a standpoint implies an interest. In fact, it is a kind of drive, a sublimated expression of an urge to dominate, and this Nietzsche calls 'the will to power'. There is, in fact, an inherent tension between the will to power and perspectivism, since the former for Nietzsche implies the predominance of one kind of perspective over and above all others. I will return to the will to power elsewhere.[28] For present purposes, it is worth addressing one important question that follows immediately from Nietzsche's analysis of the nature of human knowledge. If Nietzsche's account is persuasive, then what is left of 'epistemology'? If one had to sum up Nietzsche's overall position in the briefest possible terms, then it is clear that traditional epistemology, which seeks to uncover the basic conditions of our knowledge, is to be regarded as little more than an uncritical extrapolation of the underlying presuppositions of metaphysical philosophy. To that extent, epistemology is something that must be overcome, even if metaphysics itself cannot be entirely abandoned. The epistemological aim of presenting a transparent account of the nature of our knowledge founders upon the fact that the subject (the Cartesian 'I think') can no longer serve as the foundation of our knowledge. Subjectivity is itself, for Nietzsche, produced by environmental forces, practices, norms and linguistic conventions. All subjectivity is, in turn, essentially contextual: we all speak from a particular perspective whenever we make a judgement of any kind. In turn, what perspectivism implies is that there is no 'knowledge' as such; rather, there are many possible 'knowledges': many different possible standpoints from which the world may be viewed. Hence, any unified account of the nature of what it is to 'know' would have to reassemble all of these perspectives by subordinating them to one unifying principle. Only then would epistemology again be possible, in the traditional sense. But, Nietzsche argues, if we are to preserve a sense of 'objectivity' this must be bought at the cost of our becoming modest about what we think we know. We must be modest with regard to the status of our own beliefs, for there are other possible ones. This knowledge, alone, amounts to our objectivity. Can we, however, abandon epistemology entirely? Equally, if rationality has turned out to be instrumental, how are we to understand the significance of this fact? One possible response to these issues has been developed by the thinkers of the Frankfurt School.

3   The Frankfurt School: Horkheimer and Adorno

The Frankfurt Institute for Social Research was opened in 1924. The work of the thinkers associated with this Institute are generally grouped together as the writings of the 'Frankfurt School'. The central figures associated with the Frankfurt School are Theodor Adorno (1903–69), Walter Benjamin, Erich Fromm, Herbert Marcuse, Max Horkheimer, (1895–1973), and most recently Jürgen Habermas (1929–) and Karl Otto Apel (1921–). Horkheimer became the Institute's director in 1930, and it was his influence that initiated a turn toward developing the neo-Hegelian and Marxist approaches with which the Frankfurt School's name has become synonymous. We have already seen how Hegel articulates the problem of knowledge in terms of the principle of immanent historical development. On such a view, we do not need to look 'outside' consciousness in order to arrive at an understanding of the true nature of thinking, for the logical structure of reality is shared by thought and the world of sense experience alike. Hegel's immanent account is developed by the Frankfurt thinkers, but is articulated by them primarily in terms of the social conditions of thought.

For thinkers such as Horkheimer and Adorno, the development of thinking is intrinsically connected with the conditions of cultural life, and it is this relationship which marks out the immanent structure of thought. Contradictions, in other words, point to the capacity of thought to transcend its own particularized limitations. But the significance of contradiction is not to be understood as a mere stage in the unfolding of an inexorable progress toward the universal Hegelian Idea. Since all thinking, on their conception, is bound inextricably to its social conditions, the presence of contradiction in thought informs us that these conditions themselves do not add up to a rational and unified whole.[29] The contradictions of thought, in other words, are analogues of the contradictions present within the society that renders that thought possible. The elucidation of these contradictions is the proper role of critical reflection. And the latter, in order to remain properly critical, must continually bear in mind its own limitations. Thought must, therefore, challenge its own limitations through critical reflection, and yet at the same time renounce any claim to the possession of absolute knowledge. To this extent, critical awareness is, for Horkheimer and Adorno, an activity of dialectical reflection. One might say that thinkers such as Horkheimer and Adorno are 'Hegelians' to the extent that they perceive the importance of dialectically generated contradiction and the striving toward the universal. However, they are not Hegelians because they are highly critical of the notion of the Absolute even though they keep it in play. For them, the third moment of the Hegelian dialectic is never attainable.[30] In the same way as the particular is, for Hegel, always mediated by the dialectical movement toward the universal, so on Horkheimer and Adorno's view particular social forms are to be read in the context of the larger network of social relations that constitute them. However, where Hegel regards the desire for the Absolute as a necessary consequence of thinking, for Horkheimer and Adorno this goal is ultimately blocked by the historical and social specificity that is a necessary condition of all thought.

The emphasis upon the social dimension of thinking within the writings of the Frankfurt School is derived from a critical encounter with Marxist theory. In this connection, it is worth very briefly noting some relevant points about the thought of Karl Marx (1818–83). Where Hegel sought to understand thinking in terms of a historical process of dialectical development toward the Absolute Idea, Marx argued that Hegel had in fact got matters upside down. It is not the conditions of self-consciousness that determine the nature of historical development, but material conditions. These material conditions are to be found in the fabric of social life: they are economic. Marx, therefore, develops a variant of the Hegelian dialectic that concentrates upon articulating the conditions of human existence in terms of the economic relationships that dominate any social order.[31] Principally, Marx's analysis centres upon the phenomenon of modern capitalist society. This is a form of social and economic organization that, Marx argues, is dominated by 'production', i.e. the economic production of material goods for the purposes of consumption. Above all, Marx argues, capitalism is marked by the division of labour into classes and by the unequal distribution of goods within society. The division of labour is a direct consequence of the need inherent in capitalist social forms to organize production with a view to the maximization of profit. This need results in exploitation. The majority of individuals (in the form of those who work within the capitalist system) are treated as a means of furthering the profit of a minority (those who own the means of production: the bourgeois capitalists). Capitalist society is thus essentially a class-ridden social formation.

The issue of Marx's analysis of capitalist society will be returned to in chapter 5, in connection with the French philosopher Louis Althusser's interpretation of Marx's theory of ideology. For the moment, the key point to draw from Marx's analysis as it relates to the thinkers of the Frankfurt School is that his account of society highlights the role of economic activity in the development of cultural and intellectual life. In the most basic terms, this comes down to the claim that economic conditions (what is generally referred to as the 'economic base') determine the nature and structure of society as a whole, including its governmental, educational and cultural institutions (what is generally referred to as the 'superstructure'). To put it another way, like Nietzsche, Marx thinks that material conditions exert a decisive influence upon the way in which we think. In turn, 'history', for Marx, is to be understood in terms of changes that occur within the economic base structure. The motor of history, in other words, is to be found in the material economic conditions that operate within society, not in Hegelian Absolute self-consciousness. These changes, and thus the development of history, are the direct consequence of class struggles for power. Such struggles result from the contradictions inherent within the capitalist mode of organization itself. For capitalism creates the conditions under which the creation of classes is rendered possible. The members of classes, in turn, develop a self-conscious sense of identity in virtue of their position within society. Since the majority of social members (workers) do not share in the overall wealth of capitalist society, in so far as they work for those who possess the greatest wealth (the capitalists), their sense of identity is rooted in alienation.[32] Alienation, which is in fact a notion developed by Marx from Hegel's account of it in the *Philosophy of Right*,[33] springs from the fact that even at the level of production (i.e. on the factory floor) the worker exists in an alienated relationship to the product they are making: they exercise no control over what happens to that product. Equally, the worker finds him or herself as existing at the level of a mere commodity: what defines them is that they can sell their labour in exchange for the means of subsistence. The division of society into classes, it follows, is symptomatic of the divisive and alienating tendency of capitalism. To this extent, all class identity is also alienated identity.

Marx's theory of revolution springs from these class tensions. Alienated working-class labour will, in the last analysis, seek to overthrow the dominant bourgeois capitalist class by seizing the means of production. In the long term, this will, Marx believes, lead to a classless society, in so far as a working-class revolution will entail the destruction of the bourgeois state, and indeed all forms of state control. Marx's analysis of the nature of society is broadly accepted by Horkheimer and Adorno. In so far as it is, their central aim is to develop a critical (and indeed self-critical) account of the social and historical conditions which inhere in twentieth-century capitalist society, in the form of a 'critical theory' (to use Max Horkheimer's phrase).[34] The Marxist faith in the inevitability of social revolution, however, is not. One reason for this is that, on Horkheimer's view, the working class has been successfully assimilated within the framework of capitalism, and has therefore lost any potential for overcoming it.

Horkheimer's conception of critical theory can perhaps be best understood by contrasting it with traditional empirical 'scientific' theory. Where, following on from the philosophy of empiricism, the physical scientist regards objects of study as unproblematically given prior to observation, the critical theorist pays attention to the social and cultural influences that determine the nature of knowledge. For Horkheimer, the scientist, like everybody else, is a historically and socially situated being who does not have an unmediated access to physical phenomena, as is generally presupposed by so-called 'scientific' theories of cognition. Rather, our knowledge of objects is, Horkheimer contends, always mediated by social conditions. We can, in other words, only arrive at an adequate comprehension of the nature of scientific enquiry when we appreciate the fact that, in the modern context, science is a kind of social 'institution'. Any approach that ignores this is, for Horkheimer, philosophically naive. One of the principal targets of Horkheimer's criticism is the philosophy of 'positivism' (of which more in due course).

Equally, it is evident that adopting this position commits Horkheimer to the kind of self-reflexivity with regard to knowledge that, we have seen, is central to Nietzsche's account of perspectivism. This is no mere coincidence, since Nietzsche's thought, too, is of central importance to the work of both Horkheimer and Adorno. Their jointly authored *Dialectic of Enlightenment* (1944),[35] in fact takes up and develops many of Nietzsche's points about the nature and limits of rationality – especially its mythological and irrational roots.[36] Both thinkers thus engage in an 'immanent critique' of rationality, arguing that implicit within the ideal of reason is a tendency toward irrational, mythological forms of thought. This tendency can also be found in contemporary developments within philosophical discourse about the nature of knowledge; in a movement which Horkheimer characterizes in terms of a contrast between 'subjective' and 'objective' rationality.

3.1 Horkheimer on subjective rationality

What do we mean when we talk about 'reason'? This is a question that Horkheimer poses at the beginning of *Eclipse of Reason* (1947).[37]

> When the ordinary man is asked to explain what is meant by the term reason, his reaction is almost always one of hesitation and embarrassment. It would be a mistake to interpret this as indicating wisdom too deep or thought too abstruse to be put into words. What it actually betrays is the feeling that there is nothing to enquire into, that the concept of reason is self-explanatory, that the question itself is superfluous. When pressed for an answer the average man will say that reasonable things are things that are obviously useful, and that every reasonable man is supposed to be able to decide what is useful to him.   (p. 3)

In contemporary terms, then, reason is regarded as something that concerns what is 'useful'. This purported 'fact' is taken as self-evident: reason is always a means to an end. Taken in this way, reason does not consist in reflection upon what might be good or bad, desirable or undesirable, but only upon how to attain something that one already thinks of as 'good', as 'desirable'. This, however, Horkheimer tells us, is a particular kind of conception of reason; it is 'subjective reason'. Reason, taken in this sense, is not concerned with whether or not what is desired is itself 'reasonable'. On the contrary, questioning the nature of the purposes involved here is, from the standpoint of subjective reason, something that is regarded as wholly unnecessary. This is because the notion of subjective reason involves taking the idea of 'desirability' as a given: a subject's purposes in reasoning how to get what they want are regarded as intrinsically reasonable, since what a person wants is something that is dictated by self-interest. Likewise, this conception of reason can have a communal basis, for 'self-interest' here is also taken to mean the interest of a society composed of self-interested individuals. But what does such a conception of reason signify? Horkheimer's contention is that the very fact that reason can be taken in this way indicates that a historical shift away from an earlier conception of rationality has taken place.

  In the works of thinkers such as Plato, Aristotle, or Hegel, reason is not regarded as something merely subjective. It is not, in other words, taken as a mere instrument for the attainment of subjective interests, as something that is only subjectively 'useful'. Rather, reason for a thinker like Hegel is 'objective' to the extent that it is concerned with how reality is ordered, and it thereby provides a criterion for the evaluation of questions concerning matters of means and ends. An objective conception of rationality is not, of itself, therefore intrinsically opposed to subjective reason. It merely understands subjective interests to be 'only a partial, limited expression of a universal rationality from which criteria for all things and beings . . . [can be] . . . derived' (*Eclipse of Reason*, 4–5). The difference between them is that where subjective reason places emphasis on the notion of 'means', objective reason places its emphasis upon the notion of 'ends': it is the ends (that is, the purposes), not the means, that are regarded as being subject to rational evaluation. For subjective reason, in contrast, asking any questions about the 'reasonableness' of a purpose is meaningless.

Horkheimer himself is not going to advocate a return to objective rationality. However, he detects in the increasing predominance of subjective rationality a process of social and cultural development with important consequences. The subjectivization of reason represents, at the same time, its 'formalization'; and this has 'far-reaching theoretical and practical implications' (p. 7). This is because the formalization of reason renders it no more than a 'tool', in so far as the concepts that underlie and so justify rationality have been deprived of any meaningful content; they 'have come to be only formal shells'. Questions of knowledge, in turn, concern only what can be shown to be the case, so that what is true can only be a matter of judgements concerning facts, rather than ethical judgements. 'When the idea of reason was conceived, it was intended to achieve more than a mere regulation of the relation between means and ends: it was regarded as the instrument for understanding the ends, for *determining them*' (p. 10). In this way, the unbridled pursuit of personal interests could be opposed, for reason rather than personal interest could be claimed as the ultimate court of arbitration when it came to the issue of how to resolve disputes or decide upon a correct course of action. Reason, in this sense, functioned as a form of 'conscience', as a standard by which it could be established whether or not individual attitudes measured up to the standard of objective reality. Horkheimer illustrates this last point by alluding to Socrates's dispute with the Sophists. The Sophists, as Plato presents them, argued that there are no objective truths. One of the most famous of the Sophists, Protagoras, argued that 'man is the measure of all things': it is we who determine what is to count as true and what is not to do so. This maxim is a prime example of the 'subjective rationality' that Horkheimer is discussing. Socrates argues against the Sophists for an objective understanding of reality. He argues for the view that the question of *how* we should live is an objective issue: the 'good life' is justified because it conforms to the criteria laid down by objective reason: truth is a good, and living according to the dictates of truth means living an ethical life. So, Horkheimer argues, the term 'objective reason' in fact denotes two things: (1) the objective order of reality, and (2) the striving to reflect this order in everyday life. Objective reason, we can say, addresses itself to the issue of the purpose of human life. And it answers this question by maintaining that the purpose of life is fulfilled if we live according to the rational principles that order reality. To this extent the claims of objective rationality simultaneously parallel and challenge the claims of traditional religion. Again, the example of Socrates furnishes a good illustration. He opposed the traditional, polytheistic religion of his own society, and advocated monotheism in the name of objective reason.

However, 'In modern times, reason has displayed a tendency to dissolve its own objective content' (*Eclipse of Reason*, 12–13). This can be traced back to the eighteenth century and the thinkers of the Enlightenment.[38] They sought to overturn the authority of religion in the name of reason, but their attack 'killed . . . not the church but metaphysics and the objective concept of reason itself, the source of power of their own efforts' (p. 18). The example of Hume, 'the father of modern positivism' and one of the central thinkers associated with the Enlightenment, shows us why. In spite of Hegel's objections, the pursuit of reason ultimately leads to the conclusion that reason itself is limited, that it is essentially 'subjective' in nature, not objective. Reason, in turn, is no longer an autonomous criterion of judgement: it is a means. For Horkheimer, however, the central lesson to draw from this is that reason itself must bear its share of the responsibility for the current state of affairs. For the pursuit of rationality (in the form of the development of the physical sciences, lauded as a paradigm of rational enquiry by the exponents of Enlightenment) ultimately exposed the limitations of 'objective reason' itself, and thereby severed its supposed link with reality. The 'history of reason or enlightenment' therefore presents us with the spectacle of a process in which rationality, driven by internal contradiction, unweaves itself. In abandoning its aspiration to universality, however, reason also abandons itself to the mercy of contingent social forces. In doing so it renders itself subject to the dictates of a society that is primarily organized according to the criterion of individual self-interest. It is in this sense that reason is now merely 'subjective'. This is also manifested in current theories of knowledge advocated by philosophers who have thereby given up on the Socratic project of critical reflection.

3.2   Criticisms of pragmatism and positivism

> Having given up autonomy, reason has become an instrument. . . . Reason has become completely harnessed to the social process. Its operational value . . . has been made the sole criterion. . . . Concepts have become 'streamlined', rationalized, labor-saving devices. It is as if thinking itself had been reduced to the level of industrial processes. (*Eclipse of Reason*, 21)

According to Horkheimer, the articulation of reason, taken as mere instrument, informs much contemporary theory of knowledge. Such theories are as context bound as all other thought. Two primary culprits that he singles out in this regard are the philosophies of 'pragmatism' and 'positivism'. As the briefest possible summary of pragmatism, one could say that this is an interpretation of concepts that takes their rational significance to be limited to their use-value. In the words of C. S. Peirce (1839–1914), the founder of pragmatism:

> a *conception*, that is, the rational purport of a word or other expression, lies exclusively in its conceivable bearing upon the conduct of life; . . . if one can define accurately all the conceivable experimental phenomena which the affirmation or denial of a concept could imply, one will have a complete definition of the concept, and *there is absolutely nothing more to it.*[39]

Peirce's conception of pragmatism revolves around the notion that exclusive emphasis must be placed upon the concrete consequences of our concepts with a view to determining their epistemological value. Such consequences determine a concept's worth with regard to its being an expression of knowledge. In turn, rational thought is regarded as being inseparable from subjective purposes.[40]

This view of knowledge Peirce himself regards as springing from Kant's thought.[41] Horkheimer, however, is taken aback by this kind of claim: 'one might be tempted to deny any philosophical pedigree to a doctrine that holds not that our expectations are fulfilled and our actions successful because our ideas are true, but that our ideas are true because our expectations are fulfilled and our actions successful' (*Eclipse of Reason*, 42). Kant, according to Horkheimer, engaged in a critical reflection upon the nature of rationality that is emphatically *not* purposive in implication: the transcendental critique does not derive its authority from an instrumentalism, but from an argument about the metaphysical conditions of knowledge. Instead of seeing what is essential about pragmatism as emerging from an engagement with the philosophical tradition that Kant inhabits, Horkheimer argues that it must be comprehended in terms of its relation to modern industrial society. When pragmatism seeks to comprehend the meaning of our concepts in purely instrumental terms, this pays testimony to its complicity with cultural processes wherein the meaning of words and concepts has been reduced to their subjective function. That the meaning of our ideas is reduced to the status of 'a plan or draft' by pragmatism occurs, therefore, because the processes underlying the subjectivization of rationality are dominant within modern society. 'Subjective reason conforms to anything' (p. 25) because it has abandoned all right to claim a critical standpoint from which to judge the value and validity of its key concepts. And this entails the abandonment of all commitment to a critical attitude toward the concepts at its disposal. The significance of pragmatism's espousal of a subjective and hence instrumental understanding of our rational abilities cannot be read purely in terms of its purported status as a theory concerning how our knowledge actually works. What seems, on the face of it, to be a 'theory of knowledge' turns out, on Horkheimer's account, to be the expression of a historically situated social tendency.

Above all, this tendency finds its blueprint in the form of scientific enquiry, in so far as the rise of subjective rationality and the historical development of the Enlightenment ideal of scientific methodology go hand in hand. The pragmatist insistence that the meaning of a theory is reducible to its success or failure in terms of 'experimental' criteria thus turns out to be an uncritical acceptance of the model of scientific enquiry as the paradigm instance of 'knowledge'. As we have already seen, for Horkheimer, science can be characterized not merely by way of its instrumentalism, but also in terms of its propensity to lack self-reflection. So, too, any philosophy that uncritically adopts the experimental metaphor betrays an absence of self-reflexivity with regard to its own social context. Doubtless, some of Horkheimer's polemical comments concerning pragmatism might be objected to, at least to the extent that he does not do full justice to the rich variety of ideas and approaches contained within the pragmatist tradition.[42] But his point is, nevertheless, a germane one in so far as the question of 'purposiveness' itself is unlikely to receive the critical attention it deserves so long as one remains committed to regarding it as a kind of 'category' of rationality.

Likewise, Horkheimer's engagement with positivism presents a powerful case for the view that philosophical theories are not autonomous, but socially embedded. Positivism is a doctrine about knowledge that can be traced back to the writings of Auguste Comte (1798–1857), who argued that knowledge must always be concerned with what can be empirically observed. In the twentieth century this view has been most famously recast as 'logical positivism'. To put the matter in the simplest terms, this approach argues that if a proposition cannot be validated by way of observation in a manner whose standard is set by the example of the empirical sciences, then such a proposition has no meaning.[43] For Horkheimer, the tendency within positivism to elevate the scientific model of knowledge to authoritative status when it comes to examining philosophical issues is another example of an uncritical instrumentalism at work. In adopting this stance it conforms to 'one of the dominant trends in modern philosophy'. By accepting the view that the scientific method is the sole means of evaluating knowledge claims, positivism effectively disavows the right of philosophy to an independent stance with regard to this issue. It 'hand[s] over to science the work left undone by traditional speculation', and so renounces the autonomy of critical thought (*Eclipse of Reason*, 58). In aspiring to the status of scientific methodology positivism necessarily abandons all claim to a critical standpoint concerning science. Again, Horkheimer's argument highlights his contention that the most rigorous comprehension of the significance of scientific activity is possible if it is 'understood only in relation to the society for which it functions' (p. 59). The positivist's uncritical adoption of the methodology of the sciences as the foundation for contemporary epistemology necessarily disavows any commitment to this task. For the authority of scientific method is thereby rendered a kind of 'absolute', and those who espouse it condemn themselves to remaining blind to its historical determinations.

Horkheimer's central point, then, is that the significance of the historical transition from an objective rationality to a subjective and instrumental one is rendered invisible if one adopts a standpoint that has itself emerged out of this process. For the positivist, the question of the criteria of knowledge is taken as already settled: what counts as knowledge can be established by way of reference to the self-evident 'methodology' of empirical demonstration. But, Horkheimer again argues, by reducing the meaning of the term 'knowledge' to something equivalent to 'method' positivism conceptualizes knowledge according to the precepts of the socially determined instrumentalism he has outlined (the belief that knowledge is solely concerned with identifying the appropriate means for a given end). As with pragmatism, this entails the abandonment not only of those questionable speculative and metaphysical claims that were an essential component of objective reason, but of critical self-reflexivity, too. The very notion of a 'method' betrays this fact: a method is, like a cookery recipe for a soufflé, something that is simply 'followed', a series of directions that presuppose we already know what we want.

The positivistic abandonment of critical self-reflexivity is made evident when one turns to the question of the justification of scientific method itself. If positivism wishes to claim that other approaches to knowledge are misguided, then it must also justify itself; but this it signally fails to do. Positivism, Horkheimer notes, suffers from a tendency to 'fall back on self-evident principles': 'How is the principle of observation to be justified? When a justification is requested, when someone asks why observation is the proper guarantee of truth, the positivists simply appeal to observation again' (*Eclipse of Reason*, 72, 76). Such an appeal will simply not do, in so far as all claims to 'self-evidence' are *a priori* suspect. The reason for this is to be found in his commitment to the Hegelian (and, indeed, Nietzschean) insight that there are no 'immediate certainties', as the positivist seems to presuppose. Contrary to the spirit of empiricism, experience is no mere 'given': it is socially mediated. Any appeal to experience presupposes criteria that cannot in fact be derived from 'self-evidence'. The appeal to self-evidence thereby betrays positivism's uncritical commitment to a formalized or 'methodological' conception of reason.

But reason, when understood as critical reflection, is no mere 'method'. Reason is not the mere putting into practice of pre-existing formulas. If we aspire to attain 'true knowledge' we must, on Horkheimer's view, pay attention to ourselves, to the fact that our talk about knowledge is an activity that is always mediated by the larger domain of society and history. Self-reflexivity, in other words, means developing an understanding of where you speak from and appreciation of the fact that there is no unmediated access to truth. The conflicts and contradictions of thinking unfold by way of the fact that they are socially mediated. Contradiction, in turn, tells us something, for 'truth is forged in an evolution of changing and conflicting ideas. Thought is faithful to itself largely through being ready to contradict itself while preserving, as inherent elements of truth, the memory of the process by which it was reached' (p. 63). In other words, Horkheimer develops an approach that pays testimony to the legacy of Hegel: critical thinking involves dialectical reflection on the contradictory tensions that emerge when we think. In identifying and criticizing subjective rationality, therefore, Horkheimer's own approach embraces the metaphysical heritage of objective reason by attempting to speak in a manner that transcends social particularity and yet remains self-aware of its socially situated nature. It is, in short, a matter of keeping the tensions in play. This is because it is not possible to come out in favour of either objective or subjective reason: 'The two concepts are interlaced, in the sense that the consequence of each not only dissolves the other but also leads back to it. . . . Both the separateness and the interrelatedness of the two concepts must be understood' (p. 175). This amounts to a broadly 'Marxist' commitment to overcoming the distinction between these two types of reason by arguing for a society in which it is 'respect for individual life, [that] deserves to be called objective'. The instrumentalism of social relations must be challenged with the claim that the individual has an objective validity, the claim that ends, not means, are of primary importance. One might say then that, for Horkheimer, our knowledge must aspire to a Socratic ethical stance in order to become properly self-reflexive.

3.3   Adorno: the critique of 'first philosophy'

Adorno, like Horkheimer, aspires to the articulation of a self-critical philosophy that spurns 'method'. It is not surprising, therefore, that one of Adorno's central contributions to the debate on theory of knowledge arises from a detailed engagement with the issue of 'first principles' – epitomized by what Adorno refers to as 'first philosophy'. Many of Adorno's arguments about this are presented in *Against Epistemology*.[44] 'First philosophy' or 'philosophy of origins', according to Adorno, is marked by the desire to secure an ultimate foundation for knowledge. In epistemology, this search has derived its primary impetus from the assumed importance of the concept: 'the concept of the first' is taken by epistemologists as primary, even over and above the possible content that such a concept might have (*Against Epistemology*, 7). To this extent, first philosophy is a kind of formalism: it gives priority to the formalizable aspect of thought, that is, to its conceptual nature. Equally, first philosophy claims to start with what is immediate. The first or original principle, as a foundational principle, is unquestioningly taken as a given even as the project of its articulation is pursued. What is given in this way must not only have the status of being immediate and self-evident; it must also be taken as being both universal and necessary. In order to be what it is, the first principle can never be rendered contingent: it cannot be derived from something else, it must not be a mere accident or kind of by-product.

The question as to whether or not we ought to engage in the search for a 'first principle' is not, Adorno argues, an issue for the traditional 'critique of representation' that goes to make up epistemology. This is due to the fact that epistemology is already committed to the notion of the 'philosophically first'. It is a notion that is presupposed by any epistemology as being necessary for the elucidation of the grounds of knowledge. Adorno's primary concern is not the adequacy of any particular category as a starting point for theory of knowledge – be it subjectivity, objectivity, being, thought, experience, essence, etc. His concern is to address the very presupposition that all talk about knowledge is analysable in terms of first principles. To put the matter in different terms, Adorno's aim is to develop a critique of the philosophically articulated concept of 'universality'; namely, the view that what is first 'must always already contain everything' within it (*Against Epistemology*, 9). Such a view is, for Adorno, *a priori* suspect. It is suspect because in the desire to seek an all-encompassing first principle the epistemologist effectively subordinates to that principle everything that does not accord with it. The principle of the first, in other words, aims to rule with an iron fist, and the cost of its doing so is the transformation of all possible experience and thought into 'its property'. As such, first philosophy is an expression of a desire for mastery. Such mastery is to be understood in terms of the desire for dominion over objects and subjects alike. In seeking such dominion first philosophy is effectively committed to a form of conceptual exchange-value,[45] since the notion of a 'first principle' is accorded greater worth than other, 'secondary' concepts. In this way, the first philosopher becomes a kind of conceptual stock-taker, intent on assessing the relative value of concepts in terms of their profitability. 'The accountability of the stock becomes axiomatic', in that the *calculability* of relations is essential for first philosophy. The web of human experience becomes open to being determined in terms of what is designated as 'necessary' and 'unnecessary' solely from the standpoint of conceptual priority. In this way, the 'stock' of human life is presented with the demand that it must be ordered, i.e. sorted out according to a rule that draws a distinction between the essential (the unity of the first principle) and the non-essential (the plurality of individuated human lives and experiences). Because of this, first philosophy is always a form of system building (p. 28).

This point can be made with regard to Kant's conception of the transcendental subject. The transcendental subject is a unity (a first principle underlying knowledge), and it is its primarily conceptual nature that secures its legitimacy with regard to providing the necessary conditions of possible experience. Kant's formalism is an expression of the view that a first principle can be deduced from a non-social and a-historical account of subjectivity. In this sense Kant, too, understands our formal conceptual abilities as providing the basis for an exhaustive determination of everything else. Descartes's rationalism is another case in point. As we have seen in chapter 1, Descartes's primary concern is the construction of a body of knowledge (represented through the metaphor of a 'building') that rests upon a conceptual 'foundation'. The foundational metaphor, in its own turn, represents an articulation of the fixed, first principle of rational cognition ('clear and distinct ideas' are taken as the proof of self-evidence). In turn, the Cartesian system seeks to render all knowledge in terms of a 'method' that both asserts and legitimates the primacy of rational introspection as a means of assessing what is to count as 'knowledge'. The key point here is that this kind of urge to build a system founders upon a tension that remains inherent within all first philosophy. This is the tension between the subjective and objective conditions of knowledge. In order to aspire to objectivity, the Cartesian subject must subordinate itself to the all-encompassing demands of method. It is not individual experience that is taken by Descartes to be primary, but the rational structure of thought understood as an all-embracing methodological principle. Descartes can set himself the task of doubting everything according to the precepts of his sceptical method but whatever else he might succeed in doubting, the *method* itself is never placed in question. The Cartesian system therefore understands 'necessity' as signifying the necessity of method. But such a move conceals the subjective conditions that must operate in all thinking. However, thought, in Adorno's view, is not a metaphysical category of existence, nor is it purely 'methodological' in nature. Against this conception, Adorno argues that thinking occurs only in a web of societal relations, and subjective conditions betray the nature of these societal relations. What is presented as the exhaustive demand of Cartesian 'method' is in fact a socially determined requirement that the world of subjective experience be subordinated to the demands of conceptual control.

First philosophy can be best understood in the context of the development of an instrumental conception of rationality. The search for first principles is, in effect, the search for the most efficient means of conceptual control. This tendency, in its own turn, has a history that Adorno traces back to the pre-Socratic thought of Parmenides (*Against Epistemology*, 9ff). Parmenides equated thought with reality (being). His influence upon Plato results, Adorno says, in the earliest systematic expression of first philosophy. There is no need here to rehearse the historical analysis that Adorno provides in this context. The main thing is to grasp his central claim, following Nietzsche, that metaphysical philosophy is a form of conceptual fetishism.[46] But Adorno's interpretation of this fetishism stresses its socially mediated nature. In effect, his contention is that, in claiming access to the absolute, first philosophy 'is merely absolute delusion about its own subjective mediacy' (p. 22). According to its own governing principle, the absolutely first ought not to be mediated by the subjective and social conditions of human life. But the fact is that all thinking is always already mediated in this way. When first philosophy aims at transcendence by way of the concept this means that it must negate what is essential to it: it must deny that philosophical thought is itself rooted in social contingency. This denial necessitates the exclusion of all 'subjective' content from first philosophy's account of the nature of knowledge. Individual human life passes away, but first philosophy aspires to think immortal not mortal thoughts,[47] and it pursues this aspiration by way of the concept. Adorno's intention, therefore, is to drag first philosophy back down to earth by highlighting the subjective content in all philosophical reflection, and by noting in turn that all subjective content is itself mediated by social conditions.

First philosophy is 'metaphysical' to the extent that it seeks to deny the force of social conditions, and as such is a form of self-delusion. The account of reality offered by first philosophy is one that is emptied of genuine critical content, in so far as the attainment of a properly critical perspective demands that subjective thought must recognize itself as socially mediated; it must acknowledge its own contingency. The failure of first philosophy to do this means that it abandons all pretension to critical reflection and at the same time renders itself susceptible to being used as a tool for the furthering of individuated social interests. It is worth recalling here Horkheimer's argument concerning the increasing dominance of subjective rationality in modern society. The predominance of this kind of conception of reason is itself evidence of the increasing 'subjectivization' of modern society. The significance of the word 'subjectivity' when taken in this way is to be found in the complex web of societal relations which underlie it: 'means and ends' thinking betrays the tendency in modern society to treat human relations as purely instrumental, i.e. according to the dictates of economic imperatives. Likewise, for Adorno, the conception of subjectivity implicit within first philosophy can be interpreted in an analogous manner. First philosophy springs from mediated subjective social conditions and yet it must deny that this is the case in order to legitimate its claim to being 'objective'. It must likewise deny its own complicity in political and social relations, and by making itself blind to this possibility becomes all the more prey to them. First philosophy seeks to master the world through concepts, but in order to proclaim its universal right to do so it is obliged to deny its own subjective content: 'For the sake of mastery, subjectivism must master and negate itself . . . They use their subjectivity to subtract the subject from truth and their idea of objectivity is as a residue . . . Truth is supposed to be the leftover, the dregs, the most thoroughly insipid' (*Against Epistemology*, 15). The socially mediated conditions that underlie philosophical reflection and would give it its validity are, ironically, disregarded in the name of a timeless 'truth'. In consequence, all that is left over from this process is an empty conceptual residue masquerading as the absolute condition of all possible knowledge. In this way, rationality betrays itself by failing to fulfil its true critical potential.

If the philosophy of rationalism stands indicted on this account, then the alternative approach of empiricism is equally open to criticism. This is because the commitment to a first principle is, Adorno argues, characteristic of rationalist and empiricist theories alike. In this regard, 'they are not so radically distinguished in their internal structures as traditional history of philosophy suggests' (p. 23). Empiricism, too, seeks a first principle in the form of unmediated sensory experience. In doing so, it reduces thought to the factual conditions of consciousness. But the model of human understanding that this implies is blind to its own social determination since there are no 'facts' of consciousness that are not at the same time mediated by the social conditions in which thought necessarily occurs. But, Adorno argues, 'spirit can as little be separated from the given as the given from spirit. Neither is a first. Since both are essentially mediated by one another, both are equally unsuitable as original principles' (p. 24). The critical insight that empiricism expresses against rationalism is itself limited in that it abandons the possibility of critical reflection about the social conditions of knowledge by 'humbly deferring to sheer existence'. In this way, the subjective conditions of 'experience' are accorded the same primary status that the rationalist attributed to concepts. For example, Lockean empiricism ultimately determines the nature of knowledge in terms of the purely 'given' conditions of an isolated consciousness: sensory impressions are simply 'there' and no further context is required for their significance to be articulated.

According to Adorno, there is an important lesson to be learned from the delusion of first philosophy, be it rationalist or empiricist. The lesson is that we should abandon the notion of 'unmediated knowledge' altogether. If we appreciate that all thought is mediated this means accepting that the best we can hope for is a self-critically negative conception of the nature of our knowledge. This amounts to the adoption of a kind of 'negative Hegelianism': a dialectical conception of thinking that denies the Absolute even as it acknowledges it. Taking mediation as the universal principle of Absolute Spirit, as Hegel does, would lead to the view that the self-transcendence of thought is possible and to a regression into first philosophy once more. But mediation, in order to remain true to itself, cannot be expressed in such positive terms, since mediation itself is never universally given as a complete and realized unity of consciousness. For this reason, Adorno argues, we need a 'changed philosophy'. Such a philosophy would be one that no longer seeks to subordinate the order of things to the order of concepts. Adorno's encounter with Hegel, therefore, leads him to the conclusion that the heritage of Hegelian idealism must be turned against itself by invoking a new conception of the 'infinite'. As Adorno argues in *Negative Dialectics* (1966): 'A changed philosophy would have to . . . cease persuading others and itself that it has the infinite at its disposal. Instead, if it were delicately understood, the changed philosophy itself would be infinite in the sense of scorning solidification into a body of enumerable theorems . . . The metacritical turn against the *prima philosophia* [first philosophy] is at the same time a turn against the finiteness of a philosophy that prates about infinity without respecting it.'[48] We *can* acknowledge infinity or universality. But we can only do so by accepting that our conceptual abilities are finite. We can embrace universality only by resisting the temptation to believe that we are in possession of it.

Adorno's thought initiates a turn toward the acknowledgement of what he calls 'non-identity' through a recognition of 'the fact that the concept does not exhaust the thing conceived'.[49] For Adorno, the belief that we could arrive at an exhaustive knowledge of reality on the basis of our conceptual abilities is an illusion. At the same time, however, we cannot think at all unless we do so conceptually. For this reason, Adorno insists, the only possible course open to philosophy lies in recognizing the fundamental importance of negation. As with the second stage of the Hegelian dialectic, negation occurs as a reminder that the concepts at our disposal are limited. Through negation the supposed homogeneity of our concepts are fractured and shown to be wanting. But there is no Hegelian solace to be found as a result of this. Where Hegel seeks to subordinate negation to the positive speculative power of the *Idea*, Adorno argues that such a move would amount to an uncritical reaffirmation of the dominance of the concept. On the contrary, negation tells us that our thinking is finite and remains essentially so in its very nature. The only possible recourse we can have is to construct an epistemology that refuses to claim the right to transcend the contextual factors inherent in all thought: 'Epistemology is true as long as it accounts for the impossibility of its own beginning and lets itself be driven at every stage by its inadequacy to the things themselves. It is, however, untrue in the pretension that success is at hand and that states-of-affairs would ever correspond to its constructions and aporetic concepts' (*Against Epistemology*, 25). Epistemology must remain content with revealing that our concepts are never adequate representations of reality. They are never adequate representations of reality because all of our ideas and concepts are socially mediated and hence do not spring from a representational relation with unmediated concepts or experience. The critique of knowledge must dispense with 'the illusion that . . . the totality of consciousness, is the world, and not the self-contemplation of knowledge' (p. 27).

Since we cannot escape conceptual thought, overcoming this illusion demands at the same time that we aspire to being self-critical with regard to the nature of our concepts. For this reason, we ought not to abandon the project of attempting to elucidate a theory of knowledge, for 'Criticizing epistemology also means . . . retaining it.' What is necessary, however, is a 'metacritique' of epistemology: an account of the nature of knowledge that, at the same time, explodes the pretence that the search for first principles is a valid one.

3.4   The essay form as critique of 'method'

How, then, are we to go about articulating questions of knowledge in a manner that does not fall prey to the pitfalls of first philosophy or the illusory promise offered by conceptions of 'method'? One possible way of pursuing this project is explored by Adorno in 'The Essay as Form'[50] – written sometime between 1954 and 1958. In this work Adorno analyses the 'essay form' as a mode of social enquiry. In line with the arguments presented in *Against Epistemology*, the main point of this piece is to highlight the view that the self-reflexivity of critical thought is essential to it. The key feature of the essay form, Adorno argues, is its openness. What is distinctive about the essay is the fact that it is capable of reflecting the inherent tensions that underlie its own conditions of production without resorting to a predetermined 'method' in order to do so:

> The essay . . . does not permit its domain to be prescribed. Instead of achieving something scientifically, or creating something artistically, the effort of the essay reflects a childlike freedom that catches fire, without scruple, on what others have already done. . . . Its concepts are neither deduced from any first principle nor do they come full circle and arrive at a final principle.   ('The Essay as Form', 152)

The essay form offers an example of thinking as a mode of engagement with the social world that takes up issues from that world in order to reflect upon them. The essay is an 'unscrupulous' mode of engagement to the extent that it does not require a reason for taking up an issue. Likewise, it does not pretend to be anything more than derivative of the achievements of others. In this way, the essay rejects any claim to 'originality'. It cannot therefore present itself as an elucidation of 'first principles', nor as something that aims toward a final resolution of the issues at hand. In this sense the essay is an *anti-methodological* form of thought. The essay's 'freedom' springs from the fact that we cannot determine in advance what it ought to be about, or what it ought to say. Nevertheless, although anti-methodological the essay form is capable of expressing a kind of knowledge. To be sure, this is not the 'knowledge' that is characteristic of the positivistic understanding of the world. For the positivist, Adorno tells us, 'Presentation should be conventional, not demanded by the matter itself' (p. 153). What counts as 'knowledge' is, on the positivist's view, a matter that is decided beforehand according to the dictates of strict method. However, because its purposes cannot be defined according to the criterion of 'method', the essay contradicts the view that the investigation into what knowledge is can be approached in such conventional terms. The essay form, at its best, begins by posing a question mark over received ideas: it takes such ideas up in order to question them.

Even so, there is such a thing as 'the bad essay' (p. 154). The very ability of the essay to begin with the matter at hand can also lead to its becoming complicit with dominant ways of thinking. 'Bad' essays merely chatter 'about people instead of opening up the matter at hand; in this the essay form is somewhat complicitous'. There is, then, an inherent danger in the essay form which lies in its propensity to take what is purportedly 'given' as self-evident instead of embarking upon critical reflection concerning it. For example, in modern culture the separation of art from science can be passively reflected by the essay. This division, however, is something that the good essay can invite reflection upon by revealing the conditions of individual life within culture. And it is through aspiring to do this that the essay form can offer us the glimpse of a kind of objectivity. As is sometimes held to be the case with the physical sciences, the measure of such knowledge is to be evaluated according to experience. Yet such experience is not to be understood in terms of the conditions that predominate on the laboratory bench:

> The measure of such objectivity is not the verification of asserted theses through repeated testing, but individual experience, unified in hope and illusion. Experience, reminiscing, gives depth to its observations by confirming or refuting them. But their individually grasped unity, in which the whole surely appears, could not be divided up and reorganized under the separated *personae* and apparatuses of psychology and sociology.   ('The Essay as Form', 156)

For Adorno, therefore, the essay form presents us with the possibility of a kind of 'science of life' that does not reduce the significance of living to the merely causal terminology of scientific procedure. There is an inherent truth content in individual experience that cannot be broken down into constituent parts and then analysed without remainder. The essay offers this kind of knowledge in the form of a non-methodological grasping of particulars (individual experiences). But the presentation of these experiences, although offered in the form of a kind of unity, never submits them to the determinations of systematic principles. In this way, and in spite of its link with experience, the essay is distanced from the philosophy of empiricism: 'Even the empiricist doctrines, that grant priority to open, unanticipated experience over firm, conceptual ordering remain systematic to the extent that they investigate what they hold to be the more or less continuous preconditions of knowledge and develop them in as continuous a context as possible' (p. 157). The essay does not do this; for, through the essay form 'the unconditional priority of method' is thought to its limits 'in the actual process of thought'.

In effect, what the essay thereby achieves is a kind of metaphysical advocacy. The essay rebels against the tradition of metaphysics that thinks of truth and knowledge in terms of the articulation of a fixed relation between the order of ideas and the order of things. Traditional metaphysics regards the purposes of knowledge in terms of the conceptual grasping of objects of experience: concepts are true when they are accurate representations of the way things are. In contrast, the essay, Adorno says, 'does not strive for closed, deductive or inductive, construction. It revolts above all against the doctrine – deeply rooted since Plato – that the changing and the ephemeral is unworthy of philosophy' (p. 158). Such a view presupposes that we have access to an unmediated experience of the world, it 'is based on the insinuation that the mediated is unmediated'. But this is a delusion. There are, Adorno argues, no unmediated facts, for every 'fact' presupposes a concept. Likewise, there are no unmediated concepts, since concepts cannot be thought 'without reference to the factual'. It follows that the issue of how we have knowledge of experience is one that must always come down to the shared conditions that inhere between thought and its environment. As with Horkheimer, these conditions are for Adorno both social and historical. We can see here a variant of Hegel's view: all individuated experience is related to a whole and this whole is historical in nature. To this extent, what is immediately 'given' in experience (even in the form of Kantian preconditions of possible experience) is to be understood in terms of a temporal unfolding: the given is mediated by change. Truth, Adorno can then argue, is not the opposite of history, but is to be found *in it*. The essay pays testimony to this, in that 'the desire of the essay is not to seek and filter the eternal out of the transitory; it wants, rather, to make the transitory eternal' (p. 159). Recalling a central theme from *Against Epistemology*, we can say that the essay wants to think mortal not immortal thoughts. In doing so, it acknowledges that metaphysical categories of knowledge, which determine knowledge in terms of securing an objective relation to a natural order, are illusions. 'The essay silently abandons the illusion that thought can break out of *thesis* into *physis*, out of culture into nature. Spellbound by what is fixed and admittedly deduced, by artifacts, the essay honors nature by confirming that it no longer exists for human beings' ('The Essay as Form', 159). In effect, then, in the essay form Adorno perceives a way of thinking about knowledge that demonstrates the fundamental importance of the transitory. Concepts rely upon experience in order to give them content, but this content is never unmediated: what we conceptualize when we think of objects of experience is a cultural and historical issue.

As Adorno argues in *Against Epistemology*, this does not mean that we should abandon the project of seeking knowledge. But what it does entail is the recognition that all thinking is finite; and that we should therefore reject any parallel between truth and 'transcendence'. Following Nietzsche, Adorno argues that we must overcome 'epistemology', at least as it is traditionally conceived according to the example set by the tradition of modern philosophy. Thus, we should be suspicious of any claim that asserts a necessary connection between certainty and truth, as Descartes argues for in the *Discourse on Method*. To put it another way, a genuine engagement in the task of seeking knowledge should not be taken as a pursuit of 'first principles'. Adorno's admiration for the essay form's inherent refusal to deal in first principles is therefore rooted in his contention that thinking through problems of knowledge should be a non-systematic exercise. Although the essay starts by taking what is at hand, it thinks within a given conceptual model in order to overcome its limitations by exposing them immanently through critical reflection. In this way, 'it proceeds, so to speak, methodically unmethodically' ('The Essay as Form', 161). This is another way of saying that the *principle* of any essay's mode of organization is also open to being regarded as its subject matter. In this sense, the essay's use of concepts is in some ways analogous to 'the behaviour of a man who is obliged, in a foreign country, to speak that country's language instead of patching it together from its elements, as he did in school'. Such a man reads situations 'without a dictionary' by looking at the use of words in different contexts, by noting nuances of meaning, by making interpretative mistakes of his own. Because of this, the activity of interpreting meanings becomes an immanent one: the man learns from his mistakes, he does not need a universal principle or a method to tell him how to get things right.

In this way, the 'rules' that Descartes laid out in the *Discourse on Method* as a means of assessing true knowledge are placed in question. Where Descartes aims to break objects into their constituent parts in order to analyse them, Adorno sees the formalizing impulse to subordinate experience to conceptual order. Where Descartes aims to proceed in order from the most 'simple' to the most 'complex' ideas, Adorno notes that the essay begins with complexity and wishes to do justice to it by refusing to reduce it to basic principles. Where Descartes wishes to provide an all-encompassing enumeration of what can be known, Adorno objects; for, what can be known is itself not something that we know in advance. In this, the essay remains faithful to itself, since it is not 'a downpayment on future syntheses' ('The Essay as Form', 165).

In *Against Epistemology*, Adorno is critical of Hegel's concept of the Absolute. Now, he tells us, Hegelianism, likewise, is overturned by the essay. Hegel's dialectic, Adorno argues, ultimately cannot remain faithful to itself. When Hegel formulated a 'dialectical method' he sought to undo the dialectical movement of thought itself by reducing it to a methodological principle. Yet Adorno remains above all a dialectical thinker. But Adorno favours a very specific conception of dialectical thinking. Like the essay, dialectics is no mere 'method' for Adorno. It is not a matter of playing off the particular against the universal and then simply waiting for the correct 'result'. The result of dialectical engagement is not truth in the unmediated sense. On the contrary, it is a *mediated* sense of truth that Adorno locates as being essential to dialectical thinking: 'neither may the truth of the totality be played off immediately against individual judgments, nor may truth be reduced to individual judgments; rather, the claim of the particular truth is taken literally to the point where there is evidence of its untruth . . . the untruth in which the essay knowingly entangles itself is the element of its truth' ('The Essay as Form', 166). Truth, on such a view, is not the positive outcome of a dialectical unfolding toward the Absolute. Truth only announces itself in the negative, in the absence of the Absolute. The essay exposes the unjustified nature of all claims to a final and ultimate truth and it is this exposure that constitutes its truth content. In this way, Adorno, like Horkheimer, seeks to keep the notion of universality in play with regard to questions of knowledge. The universal announces itself, however, only as a kind of *lack*. Truth is what we do *not* have. But it stands as a reminder of the limitations of what Adorno terms 'identity thinking'. We may have to conceptualize experience, and in doing so impose 'identity' upon the objects of our experiences, but these objects themselves remain stubbornly imbued with an element of 'non-identity'.[51] Adorno's view of philosophy expresses this tension: philosophy wishes to attain a transcendental knowledge of the ultimate conditions of reality, yet it cannot because its judgements always remain historically specific and hence partial.

In this sense, Adorno adopts a position that, along with an indebtedness to Hegel, also owes something to Kant's critical enterprise. For Kant and Adorno alike have an interest in elucidating the limitations of our rational abilities, coupled with a refusal to abandon the value of reason. However, for Adorno the limitation of Kant's account ultimately resides in his formalism: the Kantian elucidation of the *a priori* conditions of the 'forms' of our sensibility and understanding indicate that, in the last analysis, Kant was an 'apologist of first philosophy' (*Against Epistemology*, 30). In other words, Kant gave form priority over content, and in doing so committed himself to the view that it is concepts that determine what is to count as reality, and nothing else. For Adorno, both the prioritizing of concepts over experience or of experience over concepts, as empiricism advocates, are equally suspect moves. Both are the consequence of the development of epistemology under the influence of 'philosophy of origins' or 'first philosophy'.

4   Mediations, not Meditations

The intellectual journey that has, over the course of these two chapters, taken us from Descartes to Adorno is not the only possible one that we could follow in a discussion of the nature of knowledge. But it is instructive. It is a journey that begins with an assertion of the positive potential of reason, engages with the problem of experience, and ends in critical reflection on the limitations of the concepts of 'reason' and 'experience' alike. Where we might choose to take things from there is to some extent an open matter, and some of the issues that have been raised will be pursued in other contexts in other parts of this book. But there are several related issues that seem to be sufficiently important to warrant comment at this juncture. The first of these concerns the relationship between subjectivity and knowledge. Whatever their respective differences, for post-Kantian philosophers like Hegel, Nietzsche, Horkheimer and Adorno, subjectivity is not something given independently of our engagement with the world of experience. Contrary to such a view, the nature of subjectivity is to be interpreted in terms of conditions that are coextensive with it. By the same token, 'reason' and 'experience' are words that must be taken in similar fashion. In so far as subjectivity is mediated so are the attributes that we associate with subjectivity. Moreover if, as thinkers like Hegel, Nietzsche and Adorno maintain, we are primarily social beings, then the process of mediation can be regarded as something in which shared subjective factors enter into play. Seeking, as Descartes does, to erect a theory of knowledge on the foundation of individual introspection becomes a rather dubious enterprise in the light of this. To reiterate the Nietzschean point, the notion of 'immediate certainty' that the Cartesian enterprise embraces as the standard of measure of true knowledge must remain an intangible goal, for doubt even concerning the 'I think' is always possible. There are simply no certainties of this kind to be had that can function as a reliable starting point for the construction of an 'edifice' of knowledge. In the light of this, we are well advised either to look elsewhere for an epistemological starting point, or abandon the task of securing one altogether.

Do we, therefore, need first principles at all? Is it meditations or mediations that we should be looking to in order to arrive at some kind of account of the nature of knowledge or human experience? This, to repeat the point, amounts to asking whether or not we ought to dispense with the aim of constructing an epistemology altogether. If our knowledge of the world is mediated, then it does not follow that we can provide an exhaustive elaboration of the conditions that make up mediation in the form of an enumerable body of theorems. In fact, for a thinker like Hume the issue of mediation remains implicit rather than explicit, but it is present within his work. Even though he contends that our sensory impressions give rise to our ideas, nevertheless Hume's emphasis upon the role that habit or custom plays in our knowledge indicates the possibility that no knowledge of objects of experience is independent of the mediating role of customs. Likewise, the Humean interpretation of the self as a mere 'bundle' of experiences brings with it the implication that subjective awareness is grounded in habit. Habits or customs are simply ways of doing things, that is, conventions. And all conventions are by definition social in so far as they must be shared and are therefore inter-subjective. At the same time, however, if our shared conventions are decisive in delineating our understanding of experience, then it follows that experience itself is something that is ultimately mediated by them rather than by the formal rational-subjective conditions that Descartes looks to as the basis of our knowledge. We can say, therefore, that Hume initiates a turn away from the disengaged conception of subjectivity that forms the foundation of Descartes's epistemology. A Humean subject is constituted by experience, and it is this mode of constitution that is essential in making it what it is.

One direct consequence of this kind of move is a turn away from the Cartesian view that the subject is rational and that such rationality implies individual autonomy of thought. In Descartes we find the most extreme expression of this conception of autonomy: the 'I' is a mental substance, unfettered by the conditions that govern the behaviour of material bodies. The Humean subject, in contrast, is ultimately fettered by the bounds of experience and dependent upon such experience for its continued survival. Hume, we might say, takes the Cartesian model and unhooks it from its rational foundations. But what Hume does not carry through is the implication that experience, no less than rationality, is mediated by conditions that are not given in the form of pure immediacy. It is Kant, whose response to Hume is to argue that experience is mediated by subjective conditions understood in the form of rules, who offers a decisive turn away from the Cartesian view. Kantian rules are not the same as Humean conventions. Habits or customs are in the end contingent, and we do not need to recognize them as compelling in order to be compelled by them. But rules, in order to be what they are, must be acknowledged as compelling. It is for this reason that they display the kind of necessity that Kant attributes to them. Kant's central contention is that the subjective conditions of knowledge are the kinds of conditions that we must both abide by and at the same time acknowledge whenever we think at all. Our ability to have knowledge of experience, in other words, pre-supposes an *acknowledgement* of transcendental conditions in the form of rules. This, in turn, implies the existence of certain abilities that are not derivable from experi-ence. The transcendental subject, understood as an assortment of rules collected together in various 'faculties' (the faculty of sensibility, the faculty of understanding, of judgement, etc.), constitutes the necessary conditions of our representations. Hence, Kant's achievement is to argue in compelling fashion that the objective conditions of our knowledge are to be found not in pure self-reflection but in the subjective conditions that make such reflection possible: our representations rest upon an *a priori* structure.

But Kant, in his turn, is open to the Hegelian criticism that what is subjectively given cannot itself stand outside the immanent conditions of historical life. Articu-lating the transcendental structure of subjectivity as something that is merely given implies that the objectivity of transcendental rules is secured by the fact that they exist independently of experience. Although it must always be conjoined with experi-ence in order to pertain to any determinate content, the transcendental structure of subjectivity remains 'outside' the world. Hegel's contribution to this debate is to point to the fact that we, as thinking beings, only have knowledge in virtue of the fact that we are engaged *in* and *with* the world. Thought and experience must be acknowledged as sharing a common structure, and that structure is objective in so far as it is impossible to draw an absolute distinction between them. Such a contention initiates a decisive move away from the Cartesian model of consciousness that Kant retains in the formal constitution of the transcendental subject. Subjectivity, on Hegel's account, is not something that can be analysed in isolation from the conditions that are immanent to it. Instead, subjectivity springs from an engagement with the world, and the world in question is intrinsically social: 'I' presupposes 'Thou', and 'I and Thou' entail 'We'. It is 'We' who are capable of having knowledge, not 'I'. For Hegel, the real significance of subjectivity can only be articulated in terms of the objective conditions of its emergence. In turn, our rational abilities are not immedi-ately given, nor are they analysable through introspection alone. We might put this another way: there are no clear and distinct Cartesian ideas that can be generated by way of a pure meditation by the mind upon its contents. Meditations presuppose mediations.

Hegel's emphasis upon the emergence of consciousness through an active engage-ment with its world also brings a turn toward a different conception of the metaphysical conditions of knowledge. The Cartesian and Kantian accounts of knowledge both proceed by drawing a line between what we think and what we are thinking about, between our ideas and what they represent, and then aim to reconcile this problem. For Kant, it is the function of metaphysics to bridge the gap between thought and experience. Metaphysics, on this view, tells us about those conditions that are necessary for us to have reliable knowledge of the world as it appears to us. For Hegel, in contrast, the metaphysical conditions of knowledge are immanent to the engagement that we, as thinking beings, have with the world. This amounts to the contention that thinking and the world both share a common metaphysical structure that is already present within thought as much as within its objects. The gulf between subject and object that characterizes the epistemological starting point for Descartes, Locke, Hume, and Kant alike is collapsed. According to Hegel, meta-physical conditions are not to be construed as functioning to negotiate the links between an isolated self-consciousness and the objects of its experience. They are to be taken as intrinsic to any engagement of thought in the world. These conditions are, in other words, immanent. Of equal significance, however, is the claim they are not to be taken as signifying an already determined and fixed structure, but a fluid one. In short, Hegel's stress on the function of mediation in all thinking brings with it a commitment to a conception of metaphysics that concentrates upon the notion of change, not fixity as an essential precondition of thought. A metaphysical structure, in this sense, is not given to us fully formed and prior to experience, but emerges out of the unity of thought and its objects.

This is another way of saying that Hegel initiates a turn toward a social and historical account of the nature of knowledge. In so far as self-consciousness is the product of a process of emergence, so our knowledge must likewise be elucidated in terms of this process. But Hegel's key to interpreting this is the Idea. He has a confidence in the ability of critical reason to overcome its own limits and, in the long run at least, yield true (Absolute) knowledge. We can say that Nietzsche, Horkheimer and Adorno between them draw in various ways upon the Hegelian metaphysical insight. But in their respective rejections of Absolutism they also deny the authority of the Hegelian Idea. There is, for them, no final positive outcome to the process of historical emergence, since the removal of the Hegelian Absolute entails abandoning the notion of a purposive structure governing history. If this is the case, we cannot stand 'outside' the conditions of our own existence in order to infer a larger order governing it. Nietzsche's attack on 'metaphysical philosophy' represents one strand of this approach. For him, the claims of critical reason advocated by both Kant and Hegel must be adandoned in favour of a contextualized account of the nature of knowledge that stresses the inevitable limitations of perspective. Speaking like Adorno, we can say that Nietzsche is a thinker who opposes the non-conceptual whole to the conceptual determinations of thought. In effect, Nietzsche argues that consciousness and conceptual thought must be understood as resting upon non-conceptual and unarticulated (unconscious) presuppositions. However, for Nietzsche, unlike Adorno or Horkheimer, this move entails the abandonment of any conception of critical reason. Since for Nietzsche it is becoming, not the conceptually determined realm of 'being', that constitutes the conditions of human knowledge, the only possible option we have is to interpret our knowledge as a mode of engagement with these conditions. This is to be taken as, above all, a kind of engagement that starts by hypostatizing becoming and only later becomes aware of what it has done. Philosophers are conceptual mummifiers to the extent that they wish to arrest change and subject it to the rule of rationality. Questions about the nature of human reason thereby become primarily instrumental questions. And, in the light of this, knowledge is to be understood as a form of mastery, an issue of power.

Some implications of the Nietzschean view are developed by a variety of thinkers. Prominent among these are the French philosophers Gilles Deleuze (1925–95) and Michel Foucault (1926–84). These thinkers concentrate on the issue of power relations, but in rather different ways. For Foucault, who takes up the Nietzschean thesis of the will to power, the problem of knowledge is to be understood in terms of socially specific relations of power: it is a political issue. Deleuze, in contrast, is interested in elucidating a variant of the Nietzschean ontology of becoming in the light of what he takes to be the key insights associated with Humean empiricism. As we have seen, Nietzsche also raises questions concerning the role of language in the constitution of both our thinking and our knowledge. This turn to language has been very influential, and lies behind many of the ideas associated with poststructuralism and postmodernism.[52]

For Horkheimer and Adorno, the claims of reason are not to be so easily dismissed. Even if our understanding is socially mediated, it does not follow that an abandonment of the foundationalist model necessitates abandoning the project of a critical elaboration of the concept of reason. The problem, for them, is that advocates of rational critique have simply not been rational enough to perceive the limitations of the kinds of epistemologies they have developed. To this extent, these thinkers cleave to the view that the Kantian and Hegelian projects of critical enlightenment ought not to be abandoned so much as modified in the light of the kind of criticisms that thinkers like Nietzsche level at them. We can, they would argue, develop a critical account of rationality that does not dispense with it altogether so long as we turn to a more socially mediated and negative conception of the kind of knowledge we are after. This means not getting rid of epistemology but thinking through the kind of issues that traditional epistemology has concentrated upon in a more contextualized form.

Notes

1   It led directly, Kant tells us, to the achievements of Isaac Newton, which placed physics on a new and firm footing (*Critique*, Bxxi, n.a).

2   G. W. F. Hegel, *Phenomenology of Spirit*, tr. A. V. Miller (Oxford: Oxford University Press, 1977). All references are given in the text with paragraph numbers.

3   What Hegel means by 'mediation' is that there is nothing that is given to consciousness immediately as it is, or in itself: 'thinking is essentially the negation of something immediately given' (*The Encyclopaedia Logic. Part 1 of the Encyclopaedia of the Philosophical Sciences with the Zusätze*, tr. T. F. Geraets, W. A. Suchting and H. S. Harris (Indianapolis: Hackett, 1991), section 12). In this sense thinking is an 'ungrateful' activity since, like the activity of eating, it consumes its objects and appropriates them to itself. It is 'the digesting of that to which it is supposed to owe itself'. What appears to be

straightforwardly given in thought is 'inwardly reflected and hence inwardly mediated; it is *universality*, the overall being-at-home-with-itself of thinking'. This is another way of saying that particulars are only possible in virtue of the universal.

4   G. W. F. Hegel, *Philosophy of Nature. Being Part Two of the Encyclopaedia of the Philosophical Sciences*, tr. A. V. Miller (Oxford: Clarendon Press, 1970), section 352.

5   G. W. F. Hegel, *The Encyclopaedia Logic. Part 1 of the Encyclopaedia of the Philosophical Sciences with the Zusätze*, tr. T. F. Geraets, W. A. Suchting and H. S. Harris (Indianapolis: Hackett, 1991). All further references are given in the text with section numbers.

6   'Ob-jective': for a discussion of the use of the neologism 'ob-ject' to translate Hegel's '*Gegenstand*', see note 7, below.

7   'Ob-ject': *Gegenstand*. The translators of the Hackett edition of the *Logic* use this neologism to distinguish between Hegel's use of '*Gegenstand*' and '*Objekt*'. Whereas the latter implies a logical notion of what an object is (i.e. the concept of an object understood from a purely logical point of view), *Gegenstand* denotes an 'ob-ject' that is encountered in experience. Such ob-jects are always mediated by the consciousness of a thinking subject.

8   'Spanish poetry, chemistry, politics, music are all very interesting, and we cannot blame a person who is interested in them. But if an individual in a definite situation is to bring something about, he must stick to something determinate and not dissipate his powers in a great many directions' (section 80).

9   In this way Hegel can be seen to be raising the classical philosophical issue concerning the relationship between universals and particulars. We can think about this question in the following ways. Do we only ever encounter, and have knowledge of, particulars (what is sometimes called the 'nominalist' view)? On such a conception, universals are merely objects of thought and have no concrete existence. Or is it the case that the universal is always manifested in the form of the particular and is its condition of possibility? Hegel, of course, argues for the latter view.

10   Consider, by way of example, the process of animal reproduction. An individual seeks what is other than it (another being of the same species of the opposite sex) in order to engage in the act of reproduction. The result of the act of union is another being that is *not* its parents. Each individual is driven to do this in virtue of its own nature. In this way each seeks to transcend its own particularity by partaking of the universality of the species of which it is a member.

11   Nietzsche's attacks on Plato and his frequently vehement remarks about thinkers such as Kant pay ample testimony to this fact.

12   Friedrich Nietzsche, *Beyond Good and Evil*, tr. Walter Kaufmann, in *Basic Writings of Nietzsche* (New York: Basic Books, 1968). Further references are given in the text.

13   See *Beyond Good and Evil*, sections 204ff, and especially section 211: '*Genuine philosophers . . . are commanders and legislators . . .* With a creative hand they reach for the future, and all that is and has been becomes a means for them, an instrument, a hammer.'

14   Friedrich Nietzsche, *The Gay Science*, tr. Walter Kaufmann (New York: Vintage Books, 1974). Further, references are given in the text.

15   Friedrich Nietzsche, 'On Truth and Lie in an Extra-Moral Sense', tr. Walter Kaufmann, in *The Portable Nietzsche* (London: Chatto & Windus, 1972), p. 42.

16   Friedrich Nietzsche, *The Will to Power*, tr. Walter Kaufmann and R. J. Hollingdale (New York: Vintage, 1968). Further references are given in the text.

17   Friedrich Nietzsche, *Human, All-Too-Human*, tr. R. J. Hollingdale (Cambridge: Cambridge University Press, 1986). Further references are given in the text.

18 See also the discussion that begins *Beyond Good and Evil* for a similar point.

19 Towards the very end of 1888 Nietzsche suffered a mental collapse from which he never recovered. He died in 1900.

20 Nietzsche is, of course, a notorious atheist and is probably best known by many people for his famous proclamation of the 'death of God' in section 125 of *The Gay Science*. The 'meaning' of this is explained later in the text (section 352). The death of God is a cultural 'event': God is dead because he has become 'unbelievable' from the standpoint of contemporary scientific and cultural life.

21 Friedrich Nietzsche, *Twilight of the Idols*, tr. Duncan Large (Oxford: Oxford University Press, 1998). The entirety of this text is also contained in *The Portable Nietzsche*. Further references are given in the text.

22 Moreover, Nietzsche also argues, even if such metaphysical knowledge were possible for us it would be completely useless: 'Even if the existence of such a world were ever so well demonstrated, it is certain that knowledge of it would be the most useless of all knowledge: more useless than knowledge of the chemical composition of water must be to the sailor in danger of shipwreck' (*Human, All-Too-Human*, section 9).

23 See, T. W. Adorno, *Against Epistemology*, tr. Willis Domingo (Oxford: Blackwell, 1982): it is an 'enlightened critique which Nietzsche revives (for it is in essence Hume's)' (p. 19).

24 Nietzsche is therefore what is called a 'nominalist', i.e. he thinks that names are *given* to objects and, as such, cannot denote any essential properties present within them.

25 Friedrich Nietzsche, *Daybreak*, tr. R. J. Hollingdale (Cambridge: Cambridge University Press, 1982), section 47.

26 The Eleatics can be traced back to around 500 BC and the thinker Parmenides. Parmenides was a monist: he argued that reality is ultimately a single, unified and eternally stable entity (i.e. a philosophy of being). The most famous thinker to fall under the influence of Parmenides's thought, via the influence of his followers, was Plato.

27 Friedrich Nietzsche, *On the Genealogy of Morals*, tr. Walter Kaufmann, in *Basic Writings of Nietzsche*, third essay, section 12.

28 See chapter 5.

29 An important influence here is the work of the Marxist thinker György Lukács. See Lukács, *History and Class Consciousness*, tr. Rodney Livingston (London: Merlin Press, 1971). In this work Lukács links contradictions in the writings of Kant and Hegel to the material economic base of the social context from which they were produced.

30 Or, we might say, the Absolute is only attainable (and can only be known or articulated) in a perfect (i.e. Utopian) society. Since we manifestly do not live in such a society, the Absolute cannot be grasped in this way.

31 To this extent, Marx's approach in fact represents a conjunction of influences that stretch beyond Hegel. Primary amongst these influences are the writings of two British economic theorists: Adam Smith and David Ricardo. See, for example, Adam Smith, *The Wealth of Nations*, eds. R. H. Campbell, A. S. Skinner and W. B. Todd (Oxford: Clarendon Press, 1976); and *The Essential Adam Smith*, ed. Robert L. Heilbroner (Oxford: Oxford University Press, 1986).

32 See Karl Marx, *Economic and Philosophical Manuscripts* (London: Lawrence & Wishart, 1981).

33 See, G. W. F. Hegel, *Elements of the Philosophy of Right*, ed. Allen W. Wood, tr. H. B. Nisbet (Cambridge: Cambridge University Press, 1991).

34 See Max Horkheimer, 'Traditional and Critical Theory', in *Critical Theory: Selected Essays* (New York: Herder and Herder, 1972).

35 T. W. Adorno and M. Horkheimer, *Dialectic of Enlightenment*, tr. John Cumming, (London: Allen Lane, 1973).

36   See, for example, Nietzsche's attack on Socratic dialectical reason in *Twilight of the Idols*, 'The Problem of Socrates', especially sections 9–11.

37   Max Horkheimer, *Eclipse of Reason* (New York: Continuum, 1974). All further references are given in the text with page number.

38   The Enlightenment was an eighteenth-century intellectual movement which originated in France (although Britain also had a 'Scottish Enlightenment' – with which Hume is most famously associated). Of the thinkers associated with the Enlightenment the most prominent were Denis Diderot, Hume, Kant, Jean-Jacques Rousseau, Adam Smith and Voltaire. Kant's maxim, 'Dare to understand!', captures the underlying optimism which inspired Enlightenment thinking, which can be characterized by a faith in the ability of reason to resolve social, intellectual and scientific problems alike. In many ways, the example of the physical sciences provides a good example of the progressive Enlightenment ideal (Kant's 'Copernican revolution' being a case in point). In turn, an at times aggressive critical stance toward what were regarded as the regressive influences of tradition and institutional religion (the statement 'Crush the infamy!', summed up Voltaire's attitude toward the Christian church), a faith in the ideal of political progress through reason, and the espousal of free thinking were also characteristics of Enlightenment thinking. See, Peter Gay, *The Enlightenment: An Interpretation*, 2 vols (London: Weidenfeld & Nicholson, 1988).

39   C. S. Peirce, 'What Pragmatism Is', in *Pragmatism: The Classic Writings*, ed. H. S. Thayer (Indianapolis: Hackett, 1982), p. 102.

40   One should add here that Peirce's is not the only version of pragmatism. His friend William James (1842–1910) developed an account of it that differs from the Peircean model in some important respects. For example, where Peirce calls himself a 'scholastic realist' (i.e. he believes that there is a mind-independent reality to which our ideas can, 'in the long run', conform), James adopts a nominalist approach. In doing this, James stresses the role that our ideas play in our individual experiences and actions rather than in their relation to an objective reality. 'Reality as such is not truth, and the mind as such is not a mere mirror. Mind *engenders* truth *upon* reality; and as our systems of truth are themselves part of reality . . . we may say that reality in its largest sense does grow by human thinking' ('Pragmatism – What It Is', in Thayer, *Pragmatism: The Classic Writings*, p. 133). Equally, Peirce is concerned with elucidating a method for making our ideas clear and hence with offering a theory of meaning (a 'semiotics'). James, in contrast, understands pragmatism as additionally offering a theory of truth, in that it seeks to describe the actual (i.e. psychological) processes of thinking that we adopt in negotiating our everyday experiences. Thinking, in this sense, denotes something purposive, something that is actively engaged in concrete practical action in that 'the *use* of most of our thinking is to help us to *change* the world' rather than to grasp how it objectively is. Whatever the differences between Peirce and James, Horkheimer's criticisms of pragmatism would doubtless be applied by him to both thinkers.

41   See Peirce, 'Definition and Description of Pragmatism', in Thayer, p. 50ff.

42   By way of example, one could turn to John Dewey's (1859–1952) penetrating criticisms of mind-body dualism in 'The Unit of Behaviour (The Reflex Arc Concept in Psychology)' (in Thayer, pp. 262–74). However, Dewey's self-avowed 'instrumentalism', and his view that scientific enquiry is, as Thayer puts it, 'a paradigm of moral conduct' (p. 259), doubtless serves as ammunition for Horkheimer's case.

43   The British philosopher A. J. Ayer's book *Language, Truth and Logic* is often seen as a seminal work in the articulation of the central tenets of logical positivism. He argued that any proposition can be characterized as either true, false, or meaningless according to a

procedure of 'verification' derived from the example of the physical sciences. Either a proposition can be verified or it can be disproven. If so, then it is either true or false. If it cannot be shown to be true or false, then it cannot be said to 'mean' anything. See A. J. Ayer, *Language, Truth and Logic*, 2nd edn (London: Victor Gollancz, 1967); and see also, A. J. Ayer (ed.), *Logical Positivism* (London: Allen & Unwin; Glencoe, Ill.: Free Press, 1959). One should also add that for thinkers such as Ayer the principal of verification extends to the domains of mathematics and logic, where verification takes the form of giving a proof by way of logical analysis rather than by way of empirical experimentation.

44 T. W. Adorno, *Against Epistemology*, tr. Willis Domingo (Oxford: Blackwell, 1982). All further references are given in the text with page number. The full title of this work is *Zur Metakritik der Erkenntnistheorie: Studien über Husserl und die phänomenologischen Antinomien* (*Towards a Metacritique of Theory of Knowledge: Studies on Husserl and the Phenomenological Antinomies*). In this text Adorno undertakes a painstaking criticism of German philosopher Edmund Husserl's phenomenological methodology. It is not necessary to enter into a detailed discussion of Husserl's philosophy here, since the relevance of Adorno's arguments is not limited to Husserl's phenomenology. A brief discussion of Husserl is offered in chapter 3.

45 Here we can see an example of Marx's influence on Adorno's thinking. The notion of exchange-value is central to the Marxist analysis of economics, and is linked to the value of commodities in the market place. There are two kinds of such value. There is use-value. This concerns a thing's ability to serve human purposes (needs, desires, etc.). However, it is also the case that commodities are produced by way of labour. In this case, the value of the thing in question will be linked to the amount of labour that is required to produce it, e.g. the number of hours required in a factory to make 100 bottles of beer or 100 pencils. Beer and pencils have different use-values (it is no use trying to get drunk on pencils; if you want to get drunk you will value pencils according to this purpose by disregarding them and going in search of beer). Beer and pencils also have different exchange-values when they are sold in the market place because of the different amount of labour required to make them under normal conditions of production. We can note this difference in the following way. If it takes 100 working hours to make 100 bottles of beer and only one hour to make 100 pencils, then we can say that one bottle of beer has the same exchange-value as 100 pencils. The difference in exchange-value between commodities is usually linked to a difference in price (monetary value), which is calculated according to the number of hours of labour required to make the commodity. See Marx, *Capital: A Critique of Political Economy*, vol. 1, tr. B. Fowkes (Harmondsworth: Penguin, 1976), p. 129ff. Adorno's argument implies that the search for first principles ultimately shares a similar logic to the one that dictates the relative values of commodities in the 'market place'. The view is that certain concepts or ideas can be allotted a greater value than others by way of the notion of 'exchange'.

46 We can also note that this discussion is linked to Marx's conception of 'commodity fetishism'. According to this conception, a central feature of the capitalist market place is that it functions in terms of the exchange of goods. Social relations come to be expressed in this way, too. Thus, people come to relate to each other primarily in terms of the exchange and consumption of goods (Miss X is a producer of such-and-such a commodity; Mr Y is a consumer of this commodity). This relation obscures the fact that real people endowed with individuality are involved in this process. The ultimate consequence of this is that a confusion arises between things and people: things are regarded as if they had personal attributes and people as if they are merely commodities, or simply the 'consumers' of commodities. See Marx, *Capital*, pp. 163ff.

47   Adorno's text is prefaced by the following quote from Epicharmus: 'A mortal must think mortal and not immortal thoughts' (p. 3). For Hegel, recall, only the Absolute is eternal – life is bounded by finitude of particularity (death). Adorno's thought is an attempt to take the transitory and make it eternal (see the discussion earlier in this section).

48   T. W. Adorno, *Negative Dialectics*, tr. E. B. Ashton (London: Routledge & Kegan Paul, 1973), pp. 13–14.

49   *Negative Dialectics*, p. 5.

50   T. W. Adorno, 'The Essay as Form', tr. Bob Hullot-Kentor and Fredric Will, *New German Critique*, spring-summer 1984, pp. 151–71). All further references are given in the text with page number. The essay first appeared in *Notes to Literature*, vol. 1 (1958), tr. Shierry Weber Nicholson (New York: Columbia University Press, 1991).

51   See in connection Adorno's *Negative Dialectics*.

52   For some discussion of these terms see chapters 4 and 5.

3

Two Ontologies:
Heidegger, Deleuze and Guattari

Traditionally, as we have seen, epistemology involves constructing theories about the kind of knowedge we can have. Such a traditional account founders upon various difficulties, by no means the least of which concerns making presuppositions about the kind of beings we are (our subjectivity) and the kind of relationship we have to the world. If we cannot offer a persuasive account of these matters, then our model of knowledge is inevitably flawed. However, it does not follow that these issues need to be approached by way of constructing an epistemology, or indeed even with the aim of doing so. Instead of epistemology, we could turn to ontology. In its most usually accepted sense, ontology is regarded as a branch of metaphysics that concentrates upon discussing questions relating to the fundamental nature of existence. In simplest terms one could say that ontology is concerned with the study of what is. Where epistemology is concerned with the nature of what we know, ontology is concerned with the nature of what exists. Generally speaking, the articulation of any kind of theory about what we know presupposes some kind of ontological commitment, however minimal. It does so in so far as if we know anything at all it must be a knowledge of something – although what one is committed to in this way is far from clear.[1]

Let us take two accounts of knowledge: Kant's and Nietzsche's. It is evident that, in their respective analyses, these thinkers are committed to two very different ontological views. For Kant, what we know is appearances, not how things are in-themselves. The very division Kant asserts between what we know and what exists independently of how we know it rests upon an ontological structure. This ontological structure posits a 'real' world, which exists independently of us, and an apparent world of our perceptual experiences. Our perceptions of objects, although only concerned with what appears to us, are in the last analysis taken to devolve from the fact that there is a mind–independent reality that just 'is', even if we can never know it in anything but the most negative of senses (in that all we know is that we don't know anything about it). As we have seen, in Nietzschean terms, Kant's epistemology can be criticized precisely because of its ontological commitment. There is, Nietzsche argues in a variant of Humean scepticism, no direct correspondence between our concepts and the world, and the reason for this is that there is simply no such thing as a noumenal realm of things in-themselves. Even in order to argue his case, however, Nietzsche is clearly committed to the view that existence has independence from thought: he, too, has an ontology. And it would not be too simplistic to say that this ontology is derived from a kind of empiricism. To the degree that our senses reveal continual change to us their evidence is true. Thus, there is no being, only becoming.

Nietzsche's development of an ontology of becoming has two distinctive elements. The first of these is expressed in a commitment to the view that existence consists of 'stuff' that is in a continual state of flux. This is what Gilles Deleuze terms the affirmation of 'the being of becoming'.[2] This 'stuff' does not have any essential or individuated properties, it just 'is' in that it becomes. Nothing underlies this process of becoming, or is 'outside' it, since it is an immanent process. Second, Nietzsche then develops the thesis that any entities that might be said to exist are constituted by relations of force, or power. Becoming, in other words, is a kind of 'flux' of forces, and the intermingling of these forces is what gives rise to various kinds of being, including ones like us. If we compare Kant and Nietzsche, then, we have two distinctive views concerning the fundamental nature of existence. One asserts that what exists simply is, and does not change, but that our knowledge of it must be mediated by our subjective make-up. The other asserts that what exists becomes, and is in essence change, and that what we call 'knowledge' is a product of negotiating with this condition. In the twentieth century, two important conceptions of ontology have been developed which arise out of the tensions inherent in this difference of view. On the one hand, the work of Martin Heidegger (1889–1976) aims at the construction of a fundamental ontology of human being that draws much of its inspiration from Kant's epistemology, even as it aims at overturning the metaphysical preconceptions that govern it. In this latter regard, important aspects of Heidegger's thought also owe a significant debt to both Hegel and Nietzsche. On the other hand, the writings of Gilles Deleuze (including his co-authored work with Félix Guattari (1936–1992)) develop the Nietzschean conception in opposition to the Kantian one. Whatever their respective merits and drawbacks, both accounts effectively argue that epistemology is an unnecessary or limited approach. What we need, rather, is to offer a different kind of analysis of the nature of existence with a view to then asking whether it is worth elaborating questions about what we can know. Likewise, both spring from a critical engagement with the Western philosophical tradition and argue that this tradition needs to be subjected to a radical reappraisal. For both Heidegger and Deleuze and Guattari, what follows from this is a rethinking not only of questions of knowledge, but also of the nature of subjectivity. We could elaborate the consequences of this in a number of ways. But, perhaps most significantly, these approaches entail an abandonment of the humanistic conception of subjectivity – a view that Nietzsche endorses, but which is rejected by thinkers like Horkheimer or Adorno.

1   Heidegger and the Question of Being

Heidegger's *Being and Time*[3] (1927) begins by asking an ontological question: do we know what we mean by the term 'Being' (*Sein*)? The immediate answer Heidegger offers is that we do not. Although it is a theme taken up in the earliest works of the philosophical tradition as far back as the Ancient Greeks, the question of the significance of Being has, Heidegger claims, been buried by the preconceptions which have underlain the western metaphysical tradition since the time of Plato (p. 21). If something has been concealed in this way, then it has simply been ignored rather than dealt with. It is an unresolved issue. Accordingly, the matter needs to be raised once more. The aim of *Being and Time*, therefore, is to 'work out the question of the meaning of *Being* . . . concretely' (p. 1). This, Heidegger contends, is to be done with reference to time (*Zeit*), which forms the 'horizon for any understanding whatsoever of Being'. But initially the question itself must be addressed with a view to clarifying three questions. First, what is it we are asking about? Second, what does it mean to ask a question at all? Third, who, or what, is doing the asking? All of these are important questions. If we are enquiring into Being, then it is necessary first to have at least some provisional understanding of what we are talking about. Likewise, since enquiring into Being involves asking questions about it, the very asking of such questions must be an essential component of any such project. We must, therefore, also address the question of what it means to raise this matter. This comes down to the contention that it is not enough simply to determine the subject matter of an enquiry; what also needs to be done is to articulate the meaning and purpose of such an enquiry. Finally, if questions are to be asked about something, we have to consider the conditions under which such questions can be raised: we need to know for whom such questions are important in order to appreciate just why they might be important at all.

1.1 What is it we are asking about?

Heidegger stakes a historical claim about the nature of ontological enquiry. Although once significant in the thought of both Plato and Aristotle, he argues, the question of Being was doomed 'to subside from then on *as a theme for actual investigation*' (p. 21). For Heidegger, the modern era can be characterized as one in which the ontological question has not been taken with sufficient seriousness. The philosophical tradition that originated this question has simply lost interest in it. The reasons for this loss of interest are 'rooted in ancient ontology itself' (p. 22). This is because ancient ontological enquiry fostered what has since become the burden of contemporary presuppositions and prejudices about the matter. Such prejudices, Heidegger notes, can be found in some of the dismissive responses that have been levelled at the project he wishes to pursue. In other words, what Heidegger is doing at this stage of *Being and Time* is arguing for the legitimacy of the approach he is going to develop. If he can persuade us that he has hit upon an important and unresolved philosophical problem, then he has justified the project of rejuvenating the thematic analysis of Being. However, in order to present his analysis Heidegger must first consider some common objections to the project of ontological enquiry he is advocating.

First, it has been claimed that Being is the most universal of concepts, and therefore requires no further clarification, 'for everyone uses it constantly and already understands what he means by it' (p. 21). In other words, 'Being' signifies a concept, the meaning of which is immediately given and self-evident because we use it every day (e.g. 'the cat *is* on the mat', 'I forget my name, but I *am* a merchant banker'). For Heidegger, however, the claim that we have an unmediated understanding of Being is problematic. Our ability to use a concept or term does not entitle us to make the further claim that we possess an exhaustive knowledge of its meaning. By implication a term's meaning cannot be reduced to a mere matter of its use, however universal such use is. Indeed, Being cannot be classified by way of the procedures by which individual entities (stones, trees, cats, people, etc.) may be assigned determinate meanings. We may use a word to signify something or other, and such use is essential to that word meaning what it means. Thus, it is indispensable to the Being of any particular entity that it can be categorized as *a something*. But Being itself cannot be characterized in this way. Since all entities have in common the fact that they exist, we can say that they all possess Being in a sense that cannot be reduced to the fact of their individual existence, nor to any particular properties they might have (such as hardness, temperature, colour, etc.). For Heidegger, this invites us to consider the view that Being is the condition of possibility for any entity whatsoever. Being is not an entity and the universality at issue is not therefore a matter of class or genus: 'The term "Being" does not define that realm of entities which are uppermost when these are Articulated according to genus or species' (p. 22). Being transcends these methods of classification and is, indeed, presupposed by them. The universality of the term does nothing to annul the opaqueness of its meaning: such meaning is not self-evident.

Second, Heidegger notes, it has been held that the attribution of universality to Being renders it indefinable. Heidegger agrees that this is the case, but only in so far as Being cannot be conceived of as an entity (it is not a 'something'), nor derived from higher concepts. What this implies, though, is that Being transcends traditional notions of definition. These traditional notions are, Heidegger argues, derived from ancient ontology and represent one reason why the question of Being has been elided within Western metaphysics. The mere lack of a formal definition here does not supply a warrant for effacing the question of the meaning of Being. Rather, Heidegger contends, this very inability to define Being demands that one takes the question all the more seriously, since the activity of supplying definitions itself rests upon this unarticulated notion. We cannot even begin to define an entity without presupposing that the entity *is* in the first place. An investigation of Being is required to tell us what is going on when we are engaged in the very activity of supplying definitions. For Heidegger, then, an '*a priori* enigma operates whenever one comports oneself towards entities as entities' (p. 23). This is because what gives the kind of intelligibility that results from defining any entity as a particular X is itself unintelligible in terms of that definition alone. When we seek to define something, we presuppose the very notion of definition, we do not prove it.

Invoking self-evidence is a 'dubious procedure' (p. 23) when it comes to articulating even the most seemingly transparent of philosophical concepts. With regard to the question of Being, what we have is not something self-evident but enigmatic that stands in need of further analysis. However, Heidegger holds that in embarking on the first of the three tasks he has set himself he has managed to clarify two things: (1) 'that the question of Being [at present, at least] lacks an answer', and (2) that this question is itself for the moment 'obscure and without direction' (p. 24). It is for this reason worth pursuing such a line of enquiry in order to arrive at some degree of clarification of these issues. In order to do so, Heidegger addresses himself to the second task of analysing how such a question might be formulated. This entails examining what it means to ask a question at all.

1.2 What does it mean to ask a question?

We can ask about Being and we have some vague and, as yet, ill-formulated conception of it. But it is important at this juncture to structure our enquiry in such a manner that we know what we are getting into when we start asking about such things. We must, in other words, engage in a form of analysis that accords with the question at hand: 'The question . . . must be *formulated* . . . in an appropriate way' (p. 24). Heidegger approaches this task by first providing an account of what it is that characterizes all questions. Once we have some idea of what is going on whenever any question is asked we may have some chance of arriving at a better understanding of what is involved when we ask about the sense of 'Being'. In this way the question of Being can be made explicit with regard to its nature.

To ask a question, Heidegger tells us, means engaging in the activity of enquiry. Any enquiry involves seeking. In so far as we are seeking something, this activity is guided by what it is that is sought. This seeking is aware 'both with regard to the fact that it is and with regard to its Being as it is'. To put it another way, such seeking is an investigation. Through an investigation both the subject matter of the question (i.e. what the question is about) and its character are disclosed. What is asked about is thereby determined and conceptualized as an object of enquiry. Additionally, any question we might ask also concerns both '*that which is interrogated*' and finally '*that which is to be found out by the asking* . . . this is what is really intended' and this is the goal of enquiry (p. 24). Heidegger claims that enquiry, as a kind of seeking, must therefore be guided beforehand by what is sought. One does not enquire without already having some purpose in mind. Therefore, the purposes of any question serve to orient us toward the object of our investigation. This is all well and good, but it will come to nothing if Heidegger cannot provide some convincing reasons to persuade us that Being already has some kind of significance for us. This he now attempts to do.

Although it is ill defined, Heidegger argues, the sense of Being is already available to us in some manner. This is because 'we always conduct our activities in an understanding of Being' (p. 25). In other words, whenever humans engage in doing things, they necessarily do so in the context of some kind of understanding of what it means for something to be (i.e. to exist) at all. Even though we do not know what Being means in the sense of having ready access to a convenient shorthand definition, the fact that we can ask 'What is Being?' implies that we are already 'within an understanding of the "is"' (p. 25). This is why Heidegger's project is not one that begins by seeking to construct a 'theory' of knowledge. If we were to stick for the moment to the question of knowledge then, for Heidegger, what would be of primary interest is the kind of *understanding* that any such theory necessarily presupposes and must rest upon. This is why, as I noted earlier, there are strong structural parallels between Heidegger's analysis of ontology and Kant's epistemology: both aim at elucidating the conditions necessary for any engagement with the world. But where Kant's model depends upon articulating this problem in terms of what we can know, Heidegger rejects the epistemological route, and begins instead by asserting the importance of our understanding as something that arises not from transcendental conditions but from the actual engagement of human beings in their world. For Heidegger, then, the goal of the enquiry into Being is already presupposed in our everyday activities and the manner in which we have a conception of them. We already have a '*vague, average understanding of Being*' (p. 25). In this way the project of ontological enquiry is already determined by the presence of this understanding. The very vagueness of this conception as Heidegger has explicated it, its indefinite nature, is in fact positive, for it presents us with the task of clarification: it justifies the task of ontology.

In asking the question of Being '*what is asked about* is Being – that which determines entities as entities, that on the basis of which entities are already understood' (pp. 25–6). Being, as we have noted, is not an entity, since all talk of entities presupposes it. One way of talking about entities is to discuss their origins: where they came from and the conditions under which they arose. But Being cannot be analysed through recourse to a narrative account which seeks to inform us about where it came from. There is no 'origin' of Being, since it itself is what allows us to talk about issues concerning matters like the origins of entities. Thus, Heidegger is arguing, we cannot adequately address the question of Being by thinking of it as a kind of entity, a 'something'. We must try to approach this matter in a different way. 'Being . . . must be exhibited in a way of its own, essentially different from the way in which entities are discovered' (p. 26).

That said, entities nevertheless serve a key function in Heidegger's analysis of Being. What is to be found out here by engaging in the activity of asking a question is Being. But all we can ever have at hand to ask about are individual entities. This is because, as Heidegger has already stated, Being is always the being of a particular entity, even if the question of what Being means cannot be reduced to the status of any such entity. What need to be interrogated in order to facilitate ontological enquiry are entities: 'These are, so to speak, questioned as regards their Being.' We can ask of entities what it is that allows them to be in the first place.

1.3   Who is doing the asking?

To address the question of Being, then, we must, Heidegger argues, turn to entities. One important point needs to be raised here. This point leads us directly into the third point that Heidegger raised early at the outset of *Being and Time*: who or what is doing the asking? We, as enquirers, exist in an immanent relation to 'being': 'what we are is being, and so is how we are.' In other words, we exist (we 'are') and this is fundamental to *how* we are. So, where does one start in order to ask the question of the meaning of Being? With which entity would it be appropriate to commence in order to disclose Being, and why? Heidegger's answer is that it is to ourselves, as a particular kind of entity, that we must turn: 'Looking at something, understanding and conceiving it – all these ways of behaving are constitutive for our inquiry, and therefore modes of Being for those particular entities which we, as inquirers, are ourselves' (pp. 26–7). Seeing entities and having concepts yielded by our understanding are all things that *we* do. They are, Heidegger is arguing, *modes* or *ways* in which we exist and are therefore ways of our Being. We are entities that exist in certain ways, and one of those ways is exhibited whenever we ask questions – in other words, whenever we engage in enquiry. Since this is the case it follows that in order to approach the question of Being, the enquirer must first must be made 'transparent in his own Being'. We need to know what it is about us that makes us what we are: what an enquirer is must be clarified. We could assume here that Heidegger is starting his ontological investigation by turning to the subject. This is, in a limited sense, true. However, as will become clear, our subjectivity, for him, is *not* to be disclosed by way of Cartesian introspection.[4] What we are will be shown in a radically different manner.

Heidegger approaches the question of what an enquirer is by arguing that an entity engaged in enquiry already possesses a *mode* of Being as one of its possibilities. If we ask a question then the very act of asking implies a *way* of Being: 'The very asking of the question is an entity's mode of *Being*; and as such it gets its essential character from what is inquired about – namely, Being' (p. 27). The activity of enquiring is one of the *ways* in which an entity that can ask the question of the meaning of Being *is*. Heidegger calls this entity '*Dasein*' (p. 27).[5] Dasein is a word that is usually used by philosophers like Nietzsche, for example, to mean 'existence'. For Heidegger, this word is given a rather more subtle significance, which comes from the two elements that make up the compound word: '*da*': 'there'; and '*sein*': 'being'. Dasein therefore can be taken as meaning 'being-there'. Heidegger is arguing that we must first provide an analysis of our existence, as the kind of entities that exist in the sense of 'being-there', in order to approach the question of the meaning of Being. This is not, Heidegger claims, a circular undertaking since, as a matter of fact, it 'arises from the average understanding of Being in which we operate and *which in the end belongs to the essential constitution of Dasein itself*' (p. 28). But, Heidegger says, we should not start by assuming that Being is presupposed as a *concept*. Being is not a concept. Rather, Being is presupposed as an essential and concrete aspect of what we, as *Dasein*, are. It has existential 'weight', so to speak, for it concerns the existence of particular beings (us) and their engagement with their world by way of an already possessed *understanding* of what 'is'. Ontological enquiry, in this sense, is for Heidegger the most concrete or substantive form of philosophical investigation.

1.4 'The Ontological Priority of the Question of Being'

We might still be tempted to ask whether the question of Being is abstract and empty or concrete (p. 29). But Heidegger thinks he has now overcome such an objection. In reply, he can contend that it is concrete because it concerns our substantive engagement with entities in the world. We ourselves are entities, but we are in such a way that we have understanding and all such understanding presupposes Being.

But a bit more work is needed in order to show precisely what is special about ontological enquiry. What is it that makes an ontological approach different from other ways of analysing entities, be they stones, cats or us? As a means of telling us about this Heidegger provides an elucidation of the question of Being through a ground-clearing exercise which contrasts scientific enquiry with ontological investigation. The purpose of this seems to be twofold: (1) to clarify what ontological investigation is by distinguishing it from the various scientific disciplines, and (2) to characterize these latter disciplines as unsuitable for the resolution of ontological issues. The sciences are unsuited to this task, Heidegger will tell us, because they are all disciplines that *presuppose* entities as existing. Since they do this, they cannot be deemed a suitable tool for investigating the theme of ontology itself.

'Being [*Sein*] is always the Being of an entity [*Seiendes*]' (p. 29).[6] There are those entities that provide the subject matter for the study of history, nature, etc. These comprise what Heidegger terms the 'basic concepts' of any science. The sciences elaborate these basic concepts. They do so by investigating those entities that fall within the field of these concepts. A science, however, can reach the point at which there is 'a crisis in its basic concepts'. In other words, the sciences are capable of reaching a state in which the concepts which ground them become open to question: 'In such immanent crises the very relationship between positively investigative inquiry and those things themselves that are under investigation comes to a point where it begins to totter.'[7] That such crises occur cannot, Heidegger argues, be accounted for from within the sciences themselves. The sciences take the conceptual ordering of reality that grounds their own possibility for granted. They presuppose the existence of entities of a particular kind (e.g. in biology, the notion of an 'organism' – an entity that lives). But they cannot investigate the condition in virtue of which an entity is an entity. They must presuppose this condition in order to investigate the entities that form their subject matter and because of this they cannot talk about it. The sciences are, for this reason, what Heidegger terms 'ontical', rather than ontological, disciplines. Put simply, the sciences are concerned with entities in the world, not the condition of their possibility. A scientific crisis, Heidegger argues, denotes the fact that a science experiences its relationship with its subject matter as problematic because its own presuppositions are being placed in question by the engagement implicit in that relationship. Hence Heidegger's contention that such crises are 'immanent' to the activity of scientific inquiry and his advocacy of the primacy of ontological enquiry as grounding the sciences. At the same time, it is not simply enough to do traditional ontology as a means of investigating what is at stake here:

> Ontological inquiry is indeed more primordial, as over against the ontical inquiry of the positive sciences. But it remains itself naïve and opaque if in its researches into the Being of entities it fails to discuss the meaning of Being in general . . . The question of Being aims therefore at ascertaining the *a priori* conditions not only for the possibility of the sciences which examine entities as entities of such and such a type, and, in so doing, already operate with an understanding of Being, but also for the possibility of those ontologies themselves which are prior to the ontical sciences and which provide their foundations. *Basically, all ontology . . . remains blind and perverted from its ownmost aim, if it has not first adequately clarified the meaning of Being, and conceived this clarification as its fundamental task.* (p. 31)

In order to further clarify his project, Heidegger then discusses '*The Ontical Priority of the Question of Being*' (pp. 32ff). This may seem paradoxical, given his assertion of ontological priority, but it both forms an important part of the overall project he is elucidating and clarifies Heidegger's view of the nature of ontology.

1.5 '*The Ontical Priority of the Question of Being*': Dasein in its world

We can define science as 'the totality established through an interconnection of true propositions' (p. 32). But this is an incomplete definition, since the sciences are a product of humanity and so exhibit the mode of Being that we are, as Dasein. The sciences, we might say, are what they are because they are the products of human activity. But Dasein (human being) also has other ways of Being: we do not merely engage in scientific enquiry but live our lives in all sorts of other ways. Dasein is distinct from other beings (entities) in this respect. Thus, Dasein is *ontically distinct*. Humans exist in a multiplicity of ways. Above all, we are entities who are concerned with our own existence. From this, Heidegger concludes that Dasein 'is ontically distinguished by the fact that, in its very Being, that Being is an *issue* for it' (p. 32). Each of us is an entity that is Dasein, and as such entities we have an ontological concern about our own Being: what we are and what will happen to us is of concern to us. It follows that we are ontically different from other entities in this respect, for other kinds of entity (stones, dogs, etc.) are not concerned in this sense with what will happen to them. This amounts to saying that 'Dasein is ontically distinctive in that it is ontological.'

Dasein is ontological in a specific sense. It is not theoretically ontological in the sense that, for example, Heidegger's enquiry is. His ontological investigation is a *theoretical* elucidation of the ontological conditions of our existence. Rather, Dasein has ' "pre-ontological" . . . being in such a way that . . . [it] . . . has an understanding of Being' (p. 32). Dasein, therefore, is that entity that recognizes the fact that its own Being can be an issue for it. Dasein has an existence to which it relates and this existence *is* its Being. This makes Dasein ontically distinctive from other entities in that no 'subject-matter' or 'material content' can be ascribed to it as a means of defining it in the manner in which we might define a stone. Dasein's 'essence lies rather in the fact that in each case it has its Being to be, and has it as its own' (pp. 32–3).

What Dasein is, it follows, can only be 'straightened out' through the actual activity of its living its own existence. What 'I' am cannot be determined according to a collection of essential properties that I 'have', but first and foremost by the fact that I exist; and it is only through the concrete process of existing that I realize what I am. To this degree '*Dasein* always understands itself in terms of its own existence' (p. 33). The kind of understanding which is involved in this context Heidegger terms '*existentiell*'. At this level, there is no requirement for an ontological theory. The existentiell mode is thus ontical: it concerns just how we are in the world. But, 'The context of such structures we call "*existentiality*".' It is this structure that Heidegger is interested in. If we address the issue of what the structure of the existentiell is (of what 'constitutes existence'; of existentiality), we are at a different level of analysis from one that concerns only the 'existentiell'. 'Its analytic has the character of an understanding which is not existentiell, but rather *existential*' (p. 33). Thus, there are two modes of understanding: the *existentiell*, which concerns the actual activity of existing (how we get around in the world, our understanding of it on a day-to-day basis); and the *existential*, which concerns the ontological structure of existence. The existentiell consists in existing, engaging with a world of phenomenal experience, matters of fact, etc. In concrete terms, one gets out of bed in the morning and goes to work on the train, etc. This involves things like recollection, recognition, getting things done (remembering where the bathroom is in relation to your bedroom, recognizing a train when you see it, boarding the train, and so on). In doing such things one simply takes one's world for granted. The existential, in contrast, constitutes the level at which the ontological analysis of the structure of existence (that in virtue of which what exists *is* and is understood as such) is made possible. The existential does not concern things like remembering where your bathroom is, but the kind of understanding you need to have of the world in order to think of bathrooms, trains and other entities in the first place. This understanding stipulates that all entities have one thing in common: they, like you, *exist*.

The sciences are ways of behaving in the world; ways of relating to entities which are not Dasein. For Dasein itself, in contrast, 'Being in a world is something that belongs essentially' to it. Dasein's understanding of Being implies both that it already has an understanding of a 'world' and of the Being of those entities that are encountered in that world. From this it follows that whenever an ontology is constructed it will always be grounded in the ontical structure which Dasein has in virtue of the fact that it exists in a concrete context that is meaningful to it. The phenomenological (existentiell) level, in other words, has priority and gives us the conditions in virtue of which any theoretical ontology is possible. What is apparent here is that Heidegger is attempting to draw a distinction between the ontical and ontological modes which does not simply erase the first of these by giving priority to an abstract notion of ontology. Heidegger's ontology is contextualized in that it depends on an articulation of the ontical mode of Dasein's existence. This articulation, however, is not itself purely ontical in its nature, for it must be theoretical in order to be truly ontological. 'Therefore *fundamental ontology*, from which alone all other ontologies can take their rise, must be sought in the *existential analytic of Dasein*' (p. 34).

The term 'Dasein' thus refers to that entity whose Being is an issue for it. Only Dasein can both ask questions about existence and the nature of entities (including itself), and only Dasein must in consequence already have an understanding of its own Being in order even to pose such questions. This is the case even though this understanding need not be regarded as anything more than vague, and certainly need not be articulated theoretically. However, one important point to grasp here is that the nature of Dasein is not to be understood in terms of self-consciousness. It is not another variant of the Cartesian 'I think': a subject that 'is' independently of its world. Instead, Dasein is characterized by its 'throwness': it is 'thrown' into its world. By this, Heidegger means that Dasein is always already 'there' in its world. For this reason, Dasein's presence in its world is not to be thought of as something that is 'necessary' or deducible from principles that are prior to its existence. The very notion of 'throwness' implies the Dasein's Being is contingent, it is simply *flung* into existence and hence cannot be accounted for in terms that are extrinsic to its existence. As such, Dasein is not something 'outside' the world that can be added on to 'empirical experience', but is *'delivered over'* to its world in a manner that is inseparable from it: 'as Being-in-the-world, it is the "there" . . . An entity of the character of Dasein is its "there" in such a way that, whether explicitly or not, it finds itself in its throwness' (p. 174). What is essential about Dasein, then, is the fact that it is already situated in a world. This is Heidegger's central point: every Dasein is a kind of entity that is what it is because it has an understanding of its world that is not rooted in its consciousness of itself apart from its world, but rather by way of its concrete engagement with that world. We will return to this point, below. For the moment, it is also important to note that the question of Being is essentially tied to the existence of Dasein. Dasein is the point of departure for Heidegger's investigation. It is only through an interrogation of the constitution of Dasein that one can approach the possibility of formulating the 'question of the meaning of Being'.

As we have seen, in order to formulate the basis of this question Heidegger draws a key distinction between the *ontological* and the *ontical* realms. The latter is the domain of the sciences (e.g. physics, chemistry, history, etc.). These disciplines deal in categorizing and describing the behaviour of entities and hence presuppose them as entities. Ontology, in contrast, is concerned with the conditions of possibility of all entities, not with elucidating the characteristics of particular entities. In this way, Heidegger's project stakes a claim for the primacy of a mode of enquiry which is radically different in kind from that of scientific investigation. In turn, Dasein is characterized as an ontico–ontological entity. It is ontical because it is instantiated in the world, and it is ontological because it is the only kind of entity that can ask questions about its own existence. As an ontico-ontological entity, Dasein already possesses an, albeit ill-defined and non-theoretical, understanding of Being. As such, Dasein is a necessary condition for the question of the meaning of Being to be raised. And, by the same token, Dasein is also what must be examined in order to elucidate the basis and nature of fundamental ontology. One thing immediately follows from this. Without Dasein there is no 'meaning' or sense that could be attributed to the question of Being. If Dasein were not then it could not meaningfully be said that entities 'are'. All talk of the *meaning* of Being, therefore, is dependent on the presence of an understanding of it, even though the existence of entities themselves is not: 'Being (not entities) is dependent upon the understanding of Being' (p. 255). By way of summary, then, we can say that Heidegger contends that Dasein has fundamental priority over all other kinds of entities with regard to the project of constructing a fundamental ontology. This priority is threefold. First, it is ontical, in that Dasein is characterized by the fact that it actually exists (there are such entities). Second, it is ontological, in that the existence of Dasein is itself ontological (its Being is an issue for it). Third, this priority is ontico-ontological: only Dasein has an understanding of all entities other than itself, and because of this Dasein itself provides the ontico-ontological condition for the construction of any ontologies whatsoever. Without Dasein, in other words, there can be no theories about the nature of Being, for there would be no meaning.

1.6   'The ontological analytic of Dasein'

'If to interpret the meaning of Being becomes our task, Dasein is not only the primary entity to be interrogated; it is also that entity which already comports itself, in its Being, towards what we are asking about when we ask this question. But in that case the question of Being is nothing other than the radicalization of an essential tendency-of-Being which belongs to Dasein itself – the pre-ontological understanding of Being' (p. 35). This may seem like a bit of a mouthful, but we can clarify it in the following way. Heidegger advocates the investigation of Dasein through its phenomenological constitution (the existentiality of its existence) in order to raise the question of its Being. This move, he argues, will yield us an ontology, namely, an account of the formal structure of the Being of Dasein. We can arrive at this ontology by looking first at the non-theoretical (i.e. 'pre-ontological') understanding of Being that Dasein has. On the basis of this, we can then raise the issue of the Being of the entities that make up Dasein's world. This, in its own turn, will equip us to ask the question of the meaning of Being. However, it is not only important to work out which entity is best suited to be the primary object for the interrogation of the question of Being, namely Dasein. In addition, we must also establish what is the 'right way of access to this entity' (p. 36).

Although Dasein has ontico-ontological priority, it should not be concluded that the kind of Being it has is presented to us with an unproblematic immediacy. For, the very fact that we are ourselves Dasein means that 'it is ontologically that which is farthest' from us. This is because we tend to understand ourselves by way of reflecting upon the world in which we live: 'In Dasein itself, and therefore in its own understanding of Being, the way the world is understood is . . . reflected back ontologically upon the way in which Dasein itself gets interpreted' (pp. 36–7). In other words, we cannot be directly aware of our own mode of Being in the world we inhabit, since that mode of Being is what reveals the world to us. What shows the world to us cannot itself be shown in an immediate and transparent fashion: you cannot 'see' what *allows* you to engage in seeing in the first place.

It is for this reason that Heidegger feels that we must first of all provide an 'ontological analytic' of Dasein: 'We must . . . choose such a way of access and such a kind of interpretation that this entity [Dasein] can show itself in itself and from itself' (p. 37). This means looking at Dasein 'in its average *everydayness*'. The analysis of this that Heidegger will provide, he tells us, is both incomplete and provisional, in that it will merely *show* the Being of Dasein, not state its meaning. He is, in other words, going to offer us a kind of description of it. In so doing, however, the horizon for interpreting the meaning of Being will be laid bare. The metaphor of a 'horizon' is an important one. A horizon is the limit beyond which it is impossible to see any further. And this limit, Heidegger contends, is to be discovered in the form of *temporality*. Thus, Heidegger is claiming that though he may not get to the point of telling us about the meaning of Being, what he can do is try to show us the limits within which we, as Dasein, exist. And it is the indication of these limits that can, in principle, allow for the possible elucidation of the meaning of Being: 'We shall point to *temporality* as the meaning of the Being of that entity which we call "Dasein" . . . In thus interpreting Dasein as temporality, however, we shall not give the answer to our leading question as to the meaning of Being in general. But the ground will have been prepared for obtaining such an answer' (p. 38).

1.7 Dasein, Being and Temporality

Whenever *Dasein* engages in understanding and interpreting Being it does so from a temporal perspective (p. 39). In this way time forms the 'horizon for all understanding of Being and for any way of interpreting it'. Time must therefore be explicated in its function as this horizon; and this means that we need to rethink what time is. 'We are accustomed to contrasting the "timeless" meaning of propositions with the "temporal" course of propositional assertions' (p. 39). This is like talking of 'being *in* time'. On this view, time functions as a means for 'distinguishing between realms of Being'. It therefore has an ontological function specific to it. But, for Heidegger, one can go further: 'our treatment of the question of the meaning of Being must enable us to show that *the central problematic of all ontology is rooted in the phenomenon of time, if rightly seen and rightly explained . . .*' (p. 40). Being must be conceived 'in terms of time'. If so, then temporality cannot simply mean being '*in*' time. Rather, Being *and* time are conjoined.

The Being of Dasein is absolutely determined by time. We simply *are* in time, and our existence cannot be separated from this 'primordial' condition. It is no use, in other words, looking for something essential about what makes us the kind of entities we are 'outside' the realm of time. We are, on this view, subject to the condition that time is essential in making us what we are. This Heidegger calls Dasein's '*"Temporal"* determinateness'. Since this is the case, working out the 'Temporality of Being' is a fundamental part of ontology simply because we cannot grasp the meaning of Being without including time within our account. In short, if the meaning of Being is to be found anywhere, then it will be located in our actual, temporal existence in the world. And since we are entities whose constitution is essentially temporal, then it follows that we are also 'historical' beings. In this way the temporality of our Being-in-the-world grounds our understanding of ourselves as intrinsically *historical* creatures, in so far as *what we are* is to be understood in terms of *what we were*: 'any Dasein . . . is its past . . . in the way of *its* own Being' (pp. 41/63). This 'pastness' or 'historicality' forms the basis for Dasein's interpreting itself, and it projects its own *future* in terms of this: 'Its own past . . . is not something which *follows along after* Dasein, but something which already goes ahead of it' (p. 41). This is what Heidegger terms the 'elemental historicity' of Dasein. To put matters more simply, we have an understanding of our existence and this understanding is necessarily articulated within the context of Being. But, equally, this understanding is not merely given in a direct and immediate manner. We do not understand our Being in terms of something that simply and essentially 'is'. Rather, we are able to understand what we are only on the basis of the understanding we already have of ourselves. This understanding is temporally determined, and this temporal determination announces itself in the fact that whenever we think of ourselves we do so in terms of our past. What I am is something that essentially concerns what has happened to me in my life: I am my history. What I will be (my projects concerning the future) is likewise something that I can only think of in terms of this past. In this sense, when I interpret the world in which I live, my past necessarily *precedes* me. Another way of looking at this is to say that all thinking is bound up with the conditions that precede it. We only think because we are historical entities, and as such we are bound by tradition.

1.8   Tradition and metaphysics

Tradition is essential to the structure of Dasein. It is a condition of our understanding. At the same time, however, Heidegger contends that tradition also 'blocks' our understanding. When we fall back upon tradition and rely upon it we lose the insight it gives us, for 'what it transmits is made . . . inaccessible' (p. 43). Thinking relies upon tradition as its condition of possibility. We only have understanding to the extent that we are beings who inhabit a world delineated by tradition, by the ways of thinking bestowed to us by the past. Yet, if we simply deliver ourselves up to the force of tradition in an uncritical fashion by accepting the ways of thinking it hands down to us as self-evident, then we lose sight of what it truly offers us: 'it blocks our access to those primordial "sources" from which the categories and concepts handed down to us have been genuinely drawn.' For this reason, Heidegger wishes to draw a distinction between the positive potential of tradition, and its negative force. This is because passively accepting the authority of tradition can cause the ontological question to be covered up. This, after all, is Heidegger's contention at the very beginning of *Being and Time*: the metaphysical tradition both articulated the problem of ontology and then veiled it. In order to reveal it we must destroy the traditional concept of ontology (p. 44). Such a destructive act, however, does not involve the mere negation of tradition. On the contrary, the destruction of the traditional concept of ontology will cause the actualization of its positive potential. In other words, Heidegger is arguing that the fundamental ontology he wishes to pursue is only possible if we recognize that the tradition of metaphysical speculation that gave rise to it must be turned against itself. To this degree, Heidegger's project also owes something to Hegel's notion of the immanent conditions of mediation that were discussed in the previous chapter (sections 1.2ff).

1.9   Phenomenology

If the metaphysical tradition is to be turned against itself, then we are entitled to ask: how is this to be done? One way is by a turn toward phenomenology. Traditional ontology aims 'to explain Being itself' metaphysically (p. 49) and, Heidegger contends, such an enterprise remains a dubious methodological procedure as long as we accept it as it has been handed down to us. The question of the meaning of Being must be dealt with *phenomenologically*. Such an approach as Heidegger conceives it is critical of the metaphysical tradition and yet does not seek to stand outside it. Phenomenology aims at actualizing the potential of traditional ontology by accepting that it has itself emerged from this tradition. Phenomenology is not a purely methodological notion, however. A method stipulates a 'how' for research, not a 'what'. Phenomenology, in contrast, concerns the 'what'.

There are two components of the word 'phenomenology': phenomenon and logos. 'Phenomenon', Heidegger claims, is derived from the Greek *phainesthi* – 'to show itself', 'the manifest'. The phenomenon, in this sense, is that which shows itself to us. This 'showing' is neither mere appearance nor semblance, and should not be confused with either. The notion of 'semblance' is structurally connected to the concept of the phenomenon: a semblance 'looks like' something, but is not it. To have semblance is to 'seem-like', which presupposes that which it is like (the phenomenon). Equally, a 'mere appearance' concerns something that does not show itself. Heidegger provides an example. An 'appearance' is what one refers to when speaking of the 'symptoms of a disease'. Such symptoms, in showing themselves, indicate something that does not show itself, i.e. the disease. Taken in this way, 'Appearing is a *not-showing-itself* . . . What appears does *not* show; and anything which thus fails to show itself, is also something which can never seem' (p. 52). All appearances and semblances are, therefore, derived from phenomena. Appearing, it follows, can only happen because something announces itself by way of that appearance. And what are thus announced are phenomena: 'phenomena are *never* appearances, though on the other hand, every appearance is dependent upon phenomena' (p. 53). We can talk of 'appearances', but when we do this we are engaged in an activity whereby what we are really referring to is the phenomenon as it announces itself to us. Thus, the term '*Phenomenon*' means a 'showing-itself-in-itself, [and] signifies a distinctive way in which something can be encountered' (p. 54).

'Logos' means 'discourse'. And to engage in a logos means 'to make manifest what one is "talking about" in one's discourse' (p. 56). Speaking of something in a discourse (logos) is 'a letting-something-be-seen'. In conjoining these two words we get 'phenomenology', and phenomenology 'means . . . to let that which shows itself be seen from itself in the very way in which it shows itself from itself' (p. 58). This is a very complex formulation, so it might be helpful to spell it out. The phenomenon is that which 'shows itself'. It is simply what we grasp whenever we engage in any activity in the world. Phenomenology seeks to allow this phenomenon to announce itself to us just as it is. Hence the maxim of phenomenology 'to the things themselves'. This phrase comes from Heidegger's teacher, Edmund Husserl (1859–1938).[8] According to Husserl's conception, phenomenological enquiry operates by adopting the method of 'bracketing' off all the presuppositions (factual, social, cultural, etc.) that an observer may have. This act of 'bracketing' is also termed the 'phenomenological epoché'. The point of this is to reveal the fundamental structure of assumptions that makes our experience of objects possible. Such bracketing does not merely involve the suspension of, say, certain theoretical principles of interpretation (such as those that the natural scientist may have), but also even the attitudes and expectations that we have when engaged in everyday life.

In adopting this approach Husserl tells us that he follows, in a modified form, the same route that Descartes takes in the *Meditations on First Philosophy*, which 'draws the prototype for any beginning philosopher's necessary meditations, the meditations out of which alone a philosophy can grow originally'.[9] However, it should be noted that Husserl's analogy between his method and Descartes's is not entirely accurate. For instance, Husserl is not interested, as Descartes is, in proving the existence of the world of empirical experience, of a world that is 'external' to the mind. What is of interest to him, rather, is to show the *sense* that the notion of an objective world of experience has for us.[10] Husserl holds that the phenomenological method of bracketing offers a means of arriving at a first principle on the basis of which such an understanding is possible. The problem with Descartes's methodology is that he fails to 'make the transcendental turn'. Descartes conceives of the ego as a substantive entity, 'a *substantia cognitans*, a separate human', which it is not. In making this error Descartes 'does not pass through the gateway that leads into genuine transcendental philosophy'.[11] Passing through this gateway involves appreciating that the ego in its transcendental form cannot be understood as an entity in the manner that entities in the world of facts and things can be. Rather, what we are faced with is 'the realm of *transcendental-phenomenological self-experience*'. This mode of self-experience bestows objectivity upon the world of empirical experience in that 'this world . . . derives its whole sense and its existential status, which it has for me, *from me as the transcendental Ego*, the Ego who comes to the fore only with the transcendental-phenomenological epoché.'[12]

The upshot of Husserl's account is to argue that we are essentially conscious beings, but that such consciousness is necessarily 'intentional'; that is, there is no such thing as a consciousness that is not the consciousness of some object or other. In other words, what is fundamental about consciousness is that it is always a 'consciousness *of* something'.[13] Such objects, it should be added, need not be material things; they can be expectations, for example 'Tomorrow I will take the train to work.' Husserl's point is that we cannot account for the nature of human experience by thinking of it solely in terms of an analysis of the material causes of our ideas (as, for example, some psychological accounts of consciousness try to do). What we need to do, instead, is to provide a descriptive account of the ways in which we have experiences and of the kinds of experiences we have. These two kinds of description are termed '*noetic*' and '*noematic*' descriptions.[14] What is important about these descriptions is that they show us that consciousness, in order to be what it is, necessarily always has an object toward which it is directed. In consequence, it is incorrect to assert a radical distinction between 'inside' and 'outside', i.e. between what perceives objects and what is perceived. For this reason it is not true to say that we simply apprehend things either as they 'are' or 'appear to be'. Rather, we tend to interpret our experiences in terms of certain expectations. I may, for example, look out of the window and see a field of grass and conclude 'This field of grass is green.' But this judgement is guided by specific expectations concerning fields of grass. In fact, a botanist with a special knowledge of grasses (i.e. someone who has different expectations) might say to me, 'This field of grass is not simply green – that's just how people tend to think of grass – in fact the grass here is all sorts of shades of green.' My mode of consciousness and the object toward which my consciousness is directed are therefore elements that are intrinsically related to one another – they are not separate or different in kind. Together these elements constitute a synthetic unity in the form of the transcendental ego. This unity, Husserl argues, is maintained by temporality. In other words, individual consciousness is what it is because it is structured by time. In effect, therefore, Husserl contends that the sense of our experience of the world can only be adequately comprehended if it is understood in terms of being produced by a transcendental ego. This sounds very similar to Kant's account (discussed in chapter 1). However, Husserl abandons the Kantian notion of things-in-themselves and hence the latter's distinction between phenomena and noumena. Equally, Husserl is not seeking to offer an account of how our knowledge of objects of experience is possible. For him, on the contrary, the point is to provide a description of the kinds of experience we have without making reference to the epistemological status of such experiences. What Husserl does cleave to is the notion of a disembodied agent, exemplified in his developing a modified version of Descartes's *cogito* as a point of departure for phenomenology.

It should already be clear that Heidegger's conception of phenomenology differs from Husserl's in so far as Heidegger rejects the latter's notion of a disembodied agent. For Heidegger, in contrast, it is our practical engagement with the world that gives rise to our understanding of it. What Heidegger is interested in is not just that which shows itself in relation to intentional consciousness. For him, phenomenology must also aim to reveal what is hidden from us whenever we encounter phenomena; namely, 'the *being* of beings' (*Being and Time*, 59), i.e. that which makes any entity an entity. In other words, Heideggerean phenomenology aims at revealing the fundamental structure in virtue of which any understanding of entities is possible. This structure is not something which can be given to us by way of a straightforward description from the standpoint of an observer who is outside of it, as Husserl would argue, but arises through an active '*interpretation*' of that structure undertaken from within it (p. 61). This is because 'the *being* of beings' is that through which we practically engage with our world. Phenomenology, in other words, takes as its starting point our activities in the world and aims to uncover the hidden ground of understanding upon which these activities rest, but not from a viewpoint exterior to that world. So, for Heidegger, we are entities who are *already* engaged in interpreting ourselves prior to any theoretical activity. The task of phenomenology is to reveal the hidden structure that underlies this activity of self-interpretation without seeking to obtain a standpoint that floats above it in order to do so. Heidegger's approach is what is termed a 'hermeneutic' one.[15]

1.10   Present-at-hand and ready-to-hand

If it is the aim of phenomenology to articulate the conditions of our understanding of Being in concrete terms, then this must be done with reference to elucidating the conditions of our actual engagement with entities. All entities can be divided into two kinds: 'any entity is either a "*who*" (existence) or a "*what*" (presence-at-hand in the broadest sense)' (p. 71). The first of these is always and only Dasein, and 'one must always use a *personal* pronoun when one addresses it: "I am", "You are"' (p. 68). This is because what essentially characterizes Dasein is its *existence*, its Being in the world; and it is we who have such Being, not what we engage with in our world. The existence that 'I' or 'You' possess is not something that can be articulated in terms of determinate properties, since it is 'I' or 'You' who encounter and understand the world in which we live. Such understanding is not thing-like, since it essentially involves interpretation. *What* we encounter, in contrast, possesses determinate properties that are interpreted by us. The term 'presence-at-hand' is used by Heidegger to denote the kind of entities that possess such properties. Whenever we think of an entity in terms of a 'what' we understand it as something that can be looked at and examined with a view to grasping the kinds of properties it possesses: a stone, a tree, a house (p. 67). Such things exist in a determinate manner: they have characteristics that make them what they are.

Dasein's existence is to be understood as 'Being-in the world'. But such 'Being-in' is not to be taken in the sense in which entities that are present-at-hand can be said to be 'in' a particular space at a particular time. We do not exist 'in' the world in the sense in which 'the water is "in" the glass, or the garment is "in" the cupboard' (p. 79). Entities of this kind 'are *worldless* in themselves, they can never "touch" each other, nor can either of them "*be*" "*alongside*" the other' (pp. 81–2). Rather, Dasein is 'in' its world in that it is already engaged with it and has an understanding of its existence in terms of this engagement. It is we who understand entities as 'being-in' or 'being-alongside' other entities, and this understanding denotes the fact that we inhabit a world in which entities exist in these ways. Heidegger, therefore, is challenging the traditional view that subjectivity can be adequately grasped and articulated apart from the conditions of its existence:

> what is known is not a process of returning with one's booty to the 'cabinet' of consciousness after one has gone out and grasped it . . . If I 'merely' know about some way in which the Being of entities is interconnected, if I 'only' represent them, if I 'do no more' than 'think' about them, I am no less alongside the entities outside in the world than when I *originally* grasp them.   (pp. 89–90)

From this it is clear that Heidegger is arguing for overturning the Cartesian epistemological conception of human understanding as something that can be spelled out without reference to the context in which it occurs. Such a context is one of practical engagement, not of disinterested contemplation. An important point follows from this contention: our relationship with entities is not merely one of presence-at-hand. It is a relationship in which a concrete grasping of them is implicit to our understanding of them as things that are present to us in our world. Entities, it follows, are not merely present-at-hand, they are also 'ready-to-hand'. By this Heidegger means that entities can be grasped *practically*. This continuous grasping of them is an essential condition of our having a world at all that we can understand. We do not merely 'look' at the world in order to understand it. We are concerned with the world in which we exist and this concern is registered in the form of our own activity. Heidegger's most famous example of this kind of relation to entities is the hammer. A hammer is a piece of 'equipment'. Equipment is simply 'put to use' (p. 98). What makes a hammer a hammer is the fact that it is used for hammering. What is ready-to-hand is hence 'not grasped theoretically at all' (p. 99) but is determined as what it is by its being subordinated to an agent's purposes: it is 'a using *of* something for something' (p. 100). Our relationship to entities that are present-at-hand, it follows, is always mediated by our practical attitude toward their possibilities for us:

'Nature' is not to be understood as that which is just present-at-hand, nor as the *power of Nature*. The wood is a forest of timber, the mountain a quarry of rock; the river is water-power, the wind is 'wind in the sails'. As the 'environment' is discovered, the 'Nature' thus discovered is encountered too. If its kind of Being as ready-to-hand is disregarded, this 'Nature' itself can be discovered and defined simply in its pure presence-at-hand. But when this happens, the Nature which 'stirs and strives', which assails and enthralls us as landscape, remains hidden. The botanist's plants are not the flowers of the hedgerow; the 'source' which the geographer establishes for a river is not the 'springhead in the dale'. (p. 100)

It is our practical grasping of the world that endows it with significance. Yet the very notion of 'a hammer' or 'a needle' informs us that 'there "is" no such thing as *an* equipment' (p. 97). Equipment does not simply happen, nor is it something 'thing-like', we make it what it is by way of our activities in the world. And since we do this, it is our existence (our Being-in the world) that renders equipment what it is. The nature of the ready-to-hand poses an ontological issue: it informs us of the hidden preconditions that underlie the phenomena of our world.

The analysis of these hidden preconditions, however, returns us to the problem of the present-at-hand. For 'only by reason of something present-at-hand "is there" anything ready-to-hand' (p. 101). Nevertheless, what is apparent here is that we do not grasp what is present-at-hand as something that simply 'is'. What is present-at-hand announces itself when our equipment fails us. When the hammer gets broken, when the car doesn't start in the morning, are instances wherein what was taken as being simply ready-to-hand manifests itself as also present-at-hand: 'what cannot be used just lies there; it shows itself as an equipmental Thing which just looks so and so, and which, in its readiness-to-hand as looking that way, has constantly been present-at-hand' (p. 103). In turn, we realize that our world is not just determined according to the possibilities of its use. The world is not exclusively 'handy' since it is also composed of entities that we do not concern ourselves with and yet which demand our attention. A tool is broken, or it is not where we expected it to be when we sought it out. Such moments throw the underlying ontological structure of our everyday world into relief, they cast ontological light on the *'phenomenon of the world'* (pp. 104ff). From this, Heidegger concludes, the world itself 'does not "consist" of the ready-to-hand' (p. 106) since 'In anything ready-to-hand the world is always "there"' (p. 114). This is a point that concerns the preconditions of our understanding of the world. Our understanding of the world is not exclusively equipmental but rests upon an *unarticulated* structure of what is taken as being already there. It is this totality of what is 'there' that ontology seeks to disclose.

1.11   The Being of Dasein as Being-with Others

Dasein exists in its world in that it is concerned with it: it is both absorbed in it and fascinated by it (p. 149). Equally, the question of Dasein's existence is to be understood not in terms of a 'what' but a 'who'. We need to ask *who* Dasein is, not what it is. The term 'Dasein', though, does not merely signify individual human Being. We have existence in that we live in relation to others: Dasein is not only 'I' but also

'You'. This condition is an ontological one. That our world is a shared world is essential to making it what it is. What Heidegger calls '*Being-with* and *Dasein-with*' are 'equiprimordial' conditions of our existence (p. 149) – you cannot have the one without the other. As we have seen, Heidegger does not start his analysis of the Being of Dasein with the 'I' that thinks. The rigours of the phenomenological method forbid this. There is no 'I' that is not at the same time associated with its world (p. 152). Since every Dasein is 'in each case mine', the 'I' is something '*which must be Interpreted existentially*', that is, according to the ontological structure that is its condition of possibility. Again, we can turn to Dasein's everyday existence as a means of explicating this matter. Our world is composed of things that are both present-at-hand and ready-to-hand. But the environment consisting of what is ready-to-hand also includes and concerns the existence of Others. We encounter Others in an 'environmental context of equipment' (p. 154). Understanding our environment as being composed of things that are ready-to-hand, a world of 'equipment' and hence of 'work', entails the existence of those for whom such work is destined. A garment is cut to fit *someone*, and we can encounter the tailor of the garment as someone who is ready-to-hand for us in that he or she serves our needs 'badly' or 'well'. However, the Dasein of others is not to be confused with what is present-at-hand or ready-to-hand, both of which are essentially characterizable as 'Things'. Other Daseins also have existence and whenever each of us understands the world we also understand it as containing other entities that are not mere 'Things' but beings in some sense 'like us'. Others are not merely 'added on in thought' to 'Things' but encountered as an essential component of that world. So, the earlier analysis of the present-at-hand and the ready-to-hand turns out to have been a limited one. This is because 'the kind of Being which belongs to the Dasein of Others, as we encounter it within-the-world, differs from readiness-to-hand and presence-at-hand.' Others are neither equipment nor Things, '*they are there too, and there with it.*'

It is because of the necessary presence of Others in the world that, though the Being of any Dasein is always and in every case 'mine', we cannot analyse Dasein by starting, Cartesian style, with the 'I'. The existence of the personal pronoun 'I' and the existence of Others is combined. When we refer to 'Others' we do not mean everybody else but 'me'. Others are 'those from whom . . . one does not distinguish oneself – those among whom one is too'. Our Being is always a 'Being-with' Others, and the 'with' tells us something essential about who we are. If we are always necessarily 'with' Others as a condition of being who we are then, Heidegger argues, it is pure folly to begin our analysis of human existence by looking to the self as an isolated entity as a means of understanding what it is to be who we are. What is 'mine' is so only in virtue of the fact that I am *with* Others. What is 'individual' turns out to be something already shared.

We all engage with Others in the world. We meet them at work, we see them 'just standing around', even (p. 156). But in all such cases, Others are never mere 'Things' that are simply present-at-hand or ready-to-hand. Somebody standing around or at work *is* in a sense that denotes 'an existential mode of Being'. We *are* with Others and to this extent we always understand them as 'Dasein-with': they, too, have an existence which is a Being-with us. 'Being-with' therefore has the significance of an 'existential characteristic of Dasein'. By this, Heidegger means that Being-with marks us as who we are, no matter where we are. We can, as a matter of fact, be with Others or be alone with ourselves, but even being on our own only has meaning because our existence is already determined as a Being-essentially-with-Others. Being alone, it follows, is 'a deficient mode of Being-with' (p. 157). Moreover, in so far as we always exist in a state of Being-with, it follows that our world is one that is characterizable in terms of our relations with Others: we are always concerned with them. Our existence is one which is determined in advance as one of 'care' or 'concern' not only for ourselves as individuated Daseins. It is true that what happens to me is *my* concern in so far as my Being is always and in each case 'mine', but I am also always concerned with Others. By this, Heidegger does not mean that we 'care for' Others in the sense of simply worrying what will happen to them, as we do in the context of personal relationships. We exist in a state of care with regard to Others in so far as we are always engaged with them, and we always have an understanding of who we are in virtue of the fact that Others are there, too. Putting it more bluntly, we are concerned about Others to the extent that we cannot ignore them: 'Being for, or against, or without one another, passing one another by, not "mattering" . . .' all exemplify this state of care (p. 158). All these are 'deficient or Indifferent' modes (or ways) of Being-with Others. Above all, though, the central point is that such modes are essentially characteristic of our *everyday* life: they tell us that there is an intrinsic difference that we implicitly hold to exist between Other people and 'Things'. Things we can be indifferent toward in the sense that they are simply 'there' and of no concern to us. Others, however, 'do not matter to one another'. Such 'not mattering' expresses something about *how* we are in the world: our 'indifference' toward one another in everyday life *shows* the degree to which we have a reciprocal relationship with one another in order to be the kind of entity we all are.

We can behave toward each other in all sorts of ways. But what is fundamental, Heidegger contends, is that we must always share a world in order even to 'not matter' to one another. Dasein 'is Being-in the same world in which, as encounterable for Others, it is there with them' (p. 160). A 'world', in other words, is always a shared world. This is an existential fact about us: it concerns the Being of Dasein, and hence is an ontological issue. Again, it is important here to note the move away from the 'epistemological' method of analysing the nature of human thought and knowledge. If human Being is always shared in Heidegger's sense, then we cannot understand ourselves by way of simple reflection upon the 'contents' of our minds. Self-knowledge rests upon an ontological precondition: 'Knowing oneself is grounded in Being-with, which understands primordially' by positing 'a relationship of Being from Dasein to Dasein' (pp. 161, 162). Equally, therefore, it is no use trying to speak of Others and the individual self in terms of which 'came first'. There is no order of priority here: the Being of Others and our own individuated Being are coterminous with one another: they are both existential characteristics of Dasein and must be understood as forming part of this totality.

1.12 The 'they'

Dasein is an entity that is absorbed in its world, and is what it is in virtue of the fact that that world is composed of Others as well. We live in the context of Others and judge ourselves by way of them. But Heidegger still has not really grappled with the problem of *who* Dasein is. Who is 'I' and 'You', and who are 'we' and 'Others'? Others '*are* what they do' (p. 163) – in other words, their practical activities in relation to us define them. In that we are concerned with Others we define ourselves in relation to them. We want to make sure that Others do not outstrip us in some way (who is paid more than 'me'?) or, if we have some kind of priority over them in some manner, we are keen to maintain this priority. This kind of relationship Heidegger calls one of '*distantiality*': we define our own Dasein (i.e. who we are) in terms of what separates us from Others. In such cases, Heidegger claims, our own Dasein 'itself *is* not; its Being has been taken away by the Others' (p. 164). Our sense of individual identity, in other words, is generated by way of reference to a normative understanding of what 'Others' are. But such Others 'are not *definite* Others': they are not 'Michael', 'Chris' or 'Andrew'. 'Others' in this sense are non-individuated, they are '*the "they"*', or people in general. Heidegger's analysis of the existential character of Dasein thus turns toward an impersonal realm of human affairs as being that on the basis of which individual identity is attributed. 'They' are there in everyday life. We judge ourselves by what 'they' do, what 'they' think. The force of the 'they' is that of conformity. The 'they' signifies a normative pressure whereby what counts as 'average' is determined in the public environment that makes up our world.

But, at the same time, each one of us is the 'they'. We all belong to the 'they' even as we assert our own identity in relation to it. This constitutes what Heidegger calls 'the real dictatorship of the "they"':

> We take pleasure, and enjoy ourselves, as *they* take pleasure; we read, see, and judge about literature and art as *they* see and judge; likewise we shrink back from the 'great mass' as *they* shrink back, we find 'shocking' what *they* find shocking. The 'they', which is nothing definite, and which all are, though not as the sum, prescribes the kind of Being of everydayness. (p. 164)

The 'they', then, is the average or normative structure of everyday life: by way of it differences are 'levelled-off', what is 'normal' is given priority. We, as individual Daseins, live out our lives in this context, which Heidegger terms '*die Offentlichkeit*': 'publicness', or the public sphere. In such a context, 'Everyone is the Other, and no one is himself' (p. 165). Heidegger is claiming that the fundamental conditions under which we become who are we rest upon the ontological structure wherein we judge ourselves by way of what 'they' think. The realm of the personal, it follows, exists in a fundamental relation to the realm of the public. In everyday life, who 'I' am is rendered understandable in terms of what 'they' think and do: 'The Self of everyday Dasein is the *they-self*' (p. 167).

The ontological structure of Dasein is, it follows, only understandable in terms of the 'they', which marks out the domain of our everyday existence. In turn, *who* Dasein is ('I', 'You') is derived on the basis of this background structure. This structure, however, is not to be confused with the structure which Kant attributed to the transcendental subject: 'the "they" is not something like a "universal subject" which a plurality of subjects have hovering above them' (p. 166). On the contrary, it is *lived out* concretely in the realm of everyday existence: it is the normative condition of our Being-in-the-world as *involved* entities.

1.13 Dasein as Being-towards-death

If we engage in an attempt to articulate Dasein as a whole we encounter one key problem. Even taken individually, Dasein is never a completed whole because its essence lies in its existence, its 'to be'. Likewise, once Dasein has ceased to be and hence is, in the vaguest of possible senses, 'complete', then there will be no Dasein left to engage in the analysis of Dasein. There is a contradiction between the attempt to articulate exhaustively what Dasein is and the fact that one cannot since, so long as it is, it is necessarily incomplete: 'When Dasein reaches its wholeness in death, it simultaneously loses the Being of its "there"', it is Dasein no more (p. 281). This is the problem of death (pp. 279ff). Death brings to completion the life of every Dasein, but no Dasein is capable of experiencing this completion. This is a somewhat long-winded way of saying that we cannot experience our own death. Of course we can experience the death of Others. But this does not entitle us to claim that we can thereby grasp their Being as a totality. What we do when we encounter the death of Others is to make sense of that death, through funeral rites, graves, acts of commemoration, etc. But making sense of the death of Others in this manner is to understand death from the standpoint of our own continued existence as living entities. 'Death', taken in this sense, is a continuation of life, for those who mourn the dead in doing so remain with them (p. 282). From this, Heidegger argues, it follows that death is, in every case, an individual matter: nobody can die 'for us' or go 'with' us: we all die our own death.

For Dasein death is not, therefore, some kind of 'limit' in the sense in which we can place limits on the jurisdiction of a country by representing its borders by drawing lines on a map. Death is not a 'boundary'. It is not some kind of line that encloses and thereby delineates the space of 'a life' in a determinate manner. If we take the example of a country's borders, there is something beyond the borders: other nations with their own national sovereignty, the spaces of oceans that do not fall under any national jurisdiction, etc. Death, in contrast, is not an 'outside', it is not 'somewhere' over the border. Death is not a 'limit' beyond which there will be 'something else'. Death is the *end* of Dasein, 'that is to say, [the end] of Being-in-the-world' (p. 292). As such, it is the end even of all borders and limits. Since Dasein and its world are conjoined, when any Dasein ceases to be in the world it simply ceases to be altogether. The death of the human body, we can say, is not another mode of Dasein's Being, it is the end of its Being *such that it is what it is*.

Humans, as *Dasein*, it follows, die in a specific sense. We can understand what Heidegger is saying by contrasting human death with the death of non-human animals. Where we can say that non-humans 'perish', we cannot say that Dasein simply does this (p. 291). Rather, Dasein *lives its life out* to the point of its 'demise'. Dasein's death differs from that of other organic entities since Dasein's Being is an issue for it. This means that Dasein's relationship with its own death will be different from that of any animal. An animal strives to survive and it does so as a part of its species. Likewise, its death has significance only as the death of a member of its species, not as the death of an entity that has a world, as Dasein does. In every case, an animal acts according to the forms of behaviour it possesses simply in virtue of being a member of its species: a cat does not 'choose' to hunt mice and birds, doing this is what cats simply 'do'. We can hunt, but we can decide not to; we can decide to live differently (the domestication of animals, vegetarianism). Dasein thus makes decisions with regard to what it will be and this matter is not determined in advance by its being a member of a species. Dasein's relationship to death, in turn, is a possible mode of its Being and is recognized as such by it. This possibility is an existentiell one: it is an empirical 'fact of life', so to speak, that can (and indeed will) happen. The possibility of death is the possibility of Dasein's running out of possibilities altogether: 'Dasein cannot outstrip the possibility of death. Death is the possibility of the absolute impossibility of Dasein' (p. 294).

As a possibility of Dasein's Being-in-the-world death is present at every moment of life. Equally, the inevitability of death makes it Dasein's 'ownmost possibility'. No action can ever remove the possibility of death from Dasein's life, and death is always and in each case a personal event. Every moment of Dasein's life, it follows, can always be its last. Thus, Dasein's Being is always a 'Being-towards-death'. As the threatening of Dasein with its own destruction death highlights Heidegger's contention that Dasein's Being is an issue for it: 'In Dasein there is undeniably a constant "lack of totality" which finds an end with death. This "not-yet" "belongs" to Dasein as long as it is; and this is how things stand phenomenally' (p. 286). Since what we are is never given as a completed totality, what we can become remains an issue for us. We are not like ripening fruit, which reaches a point at which its end is fulfilled and dies in fulfilling that end. We can die too early, for 'Even "unfulfilled" Dasein ends' (p. 288); and we can die too late.

The spectre of death, however, is avoided in everyday life. Indeed, as a rule we greet the possibility of death by running away from it. By fleeing in the face of death we embrace what Heidegger calls an 'inauthentic' mode of Being. More will be said about the notions of authenticity and inauthenticity in due course (see section 1.14, below). But for the moment we can say that being inauthentic in this context means refusing to face the fact that we are intrinsically mortal. For example, today people might place hope in a 'healthy' life-style, or in the power of technology, as a means of deferring death; or we might turn our backs on it by immersing ourselves in the world of our everyday concerns, or losing ourselves in various narcotics. There are numerous ways of being inauthentic in this sense. In contrast, an 'authentic' attitude toward death means acknowledging our mortality as *our own*. This does not mean that to be authentic we must become obsessed with our own forthcoming death (morbidity). It merely means that we must accept that death is the ever-present possibility that accompanies our existence and is essential to it. Such acknowledgement entails three things. First, that Dasein is aware of itself as an entity whose Being is an issue for it. Second, death obliges Dasein to accept that what matters about its existence is not just mere parts of it but the totality, for death is a possibility which accompanies living at all times. Third, death forces the recognition of the fact that life generally is lived in relation to others, who dictate the terms upon which much of life is lived (the 'they'). Being authentic means not accepting death as 'they' do, i.e. as something merely 'factual' about which one can afford to be 'indifferent' (p. 298).

Finally, as a non-relational possibility, death forces Dasein to accept that its Being is its own responsibility. To live authentically means not letting oneself become distracted by the attitudes of others or by the material world. Further, as a non-relational possibility death obliterates any sense of necessity or inevitability in life. Dasein must accept that death is inevitable. Therefore, whatever we do is a contingent matter, since we are ourselves contingent. Since this is the case, it is also the case that we need to recognize that there are no higher courts of necessity which determine what we are (the realm of the social has its limits when it comes to such an issue). If there are no higher courts of necessity then what we are and can become is a matter for us, not for 'society' or others, etc. Living authentically means accepting that we are ourselves responsible for changing the way things are with regard to the life-situation that has been forced upon us as entities which have been 'thrown into the world'.

1.14 Authenticity, inauthenticity and the 'call of conscience'

The ontological structure of Dasein's existence is rooted in the everydayness of the 'they'. But, Heidegger contends, it does not follow from this that Dasein is thereby condemned to conformity. Since Dasein's ' "essence" . . . lies in its "to be" [*Zu-sein*]', or to put it another way, '*The essence of Dasein lies in its existence*' (p. 67), *who* Dasein is not something determined in advance. The 'they' may comprise the ontological structure of Dasein's everyday world, but this structure does not prescribe how we, as individual Daseins, are to live our lives. It merely stipulates the conditions that comprise the everyday and so go toward making us who we are. Dasein's characteristics 'are in each case possible ways for it to be, and no more than that . . . [Hence] . . . when we designate this entity with the term "Dasein", we are expressing not its "what" (as if were a table, house or tree) but its Being'. Arguing that what we are is exclusively determined by the force of normative opinion, therefore, would be to treat us like 'Things', which we manifestly are not.

Moreover, Dasein is not only 'mine'. Equally, it is also 'mine to be in one way or another'. In other words, Dasein's Being-in-the-world is understood as a range of possibilities, not one determinate mode of Being (as, for example, plants *are* in a determinate sense: they cannot choose to be in any manner other than the one in which they exist). 'I' exist not just in one determinate manner, but as an entity that can make choices with regard to *how* I will be. In this way, Dasein always makes some kind of decision with regard to the *manner* in which is. It is clear, then, that for Heidegger, Dasein's *Being* is always an immanent condition of the existence of this entity in the context of the everyday. But this itself always involves Dasein's *recognizing* in some manner (or at least tacitly acknowledging) its Being as its own. As such, Dasein's Being is that toward which it therefore comports itself (i.e. that in relation to which it is always oriented) and it is therefore that with regard to which it has in some sense a role in deciding what it is (how it will be). We can, it follows, choose the path of conformity and be an instance of 'the "they self"', or we can resist it: 'because Dasein is in each case essentially its own possibility, it *can*, in its very Being, "choose" itself and win itself; it can also lose itself and never win itself; or only "seem" to do so' (p. 68). Dasein can make decisions about its own existence and in making these decisions it can recognize itself for what it is, or fail to do so. Such decisions are issues that concern what Heidegger calls Dasein's 'authenticity'.

Heidegger identifies the question of 'authenticity' in terms of Dasein's Being: authenticity, like 'Being-with' and the existence of the present-at-hand and the ready-to-hand, is a way of Being and essential to Dasein's existence. It, too, is an ontological matter. It is worth noting that Heidegger's argument is derived from a Kantian-style move: it is a conditions of possibility argument such as is laid out in the first *Critique*. But Heidegger has transposed it from the epistemological realm (which concerns the nature of knowledge) into the realm of existence/ontology. Whereas for Kant, knowledge is to be examined in terms of those conditions that allow for its possibility, for Heidegger, Dasein's Being-in-the-world as a Being that is characterized by 'mineness' *is* an essential component of its possibility. There is a sense, then, in which all Daseins are their own conditions of possibility, i.e. with regard to the decisions each of us can make concerning what we will become. The everyday world of the 'they' comprises an essential ontological condition, in that we *are* only in relation to Others. But *how* we are in relation to them is not a foregone conclusion: we can recognize our Being as our own (authenticity) or we can deliver it over to Others (inauthenticity).

Given Heidegger's characterization of Dasein in terms of its possibilities, it follows that inauthenticity is something that already presupposes authenticity. We can only be inauthentic in the sense of letting our existence be determined by the 'they self' because we can can recognize our existence as essentially our *own*: 'only in so far as it is something which can be *authentic* – that is, something of its own – can it have lost itself and not yet won itself' (p. 68). We can choose an authentic or an inauthentic mode of existence: we can embrace the 'they self', or we can recognize that who we are is a matter that concerns us. Authenticity and inauthenticity are, it follows, in equal measure derived from the fact that the Being of any particular Dasein is always characterized by its 'mineness'. It is worth noting, though, that 'to be inauthentic' does not denote any 'less' Being; nor a 'lower' form of Being: 'even in its fullest concretion Dasein can be characterised by inauthenticity – when busy, when excited, when interested, when ready for enjoyment.' Inauthentic existence is not a 'lesser' form of existence, since it *is* a way of Being no less than authentic existence.

Heidegger then turns to an analysis of 'conscience' as a means of explicating his case. It is conscience which 'summons Dasein's Self from its lostness in the "they"' (p. 319). The call of conscience just comes: it is not a matter of volition ('I' cannot 'choose' to be stung by my conscience, I simply am taken by it). 'The call comes *from* me and yet *from beyond me*' (p. 320). The call to authenticity is, in other words, a phenomenon of Dasein's Being. But what is the 'it' that does the calling? We have already noted (see section 1.6 above) that Dasein is characterizable as an entity that is 'thrown *into existence*', i.e. that it *is* its world. By being thrown into existence what is revealed to Dasein is the fact that it and its world are simply 'there'. That it exists in a world that is already understood in such terms characterizes what Heidegger calls Dasein's 'state of mind'. Such understanding need not be overt. Either *implicitly*, or *explicitly*, we understand we are in a world that is 'there' in this sense. This understanding is something we can turn away from (though by so doing we still cleave to it implicitly) by retreating into the everyday realm of the 'they'. We can turn our backs upon the issue of who we are and who we will become by just living according to the norm, by immersing ourselves in the everyday world and hence feeling 'at home' in it. But human Being is such that it is not at home in its world. This fact is attested to by the 'thrownness' (*Geworfenheit*) that Heidegger has already claimed characterizes Dasein's existence: it is thrown into its world, and as such its world is, at the same time, strange to it, 'uncanny' ('*unheimlich*': 'un-homely'). We can become anxious about ourselves on this account. This does not mean being anxious about something in particular ('will I get that pay-rise next month?', 'will I be able to afford a new car?'), but being anxious about *who* we are and *how* we are living, and hence whether we can live and *be* differently. The call of conscience, therefore, comes from our ontological composition; it is 'Dasein in its uncanniness: primordial, thrown Being-in-the-world as the "not-at-home" – the bare "that-it-is" in the "nothing" of the world. The caller is unfamiliar to the everyday they-self; it is something like an *alien* voice' (p. 321). Such a call to authenticity does not tell us that we should be such-and-such, or carry out some particular action. It merely indicates that we could be differently from how we are at present. The call of conscience is something that is characterized by its 'silence': it is not the chatter of the public sphere, but that which can call each Dasein '*back* from this *into the reticence of his existent* potentiality-for-Being' (p. 322). It is, in short, the call of the concern or 'care' which, as we have seen, characterizes our existence even in the public realm of Others and the 'they'. But, such a call of conscience is neither that of the public sphere nor of individual 'subjectivity'. It is, rather, an ontological characteristic of Dasein's Being.

1.15 The 'meaning of Being'

Heidegger never gets around to answering the question of the 'meaning of Being' directly, and there is at least one central reason for this that I will come to. But, for the moment, it can be noted that, for him, such a question must revolve around the ontological constitution of Dasein. We have seen that Being is not a 'something' that can be treated of in the manner appropriate to entities that are other than Dasein (in the manner, for instance, in which the botanist analyses plants). Being, rather, is that in virtue of which all humans, as Dasein, have an understanding of their world; and Being thereby essentially characterizes Dasein's engagement with that world. One point certainly follows from this fact: the question of the *meaning* of Being cannot be separated from the existence of Dasein as an entity that *interprets* its world. Since this is the case, we can say that the issue of meaning is one that must revolve around the problem of what interpretation is.

In line with the rigours of the hermeneutic model of understanding that he has formulated, all 'interpretation', Heidegger tells us, 'is never a presuppositionless apprehending of something presented to us [i.e. of something simply 'fore-given', *Vorgegebenen*]' (p. 192). To put it more simply, any act of interpretation necessarily brings with it some presupposition or other. The central question, though, concerns how one is to understand the nature of presupposition: 'How are we to conceive of the character of this "fore" [*Vor*]?' (p. 192). We do not, Heidegger notes, perceive Things as purely being present-at-hand and *then* interpret them as this or that particular '*x*' ('this dog', 'that stone'): 'In interpreting, we do not . . . throw a "signification" over some naked thing which is present-at-hand, we do not stick a value on [to] it' (p. 190). Our interpretation of any entity is not something that is subsequently *added* to our experience of some unmediated '*x*' as, for example, an empiricist would contend. Rather, one might say that for Heidegger *interpretation* is essential to our encountering any entity whatsoever, in that it forms the precondition of any such encounter.

But this position requires some modification, for even though interpretation is essential, it does not follow that interpretation 'goes all the way down', as a thinker like Nietzsche would argue. All interpretation presupposes an understanding within which it takes place. Whenever we encounter an entity within the world we encounter it as something that exists within-the-world 'as such'. We do not, in other words, 'interpret' our world into existence: it is 'there' already as that whereby we can interpret and attribute meaning to what we encounter in it. We already presuppose that there 'is' a world, that there is a totality ('world') of which any entity is a part. Any particular '*x*' is necessarily already understood as being part of our world, it already has 'an involvement which is disclosed in our understanding of the world, and this involvement is one which gets laid out by the interpretation' (pp. 190–1). Any act of interpretation is thereby a kind of exposition of what we encounter in our world that is itself 'grounded in *something we have in advance* – in a *fore-having* [*Vorhabe*]' (p. 191). And 'fore-having' is an intrinsic aspect of any act of understanding. Interpretation is thus what Heidegger terms 'the appropriation of understanding'. It seizes hold of what is already understood, and what is already understood is 'a totality of involvements . . . which recedes into an understanding which does not stand out from the background'. Interpretation always operates in relation to a 'fore-having'. This fore-having offers the possibility of interpretation; but the determination of what it is that is to be interpreted as a particular '*x*' is 'grounded in *something we see in advance* – in a *fore-sight* [*Vorsicht*]'. Fore-sight ' "takes the first cut" out of what has been taken into our fore-having, and it does so with a view to a definite way in which this can be interpreted'. In turn, fore-sight 'is grounded in *something we grasp in advance* – in a *fore-conception*' whose function is to provide a determinate sense concerning what it is that we are interpreting. This is the case even if that sense turns out to be the wrong one: our interpretation of an entity can be challenged by the fact that it does not always behave in the manner in which we expected it to.

Interpretation thereby rests upon understanding. And understanding itself is structured by these three 'fores': 'fore-having' sets up the possibility of interpretation; 'fore-sight' determines that there is a something to be interpreted; 'fore-conception' determines in a preliminary way what that 'something' is. The interpretation of any entity *as an entity* presupposes these three elements. That is why any act of interpretation is never without presupposition: understanding involves projection, and projection always requires presuppositions that constitute a structure within which it can take place. What an entity '*is*' has a fundamental relation to this structure, since this structure comprises an entity which itself has Being, namely Dasein. Understanding is something that we, as Dasein, have. Meaning flows out of this. When 'entities within-the-world . . . have come to be understood we say that they have *meaning* [*Sinn*]', i.e. that they make 'sense' to us. 'Meaning', for Heidegger, thus entails that some particular '*x*' ('this dog', 'that flower', etc.) is encountered within a totality of relations. Meaning is thereby always a matter of 'reference-relationships': the sentence '*x* is to the right of *y*' expresses a meaning, i.e. the relationship between *x* and *y*. These reference-relationships are rendered possible by understanding.

But what is understood 'taken strictly is not the meaning but the entity, or alternatively, Being' (pp. 192–3). In other words, we encounter entities in our world, and what is thereby disclosed is our relationship with them as one of Being: meaning discloses our world to us as it is. This is because *'Meaning is the "upon which" of a projection in terms of which something becomes intelligible [verständlich*, i.e. understandable] *as something; it* [i.e. meaning] *gets its structure from a fore-having, a fore-sight and a fore-conception'* (p. 193). Putting the matter more simply, 'meaning' springs from the existence of Dasein, and is hence 'not a property attaching to entities'. From this it follows that *'only Dasein can be meaningful [sinnvoll] or meaningless [sinnlos]'*, and that any other kind of entity can only be thought of as *'unmeaning [unsinniges]'*, i.e. as 'essentially devoid of any meaning at all'. That is why certain events in life, like natural disasters (earthquakes, floods, etc.), are not meaningful for us but *'absurd'*. Such events 'can break in upon us and destroy us' but we cannot assign them a 'meaning' in the sense in which we can do so with regard to the actions of other people or ourselves.

From this we can conclude that Heidegger believes that entities have some degree of independence from our thought. Natural forces can impinge upon our lives and even sweep them away. Entities, if they could be taken independently of us, would be 'real', but there would be no 'reality', since this is a word that expresses our relation with entities. The significance of the world, in so far as it can have any significance at all and so be called a 'world', is a matter that concerns us alone:

> Of course, only as long as Dasein *is* (that is, only as long as an understanding of Being is ontically possible) 'is there' Being ['*gibt es*' *Sein*]. When Dasein does not exist, 'independence' 'is' not either, nor 'is' the 'in-itself' . . . *In such a case* it cannot be said that entities are, nor can it be said that they are not. But *now*, as long as there is an understanding of Being and therefore an understanding of presence-at-hand, it can indeed be said that *in this case* entities will continue to be. (*Being and Time*, 255)

Dasein, it follows, is a necessary condition for the question of the meaning of Being to be raised: Dasein itself bestows Being. Without Dasein there is no meaning of any kind which can be attributed to the Being of entities. If Dasein were not, then it could not meaningfully be said that entities 'are'. The sense of 'Being', it follows, is dependent on the presence of an understanding of it: 'Being (not entities) is dependent upon the understanding of Being; that is to say, Reality (not the Real) is dependent upon care.' The 'Real', we might say, consists merely of entities, and without us entities cannot be endowed with the characteristic of 'Reality', for it is our concern with our world that engenders this possibility. That is why Being is always the Being of *an* entity; which is to say that Being is always the Being of Dasein.

1.16   Three criticisms

Even so, the question of Being has not been answered. Nor, to be fair, did Heidegger intend to answer it in *Being and Time*. All this text seeks to do is to articulate the terrain upon which such a question may subsequently be addressed and Heidegger planned a further volume to take us the rest of the way. But this projected work never came to fruition. The later Heidegger does not abandon the problem of Being. However, he chose to address it from a different perspective which turns away from asserting the ontological priority of Dasein. Three criticisms of the ontology of *Being and Time* might suggest why Heidegger chose to pursue the problem of Being from other angles. The first of these concerns the question of authenticity.

We might well ask how authenticity is possible at all, given the sheer force of the normative structure of the 'they'. If 'we' are 'they', as Heidegger contends, and 'they' are inauthentic, it is hard to see how the 'call of conscience' that summons us to address the question of the kind of existence we are leading is genuinely possible. If such a call is an 'alien voice' that tells us we are not at home in our world then there is a sense in which we are not our world, as Heidegger ultimately contends: the Being of Dasein cannot be identical with the conditions of its possibility. If this is so, then Dasein's Being cannot be determined merely by way of an existential analytic of its everydayness. True, the hidden ontological structure which underlies the every-day world of Dasein's life is not itself inauthentic, but neither need we be committed to determining it *a priori* as 'authentic', as Heidegger seems to do in order to argue the case for authenticity. The 'it' which calls us to authenticity, which in the end means acknowledging that one's existence can always be different, that one need not be determined in one's Being by the forces of social conformity, ultimately fractures the ontological model. By arguing that this 'it' is located within Dasein itself, and despite himself, Heidegger recapitulates a version of the transcendental subject. 'It' is the continual precondition of the possibility of Dasein, and as such 'it' under-lies the social fabric that comprises Dasein's everyday world and calls to us from 'beyond' that world. In this manner, we become the 'cause' of our own subjective Being-in-the-world by transcending its determinacy: what 'I' am authentically means not letting my life and hence my identity be determined by the normative force of the 'they'. The later Heidegger is to maintain that such 'transcendence' is indeed possible, but that this possibility cannot be developed on the basis of an analysis of Dasein alone: existential ontology must give way to a poetic language which *shows* Being rather than says (i.e. analyses) it.

Amongst Heidegger's contemporaries, Adorno is probably his most outspoken critic. For Adorno, Heideggerean ontology is merely another recapitulation of first philosophy. Turning to an analysis of Dasein's everydayness as a means of explicating its ontological structure involves making a move which ignores the socially mediated conditions of thought and thereby covers over its inherently political nature. Foremost amongst Adorno's targets is Heidegger's conception of authenticity. Any appeal to authenticity, he argues, can all too easily validate slipping into the very conformity that it purportedly rejects by becoming a mere 'jargon'. In turn, the real problem of subjectivity, namely its mediating and inherently unpredictable role in the determina-tion of conceptual thought, vanishes beneath an ontological 'aura' which naturalizes the inherent tensions within social relations even as it claims to reject their authority. Moreover, Adorno claims, despite Heidegger's protestations to the contrary, Dasein in fact represents another variant of the conception of subjectivity that defines it primarily in terms of individual self-consciousness. Although Dasein is engaged in a world that is structured by the activity of practically grasping it in the form of the 'ready-to-hand', and its world is mediated by the 'they', nevertheless this entity's self-consciousness is taken as ontologically significant, as an unmediated fact:

> Heidegger supplants the traditional category of subjectivity by Dasein, whose essence is existence. Being, however, which 'is an *issue* for this entity in its very Being, is in each case mine'. This is meant to distinguish subjectivity from all other existent being . . . to prohibit existence from being 'taken ontologically as an instance or special case of some genus of entities as things that are present-at-hand'. This construction . . . would like to make possible a starting out from some element of being. This latter is valued as the immediate givenness of the facts of consciousness in traditional epistemology; yet, at the same time, this element of being is supposed to be more than mere fact . . . Behind the apersonal 'is concerned' is hidden nothing more than the fact that Dasein is consciousness.[16]

In turn, Heidegger's characterization of Dasein as 'in each case mine', Adorno argues, can be interpreted as a naturalization of the power relations inherent within modern society. As modern society is structured by relations of power and ownership so Dasein, too, is a piece of property. It is something that is owned in a manner akin to the way in which a merchant owns goods. In this way, socially mediated relations of possession are 'ontologized' and rendered natural; they are taken as 'given' in the same way in which empiricism thinks of facts as mere givens that require no critical interrogation.[17]

That said, there is in fact much that Adorno's and Heidegger's thought have in common. Both turn away from the foundationalism of traditional epistemology and metaphysics toward a more contextual understanding of human life. Equally, we can find an analogy between Heidegger's conception of the 'they' and Adorno's claim that subjective conditions are mediated by objective (normative) conditions. There may, therefore, be another contributory reason for Adorno's virulent polemic against Heideggereanism: the fact of Heidegger's own political involvement with the Nazis in the 1930s. This is not the place to get into this issue, but it is certainly the case that Heidegger, albeit perhaps for a comparatively brief period, saw German National Socialism as being conducive to the furthering of his philosophical vision. For the moment, all I will say is that it is quite possible for a philosopher, as someone who is a 'lover of wisdom', to be unwise and still be a great philosopher (although someone's being a great philosopher does not mean that we need to agree with them).

By way of a third point against the project of *Being and Time* we might well ask 'Why Being at all?' Why privilege the tradition of Greek thought as Heidegger does and then use this as the justification for pursuing fundamental ontology? Of course, plenty of other philosophers have expressed an admiration for Ancient Greek culture, including Hegel and Nietzsche (who seems to have felt his relation to the Greeks in very personal terms). It is true that the philosophical tradition owes much, if not everything, to the writings of figures like Plato and Aristotle. Heidegger makes very explicit claims concerning the importance of the western 'metaphysical tradition': it is, in 'inauthentic' form, the medium through which the question of Being has been 'passed down' to us and we need to destroy it in order to develop an authentic ontology. But, as Nietzsche has argued, does destroying this tradition, if such an act is possible and such a monolithic 'thing' like this tradition really exists, entail a return to Being, even if it is understood by way of a turn toward temporality? Why not becoming, as Nietzsche urges us? Two thinkers who take Nietzsche's challenge seriously are Deleuze and Guattari.

2   Deleuze and Guattari: An Ontology of Becoming

The French philosopher Gilles Deleuze's name is often associated with 'poststructuralism'.[18] His work, a good deal of which was co-authored with Félix Guattari, encompasses a wide range of influences and an equally diverse range of areas: for example, questions in epistemology and metaphysics, an engagement with Freudian psychoanalysis, semiotics, and theories of meaning. Deleuze's influential interpretation of Nietzsche's thought in *Nietzsche and Philosophy* (1962) offers an approach that contrasts starkly with those of Anglo-American and German commentators on Nietzsche's work. And it is in large part from Nietzsche that Deleuze, both alone and in conjunction with Guattari, develops an approach which advocates an ontology of 'becoming' and a 'polymorphous-perverse' conception of subjectivity. The ontology of becoming, however, is not for Deleuze something that begins only with Nietzsche. Just as Nietzsche revives aspects of Hume's empiricism in order to attack the 'mummifying' tendencies of non-historical philosophers, so Deleuze turns to the example of empiricism as a means of furnishing an elucidation of his conception of becoming. As Deleuze says in *Dialogues* (1977) 'I have always felt that I am an empiricist, that is, a pluralist'.[19] What he means by this can be explained most clearly by contrasting his conception of empiricism with rationalistic philosophies. Rationalism, Deleuze argues, is a philosophical enterprise that proceeds by way of abstract concepts and seeks to determine the nature of reality by presupposing that it will ultimately in some way match these concepts: 'One starts with abstractions such as the One, the Whole, the Subject, and one looks for the process by which they are embodied in a world which they make conform to their requirements.' The rationalist begins with a particular kind of judgement concerning the relationship between our concepts and what we conceptualize. Empiricism, in contrast, 'starts with a completely different evaluation'. Instead of beginning with abstraction, empiricism begins with 'states of things' and seeks to extract concepts from them. Empiricism, in other words, generates its concepts out of an engagement with the material world. As such, empiricism does not proceed from a theoretical starting point. Indeed, it does not have a first principle at all:[20] 'Empiricists are not theoreticians, they are experimenters: they never interpret, they have no principles' (*Dialogues*, 55). Such an account of empiricism actually entails turning 'experience' into a pseudo-starting point, one that is immediately open to challenge as soon as a thinker like Hume begins to experiment. For Hume, Deleuze contends, is a philosopher who thinks 'AND' not 'IS': he is someone who always makes links and connections and thus continually invokes multiplicity, not unity.

But what, we might ask, are the 'states of things' with which empiricism deals? This is an important question. For Deleuze, 'States of things are neither unities nor totalities, but *multiplicities*.' By this he means that 'states of things' are never them-selves determinate 'things'. All such states 'are irreducible to one another' and hence cannot be added together to make up a unified 'whole', for all 'wholes' are themselves composed of multiplicities. The word 'multiplicity' in this way 'designates a set of lines or dimensions which are irreducible to one another'. Although Deleuze rejects all talk of language as either being literal or metaphorical, we can use a metaphor to illustrate this point: the image of the 'line'. Imagine a set of lines strung out across one another. Wherever two or more of these lines cross we get the conjunction of each different line, which forms the 'point' of their intersection. Think of such points of intersection as 'states of things'. We can now develop this metaphor one stage further. Instead of thinking of these lines as being like finite 'pieces' of string that stretch from one point to another in two dimensions, put them into three dimensions and think of them as being in a constant state of 'growth'. The most informative example Deleuze uses to illustrate this is that of the 'rhizome' (a notion which will become central to his and Guattari's approach). A rhizome is a kind of plant that does not germinate in the ground and develop a root structure like a tree, which puts down roots. A rhizome, in contrast, has no 'foundations' and is not fixed to the spot. Instead, rhizomes throw out tubers. These tubers move over surfaces putting down temporary instead of permanent roots, and then they carry on moving. Imagine a number of rhizomes in a wood, blackberries for example, throwing out tubers, moving through the wood, entwining with one another. Now remove the wood so you just have the tubers. The points of intersection are the consequence of this process of growth, and this process is what Deleuze calls 'becoming'. Becoming therefore constitutes a process of movement. Such movement cannot be grasped conceptually, it 'always happpens behind the thinker's back, or is the moment when he blinks' (*Dialogues*, 1). 'Becoming' signifies a plurality of events and is not deter-mined by how things are. It is not, to put it another way, 'rooted' in determinate states of affairs or things. As such, becoming never involves imitation or mimicry because it does not concern a '*what*': 'The question "What are you becoming?" is particularly stupid' (p. 2).[21] Why? Because when someone or something becomes, what he, she or it is becoming also changes. Becomings do not concern the nature of 'things', in so far as things (states of things) *emerge out of becomings*.

The notion of the rhizome, it follows, offers us a different model of thought from that presented by traditional epistemology. Thought does not involve the forming of representations of the world of 'experience' but forms a rhizome with it. We, as bodily beings, form a rhizome with the world. If we get drunk, for example, we form a particular kind of rhizome with another form of life: the human combines with what is produced by the living process of fermentation. Talk about rhizomes does not, it follows, consist in providing an account of our representations of states of affairs (how things are), but an analysis of the congruence of different bodies and forces interacting in a reciprocal fashion. Rhizomes give rise to 'assemblages': ensembles of heterogeneous (i.e. different in kind) forces situated in relation to one another. We can say of an assemblage that it is 'a multiplicity which is made up of many heterogeneous terms' (*Dialogues*, 69). Any assemblage is a kind of unity that is the consequence of the 'co-functioning' of different elements, e.g. 'MAN-HORSE-STIRRUP'. Out of these co-functioning elements we get an assemblage. Clearly, this kind of conception requires that we no longer think of human beings, for example, as conceptualizable in a manner that separates them from their environment. When humans came to form a relationship with horses a new unity was produced that is neither that of 'man' horse or stirrup (i.e. tool) alone. What we get is 'a new man-animal symbiosis, a new assemblage of war' (p. 70). In such a symbiosis 'humans' change just as much as horses do. This assemblage represents a 'becoming-different'. A rhizome, then, operates by connecting heterogeneous parts; it is a unity composed of multiplicity, and its parts are themselves multiplicities. In turn, rhizomes have no beginning or end. A rhizome is 'always a middle', a 'plateau' composed of multiple elements (see *A Thousand Plateaus*, 21).

We can illustrate this conception further by turning to the notion of subjectivity. On a Deleuzean view, what we term 'subjectivity' does not denote a 'something' that is determinate and unified. Rather, subjectivity is itself both produced by and composed of a multiplicity of lines of becoming, in the same way that 'the skin is a collection of pores, the slipper, a field of stitches.' Any given multiplicity can have concepts 'extracted' from it. 'To extract the concepts which correspond to a multiplicity is to trace the lines of which it is made up, to determine the nature of these lines, to see how they become entangled, connect, bifurcate . . . These lines are true *becomings*, which are distinct not only from unities, but from the history in which they are developed' (*Dialogues*, viii). Thus, for Deleuze, the word 'becoming' signals a vitalistic process composed of a multiplicity of forces that have ontological priority over the domains of 'society' and 'history'. 'Reality', we might say, becomes. Reality is not a 'whole', a unity that can be articulated by way of reference to prior concepts, but a constant becoming of forces that, when they intersect, create wholes. Following Nietzsche, the truth is that there is no 'Reality'. We can think in concepts, but concepts, too, are *created* out of multiplicities and are themselves multiple. As Deleuze and Guattari put it in *What is Philosophy?* (1991): 'There are no simple concepts. Every concept . . . is a multiplicity, although not every multiplicity is conceptual.'[22] In other words, the multiple conditions that give rise to concepts are not themselves conceptual, for the word 'becoming' does not denote a concept, it denotes a plurality of possible intersections, of 'events'.

It is, Deleuze tells us, to the credit of empiricism that it realizes this fact in philosophical form. As a philosophical approach, empiricism concentrates on creating concepts out of 'states of things' rather than beginning with an act of conceptual abstraction and trying to fit the world into the concept: 'Empiricism knows only events and other people and is therefore a great creator of concepts. Its force begins from the moment it defines the subject: a *habitus*, a habit, nothing but a habit in a field of immanence, the habit of saying I.'[23] The subject, too, is a mere intersection of lines of force, a (linguistically determined) habit that has no essential 'core' that makes it what it is in virtue of its concept. The concept comes *after* the habit of 'saying I', it is an 'event'. We need, at this juncture, to clarify two points. What is an 'event'? Moreover, what are the conditions that give rise to subjectivity? These two questions can be addressed by turning to two different but related works: Deleuze's *The Logic of Sense* (1969) and Deleuze and Guattari's *A Thousand Plateaus* (1980).

2.1 'Pure Events'

At one level, *The Logic of Sense*[24] deals with the writings of someone most famous for his 'childrens' books', such as *Alice in Wonderland*: Lewis Carroll. But Carroll's works are not mere children's stories, any more than an eminent logician like Carroll is merely a writer of 'fantasy'. For Deleuze, Carroll's works present the reader with something out of the ordinary. This 'something' is neither a matter of mere fantasy nor of 'nonsense'. Carroll's writings are concerned with 'a category of very special things: events, pure events' (*The Logic of Sense*, 1). Deleuze seeks to analyse the nature of these pure events. In doing so he will raise two issues. First, there is an ontological issue about the nature of existence, its ground and basis. For Deleuze, this problem can be explored and clarified by way of a critical engagement with the platonic conception of 'being'. Second, there is a question concerning 'sense' or meaning. This is a conceptual matter that concerns the nature of language, and especially propositions. These two issues are related, for language and becoming are, in Deleuze's conception, essentially conjoined. According to Deleuze's view, then, it must be noted that questions about language and sense are also ontological questions: they concern becoming.

On a Deleuzean account, a 'pure event' is, one might say, a mere 'happening'. It is a 'going-on' that does not pertain to a determinate content with regard to its identity. Strictly speaking, one may say that *it has no identity*. As a means of elucidating this claim one may turn to Deleuze's comments, in the first of his discussions of what he calls 'the paradoxes of pure becoming', concerning a distinction drawn by Plato between two 'dimensions' of existence. The *first* dimension is the realm of determinate identities, of fixed properties, of entities and speakers who dwell in a temporally situated and structured present that has horizons and therefore limits or boundaries. Within this realm, a speaker can assign an entity a set of determinate characteristics. These characteristics, taken at any given moment, designate what an entity is, and as such they constitute its identity. Thus, a thing has a particular size, weight, colour, etc., and attributing these kinds of characteristics to the thing tells you something about it: they allow you to determine *what it is*. The *second* dimension, however, undercuts the possibility of such conceptualization. It is the realm of 'pure becoming without measure, a veritable becoming-mad, which never rests' (*The Logic of Sense*, 1–2). In this domain there is a confusion of temporal relationships and a resultant overturning and disordering. As such, it 'eludes the present' since ceaseless change and alteration does not so much occur 'within' this realm as constitute it as what it is. Such an elision precludes the possibility of speaking of entities with determinate properties. Thereby the notion that reality can be understood solely in terms of determinate states of things which may be ascribed a truth-value[25] is overturned.

Deleuze claims that a dualism is instigated within the platonic account. On the one hand, we have the fixed and determinate states that pertain to the identity of entities located within a temporal series of causes and effects. On the other, there is 'pure becoming'. Such becoming 'always eludes the present, causing future and past, more and less, too much and not enough to coincide in the simultaneity of a rebellious matter' (p. 2). In other words, it is a topsy-turvy realm, one dominated by becoming. And this realm has nothing to do with the definitions and modes of categorization that serve to structure and fix meanings. The process of becoming inherent in such a realm disrupts the coherence that the attribution of stability presupposes. It may be helpful to offer an example of this. Plato notes in the dialogue *Philebus* that the words 'hotter' and 'colder' signify a process that is interminable. That which 'becomes hotter' can never finally become so; for, if it could, 'hotter' would signify a determinate state of existence, and that which becomes hotter would then *be* hotter which is impossible, since 'hotter' signifies becoming not being. The word 'hotter' cannot signify a definite quality that a thing might have, since a thing's having a definite quality means that it has 'stopped going on and is fixed'.[26] It follows that becoming is thereby opposed to being, since becoming is that which disrupts the possibility of fixing and thereby determining identities, which in turn constitutes the possibility of conceptualizing the realm of being.

Deleuze argues that what is at work within Plato's distinction between being and becoming is 'a subterranean dualism between that which receives the action of the Idea and that which eludes this action'. In other words, this model draws a distinction between two incompatible realms. The one is conceptualizable (being), the other is not (becoming). What is at stake within this subterranean duality? Whatever it might be it is not, Deleuze holds, to be understood in epistemological terms. It is not a matter of drawing distinctions between, for instance, the realms of the sensible and the intelligible, between empirical experience and our concepts ('Ideas'). On this epistemological view, the duality would merely concern the disjunction between the material existence of entities and the conceptual scheme of ideas that we, as thinking subjects, employ in order to comprehend them. Concepts would be copies of sense-data, and such copies would be adequate to the representation of such data to the extent to which they correspond in some way to them. But what is at stake here is not epistemological, in that it concerns the fact that becoming places a question mark over the very positing of such distinctions and dualities. What we are faced with is a matter of 'simulacra'. The realm of simulacra is one in which the divisions that are generally held to exist between appearance and reality collapse, and in this way the distinction between 'sensible' and 'intelligible' is subverted. In this realm we cannot have recourse to any epistemological theories about what we know that start from a ready-made distinction between subject and experience, between mind and world: 'Pure becoming, the unlimited . . . eludes the action of the Idea . . . it contests *both* model *and* copy at once. Limited things lie beneath the Ideas; but even beneath things, is there not still this mad element which subsists and occurs on the other side of the order that Ideas impose and things receive?' (*The Logic of Sense*, 2). Even the realm of 'sensibility' (to use a Kantian term) is not coterminous with becoming, for becoming is not a matter of existence but *subsistence*. Becoming is not *opposed* to the being of entities: it subsists within them as the condition of their possibility.

2.2   Language

Significantly, Deleuze poses the question as to whether this 'mad element' may not be 'essential to language, as in the case of a "flow" of speech'. Equally, he wonders, might there not be *two* languages, one designating those moments in which a concept determines an entity as being in a particular state at a particular time (i.e. as having determinate identity), the other 'expressing the movements or rebel becomings'? Or, again, is it not possible that being and becoming signify two realms 'internal to language in general'? Language might be both that which fixes and determines the limits of its referential use, and yet at the same time 'transcends' these limits in a flow of ongoing meaning.[27]

Taken in this last way, 'language in general' will constitute a process of continuous reversal; a process in which identities are both stipulated and subsequently overturned, in that language both establishes limits and at the same time overcomes those limits. When I refer to an entity, the very act of referring provides a range within which what is referred to can be stipulated. Yet, the 'movement' (to speak in metaphor) of language is a simultaneous transcendence of those limits: language itself provides a context that it then immediately escapes from. This transcendence, says Deleuze, is 'the paradox of infinite identity'. In infinite identity determinate senses which are opposed in simultaneity – for instance 'future and past . . . the day before and the day after . . . more and less, . . . too much and not enough, . . . active and passive, . . . cause and effect' – are juxtaposed at one and the same time. Infinite identity is thus a moment at which no single sense could be said to function in a manner unfettered by the presence of its opposite. The present, likewise, is 'always being eluded – "jam tomorrow and jam yesterday – but never jam *to-day*" ', to cite a passage from Carroll (*The Logic of Sense*, 3). Indeed, the text of Lewis Carroll's *Alice*, Deleuze claims, both presents and revels in such paradoxes. Alice becomes larger, but in becoming larger she is simultaneously smaller than she will become; she exists in a domain in which it is possible 'to be punished before having committed a fault, to cry before having pricked oneself, to serve before having divided up the servings'. Such disorderings have a single result: Alice's identity is thrown into question; her proper name is lost in a barrage of verbs, a realm of pure events. What is thereby rendered problematic is the singularity of the name, its determinacy. For, to possess a proper name one must have recourse both to words that describe and words that are cognitive.[28] Where these words are subverted by the predominance of verbs the linkings necessary for the constitution of personal identity are no longer possible: 'when the names of pause and rest are carried away by the verbs of pure becoming and slide into the language of events, all identity disappears from the self, the world, and God.'

2.3   A Stoic ontology

The Stoics,[29] Deleuze tells us in the second elucidation of paradoxes of pure becoming, also offer us a dualism as Plato does. But it is not the duality of the sensible and the intelligible. In the first place, there is a domain of bodies. Bodies possess physical characteristics; agency (activity) is one of their features. 'States of affairs' are for the Stoics constituted through the 'mixtures of [such] bodies' (p. 4). Both bodies and states of affairs exist in the present, which is a 'temporal extension' of their activity. All bodies are situated in relation to other bodies and this relation constitutes a holistic unity 'called Destiny', a 'cosmic present [which] embraces the entire universe: only bodies exist in space, and only the present exists in time'. The present is the whole articulated at any one point in terms of the totality of relations between bodies. All bodies pertain to a *causal* relationship with one another, which takes the form of a reciprocal tension. As such, they are none of them the *effects* of the activity of others, in so far as all bodies both act and are acted upon in a condition of mutual reciprocity. To put it more or less simply: a body, X, is a cause of its relationship with another body, Y; but Y, too, is also a cause of its relationship with X. Thus, X is a cause for Y, and Y is a cause for X, but neither is an effect produced by the other in the capacity of its status as a body. According to such a view bodies are, Deleuze tells us, to be understood as 'causes in relation to each other and for each other'.

In the second place, however, there is the question of what such bodies are causes of. What, in other words, are their effects?

> These *effects* are not bodies, but, properly speaking, 'incorporeal' entities. They are not physical qualities and properties, but rather logical and dialectical attributes. They are not things or facts, but events. We cannot say that they exist, but rather that they subsist or inhere (having this minimum of being which is appropriate to that which is not a thing, a non-existing entity). They are not substantives or adjectives, but verbs. . . . They are not living presents, but infinitives . . . the becoming which divides itself infinitely in past and future and always eludes the present.   (pp. 4–5)

In other words, the effects of bodies are *attributes* not properties. These attributes do not exist, they *subsist*. The Stoic cosmos is, in this way, a temporal duality: a totality which constitutes the unity of the living present of relations between bodies acting upon one another, and additionally a realm of incorporeal surface-effects produced by these relations. *These incorporeal effects or entities are events.* A body can be cut by a blade, or it can become larger or smaller, but such happenings are not matters concerning the properties which a body may have, taken in terms of a range of 'quantitative and qualitative states of affairs' (p. 6). Events are the effects of these states of affairs, and occur at the level of surfaces.

Deleuze claims that Stoicism initiates a 'new dualism of bodies or states of affairs and effects or incorporeal events'. In doing so, it engenders a reversal of platonism. If we follow this reversal we enter into the realm of the simulacrum, a domain of images 'without resemblance' (p. 257), for events do not pertain to the determinacy of objects endowed with quantifiable characteristics. Indeed, even the notion of 'resemblance' eludes the domain of the simulacrum, because becomings do not 'resemble' anything. They are not copies of bodies, but their effects, a matter of surfaces and their manifestation.

2.4   *'Becoming is . . . coextensive with language'*

For Deleuze, such things are not a matter only of ontology. What we are presented with is an overturning of at least one kind of ontology – that which draws a distinction between an entity and its intelligibility, between 'appearance' and 'reality', and between our conceptual language and the 'world'. This is because events are not intelligible in terms of the determinate properties of entities, since they relate to becoming: 'The event is coextensive with becoming, and becoming is itself coextensive with language' (p. 8). Language, in turn, instantiates becoming through verbs ('to grow', 'to shrink', 'to cut') and through linguistic paradoxes: '[T]he paradox is . . . essentially . . . a series of interrogative propositions which, following becoming, proceed through successive additions and retrenchments. Everything happens at the boundary between things and propositions' (p. 8). In paradox, the ontological metaphor of 'depth' (the distinction between the apparent and what lies *underneath*, the 'real') is overturned. In the humour of Stoic paradox ('Chrysippus taught "If you say something it passes through your lips; so, if you say "chariot," a chariot passes through your lips') such depth is denied.

All propositions are, of course, linguistic. Deleuze's analysis is, therefore, intimately bound up with an account of the nature of language. As we have seen, he argues that language is coterminous with becoming, with events: 'the surface effects in one and the same Event, which would hold for all events, bring to language becoming and paradoxes' (p. 11). Language is not, it follows, a matter of plumbing the depths, but of skirting the surfaces between bodies, of non-senses and superficialities. But what, then, is the relationship between language and effects, between language and pure events?

2.5 Three relations of propositions: denotation, manifestation and signification

One thing can be said straight away concerning the relation between language and events. All events can be characterized as being, at least in principle, 'expressed or expressible, uttered or utterable, in propositions' (*The Logic of Sense*, 12). Events, in short, are coexistent with the *form* of propositions. Deleuze sets out an analysis of propositions in terms of three relations.

The first relation: a proposition denotes states of affairs. It expresses a relationship between things by associating words with '*particular* images' and individuating the properties that constitute particular states of affairs. The selection of words which correspond to the images, and which in turn correspond to states of affairs, allows for the identification of a state of affairs to be determined: ' "it is that," or "it is not that".' However, there are specific words within any proposition that do not pertain to any determinacy with regard to its content. These are deictic words (Deleuze calls them 'indexicals' or 'designators'): 'here', 'there', 'now', 'that', 'this', etc. Deictics are words that point to things. But they do not stipulate which things. They allude to states of affairs, but they do not state and thereby specify *which* states of affairs they allude to. Likewise, proper names are deictics, but have a special place, since they denote 'properly material singularities' and are thus privileged instances of them. With denotation we are in the logical domain of truth and falsity. Having the property of 'being true' means that the state of affairs denoted by the proposition and its deictic elements is fulfilled and is the case, while being false means that it does not and is not the case.

The second relation is the relationship between a proposition and a speaker who, in uttering the proposition, is engaged in expressing their own dispositions, attitudes, etc. This relationship is 'often called "manifestation"'. Manifestation appears as 'a statement of desires and beliefs which correspond to the proposition' (p. 13). That is, desiring and believing are states that reflect in some manner the content of the proposition itself. Desires, Deleuze claims, are the 'internal' causes of images with regard to what is being spoken about (i.e. a thing or state of affairs). Beliefs are those presuppositions that take there to be an external realm of causality which gives rise to states of affairs. Propositions contain 'manifesters', 'I, you, tomorrow, always, elsewhere, everywhere, etc.', of which 'I' is necessarily a privileged case (for the manifester 'I' is always presupposed in the expression of a speaker's dispositions). Manifestation, Deleuze argues, is primary with regard to denotation – it has priority over it. Without manifestation denotation would not be possible. This is because speaking always presupposes a relationship which can be inferred with regard to what is being spoken about *prior* to the indication or denotation of states of affairs which constitute instances of that relationship. Without the manifester 'I' denotation could not occur: the 'I' 'constitute[s] the domain of the *personal*, which functions as the principle of all possible denotation'. In other words, all denotation presupposes that one speaks from *somewhere* as *someone*. In turn, a logical displacement occurs in moving between denotation and manifestation: one moves from the realm of truth and falsity to that of truthfulness and illusion, from states of affairs to the Cartesian *cogito*. The veracity of the 'I think', in short, grounds the identification of states of affairs as being true.

The third relation is 'signification'. This constitutes an 'order of conceptual implication' (p. 14) whereby one infers one proposition from other propositions. Signification, therefore, is about premises and conclusions (as, for instance, occur in the construction of deductive arguments). Hence, there is '*implication*' which 'defines the relation between premises and conclusion', and '*assertion*', which allows for the affirmation of a conclusion on the basis of its implications. Signification, it follows, is about *demonstrating* relations between propositions. Either one proposition has a relation to others (for example, it can be inferred from them, as in the case of a conclusion) or others have a relation to it (for example, they allow it to be inferred, as in the case of premises). Demonstration, though, is not merely a matter of the construction of syllogisms; it does not simply concern deductions and their logical form. Equally, one can demonstrate probabilities (which concern the realm of the physical) or engage in the analysis of the links between promises and commitments (which concerns ethics) whereby what is demonstrated is the fact that, for example, a promise is kept.

If signification is what allows us to demonstrate how different propositions relate to one another, it follows that 'The logical value of signification or demonstration thus understood is no longer the truth . . . but rather *the condition of truth*, the aggregate of conditions under which the proposition "would be" true.' A proposition can state something to be the case that is not the case (it can be false). But this is not the *opposite* of truth, since what is at stake from the point of view of signification is not whether a proposition is true or false, but what conditions would make it so. Only if we already know these conditions can something be said to be true or false. Truth and falsity, therefore, are not 'opposites'. They come together as equally necessary in order for truth-talk to be possible at all. Only in the case of either of the attributions 'true' or 'false' being given would a proposition have a truth-value. We cannot, from a logical point of view, it follows, think of truth as the opposite of falsity. But what, then, is the opposite of truth-talk? Deleuze's answer to this question is that what is opposed to truth is 'the absurd: that which is without signification or that which may be neither true nor false' (p. 15) – in short, nonsense.

Traditionally, signification, like denotation, is accorded a role that makes it subservient to manifestation. We can only have truth-talk so long as there is already somebody who is able to speak and so engage in such talk. But, Deleuze argues, this is the case only so long as we think of 'speech' as the sole realm in which propositions are held to occur. 'In the order of speech, it is the I that begins, and begins absolutely. In this order, therefore, the I is primary.' In speech, the Cartesian *cogito* is understood immediately in the very uttering: as soon as I say 'I think . . .' I have already grasped who I am in the very uttering. But this claim itself presupposes that signification is a matter that concerns *only* the presence of living speakers, their intentions, dispositions, etc. However, if there is another realm of signification, one in which 'significations are . . . valid and developed for themselves' then such significations would have primacy over and above speech. They would provide the basis for manifestation, for the I that thinks, and thereby also for denotation. 'This domain is precisely that of *language*.'

2.6 The primacy of language over speech

We need not look to the subject (the speaker) as the ground of signification, but to language itself. This is because within language propositions are only possible in virtue of the fact that they signify concepts *prior* to the manifestation of a thinking subject who utters them. In language, then, spoken words relate to their concepts *necessarily*; and in this relation concepts take priority over spoken words. The notion of necessity is important here, for Deleuze holds that the necessity engendered by this relation is of a kind that no other relations within propositions have. The kind of necessity involved is not a matter of denotation, manifestation, or spoken signification. What we are really talking about here is the priority and necessity of a particular mode of *reference*: 'the possibility of causing particular images to be associated with the word to vary, of substituting one image for another in the form "this is not that, it's that," can be explained only by the constancy of the signified concept' (p. 16). In its 'constancy' the concept provides the basis for articulating reference. What I refer to in speech, on this account, would not be the object or state of affairs I am talking of, but the concept; and it is the concept that remains constant no matter which 'images' I think in relation to a word. The words in which images are made manifest, it follows, have as their referents *concepts*. Implications are drawn only in virtue of the structuring force of concepts.

However, there is another problem. When we draw an implication in virtue of the order of concepts in language and conclude with a 'therefore . . . etc.', a proposition thereby gains autonomy from the premises which grounded it: 'We set aside the premises and affirm it for itself, independently.' Such a proposition denotes a state of affairs *without reference to its order of signification*; it becomes a matter of denotation only. In order for it to do this, however, we are obliged to presuppose that the premises in question are true. Once we have done this we can detach the conclusion from the premises by constructing a further proposition that states the conclusion is true if and only if the premises are true. The problem is that this proposition, too, remains within the same order of implication and hence requires another proposition to state that it, too, is true, and so on *ad infinitum*. Thus, premise 1: 'Socrates is a person'; premise 2: 'All people are mortal'; conclusion: 'Therefore Socrates is mortal'; gives rise to a further proposition 'The proposition "Socrates is mortal" is true if and only if premises 1 and 2 are true', which requires yet another: 'The proposition "The proposition. . . ." etc.'. This, Deleuze tells us, initiates an infinite regress of denotation. Because of this the structure of language itself cannot offer us a means of attributing a final and determinate sense to any proposition.

2.7   Sense: the fourth dimension of the proposition

But where should one look for sense (or meaning) within such a model? Should one bother at all? Certainly, sense is not a matter of denotation, since denotation is to do with those conditions which make propositions true or false, not with their sense: 'It is undeniable that all denotation presupposes sense, and that we position ourselves *straight away* within sense whenever we denote' (p. 17). Likewise, manifestation will not do, for (as already noted) beliefs and desires are founded upon the order of signification. Only signification remains as a possible source of sense/meaning. But this, likewise, rests upon an infinite regress of denotation.

Sense, Deleuze therefore concludes, is itself a necessary dimension of the proposition, just as much as denotation, manifestation and signification constitute its necessary relations. Sense is 'that which is expressed by the proposition, [and] would be irreducible to individual states of affairs, particular images, personal beliefs, and universal or general concepts' (p. 19). To uncover sense would thereby be something of a problematic undertaking, for sense cannot be instantiated in any of the three relations of the proposition. Sense cannot be denoted: you can't point at it. Sense cannot be manifested: a speaker 'makes sense' or does not, but a *speaker* is never the 'sense' of a proposition. Sense cannot be signified: you cannot say that sense is the same as the order of conceptual implication, which is what allows you to make inferences and thereby link different propositions together. 'In truth,' Deleuze notes, 'the attempt to make this fourth dimension evident is a little like Carroll's Snark hunt. Perhaps the dimension is the hunt itself, and sense is the Snark' (p. 20). Sense does not even pertain to utility: it does not need to be shown to be 'at work' in language in order for language to work. Thus, 'it is endowed with an inefficacious, impassive, and sterile splendour' which can be inferred only indirectly from the circularity and paradoxical nature of the proposition itself.

Sense is not external to propositions, since what is expressed cannot be external to its expression. Sense, it follows, does not 'exist', but like becoming 'it inheres or subsists' in relation to the form of its expression. In this regard, sense depends upon the *form* of the proposition. Yet, sense 'does not merge at all with the proposition, for it has an objective which is quite distinct. What is expressed has no resemblance whatsoever to the expression' (p. 21), nor to its form. This is because sense is an attribute not of propositions but of things and states of affairs and what is expressed by a proposition does not concern the proposition itself, but what the proposition is *about*. Whereas the attribute of a proposition is its predicate, the attribute of 'the thing is the verb: to green, for example, or rather the event expressed by this verb . . . [The word] "[g]reen" designates a quality, a mixture of things, a mixture of tree and air where chlorophyll coexists with all parts of the leaf. "To green", on the contrary, expresses not a quality in the thing, but an attribute which is said of the thing.' Yet, such an attribute still cannot exist outside the proposition, and so we are again within an apparently vicious circle.

'But', Deleuze holds, 'this is not a circle. It is rather the coexistence of two sides without thickness, such that we pass from one to the other by following their length. *Sense is both the expressible to the expressed of a proposition, and the attribute of the state of affairs*. It turns one side towards things and one side towards propositions . . . It is exactly the boundary between propositions and things' (p. 22). This constitutes an *event*. An event, it follows, is not a temporal and spatial happening which occurs to things within states of affairs, but a *pure happening*, one which does *not* occur in relation to a 'somewhere': 'We will not ask therefore what is the sense of the event: the event is sense itself.' In other words, sense 'is' becoming.[30]

2.8 Some comments

Before moving on to *A Thousand Plateaus*, let us raise some questions with regard to this account. First, Deleuze seeks to ground his reading in the metaphor of the surface, in surface effects. Sense, in turn, is identified as a surface effect that occurs in a Stoic universe of bodies and their attributes. But is it sufficient to render language in terms of pure becoming, to make it 'coexistent' with pure becoming and hence dependent upon 'non-sense'? Sense, on this view is the product of 'nonsense and its perpetual displacement' (*The Logic of Sense*, 71). Although nonsense always lacks a determinate sense Deleuze nevertheless assigns it a privileged role, in so far as nonsense becomes the necessary precondition of sense. But how ought one to characterize nonsense? Certainly, one could claim that nonsense is that which has no determinate content. Any proposition that is nonsense expresses nothing. But by accepting this claim we have in fact already assigned 'nonsense' a determinate content (a sense). We have done so simply by way of our accepting this view and propounding it within a proposition: we cannot talk about nonsense at all without making sense of it. But this cannot be acceptable according to Deleuze's own account, since sense is predetermined ultimately by and through the existence of bodies.

In a proposition, sense expresses the relation between bodies; it involves a mode of reference that ultimately must be produced by these bodies themselves. If this is the case, then Deleuze has in effect 'ontologized' sense by situating it within a model that determines the existent as its precondition and so rendering it subservient to the realm of the existent. To claim that it 'flows' over the surfaces which exist between bodies does not, in effect, overcome the platonic duality. It merely reverses the platonic model in a gesture that denies that sense has independence from bodies. The realm of bodies now takes on the role of ideas, as they are outlined within so-called 'platonic' metaphysics. But a mere reversal is not an escape from something: we can claim that sense inheres in the relations between bodies, but if we do so then we are merely privileging bodies over sense. But privileging bodies over sense instead of sense over bodies is still to remain trapped within the duality of senses and their referents. Likewise, it does not follow that language itself can be rendered coterminous with becoming. That we are able to affirm that language changes, flows, etc., does not entitle us to make the further claim that it must share something in common with the causal realm of bodies, namely that it is one of their effects, that 'language is coextensive' with the becoming of bodies.

Moreover, Deleuze's reading ignores one important element: the question of rules in language. If we turn to Lewis Carroll's writings, then Humpty Dumpty, for Deleuze, is a Stoic, and Alice his pupil (p. 142). As such, he is a pedagogue. But Humpty Dumpty himself is a voice which operates within the text of *Through the Looking Glass* not with any Stoical pedagogical force, but through the overturning of rules of meaning with regard to the nature of words. It is neither denotation, nor signification, nor sense that is at work here, but pure manifestation. That is why Humpty Dumpty states 'When *I* use a word . . . it means just what I choose it to mean – neither more nor less.' In this regard, Humpty Dumpty formulates his own rules of meaning. Meaning here is pure intentionality; it is not becoming, but the immanence of a voice which is itself a giver of rules. Humpty Dumpty in this regard speaks a 'private language': he himself is his own rule of speech; and the privacy of his language is not the language of the pure event, but a language which is not a language at all, because it has no normative underpinnings. For Deleuze, Carroll presents us with games devoid of rules (pp. 58ff): 'There are no pre-existing rules, each move invents its own rules' (p. 59). Humpty Dumpty would, on this view, be playing a game with no purpose, and as such would reflect the ontological lack of purpose at work in the play of surfaces that constitute the pure event and becoming. But such a view overlooks the normative component of language. It ignores the fact that language itself presupposes shared rules or conventions. That is why a private language like Humpty Dumpty's is not really a language at all. But let us leave *The Logic of Sense* to one side, and instead turn to Deleuze and Guattari's *A Thousand Plateaus* as a means of further developing an account of this ontology of becoming.

2.9   A Thousand Plateaus

Deleuze and Guattari's *A Thousand Plateaus* is a book that may rightly be said to defy simple exegesis. For one thing, Deleuze and Guattari renounce any straight-forward mode of 'logical' analysis. This is not a systematic work. Instead, and in keeping with the account of becoming offered above, it is one which develops an approach which envisages the world as a phenomenon consisting of a multiplicity of 'rhizomatic' structures that are themselves multiple. But this text also offers a further elucidation of the rhizome as a multiplicity. 'A rhizome has no beginning or end; it is always in the middle, between things, interbeing, *intermezzo*' (*A Thousand*

Plateaus, 25). This multiplicity constitutes a quasi-organic machine. As a 'middle', this machine has no origin: it is locked into a fluid process of ceaseless becoming, 'a stream without beginning or end' (p. 25). The structures that erupt from this stream of becoming can only be delineated in terms of relative relationships of force.

Phenomena in general are open to being analysed as 'assemblages' that are capable of joining or connecting in an infinite number of possible ways (p. 4). Any machine-like assemblage, as 'a kind of organism,' thereby constitutes a series of power relations. In turn, Deleuze and Guattari consider these relationships of force in terms of a pure plenitude of positively charged elements. These elements interact in such a manner as to produce 'phenomena of relative slowness and viscosity, or, on the contrary, of acceleration and rupture'. Meaning, too, is reinterpreted within the framework of this line of thought: 'There is no ideal speaker-listener . . . There is no mother tongue, only a power takeover by a dominant language within a political multiplicity' (p. 7). Even books are machines that only produce meaning through a process of intersection and subsequent interaction with other forces. Literature, for example, is regarded as a form of 'assemblage'. Since the conditions which give rise to such assemblages are rooted in becoming not history, the meaning of a text cannot be reduced to historical or social contexts, such as questions of ideology. Indeed, 'There is no ideology and never has been' (p. 4). This is because there are, in Deleuze and Guattari's view, only lines of force which join and break to form stratified 'rhizomatic' wholes, or 'haecceities',[31] devoid of permanence.

This is an 'anti-theoretical' position, in so far as it spurns any claim that there is a conceptual priority with regard to how becoming can be interpreted. It may be best to understand Deleuze and Guattari's position in terms of a rejection of both ideological analysis and dialectical thinking which, for them, are opposed to any affirmation of rhizomatic multiplicities. Dialectics, they tell us, is 'the most classical and well reflected, oldest, and weariest kind of thought' (p. 5). Given that the 'world' is interpreted as a rhizome or 'middle', Deleuze and Guattari reject a unified conception of reality in favour of the affirmation of a diverse plurality of forms. Human histories and cultures are understandable in terms of competing forces. Cultures, like 'states of things', arise from this stream of becoming and when they encounter one another it is in the form of a struggle. In turn, since humans are linguistic beings, such struggles are fought out in contending regimes of signs. Any language of mediation, such as might be sought by way of dialectics, is therefore abandoned in favour of an approach that concentrates on the thematics of struggle, seizure and take-over. Following *The Logic of Sense*, we have a model in which an account of the nature of language is primary. But, for Deleuze and Guattari there is no such thing as 'Language', with a capital 'L'. There are only *languages*, multiple rhizomatic systems of signification that encounter other systems of meaning, other bodies. Questions of language are always issues of power: different systems of meaning embody different power relations. In turn, what we are presented with is a rejection of transcendental critique. In its place we are offered a viewpoint which concentrates upon 'lines of flight' as constituting the only means of escape from the enclosed and stratified systems of authoritarian thought which map out social and cultural 'reality'. A 'line of flight' is an escape from the stratified hierarchy of meaning that authoritarian semiotic systems impose, and this escape is one that takes thought into a 'smooth space', a realm that is not pre-determined by hierarchies of significance but by multiplicity. What Deleuze and Guattari call 'nomadic thought' engages in such lines of flight.

2.10   Three semiotic regimes

What, then, constitutes authoritarianism? How, according to Deleuze and Guattari, is the world mapped and stratified? Their answer is that this is done by particular semiotic systems (i.e. regimes of signs which endow meaning and significance upon reality) that invoke transcendence, 'a specifically European disease' (*A Thousand Plateaus*, 18). Such semiotic systems are instances of 'haecceities'. We have already noted that an assemblage is a kind of unity composed of the conjunction of hetero-geneous elements. A haecceity is to be understood in relation to this. Any haecceity is an 'entire assemblage in its individuated aggregate' (p. 262). 'Climate, wind, season, hour are not of another nature than the things, animals, or people that populate them, follow them, sleep and awaken within them' (p. 263). Taken together, all these elements form a haecceity. Individuated elements, like subjectivity, are situated within haecceities and are what they are in virtue of this fact. A haecceity, therefore, makes us what we are as individuated beings: 'You will yield nothing to haecceities unless you realize that that is what you are, and how you are' (p. 262). Haecceities, it follows, can be identified in such a way that their meaning may be read in terms of specific sets of characteristics. In turn, semiotic systems (i.e. systems of meaning and signification) are likewise haecceities.

There are, Deleuze and Guattari argue, a number of signifying regimes, and they offer us an analysis of three. First, there is the 'presignifying semiotic', which is pluralistic, polyvocal (i.e. many-voiced) and wards off the tyranny of universality. Second, there is the 'countersignifying semiotic', which is 'nomadic' in character. And third, there is the 'postsignifying semiotic', which embodies the process of 'subjectification', i.e. it is one in which modes of subjectivity are constituted (pp. 117–19). These three different semiotics may be mixed together. But, since they are necessarily connected with assemblages that 'determine a given people, period, or language, and even a given style, fashion, [or] pathology . . . the predominance of one semiotic or another' is inevitable (p. 119).

In addition, Deleuze and Guattari draw a distinction between a 'paranoid, signify-ing regime of signs and a passional or subjective, postsignifying, authoritarian regime' (p. 121). Both types of regime embody forms of delusion, in spite of the fact that it is accepted that they differ in terms of their respective force and 'direction' of movement. The paranoid regime arises from the development of forces 'organized around an idea'. This is another way of saying that it starts with a concept (p. 120). Because of this, the paranoid regime embodies an 'internalization' of forces, and it proceeds to interpret the world on the basis of this. By way of illustration, we might say that any imperial form of rule is essentially paranoid-despotic in form. In contrast, the passional-subjective semiotic is the consequence of external forces – for example, a reaction to an event – which is expressed emotionally rather than conceptually. As delusions, both can be characterized as types of 'madness'. In the first case (the paranoid form), the madness takes the form of a radiating, despotic paranoia that functions to extend the paranoic nature of the regime's *idée fixe* outwards from itself. The paranoid form's madness is overt, in so far as it is immediately clear that any despotic mode of interpreting the world wants to subordinate everything to its own conceptual power. The subjective semiotic, on the other hand, includes characteristics which 'do not seem mad in any way but are'. The latter fact is born out, Deleuze and Guattari maintain, by the passional-subjective semiotic's historical connection with 'monomanias' and authoritarian hierarchies. This distinction forms the basis for what follows in Deleuze and Guattari's argument.

2.11   The passional and the nomadic semiotics

The passional and subjective semiotic regime is, in fact, linked to the historical heritage of Judaism: 'There is a Jewish specificity immediately affirmed in a semiotic system' (p. 122). This system is a 'mixed' one, in so far as it is composed of both paranoid and passional-subjective elements. Historically, this fact can be traced back to the enslavement of the Jews in ancient Egypt. 'In the case of the Jewish people, a group of signs detaches itself from the Egyptian imperial network of which it was a part and sets off down a line of flight into the desert' (p. 122). We can conclude three things from this. (1) All 'peoples', all 'identities', are the result of certain kinds of bodies (our kind of bodies) being seized by signs. Regimes of signification take hold of 'us' and make us what we are. (2) The ancient Jews are interpreted by Deleuze and Guattari as emerging from their enslavement in Egypt as a nation (a rhizome) that embodies a mixture of the paranoid-despotic and passional-subjective semiotics. (3) Different systems for the organization of signs are linked to different cultural forms.

Above all, the significance of the Judaic passional-subjective semiotic is to be found in its contrast with nomadic regimes of signs. In fact, Deleuze and Guattari claim that a nomadic element constitutes a part of the Judaic past: the escape from enslavement in Egypt into the desert wilderness that is described in the Old Testament is an escape into a life of nomadism. But this nomadic element has subsequently been eroded by way of the authoritarianism of the passional-subjective semiotic. For Deleuze and Guattari, the passional regime constitues a particular mode of subjectivity, one which derives a racial identity from the yearning for homogeneity that the escape from Egypt initiates. The latter reaches its height of authoritarian expression in the notion of the transcendent subjectivity of God. It also implements the idea of the book as the body of passion: 'If passional delusion is profoundly monomaniacal, monomania for its part found a fundamental element of its assemblage in monotheism and the Book. The strangest cult' (p. 127). The Book becomes the sacred text, the object that, as holy, signifies the 'origin and finality of the world'. It is this that constructs the meaning of 'God' as representing a transcendent mode of subjectivity. God, the eternal self, looks down upon the world, and sees all; he is the divine authority of subjectivity expressed through the Book. In turn, the monotheist articulates his or her identity in terms of a specific relationship with God. This is a 'reactive' relationship. The Jewish prophet, for example, does not interpret God, he merely reacts to God as the supreme authority: 'the prophet interprets nothing' (p. 124). This reaction, in its own turn, engenders the possibility of a betrayal of God, since reacting to God does not imply the simple carrying out of his will. For instance, in the Old Testament, Jonah resists God's command to travel to Nineveh and in this way he betrays him. But Jonah ends up by being compelled to do as he is told anyway: he is taken to Nineveh in the belly of a fish and so fulfils his task even as he seeks to escape it.

Deleuze and Guattari read the Christian tradition, too, as a mixed form of semiotic that combines the passional-subjective and the paranoid-despotic forms. Above all, it is linked to the Cartesian *cogito*, which signifies a form of slavery to the rational self: 'Passional delusion is a veritable cogito' (p. 128). Above all, the Hebraic semiotic becomes interpreted as the origin of reason. Out of the postsignifying, subjective regime 'A new form of slavery is invented, namely, being a slave to oneself, or to pure "reason", the Cogito' (p. 130). In line with Deleuze's 1962 reading of Nietzsche, reason is construed as an essentially 'reactive' force, which is situated in the larger context of positive multiplicities. Reason is the result of a particular semiotic system that is the direct consequence of the interaction between body and world. Deleuze and Guattari's analysis thus advocates an account of rationality that reduces it to no more than a mere adjunct of a particular series of historical conjunctions. The passional-semiotic embodies a negative interpretative reaction to the world. This reaction is directly contrasted with the affirmative pluralism of the 'nomadic' semiotic.

The nomadic semiotic is a 'countersignifying' semiotic, which resists the authoritarian regime of Hebraism, and other apparatuses of control, like the state. Nomadism epitomizes becoming, and its defining effect is to produce an affirmative 'line of flight' from the confines of restrictive semiotic systems. For example, in fleeing from Egypt the Jews embraced a nomadic line of flight, even though they remained ultimately passional. Likewise, nomadism's affirmative rhizomatic nature is a reflection of the cosmic 'order' of chaos which embodies becoming: 'The life of the nomad is the *intermezzo*', i.e. the affirmation of the 'middle', of becoming (p. 380). Not only is the nomadic therefore a living refutation of all thinking of origins, in addition it also brings a 'war machine' to bear on all systems of containment. Nomadic thinkers, such as Nietzsche, present us with the question of the 'outside', they articulate a counter-thought which aims to overturn the authoritarianism of the 'I think', of reason, in favour of the affirmation of pluralism (pp. 376–7). From this we can conclude that nomadic thought attacks the notion of totality and its doing so involves 'making thought a war machine'. However, in spite of their contention that semiotic regimes are always mixed there is a firm dichotomy (dare one say a dualism?) that characterizes Deleuze and Guattari's approach. This is the duality of nomadism versus rational subjectivism. Nomadism is by definition opposed to 'universality' in the sense of the universal *cogito* of God. Instead, it is found in expressions of specificity: 'It [nomadism] does not ally itself with a universal thinking subject, but on the contrary, with a singular race' (p. 379).

This, in fact, seems a somewhat contradictory statement in light of the fact that elsewhere Deleuze and Guattari argue against identifying any single regime or semiotic with particular races or historical epochs (p. 119). But this latter claim seems to run counter to the general thesis that is advocated concerning semiotic regimes in

A Thousand Plateaus. Deleuze and Guattari's rejection of universalism, and of any general theory, along with their explicit association of particular semiotic forms with particular races (e.g. the passional-subjective semiotic with Jewish 'specificity') appears directly contrary to such a claim. It is perhaps sufficient to recall that the *cogito* and universality are directly linked by them with the Hebraic tradition and thus to a specific racial and historical context: 'the authoritarian process of subjectification *appears most purely in the destiny of the Jewish people*' (p. 182, italics added). The emphasis in their account is in this way shifted from a historical to a racial orientation. But, if Deleuze and Guattari recognize the dangers of such a move as representing the possibility of providing a justification for racism, they nevertheless try to resist such a conclusion on the grounds that races only exist at the level of oppression. As opposed to the 'striated', quantified space of authority, races only exist in the construction of a 'smooth space' that resists such authoritarianism: 'Bastard and mixed-blood are the true names of race' (p. 379). So, they claim, nomadism, like Judaism, may be monotheistic in the sense of pertaining to a 'sense of the absolute' (p. 385). But even where this is the case, the nomad's is an atheistic 'monotheism', in other words, it is one that is resistant to the universalized conception of subjectivity that defines authoritarianism.

Ironically, perhaps, Deleuze and Guattari construct a model of signification which, behind an overtly presented 'polyvocality', conceals an essentialism that envisages becoming in terms of '*nomadic essences*', 'essences that are vagabond, anexact, and yet rigorous' (pp. 407, 411, 507). Their semiotics rests upon a conception of becoming which embraces a particular conception of vitalism. In its traditional sense, a vitalist is someone who contends that all life can be accounted for in purely materialistic terms (i.e. without reference to concepts that invoke substances like 'mind'). However, for Deleuze and Guattari, life is not something that is 'material'. In terms of Deleuze's arguments in *The Logic of Sense*, we might say life 'subsists' in the relations between bodies and is 'incorporeal' – it is becoming. Vitalism, Deleuze and Guattari argue in *What is Philosophy?*, can be interpreted in terms of 'a force that is but does not act – that is therefore a pure internal Awareness . . . Even when one is a rat, it is through contemplation that one "contracts" a habit. It is still necessary to discover, beneath the noise of actions, those internal creative sensations or those silent contemplations that bear witness to a brain.'[32] In other words, there is a kind of vital force underlying all forms of organic life, and this force pre-exists individual identity.[33] This vitalism, Deleuze and Guattari contend, is not to be found in the codified annals of history. Nomads 'have no history', since history is the product of the very authoritarianism from which the nomadic 'line of flight' seeks to escape (*A Thousand Plateaus*, 393). It is this vitalism which allows for the construction of the opposition between the fluid 'becoming' of essences and the stability of 'being' to be articulated in such a manner as to erase any positive content that might be otherwise appended to history.

2.12 The innocence of becoming; the innocence of the nomad

Deleuze and Guattari's maintaining of a link between nomadism and the war machine requires that the war machine itself be cleansed of any connection with actual, historical (that is, real, and therefore bloody and unpleasant) war. It is perhaps for this reason that war is understood by them as being a kind of 'supplement' to the war machine. Actual war, they argue, is neither the condition nor the object of the war machine, but nevertheless necessarily accompanies it. Turning once more to the Old Testament, Deleuze and Guattari cite the example of Moses's introduction of a war machine as a means of flight from the Jews' enslavement in Egypt. Moses constructs a war machine and with it enters a smooth space (the Jews escape into the desert). But the supplement (i.e. actual war) only occurs when it is realized that war necessarily follows from the Hebrews encountering other cities, states and cultures. This is how Deleuze and Guattari account for this: 'speaking like Kant, we could say that the relation between war and the war machine is necessary but "synthetic" (Yahweh is necessary for the synthesis)' (p. 417). Or, to put it another way, war is the direct consequence of the cross–fertilization between the passional semiotic and the otherwise 'pure' nomadic semiotic. When *actual* war occurs, then Yahweh is to blame.

What is so curious about this is that, in addressing the historical fact of fascism, which also 'involves a war machine . . . [that results in] . . . a realized nihilism' (p. 230), Deleuze and Guattari cannot ignore the possibility that it, too, embodies a line of flight – that it, too, involves nomadism. They account for the historical phenomenon of fascism as a nomadic line of flight that, in the form of a 'realized nihilism', abandons the creativity of nomadism through its being dragged back down to earth by the force of the semiotic from which it was attempting to escape. This is due to the fact that 'lines of flight . . . always risk abandoning their creative potential and turning into a line of death, being turned into destruction pure and simple (fascism)' (p. 506). What is unsettling about this account is the fact that it is the passional–subjective semiotic that finally gets the blame for this. Only because the authoritarianism that typifies the passional–subjective semiotic (associated with 'Jewish specificity') prevents a nomadic line of flight from taking leave from its confines does that nomadic form return in the form of fascistic nihilism and death.

It is possible to account for this conclusion by addressing Deleuze and Guattari's conception of the relationship between history and the ontology of becoming. History, of course, is something that is linked to memory. We only have any history, both culturally and individually, in so far as we are necessarily beings who are capable of remembering. Such a possibility, on Deleuze and Guattari's account, is the result of ' "history-memory" systems' (p. 296). But, tellingly, the phenomenon of life is not grounded in history. On the contrary,

> The dividing line passes . . . between punctual 'history-memory' systems and diagonal or multilinear assemblages, which are in no way eternal: they have to do with becoming; they are a bit of becoming in the pure state; they are transhistorical. There is no act of creation that is not transhistorical and does not come up from behind or proceed by way of a liberated line . . . [It is a matter of] . . . becoming, the innocence of becoming (in other words, forgetting as opposed to memory, geography [i.e. nomadism] as opposed to history . . . the rhizome as opposed to aborescence).   (p. 296)

What might we take 'the innocence of becoming' to signify here? Certainly, it is the ontological condition of all life. Moreover, this condition must be *affirmed*. In other words, Deleuze and Guattari oppose the act of affirmation that they identify with the ontology of transhistorical becoming to the act of negation that they associate with the history of being. Given that the Hebrews are held responsible for the imposition of the subjective mode of interpreting the world in terms of the being of God, it follows that they stand on the side of negation. They stand, in other words, in history as its originators. Equally, they stand as its victims: the victims of a nomadic 'line of flight' that is dragged back down in the form of fascism. In this way, the Judaic imposition of the subject (p. 379) as a betrayal of the body and of the innocence of becoming, and as a containment of lines of flight, creates the historical conditions which lead to their own persecution. Take the example of the Flood. God warns Noah that a deluge will engulf the earth. So, very sensibly, he builds a boat (the Ark) to avoid death by drowning. But, Deleuze and Guattari claim, 'the ark is no more than a little portable packet of signs' (p. 122). In other words, the Ark pays testimony to the Judaic reluctance to embrace the smooth space of nomadism (of becoming). The building of the Ark is an attempt to preserve Jewish identity, to prevent it being encroached upon by the fluid and unknown forces of becoming symbolized by the Flood. Noah, then, does not wish to embark on a voyage that cannot be charted out and delineated in advance by terms dominant within his own semiotic regime.

2.13 A retreat from becoming into pragmatic 'rules'

In the end Deleuze and Guattari are faced with a stark choice. Either their affirmation of the nomadic must face the inherent danger of collapsing under its own weight into the nihilism they dread (fascism) or they must impose limiting formulations (i.e. in their terms, what we might call 'passional-subjective' 'Thou shalt nots'), namely 'Concrete Rules' ('Conclusion: Concrete Rules and Abstract Machines', pp. 501–14). These rules take the form of definitions concerning their own terminology. Such rules are required because the 'smooth space' of nomadism is not itself capable of redeeming us from authoritarianism: 'Never believe that a smooth space will suffice to save us' (p. 500). This amounts to a warning: we strive to escape from the stratified structures of authoritarianism at our own peril.

> Every understanding of destratification (for example . . . plunging into a becoming) must . . . observe concrete rules of extreme caution: a too-sudden destratification may be suicidal, or turn cancerous. In other words, it will sometimes end in chaos, the void and destruction, and sometimes look back into the strata, which become more rigid, losing their degree of diversity, differentiation, and mobility.   (p. 503)

So, even the nomadic, it seems, needs in the end to have its dangerous potential fenced off by rules. The pure affirmation of becoming and multiplicity is never *really* possible because such an affirmation means embracing what is terrible just as much as what is liberating. Deleuze and Guattari's affirmative vision of 'A powerful inorganic life' (which they otherwise refer to as 'a body without organs', the realm in which 'essences' of becoming are manifested) is in the end given its prescribed limits. What are these limits? Little more than points arbitrarily imposed on the vitalistic principle that underpins all notions of essence. The 'earth', they tells us, 'belongs to the Cosmos, and presents itself as the material through which human beings tap cosmic forces' (p. 509). But these forces must be subjected to pragmatic limits. However, it is difficult to see how such rules could be more than merely arbitrary impositions that serve to contain the more unsettling implications of their own discourse. All rules, on their own account, are generated by specificity. Why, in that case, avoid suicide, or worse? Why worry about ending up in the void, or in destruction? Any attempt to answer such questions must initiate a move away from the affirmation of plurality and pure becoming that is so central to Deleuze and Guattari's approach. Either we observe limits on what we can or ought to do, and in this way also with regard to what we ought to think, because those limits are arbitrarily forced upon us, or because we choose to acknowledge limitations as constituting an essential component of what we are. This is another way of saying that human existence cannot be understood in terms of becoming alone when such becoming is severed from history.

We might say that Deleuze and Guattari's approach is one that takes much from Nietzsche's conception of the primacy of becoming. As Nietzsche puts it in a note included in *The Will to Power*: 'The world exists; it is not something that becomes, not something that passes away. Or rather: it becomes, it passes away, but it has never ceased from passing away – it maintains itself in both. – It lives on itself: its excrements are its food.'[34] But, in advocating this view, Nietzsche does not argue for an *escape* from the conceptually determined realm of 'metaphysical philosophy' into pure becoming. For him, the 'tyranny' and hierarchy of normatively determined modes of life does not of itself constitute an objection to them. Nor is the fact that subjectivity is the result of 'authoritarian' practices a good reason to reject it out-right. Nietzsche, too, is a highly problematic thinker in this regard. But we can also note that for him what is most interesting is the fact that things can emerge from their opposites: truth from untruth, knowledge from error, individual autonomy from collective coercion. Likewise, and in spite of his view that becoming must be affirmed, the approach of 'historical philosophizing' that Nietzsche consistently advocates is far more modest in its ambitions than the advocacy of a 'line of flight' from history that Deleuze and Guattari envisage.[35]

We cannot stand outside our 'world', or outside our conceptual and practical grasp of it. Even as they urge us to pluralism, Deleuze and Guattari must crave just that. In their attempt to elucidate the conditions of pure becoming that are imma-nent in all systems of language they ultimately strive to step outside of the historical conditions that make signification, speech, thought, and action possible. Doubtless, their rejection of dialectical thought is important in this regard. But, though there may be some reasons to suspect that thinking is not, in itself, dialectically determined, the conditions of possibility of thought require that, as soon as we act or open our mouths, we do so in the context of others. In this sense, at least, dialectic cannot be elided so easily. Deleuze and Guattari may oppose ' "history-memory" systems' to becoming, but in order even to notice such becomings these 'systems' are essential. One might say that, without 'being' there is no 'becoming', or vice versa.

3   Is Ontology Authoritarian? The Heidegger Question

I have argued that Deleuze and Guattari's ontology of becoming leads them to construct an argument that has implications that are antithetical to the spirit of their own thinking. Given that this discussion is situated within a chapter that began with an account of Heidegger's ontology I might reasonably be expected to broach another issue in similar vein. This is the problem already alluded to at the end of the discussion of Heidegger: the question of Heidegger's own political affiliation with Nazism in the 1930s. There is no doubt that Heidegger is a compromised figure in this regard, for he is a thinker whose personal complicity with Nazism went far beyond 'mere' party membership – as if that were not of itself sufficient to give us pause. Additionally, Heidegger's behaviour during the Nazi period led, as Richard Wolin reminds us, to his being convicted of political crimes at the end of the Second World War by a committee that was actually *sympathetic* toward him.[36] As Wolin points out, one central question concerning Heidegger's relationship with Nazism is 'to what extent is Heidegger's philosophy implicated in his ignominious life-choice of the early 1930s?'[37] I do not propose to offer here a simple answer to such a difficult problem, but some things do need mentioning. The first is that Heidegger was certainly not ill-disposed to invoking terms associated with his philosophical ontology as a means of justifying Nazism.[38] Terrible as this may seem to any admirer of Heidegger, it does not of itself really pose a problem concerning the value of Heidegger's philosophical contribution. That terms from *Being and Time* could be transposed even by Heidegger himself into a different context from the Classical Greek terrain from which they are derived is one essential condition of their existing at all. We can all have what we say or write resituated in this way – and doubtless people are frequently tempted to do this very thing in everyday life, albeit with far less severe consequences. This kind of 'transposition' of terms does not mean necessarily that these terms themselves have the kind of essential link with Nazism that may be inferred from Heidegger's invoking them in this way.

More worrying, as Wolin notes, are Heidegger's *reasons* for sympathizing with the political programme of National Socialism, such as it was, and the connection between these reasons and his philosophy. That these connections were felt to exist by Heidegger seems evident. That Heidegger's critique of the Enlightenment project, which in its essentials may be called a Nietzschean one, is marked by the cultural prejudices at work within his own society is a pertinent point to raise. This is how Wolin puts the matter: 'Could it be that Heidegger's own philosophical shortcomings parallel those of his nation's own historical formation? That his thought, too, in significant respects fails to make the transition to modern standards of philosophical and political rationality?'[39] Wolin has a good point, in so far as Heidegger's project does indeed take on board aspects of what we might call the 'conservative' (i.e. anti-Enlightenment) critique of modernity offered by Nietzsche. But it is not clear that Nietzsche himself, although avowedly anti-democratic, can be regarded as simply an anti-Enlightenment thinker – the text of *Human, All-Too-Human*, after all, is one that takes much of the Enlightenment spirit on board. This book, in its first edition, was dedicated to that paradigm figure of Enlightenment, Voltaire. And Voltaire was no democrat. It is not clear that this anti-Enlightenment critique is in itself the basis for establishing Heidegger's affiliation with Nazism. After all, Nietzsche's critique of modernity has its adherents on the left as well as the right – Adorno, one of Heidegger's sternest critics, being a case in point. Is there, then, not something else in Heidegger that might help to explain his repugnant political affiliation?

One prominent factor here might perhaps be the kind of 'nostalgia' for Being that marks out the project of *Being and Time*. Heidegger's attempt to reclaim the 'original' meaning of Being implies a diagnosis of modernity as existing in a 'fallen' state, and hence legitimates its dismissal as worthless. Even this kind of explanation, though, is not sufficient, even if it is instructive.[40] Nor, for that matter, is the authoritarianism that seems to be implied in Heidegger's appeal to Being in *Being and Time* sufficient to warrant the view that his philosophy has much in common with the authoritarianism of Nazism. Authoritarianism, while another *necessary* ingredient of Nazism and other forms of dictatorship, is not of itself a *sufficient* one for providing a definition of it.

I do not propose to offer a straightforward answer to these complex matters here. However, I will stake one claim. However obnoxious Heidegger's personal views might be; however idiotic, however *evil* we might with good reason think the ideas and attitudes expressed in the so-called 'Political Texts' of the 1930s, it does not follow that the central insights of *Being and Time*, or even of Heidegger's later writings, are thereby invalidated. These insights may be doubted for other reasons and, as we will see by way of the thought of one thinker who was hugely influenced by Heidegger, Emmanuel Levinas, an ethical mode of questioning is one effective way of doing this. Nevertheless, the insights of *Being and Time* are neither entirely invalidated due to Heidegger's personal beliefs or actions, nor can they be shown to be *the* determining ingredients of the evil views that Heidegger adopted. Of course, we *must* be troubled by Heidegger's heritage in all its ambiguity, and I do not seek to foreclose the issue by making these observations. For that heritage is also part of the European tradition.

Other interpretations of Heidegger's relationship to Nazism have been offered – not least by Jacques Derrida, whose work is discussed in the following chapter.[41] Since I do not intend to return to this matter in the context of a discussion of Derrida let me say that I agree with Wolin in not finding Derrida's account of this terribly convincing. Derrida argues that it was Heidegger's remaining prey to certain key notions within the very metaphysical tradition he criticized that led him to identify with National Socialist ideology (in Derridean terms, these notions fall under the banner of 'phonocentrism'). However, as Wolin says, it is arguable that it was precisely 'insofar as Heidegger remained wedded to the discourse of humanism and to the heritage of western metaphysics . . . as he understood it, [that] he was *prevented* from identifying wholesale with Nazi ideology as it was historically constituted – that is, in the first instance as a discourse on biology and race'.[42] At the same time, Heidegger's talk of 'authenticity' (so vehemently criticized by Adorno) may well have served a function in the Nazi context. I have already rehearsed some of Adorno's views concerning authenticity and will not repeat them. What I will add concerning Heidegger is a view that, in Derridean and associated circles, might be regarded as primitive and unfashionable in equal measure. It is this: the possibility arises that Heidegger's collaboration with Nazism may not simply have been inspired by his own conception of the nature of his philosophical vision so much as by personal *greed*. We live in an age of consumerism and maybe because of this greed does not always receive its due as the dangerous phenomenon it can be. It can nevertheless be said that Heidegger's personal ambitions (not least concerning his advancement in the university hierarchy) were considerably furthered by his Nazi connections. Indeed, some of Heidegger's personal resentments were also given free reign by this association. Could it be, one wonders, that there is nothing purely 'philosophical' about the kind of greed that would lead a person to collaborate with forces that, whatever his sympathies with them, he knows to be dreadfully compromised? I cannot offer a simple answer to this question. At the very least, Heidegger *did* regard Nazism as 'imperfect' and in need of the guiding hand of his own philosophical wisdom. Such an observation does not seek to distract from the question of the relationship between Heidegger's thought and Nazism or the question of the link between 'thought' and 'life'. It serves, rather, to highlight them. If Heidegger was driven by greed or selfishness to throw in his lot with National Socialism and identify aspects of his philosophy with it, then we must also ask to which extent *any* 'philosophy' is potentially prey to this kind of danger, to being rendered in terms of the instrumental pressures that Adorno and Horkheimer, at least, identify as characteristic of the subjective rationality of modern society. In any case, since we are now embroiled in what are obviously ethical issues let us therefore pursue some of them in relation to the work of thinkers who, although both influenced by Heidegger, respond to his thought and its anti-humanist heritage in quite different ways: Levinas and Derrida.

Notes

1 One could, after all, construct a 'minimalist' ontology. This kind of ontology would hold that there is 'stuff' out there, but deny the relevance of any further deliberation concerning what this stuff is. We could interpret aspects of Nietzsche's thought as adopting this view, although it is not clear that he is consistent in this respect.

2 See Gilles Deleuze, *Nietzsche and Philosophy*, tr. Hugh Tomlinson (London: Athlone Press, 1983).

3 Martin Heidegger, *Being and Time*, 'Introduction', tr. John Macquarrie and Edward Robinson (Oxford: Basil Blackwell; New York: Harper and Row, 1962). The 'Introduction' to *Being and Time* is also contained in *Martin Heidegger: Basic Writings*, ed. David Farrell Krell, tr. Joan Stambough and J. Glenn Gray (London: Routledge, 1993). All quotations are from Macquarrie and Robinson. For readers who are interested, there is also a new translation of this work by Joan Stambaugh (Albany, New York: State University of New York Press, 1996).

4 For Heidegger's comments concerning Descartes see *Being and Time*, pp. 122ff.

5 *Dasein*: lit. 'Being-there': generally, this term is used in German philosophy to denote the Being or existence of any kind of entity; in everyday use it is generally used to stand for the kind of existence that people have – see, *Being and Time*, p. 27, n. 1.

6 We could also phrase this as 'Being is always the Being of a being.' However, I shall retain the English 'entity' in the present discussion.

7   One could, by way of example, cite the crisis in physics caused by relativity theory in the 1920s. This theory challenged the basic concept of what an entity is that nineteenth-century physics relied upon in order to construct its theories.

8   See Edmund Husserl, *Ideas*, tr. W. R. Boyce Gibson (London: Allen & Unwin, 1931).

9   Edmund Husserl, *Cartesian Meditations*, tr. Dorion Cairns (The Hague: Martinus Nijhoff, 1960), Introduction, section 1.

10   See, for example, Edmund Husserl, *The Crisis of the European Sciences and Transcendental Phenomenology*, tr. David Carr (Evanston Ill.: Northwestern University Press, 1970), p. 189. Here Husserl argues that the transcendental ego is not to be taken as the foundation on the basis of which absolute knowledge may be 'secured'. The point, rather, is to 'understand' the meaning of the kind of objectivity the world of experience has for us.

11   Ibid., First Meditation, section 10.

12   Ibid., First Meditation, section 11.

13   Ibid., Second Meditation, section 14.

14   Ibid., Second Meditation, sections 15ff. 'Noetic' and 'noematic' are Greek terms. For a discussion of them, and a detailed introduction to Husserl's phenomenology, see Michael Hammond, Jane Howarth and Russell Keat, *Understanding Phenomenology* (Oxford: Basil Blackwell, 1991). Noetic 'is the adjectival form of "noesis", which is the Greek noun corresponding to the Latin verb "cogito"' (p. 47). Thus, the term 'noetic' 'describes the mode of consciousness' that is involved when perceiving an object. What is thereby described is a subject (a *cogito*, an 'I think') in the act of perceiving. Noematic 'is the adjectival form of [the Greek word] "noema" . . . and means the same as "cogitatum" in Latin'. The cogitatum is the object of any particular experience. Hence, a noematic description is a description of an object in terms of the mode in which that object is perceived by a subject.

15   Hermeneutics is a theory of interpretation which states that all understanding is circular (exmplified in the notion of the 'hermeneutic circle'). By way of analogy, one can say that if we take a sentence, then the meaning of the sentence is dependent upon the words that make it up. However, at the same time, the meaning of the words can only be understood in the context of the sentence. There is, it follows, a reciprocal dependency between the two, and neither can be privileged with regard to elucidating what meaning is. The work of Heidegger's pupil, Hans-Georg Gadamer, develops this view in the form of a 'philosophical hermeneutics'. Following Heidegger, Gadamer argues that all understanding derives from the *activity* of interpretation. Interpretation, in turn, rests upon 'prejudice', i.e. pre-judgement. The point is that, for Gadamer as for Heidegger, there is no such thing as value-free interpretation. The understanding we bring to bear whenever we interpret, say, a text, is rooted in tradition and shared evaluative norms. This does not mean that we are confined by tradition: a text can challenge our preconceptions. However, it does mean that all interpretation begins with preconceptions, and that no final interpretation is possible. See, Hans Georg Gadamer, *Truth and Method*, tr. Garrett Barden and John Cumming (London, Sheed & Ward, 1975).

16   T. W. Adorno, *The Jargon of Authenticity*, tr. Knut Tarnowski and Frederic Will (London: Routledge, 1973), p. 113.

17   Ibid., p. 114.

18   For a succinct definition of this term see chapter 4, note 33.

19   Gilles Deleuze, *Dialogues*, tr. Hugh Tomlinson and Barbara Habberjam (New York: Columbia University Press, 1987), p. vii. All further references are given in the text with page number.

20   Such a claim is, of course, highly disputable; see the discussion of Adorno in chapter 2.

21   See also Gilles Deleuze and Félix Guattari, *A Thousand Plateaus: Capitalism and Schizophrenia*, tr. Brian Massumi (Minneapolis: University of Minnesota Press, 1988), p. 11. All further references to *A Thousand Plateaus* are given in the text with page number.

22   Gilles Deleuze and Félix Guattari, *What is Philosophy?*, tr. Graham Burchell and Hugh Tomlinson (London: Verso, 1994), p. 15.

23   *What is Philosophy?*, p. 48.

24   Gilles Deleuze, *The Logic of Sense*, tr. Mark Lester, with Charles Stivale (London: The Athlone Press, 1990). All further references are given in the text with page number.

25   By 'truth-value' I mean a determinate meaning. Thus, a proposition, if it can be said to be either 'true' or 'false', has a truth-value. For example, the statement (much beloved by some philosophers) 'The cat is on the mat' has a truth-value because it can be either true (there is a cat on the mat) or false (there isn't a cat on the mat). In order to be able to be true or false propositions like this must refer to determinate states of affairs. Not all propositions have a truth-value. For instance, a judgement of taste: 'What a pretty flower!' That a particular person expresses such a judgement ('X thinks that the flower is pretty') may be a matter of truth or falsity, but the judgement itself is not susceptible to being taken in this manner.

26   Deleuze's references here are to Plato, *Philebus*, 24d and *Parmenides*, 154–5.

27   This kind of view can be compared with that offered by Jacques Derrida in his essay 'Force and Signification', in *Writing and Difference*, tr. Alan Bass (London: Routledge & Kegan Paul, 1978). This text is discussed in chapter 4, section 3.2.

28   I use the term here in the sense employed by Jean-François Lyotard, see *The Differend: Phrases in Dispute*, tr. Georges Van Den Abeele (Manchester: Manchester University Press, 1988). A cognitive phrase is one in which truth and falsity are at stake; and cognitives are those kinds of phrases which concern the reality of a referent. For a discussion of Lyotard's philosophy see chapter 5.

29   Stoicism was a philosophy first advocated *c*.330 BC by Zeno of Citium. Stoical philosophers embraced materialism: they did not believe that anything exists that does not have a body. They argued that the world itself is a kind of living being and that all actions are ultimately determined by fate. Hence the modern meaning of the phrase 'being stoical': accepting one's fate.

30   It is worth noting here that another source of inspiration for many of these ideas is the Jewish philosopher Baruch Spinoza (1632–77), 'the Christ of philosophers' (Deleuze and Guattari, *What is Philosophy?*, p. 60). Spinoza, who was born and lived in Holland, was not a professional (i.e. academic) philosopher, but a lens-grinder by trade. Like Descartes, he is generally numbered among the 'rationalist' thinkers. However, Spinoza rejects Descartes's substance dualism of mind and body in favour of a monistic philosophy. According to this philosophy there is one single substance, which Spinoza calls 'God or nature' (see Spinoza, *The Ethics*, tr. R. H. M. Elwes (New York: Dover Publications, 1955)). What is important about Spinoza for Deleuze is that he, like Nietzsche, questions the primacy of consciousness, arguing that it is constituted as an effect of the interaction between bodies. In turn, concepts or ideas can be interpreted in similar vein. In so far as ideas represent things they do so 'because they "express" their own cause' (Gilles Deleuze, *Expressionism in Philosophy: Spinoza* (1968), tr. Martin Joughin (New York: Zone Books, 1992), p. 138). In this way, our ideas are understandable as images that are generated by way of our state of existence: we do not create them, rather they are 'impressed in us' by way of the relations between bodies (ibid., p. 147). Thus, Deleuze argues, for Spinoza, 'An image is, in the strictest sense, an imprint, a trace or physical impression, an affection of the body itself, the effect of some body on the soft and fluid parts of our own body' (ibid.). To this degree, Deleuze understands Spinoza as a thinker

who is not to be simplistically counted a 'rationalist', but is 'profoundly empiricist . . . One of the paradoxes of Spinoza . . . is to have rediscovered the concrete form of empiricism in applying it in support of a new rationalism, one of the most rigorous versions ever conceived' (ibid., p. 149). It is worth comparing this side of Spinoza's influence with his impact on other philosophers. Nietzsche also expresses admiration for Spinoza (although not for the 'hocus pocus of mathematical form with which . . . [he] . . . clad his philosophy' (*Beyond Good and Evil*, section 5). Likewise, the French structural Marxist Louis Althusser also found much of importance in Spinoza's thought (see chapter 5, note 18).

31   Haecceity: from the Latin term 'haecceitas', which denotes an individual essence.

32   *What is Philosphy?*, p. 213.

33   One source for this conception is the work of the French philosopher Henri Bergson (1859–1941). According to Bergson, all living organisms are subject to an '*élan vital*', a 'life force' or drive. This produces an ever increasing variety of life forms but does not do so according to any final purpose. See, Henri Bergson, *Creative Evolution*, tr. A. Mitchel (New York: Henry Holt, 1911).

34   Nietzsche, *The Will to Power*, tr. Walter Kaufmann and R. J. Hollingdale, section 1066.

35   Although, it has to be conceded that Nietzsche's association of Jewish morality with an anti-affirmative mode of thought is certainly something that he shares with Deleuze and Guattari. See Nietzsche, *The Antichrist*, tr. Walter Kaufmann, in *The Portable Nietzsche* (London: Chatto & Windus, 1972), and *On the Genealogy of Morals*, tr. Walter Kaufmann, in *Basic Writings of Nietzsche* (New York: Modern Library, 1968). That said, as Walter Kaufmann powerfully argued in his *Nietzsche: Philosopher, Psychologist, Antichrist* (Princeton NJ: Princeton University Press, 1974), Nietzsche is no anti-semite.

36   See Richard Wolin (ed.), *The Heidegger Controversy: A Critical Reader* (Cambridge, Mass.: The MIT Press, 1993), p. 3.

37   Ibid.

38   For example, the invocation of Being in relation to the spiritual mission of the German *Volk* in 'The Self Assertion of the German University' (in *The Heidegger Controversy*, pp. 29–39).

39   Ibid., pp. 18–19.

40   It is instructive to the extent that Heidegger's treatment of true knowledge as being independent of the ontical disciplines of the sciences legitimates this kind of talk: 'the knowledge of true *Wissenschaft* [science] does *not* differ *at all* from the knowledge of the farmer, woodcutter, the miner, the artisan. For knowledge means: *to know one's way around* in the world in which we are placed, as a community and as individuals' ('National Socialist Education', in *The Heidegger Controversy*, p. 58). This charming piece ends with 'threefold "Sieg Heil!"' for good measure. We could say that implicit here is the kind of analysis of the everday structure of Dasein's Being-in-the-world as a practical grasping of it that Heidegger presents in *Being and Time*. But, again, does it follow that adopting this kind of analysis leads one invariably to become a Nazi – American pragmatists, whatever else they may be, are certianly not characterizable in such a way, and yet their emphasis upon practical engagement as fundamental to our conception of knowledge has much in common with Heidegger's.

41   See Jacques Derrida, *Of Spirit: Heidegger and the Question*, tr. Geoffrey Bennington and Rachel Bowlby (Chicago & London: University of Chicago Press, 1998).

42   Wolin, p. xvii.

4

Anti-humanism and the Problem of Ethics: Levinas and Derrida

One thing should be clear from the discussion that I have offered of Deleuze and Guattari in the preceding chapter. My criticism of them is essentially an ethical one. At the same time, it is a criticism that seeks to analyse the implications of their thinking in the form of an 'immanent critique'. The adoption of such an approach means that we need not step outside the domain of their own thinking in order to criticize them, for the problem I have located is one that can be derived from the elements that make up the text of *A Thousand Plateaus* itself. It is, though, important to note what I *have* argued and what I have *not* argued about *A Thousand Plateaus* and about its authors. I have *not* claimed that Deleuze and Guattari 'themselves' are fascists, for it is evident that they have a quite understandable dread of fascism. Their political and ethical stance is avowedly anti-authoritarian. The central contention, rather, is that the *structure* of their argument leads them to develop an account of the history of the Hebraic semiotic that effectively holds it responsible for the phenomenon of fascism. Fascism, recall, is a consequence of a trapped 'line of flight': it is a nomadism 'gone bad', a defeated attempt at escape from the confines of (Hebraic) subjectivism that rains back down on the earth in the form of 'realized nihilism'. What, though, are we to make of this?

Above all, we might be tempted to draw one conclusion from the kind of analysis I have already offered. We need to pay heed to the ethical implications implicit in the ontologies we construct in our attempt to understand ourselves and our world. We need to heed the fact that our language, concepts and argumentation do not of themselves ensure that we will end up producing the kinds of conclusions that we might be tempted to think they will. This is another way of saying that we are not always in complete control of the implications of our own ideas. At least, we might say, Deleuze and Guattari did not actively participate in or collaborate with any form of authoritarianism, as Heidegger certainly did. But, as we have seen, the question is: is the *philosophical thought* of a figure such as Heidegger in any degree tainted by aspects of his biography? Can we read implications out of a life in the same way that we can read inferences out of an argument? I have already offered some comments concerning Heidegger in this connection. So, at this juncture,

I will only venture to say that attempts to reduce philosophy to biography are always *prima facie* doubtful. A series of arguments, of words and concepts hooked together, only have implications in virtue of their relationship to other arguments, not in virtue of the personality that 'produces' them. At the same time, however, it is evident that the question of the ethical and political implications of the arguments and ideas that we might be tempted to *endorse* needs further clarification – especially in the context of the anti-humanistic approach that Heidegger and Deleuze and Guattari share.

Let me stake a claim here: in turning away from a subject-oriented conception of epistemology we also turn toward the broader domain of human relationships, and all such relationships are, if only in principle rather than as a matter of fact, implicitly 'ethical'. Ethical issues are not matters that occur in isolation from the study of our knowledge, or the examination of ontological issues about the nature of human identity and the broader conditions within which human life is situated. These are all related matters. In spite of the problems that I have argued beset their approach, Deleuze and Guattari's advocacy of nomadic thought can be read as an assertion of the positive value of a particular mode of life (nomadic pluralism). In short, it involves the endorsement of a kind of ethics. Equally, Heidegger's analysis of authenticity, although falling short of being concretized into a 'theory of ethics', is concerned with the kind of existence that we ought to pursue – even if he fails perhaps to live up to this himself. Recall, also, that Nietzsche's analysis of the problem of 'truthfulness' in section 374 of *The Gay Science* pointedly notes that as soon as we want to have knowledge 'we stand on moral ground.' In other words, wherever one may begin philosophizing, whatever issues one may be tempted to ask about, ethical questions have a habit of cropping up. Indeed, one might with good reason view philosophical enquiry as being essentially ethical in concern. We ask philosophical questions because we want to know, because we desire knowledge rather than ignorance, because we wish to illuminate our world in a manner that endows our actions with significance.

If Heidegger's analysis of the Being of Dasein has any persuasive force, that force gains its purchase from the fact that he articulates the problem of what humans are in terms of their *shared understanding* of the world. As an entity, each Dasein sees itself in other entities that are also Dasein, and thereby already understands them differently from other entities. We realize that others who are part of our world also have a world that we, in our own turn, are part of. We, it follows, necessarily act meaningfully not simply in virtue of our having our own dispositions and desires, but in virtue of the fact that others are there, too. Although we do not always *have* to treat others differently from the way in which we are usually disposed to treat stones, trees, other animals, and the like (i.e. instrumentally), we are at the same time always disposed to *understand* them differently from such entities. One person can choose to ignore another, but such an attitude does not amount to the same thing as ignoring the weather, passing oblivious through a landscape, or not acknowledging your pet cat. It is a way of behaving toward someone else that is significant because they are *someone else*, not some*thing* else. Ignoring someone, to put it simply, is already a way of behaving toward them *as someone*. It can mean things like 'I don't like you', or 'you are not important.'

The study of ethics concerns this kind of understanding of others. Ethics is not merely the study of *how* we treat one another, but of the principles according to which we have an understanding of how we *ought* to behave with regard to one another. Our relationship with other people is a matter that is shot through with evaluations; it presupposes that we recognize in others something distinctive concerning their value both *to us* and *for us*. Ethics, or 'moral philosophy' as it is also called, is the study of values. But it does not follow from this fact that there is a ready-made 'method' for doing moral philosophy. We can engage in theorizing about morals in quite different ways. For example, we might begin by examining a set of values that are adopted by a particular society or culture (say, Christian values), and then seek to provide an account of those values in the everyday context in which they are observed. This kind of study necessarily involves an analysis of the norms of behaviour that govern a particular community; it is, loosely speaking, 'descriptive'. We can also offer an evaluation of morals. This starts with a kind of description of norms of behaviour, but then aims to argue why one set of values is better. Or, we might start by asking what kinds of action can legitimately be designated as 'good' or 'bad'. This kind of approach involves advocating a method for sorting out good actions from bad actions. A large number of philosophers have taken this latter approach. Amongst British philosophers, for instance, the philosophy of 'Utilitarianism' advocates the view that the value of an action can be determined according to the criterion of whether or not it creates the greatest happiness of the greatest number of people.[1] According to such a view, it is the *consequences* of an action that determine its moral worth. An account of this kind offers an essentially instrumental basis for the interpretation of moral values. The Utilitarian 'greatest happiness' principle, otherwise known as the 'principle of Utility', holds that 'happiness' means nothing more than the feeling of pleasure and absence of pain, while 'unhappiness' signifies the feeling of pain or denuding of pleasure. Humans, on this conception, have a natural tendency to prefer to be happy rather than unhappy, and any action that would make most humans happy is regarded as having some justification.

There are some immediate problems with the utilitarian approach. Slavery might make a lot more people happy than unhappy, at least if there were fewer slaves than non-slaves. But few of us would regard this as a sufficient justification for the enslavement of others. Likewise, I might decide to kill my sole surviving relative, say my rich grandmother, in order to inherit her wealth with a view to sharing half of the proceeds with an orphanage. This might make a lot more people happy than it would make sad – after all, what's one dead old lady, who in being dead is neither happy nor unhappy, compared to lots of happy children? But, again, few people (I hope) would think this a justifiable attitude. What if everybody acted like that?[2] In the same vein, it is not clear that we can always assess the consequences of any action exhaustively: what seems to have beneficial consequences at any one time might well turn out to have very different ones in the long run. Finally, it is not really very easy to provide an exhaustive elaboration of just what 'happiness' is. Surely, 'being happy' does not necessarily mean the same thing as having pleasure or not having pain. In fact, 'happiness' is, strictly speaking, indefinable. It is a truism, but no less true for all that, that one person's pleasure might well be another's displeasure and that their respective understandings of what is 'good' in this sense would be incommensurable with one another. To this extent, it is not very persuasive to reduce the significance of the complex web of cultural and social relations that human life consists in to a matter of the pursuit of happiness/pleasure. As Nietzsche once noted, with typical acidity, only the 'English' (i.e. utilitarians) seek happiness, not the rest of humanity.

Instead of arguing for a view that stresses the consequences of actions as determining their moral worth, we could take what is termed a 'deontological' approach to constructing a theory of ethics. A deontological theory emphasizes the importance of *duty* in ethics. This kind of view was developed by Kant in the *Critique of Practical Reason* (1788) and elsewhere. Kant offers an account of the formal conditions required for the exercise of reason in the field of practical action, principally in terms of the capacity that reason has to impose moral obligations upon us through *a priori* principles which are then applicable to the domain of human practices. In this sense, reason is deemed to lay down the basis of freedom and moral law. Kant's analysis produces the formulation of the famous 'categorical imperative', which states that in order to be moral an action must always be affirmed in universal terms: 'I ought never to act except in such a way *that I can also will that my action should become a universal law.*'[3] In other words, it is not the particular consequences of an action that determine whether or not it is moral, but the whether or not it satisfies the criterion of universality (the 'what if everybody acted like that?' principle). If any action can be affirmed in this way, then one ought, as a matter of duty, to undertake to perform it irrespective of the immediate consequences that it might have. Recalling our earlier discussion of Kant's epistemology, it is evident he is arguing in a manner analogous to the case presented in the first *Critique* that we can derive a rule for practical moral activity that is not subject to the contingent determinacy of empirical experience, but rather to the rule of reason. In effect, this notion comes down to asserting that we ought to behave toward others in the manner in which we would expect them to behave toward us. If it could be said of any action that it can be affirmed as a universal law this involves imagining yourself to be on the receiving end of it.

Whatever their respective differences, the utilitarian and deontological approaches both offer theories about how we ought to evaluate our actions in order for them to count as 'moral'. Both, in other words, seek to understand morality in terms of the view that the word 'human' has a predetermined meaning and value. These views imply that we can arrive at an evaluation of an action simply by resorting to a 'method' or a 'rule' that is not itself embedded in the social context that makes up the domain of our actions, but is a standard of measure that transcends this domain. In turn, as individual agents, we are to be taken as moral beings to the extent that we submit ourselves to the dictates of such rules. But is it sufficient to offer an account of the nature of right action that takes the meaning of 'human nature' as already given? Also, we might ask whether it is sufficient to start with talk about methods and rules for right action without first raising some questions about the nature of the individual agent who is supposed to be subject to them? If we take the notion of the 'human' as signifying something that is predetermined, as meaning something like 'self-conscious' and 'free-willed', and base our account of ethics upon this, are we not already presupposing too much? Adopting the view that the word 'human' has such a determinate range of significance is to adopt a position that is generally associated with *humanism*.

Both the utilitarian and deontological accounts of morality have in common the fact that they have an investment in a form of humanism that harks back to the Cartesian 'I think'. In contrast, and whatever we might make of their respective approaches, Heidegger's analysis of the problem of Being and the Deleuzean account of becoming share one common feature: a decisive turn away from the Cartesian conception of the self as an entity that is definable independently of its environment. In this, they follow a thinker like Nietzsche. As we have seen, Nietzsche, in constructing arguments that challenge the subjective transcendentalism of Kant, effectively challenges the claim that subjective conditions determine the scope of human knowledge. For Nietzsche, human subjectivity is itself a product of socially and linguistically mediated forces. But Nietzsche's arguments, if we take them seriously, have more far-reaching implications than the mere overturning of epistemology or of providing us with another way of thinking about ontology. They also have ramifications for how we might think about the nature of ethics and politics. We will consider some of these ramifications in the next chapter in the context of a discussion of Nietzsche's conception of the 'will to power'. For the moment, we can make a more general assertion. What Nietzsche has in common with both Heidegger and Deleuze (and not only with them), is a view that implies the rejection of an attitude toward the understanding of human beings that has been given the name 'humanism'. It is this rejection that characterizes two significant and closely related developments in post-war European thought: postmodernism and poststructuralism.

The word 'humanism' in fact has a number of meanings, so it might be helpful to clarify just what is at stake here. In the Renaissance period, a 'humanist' was someone who studied the ancient classics of Greece and Rome. Looking to more recent times, however, we can define a humanist as being someone who advocates the value of human beings above all else. In the twentieth century, the designation 'humanist' has come to imply the adoption of an attitude that is opposed to the primacy of religious beliefs and ideals. In this sense, a 'humanist' is someone who asserts the positive potential of the human species independently of any reference to a divine nature. As a matter of fact, this view is not very 'modern' at all. It is a thesis advocated by the Ancient Greek thinker Protagoras: 'For he says, as you know, that "Man is the measure of all things: of the things which are, that they are, and of the things which are not, that they are not." '[4] Ancient or modern, the point is clear enough: for the humanist it is human thought and subjectivity that sets the standard for what is to count as 'reality'. Within the context of modern humanism, then, we are talking about someone who holds that there are specific characteristics beyond the mere possession of particular physical properties (having a large brain, being able to walk in an upright position, etc.). These characteristics define what human beings are and what their world consists in. Thus, humanists believe that we can be defined primarily in virtue of the possession of individual self-consciousness and freedom, and that it is this self-consciousness that in its own turn provides the criterion for determining the nature of what is. This latter espousal of humanism has come to be associated in particular with the brand of 'existentialism' advocated by the French philosopher Jean-Paul Sartre (1905–80).

1   Sartre's Cartesian Humanism

Sartre, in his *Existentialism and Humanism*[5] (1946), argued that there are two kinds of existentialist: Christian existentialists and 'existential atheists' – the latter including himself and Heidegger (p. 26). What both types have in common is the view that '*existence* comes before *essence* – or, if you will, we must begin from the subjective.' In other words, for Sartre, humanistic existentialism can be defined by way of its contention that human beings do not have a pre-determined nature that makes them what they are prior to their engagement in the world. In turn, since he is an atheist, Sartre contends that what we are is a matter that cannot be settled by way of reference to some divinely articulated and timeless notion of 'human nature' that exists prior to each of us being born. What we are is something that can only be realized concretely by way of individual experience: 'man first of all exists, encounters himself, surges up in the world – and defines himself afterwards' (p. 28). So, Sartre claims, there is no 'human nature', for what we are (our nature) is what we make of ourselves through the concrete activity of living. Such an understanding, however, implies one thing. Although our nature is not determined in advance, what is determined is the fact that what we become is a matter that comes down to us alone, to our life choices: 'man is responsible for what he is. Thus, the first effect of existentialism is that it puts every man in possession of himself as he is, and places the entire responsibility for his existence upon his own shoulders' (p. 29). People, in short, are what they make of themselves.

What, though, does Sartre mean by the claim that we must always begin with 'the subjective'? He offers two responses to this question. First, 'subjectivism' implies that every individual subject (each one of us) is essentially free to choose what he or she will be. Second, however, this subjective condition is essentially shared – all human beings have in common the fact that they are subjective beings (selves). Sartre's existentialism thereby argues for an affirmation of the 'I think' (the Cartesian *cogito*) as the fundamental condition of human subjectivity. But he in turn adds that the presence of one thinking subject rests upon the discovery of others as its condition of possibility (pp. 44–5). To this extent, all subjectivity is *inter-subjective*.[6] From this it follows that 'man cannot pass beyond human subjectivity', since this subjective condition is the necessary condition of being human at all. In consequence, individual human choices are, at one and the same time, *shared* choices: 'everyone must choose himself; but by that we [i.e. existentialists] also mean that in choosing for himself he chooses for all men.' The responsibility of the individual toward him or herself is hence one which at the same time 'concerns mankind as a whole'. This is because each of us, in choosing what we will be also chooses what humanity will be (p. 30). Significantly, since there is no God to determine what is right and wrong and since we are free beings, all such choices are necessarily ethical choices.

As should be clear given his avowed atheism, for Sartre ethical choices are not to be made by way of reference to already existing criteria. There is no pre-given 'rule of general morality' that can tell us how to resolve the ethical dilemmas we inevitably face when we have to decide upon how we should act (p. 38). Sartre's existential humanism rests upon the recognition of this condition. For him, humanism means embracing the fact that humans have no determinate properties. It is because they have no properties of this kind that they are capable of transcending themselves through choice and action: through action we become ourselves. By the same token, we stand continually 'outside' ourselves as 'self-surpassing' beings. As such, 'man . . . is himself the heart and centre of his transcendence. There is no other universe except the human universe, the universe of human subjectivity' (p. 55). Sartre's humanism thus involves the affirmation of the essentially 'subjective' nature of reality, i.e. it takes reality to be determined according to the criterion of human self-consciousness.

Sartre's emphasis upon the fundamental importance of self-consciousness is, in fact, the defining feature of his existential humanism. This approach can be traced back to his earlier work, especially *Being and Nothingness* (1943), which seeks to investigate the universal conditions of human individuated consciousness through an analysis of its engagement with the world.[7] One can say that Sartrean humanism begins by affirming the fact of consciousness as fundamental to human existence – as its defining feature. But what is also notable is that he explicitly claims Heidegger is a fellow traveller upon this road. This is because Sartre's conception of existentialism is largely inspired by his reading of Heidegger's *Being and Time*. Sartre, then, argues for a kinship with Heidegger's existential ontology. The later Heidegger, however, does not respond in kind.

1.1 Heidegger against Sartrean humanism: the problem of causality

Published in 1947, the year after *Existentialism and Humanism*, Heidegger's 'Letter on Humanism'[8] is often taken to be his response to Sartre's conjoining of existentialism and humanism – and with good reason. At the same time, the 'Letter on Humanism' is significant not merely as a response to Sartre's philosophy. It also presents us with Heidegger's own interpretation of his philosophical development. Heidegger, we can say, offers an outline of his views on humanism and subjectivity in the form of a kind of supplemental revision of the existential analytic of Dasein presented in *Being and Time*. This revision helps clarify the question as to why Heidegger later turned away from the project of *Being and Time*. At the same time, a consideration of it provides a means of access into the anti-humanism of those thinkers who emerge in the period after the Second World War.

Heidegger's essay opens by engaging with a theme that relates to Sartre's key argument concerning the human essence in *Existentialism and Humanism*. Sartre, we have seen, argues that the human essence is its existence, and that we therefore discover ourselves only in and through *action* and engagement with our world. In this way, Sartre effectively defines the human subject as, above all, an entity that can make *choices*. This is a view with which Heidegger will disagree in one very important sense. The central bone of contention concerns the manner in which we interpret the claim that 'Dasein's essence lies in its "to be".' Such a conception is akin to Sartre's contention that existence precedes essence, but Heidegger is going to clarify why he disagrees with the 'humanistic' conception of subjectivity that Sartre infers from this.

In the light of Sartre's emphasizing the importance of choice and action, it perhaps comes as no shock that Heidegger begins the 'Letter' with a consideration of the nature of *human action*, of what it is we refer to when we talk of 'human agency':

We are still far from pondering the essence of action decisively enough. We view action only as causing an effect. The actuality of the effect is valued according to its utility. But the essence of action is accomplishment. To accomplish means to unfold something into the fullness of its essence, to lead it forth in this fullness – *producere*. Therefore only what already is can really be accomplished. But what 'is' above all is Being. (p. 217)

For the humanist, people 'create' themselves in the activity of living: they are, to this extent, self-causal beings. But, Heidegger argues, viewing agency in terms of mere cause and effect is insufficient for an adequate understanding of it. To understand action solely in terms of 'cause' and 'effect' is to reduce its meaning to utility (i.e. the view that the meaning of action is the sum of its effects). However, the meaning of action is not to be understood merely in terms of the consequences that arise from a cause 'acting upon' things in the world. This conception of action is insufficient because what makes any action what it is (what Heidegger refers to here as its 'essence') is 'accomplishment'. 'Accomplishment' in this context means 'unfolding'. In other words, Heidegger is claiming that an action is an unfolding of what is already possible within the web of relationships that make up human existence. What is possible in action cannot be reduced in its significance to the existence of an independently constituted subject acting 'upon' the world, for subjectivity is always part of its world and constituted by it. There is therefore a reciprocal relationship between subject and world such that the one cannot be defined without reference to the other. If subjectivity cannot be divorced from its world, then it cannot make sense to speak of a subject 'acting upon' something (even itself) so as to produce an 'effect' in the form of the consequence of an autonomous 'act of will'. From this it is already clear that Heidegger is not going to support the Cartesian view of human agency which is necessary for Sartre's humanism to get off the ground in the first place.[9] Heidegger claims that we need first and foremost to see in action the 'accomplishment' of something that is already possible within, and fundamental to, the structure of the world of which we are a part. He claims that what is fundamental in this sense 'already is'. What 'is' must always be understood in terms of Being, since 'what "is" above all is Being.' Action, Heidegger is arguing, can only be properly understood once we have fully appreciated the importance of the relationship between subjectivity and Being, i.e. that Being is the enabling condition of all subjective accomplishment (its condition of possibility).

Whenever we talk of 'action' what we are considering involves not only physical actions, in the sense that 'catching a bus' or 'cleaning your teeth' denote actions. Thinking, Heidegger argues, is also a form of action. The activity of thinking achieves something quite specific: 'Thinking accomplishes the relation of Being to the essence of man.' In thinking what is accomplished is not some particular result, in the form of a consequence or effect. What is accomplished is the articulation of our essential nature by way of its relationship to Being. Again, however, one should not think of this relationship in terms of a model of causality in which thinking (as willing and acting, and hence 'cause') posits Being and thereby *asserts* its relationship to it. Thinking, in short, does not set the standard according to which Being is determined since action is an unfolding of an already existing possibility, in so far as the activity of thinking is an unfolding of what is already given in the relationship that thought has with Being. As such, thinking 'does not make or cause the relation' to Being. Rather, in thinking, this relationship is taken up as 'something handed over to . . . [thinking] . . . from Being.' So, Heidegger is arguing that the activity of thinking, as an 'unfolding', takes up something which has already been handed to it and brings it to a kind of fruition.

1.2 Heidegger's turn to language

What is 'handed over from Being', Heidegger claims, is something quite specific, for in the activity of thinking 'Being comes to language' ('Letter on Humanism', 217). When thinking occurs it expresses something essential concerning the relationship between humanity and Being. But thinking, as an occurrence, necessarily involves language: we who think do so in language. To put it another way, we only have an understanding of Being because our world is constituted by language. Moreover, if thinking expresses a specific relationship between humans and Being, and if this relationship is essentially articulated in the domain of language, then, Heidegger claims, we cannot grasp the significance of Being without also recognizing that it is presented to us *as* language: 'Language is the house of Being. In its home man dwells.' Humans, therefore, live 'in' language because it is only by way of it that they think and have a world. Understanding this fact involves a reappraisal of the notion of action, since the activity of thought must, by definition, be undertaken within the domain of language. If the activity of thinking 'concerns the relation of Being to man', and this relation is expressed in language, then it follows that language is that structure within which Being is encountered (p. 217).

What is evident here is that Heidegger is offering a combined account of meaning, language and subjectivity in which all three can be understood as expressing a fundamental relationship to Being. Above all, Heidegger's account of subjectivity flows from his argument concerning the primacy of language and Being in relation to thinking. He claims that 'Thinking . . . lets itself be claimed by Being so that it can say the truth of Being' (p. 218). Moreover, Heidegger contends, it is 'Thinking [that] accomplishes this letting'. Such a contention has important implications, not least for the subject–object distinction within metaphysics. The subject–object distinction, wherein a speaker (the subject) talks about something (the object), cannot hold in this case. This is because if thinking really does let itself be claimed by Being so as to speak the truth about it, then what claims thought in order to speak (Being) is also what is spoken of (Being): subject and object collapse into one (p. 218). Heidegger, though, does not take this to indicate that he is mistaken in his analysis, or that he has produced a mere tautology in which subject and object are rendered identical. Instead, he argues from this that the concepts of ' "subject" and "object" are inappropriate terms of metaphysics, which very early on in the form of Occidental "logic" and "grammar" seized control of the interpretation of language.' The subject–object dichotomy has, in other words, concealed something fundamental about language, something that can only be realized when our understanding of language is freed from the constraints of the grammatical model of interpretation that has dominated within the western tradition. Heidegger urges us to rethink language in a manner that is not indebted to grammar and, thereby, to liberate it.

1.3   Liberating language from grammar

Heidegger talks of this 'liberation of language from grammar' in terms of a transposition of our understanding 'into a more original essential framework'. We can say that whatever he is going to argue for as being suitable to replace grammar as the basis of our comprehension of language, it will be a model which is more 'fundamental' in two senses. First, it will be 'more original' and connected in some direct manner with the origins of language (both the preconditions of language and its source). Second, it will be 'essential' in that it will concern itself with what is *necessary* in order for language to be truly itself. Significantly, the outlining of this 'more original essential' basis of language is conceived by Heidegger in terms of a *structure*: it is a 'framework'. He is, in short, arguing that there is a conceptual framework within which we will be better able to understand what language really is. But what forms the basis for this framework? *Through what* are we to approach the question of what language is? This, Heidegger tells us, is a task 'reserved for thought and poetic creation' ('Letter on Humanism', 218). So, it is immediately clear, *'thinking', taken in the sense of a poetic engagement of language by language*, is, according to him, what can liberate our understanding of language from the confines of the grammatical paradigm. Notice, above all, that on the basis of this model there is no question of allotting the role of arbitrator over meaning and language to an autonomous, thinking subject (such as the 'I think' which grounds Sartrean existentialism). What is also ruled out of court is the possibility that it is the subject that articulates and is thereby responsible for establishing its relationship to its own condition of possibility (Being). Thinking is not to be reduced to the intentions of autonomous subjects who live 'in' the world, since the subject and its world come together as a single package (we 'dwell' in language), and this package (language) is rendered possible by Being.

But what is it, then, to act, and hence to think? 'Thinking is not merely *l'engagement dans l'action* for and by beings, in the sense of the actuality of the present situation. Thinking is *l'engagement* by and for the truth of Being. The history of Being is never past but stands ever before; it sustains and defines every *condition et situation humaine*' (p. 218). Thinking is not to be taken as entities (such as us) themselves acting upon a situation exclusively with a view to their own interests and purposes. Thinking is not essentially or intrinsically *instrumental*. It is an activity in which 'the truth of Being' engages with the world for itself. That is why, paradoxically, the 'history' of Being is not something that can be demoted into the past as that which has no bearing upon the present or future. On the contrary, Being is the ever-present condition of possibility of all human action. As such, Being is responsible for the continuation of all that is human and simultaneously defines our 'humanity'. Even if we might entertain doubts about the kind of priority that Heidegger affords to Being, in so far as he presupposes that there is a kind of unity that can be said to characterize the 'there is', his argument that our 'humanity' derives from a linguistic precondition that is not of itself 'instrumental' is an interesting and important one.

If we were to accept that this is the case, then 'humanism', as it is understood by Sartre at least, begins to look less and less tenable. It is not our humanity ('Man') that sets the measure of all things, but our condition of possibility (in this case 'Being') that sets the measure of the human. Humanity, it follows, does not define itself through autonomous action, but is defined as that which is able to embark upon action freely only in virtue of its essential relationship to what makes it human.

How, though, does one actually 'experience the . . . essence of thinking' that Heidegger is alluding to? First, it is important to recognize that experiencing thinking in this essential way involves 'carry[ing] it through' (p. 218). In other words, to experience what is essential about thinking we must actually *think the essential.* For this reason, there would be no use in Heidegger providing us with a 'concept' that we can then use to 'refer' to this essential form of thinking. It is not a matter of developing a 'method' or a set of rules that we could apply in order to experience genuine thinking. Such thinking must be *lived through* if it is to be experienced 'genuinely', that is to say, if it is to be experienced concretely. What Heidegger then offers are some points concerning what would be required for such a genuine approach to thinking to be attempted.

Above all, 'we must free ourselves from the technical interpretation of thinking' (p. 218). Plato and Aristotle get a slap on the wrist in this connection, for both of them conceived of thinking as a *technē* (craft). If thinking were a craft, then it would, in common with every other craft, have to serve a specific *purpose.* That is why both Plato and Aristotle 'take thinking to be . . . a process of reflection in service to doing and making'. But thinking, Heidegger argues, is *not* instrumental. Indeed, he argues, this very insight is already implicit within Plato's and Aristotle's definition of thinking. If thinking is already taken to be a reflective activity that serves concrete purposes, then this very fact can allow for it to be detached from the material activities of doing and making which it is supposed to serve. In Heidegger's words, 'here reflection is already seen from the perspective of *praxis* and *poesis*. For this reason thinking, when taken for itself, is not "practical"' (p. 218). Moreoever, Heidegger continues, if we understand thinking purely in terms of ' "theoretical" behaviour', i.e. in a sense which allows thinking to be opposed to *practical* action, then this is only because we have already accepted the instrumental view: 'The characterization of thinking as *theoria* and the determination of knowing as "theoretical" behavior occur already within the "technical" interpretation of thinking' (p. 218). So, Heidegger is arguing, the definition of 'knowledge' as always something that is essentially 'theoretical' is only possible if one has already accepted that thinking itself can be defined primarily in terms of 'technical' criteria: as an instrument serving specific purposes and, therefore, as the handmaiden of supposedly 'genuine' activity. The acceptance of this view betrays the fact that by defining thinking in this manner one has already engaged in 'a reactive attempt to rescue thinking and preserve its autonomy over [and] against acting and doing' (p. 218). We are, Heidegger argues, presented with a model in which thinking has come to be regarded as a purely 'theoretical' matter precisely *because* it has been contrasted with practical activity.

One important consequence has flowed from this model, in which 'thinking' is contrasted with concrete, practical 'doing'. Thinking is judged according to the standards of the sciences. Where thinking is traditionally taken to be synonymous with non-active 'reflection', the sciences are taken to be paradigm examples of active 'doing'. In other words, accepting the primacy of science has produced a need on the part of philosophers to seek to establish their own discipline's credentials. They have thereby defined philosophy according to scientific criteria. Some philosophers have, in other words, sought to show that philosophy, too, is a science (positivism) because they are 'hounded by the fear that it [i.e. philosophy] loses prestige and validity if it is not a science' (p. 219). But, Heidegger argues, any attempt to present philosophical thinking as another manifestation of scientific enquiry entails 'the abandonment of the essence of thinking' (pp. 218–19). This is because if we accept the scientific view and articulate thinking solely in terms of instrumental considerations, then the essence of thinking (what makes it what it is) is thereby concealed. This is because, according to Heidegger, what is essential about thinking is that (1) it is itself essentially an *activity*, and (2) this activity always occurs in a relationship with Being, and 'Being, as the element of thinking, is abandoned by the technical interpretation of thinking' (p. 219).

In a manner that parallels another of his essays, 'What is Metaphysics?',[10] 'logic' is singled out by Heidegger as bearing some responsibility for this reductive conception of thinking. Logic 'sanctions' the assumed primacy of the instrumental conception of thought. But, says Heidegger, if one evaluates thinking according to the dictates of logic then this involves it being 'judged by a standard that does not measure up to it. Such judgment may be compared to the procedure of trying to evaluate the essence and powers of a fish by seeing how long it can live on dry land. For a long time now, all too long, thinking has been stranded on dry land' ('Letter on Humanism', 219). What is immediately apparent is that Heidegger is using a metaphor here. Thinking is essentially a form of life and what lives can only be properly understood and evaluated if it is studied in the context of its own environment. In the same way as a fish does not live on dry land, so thinking does not live 'in' logic or instrumentality. The environment proper to thinking is the Being of language, and it is only by way of recognition of this fact that the 'multidimensionality peculiar to thinking' can be fulfilled.

1.4   Do we need humanism?

In the 'Letter' Heidegger is replying to some questions put to him by the French philosopher Jean Beaufret. He now comes to the first question: 'How can we restore meaning [*sens*] to the word humanism?' In the light of what has already been noted, Heidegger's response is unsurprising: 'I am not sure whether that is necessary. Or is the damage caused by all such terms still not sufficiently obvious?' (p. 219). Heidegger is, in other words, suspicious of all '-isms' and their kin. Even terms like ' "logic," "ethics," and "physics" ' are the consequences of a situation in which 'original thinking' appears to have run its course and come to an 'end'. Thinking ceases when it is no longer conducted in the 'element' proper to it (i.e. Being) – and the Greeks, Heidegger claims, in so far as they engaged in genuine thought 'did not even call thinking "philosophy" ' (p. 220). It is Being that makes thought possible and Heidegger therefore urges us to the task of rethinking the relation between Being and thought.

This, as we have seen, means turning to language. Such a turn does not involve doing what Heidegger calls 'mere philosophy of language' (p. 222). It is not, in other words, a matter of simply looking at different parts of language (nouns, proper names, verbs, deictics, etc.) and seeing how they 'work' or what their function is. This would amount to adopting the instrumentalist approach that Heidegger has already castigated. Instead, we must 'learn to exist in the nameless' (p. 223). That is, we must first desist from embracing the preconceived notion concerning what we are as it is offered to us by instrumentalism. This means turning away from the metaphysically determined mode of understanding that characterizes the Western tradition. This tradition presupposes an already adequate interpretation of the nature of entities that does not think the difference between them and Being. To ignore this difference is a metaphysical mode of thought because it concerns itself only with particular entities (with what they purportedly 'are'), not their condition of possibility: 'Metaphysics [thereby] closes itself to the simple essential fact that man essentially occurs only in his essence, when he is claimed by Being' (p. 227). We 'are' in so far as we are claimed by Being, and it is in virtue of this that we dwell 'in' language. Moreover, it is because we are entities that live in language, Heidegger argues, that we have 'a way of Being that is proper only to man' (p. 228). What makes us what we are cannot be accounted for by way of an examination of the kinds of 'material' entities that we are. We have bodies, and these can be analysed physiologically: we can look at the organs of the body such as the liver or the brain, or we can examine its other constituents – its muscles, bones, blood, etc. But our understanding of the world, and the fact that this understanding is essentially articulated in and through language, is impervious to reduction by way of such methods. We cannot cut language up into pieces and then analyse the bits, for what language 'is' is a matter that solely concerns its unity as language, and this unity is bestowed upon it by Being. In turn, Heidegger offers an account of the essence of the human not in terms of its 'existence', which signifies a way of Being that is usually regarded as appropriate to non-linguistic entities (rocks, plant-life, animals), but its 'ek-sistence'. Ek-sistence does not denote a way of Being in a manner akin to any 'specific kind of living creature among others'. Our ek-sistence denotes the fact that we differ from all other entities in virtue of the fact that we live in the world in a manner in which no other kind of entity can: 'man occurs essentially in such a way that he is the "there" [*das "Da"*], that is, the clearing of Being. The "Being" of the *Da*, and only it, has the fundamental character of ek-sistence, that is, of an ecstatic inherence in the truth of Being' (p. 229).

This may all seem rather dense, so it is worth trying to sum it up more clearly. In effect, Heidegger is arguing that he is not a humanist because humanism presupposes an instrumentalism. Instrumentalism involves thinking of individual subjects as 'causes', but causality is only possible in virtue of the condition that enables it. This condition is Being. Thinking, as an activity, does not happen in the domain of cause and effect, wherein a 'thought' produces (or 'wills') an effect. Thinking happens only in virtue of the fact that it does so in relation to its condition of possibility. If this is so, then 'man' is not the measure of all things. The condition of our own possibility announces itself in and by way of language. It is because we are linguistic entities that we can think at all. Language is what posits the 'there' and no other entity apart from Dasein lives as something which itself is 'there' in its world with an understanding of it. Doubtless, there are problems with such an account. It is not clear, for instance, that we need to talk of the precondition of language in terms of 'Being'. As Deleuze might say, language is just as much a matter of becoming as of Being. But let us leave such problems to one side and follow Heidegger's argument further in order to see where it leads.

It is not enough to say that we are linguistic beings in the sense that we 'use' language. Heidegger's anti-instrumentalism requires that language itself is not to be taken as 'something' that is 'used' by us. Language is not an instrument that we can pick up and put down when necessary, like a carpenter does a hammer. We *are* to the extent that we exist as linguistic creatures and we cannot be otherwise. Language, therefore, is not a matter concerning the uttering of propositions by individual agents: 'In its essence, language is not the utterance of an organism; nor is it the expression of a living thing. Nor can it ever be thought in an essentially correct way in terms of its symbolic character, perhaps not even in terms of the character of signification. Language is the clearing-concealing advent of Being itself' (p. 230). Language, we might say, is a permanent 'happening'. Language is an 'occurring', a kind of event in which we are situated in relation to Being. To say that we have ek-sistence rather than existence means holding that we are entities who exist by 'standing out' in the context of this occurring, that our Being is different from the Being of other entities in so far as its significance cannot be swallowed up within them. Understanding what we are in humanistic terms covers over the genuine issue. What we are is only given by way of the fact that *language constitutes us*, not the other way round. Humans, it follows, do not 'use' language when they think. Language is not a means to the expression of our needs, intentions or dispositions as organic creatures, for we are able to talk of such things only in virtue of the fact that we are in language already. Heidegger's contention leads him to question the validity not only of humanism but also of those discourses conjoined with it. It is not only logic or physics that he singles out in this regard, but also ethics. Talking about human action in terms of the discourse of 'ethics' means talking in a manner that has already presupposed language and thought to be mere instruments for action: it means skirting over the question of how we are 'human' in the first place.

1.5   Ethics and being

Heidegger's approach, it seems, means leaving the question of ethics to one side in favour of more 'original' thinking; or at the very least, rethinking what it means to speak of 'ethics' at all. The 'human' is rendered a secondary concern, for in the determination of what makes us human 'what is essential is not man but Being' (p. 237). We might make at least one observation here with regard to *Being and Time*. The Heidegger of the 'Letter on Humanism' has in fact offered us a radical (and we might say, not necessarily faithful) reinterpretation of the significance of this work. This is not to say that Sartre's humanistic interpretation of existential ontology cannot be criticized in the way in which Heidegger castigates it. But the claim in *Being and Time* that it is 'only as long as Dasein *is* (that is, as long as an understanding of Being is ontically possible) "is there" Being[11] is presented in the 'Letter' as signifying the primacy of Being, not Dasein: 'The sentence does not say that Being is the product of man' (p. 240). Heidegger has, it follows, moved away from the view that existential *ontology* can succeed in disclosing Being through an analysis of Dasein alone. What we are presented with is a turn away from Dasein toward Being itself. The 'clearing' that marks the advent of Being is prioritized over and above the human. For, humans dwell in the 'there' that is made possible by Being, and 'Being . . . is the clearing itself.'

Heidegger claims that such an account does not of itself negate the notion of the 'human' implied in the term 'humanism'. What it does do, though, is offer other possibilities for thought (p. 250). This is because thinking against something, Heidegger argues, is not the same as negating it. If we think against logic or ethics, this does not mean engaging in battle *for* the 'illogical' or *for* the 'unethical'. 'To think against "values" is not to maintain that everything interpreted as "a value" – "culture", "art", "science", "human dignity", "world", and "God" – is valueless. Rather, it is important finally to realize that precisely through the characterization of something as "a value" what is valued is robbed of its worth' (p. 251). In other words, we only engage in thought about the value of the 'human' when we have already ceased to value it. Arguing about values in this way means thinking of what is valued as an object, as something existent (an entity). Can we derive an ethics from the project set out in *Being and Time*? The answer to this question is 'No', not in a straightforward manner. Heidegger's criticism of the very notion of the 'disciplines' of 'philosophy', 'ethics', 'logic', 'physics', etc., in favour of a turn toward more 'original' *thinking* implies that the relationship between ontology and ethics needs further clarification before any such project is possible. This, in its own turn, means understanding ontology as a mode of analysis that ultimately rests upon the primary thought of Being. Thinking the 'truth of Being . . . is not ethics in the first instance, because it is ontology' (p. 258). But the ground of such thinking is itself neither ontology nor ethics. Such thinking 'has no result. It has no effect. It satisfies its essence in that it is' (p. 259). Since this is the case, we cannot derive an ethics (a series of rules that tell us how we ought to behave) directly from ontology or even from this kind of essential thinking itself, which is 'more essential than instituting rules' (p. 262).

However, what we do get from this essential mode of thinking, Heidegger argues, is 'the experience of something that we can hold on to'. We have a world about which we can concern ourselves in an ethical manner. Nevertheless, what remains 'essential' for the later Heidegger is the primacy of this fundamental thinking of Being. This is a thinking that is neither an 'action' nor a 'production' of something, 'For thinking in its saying merely brings the unspoken word of Being to language.' It is, in short, 'an *adventure* not only as a search and an inquiry into the unthought' (p. 264). Thinking is not a formal engagement with a view to obtaining 'knowledge' by way of a 'method'. As an 'adventure' it is a pursuit of what has not yet been thought. The question of the possibility of ethics only arises in connection with this: 'It is equally essential to ponder *whether* what is to be thought is to be said – to what extent, at what moment of the history of Being, in what sort of dialogue with this history, and on the basis of what claim, it ought to be said' (pp. 264–5). The question of the 'ought', that is, the ethical question of how we should act, only arises when we have engaged in a thinking that is neither an action nor a making of something. And this question shows itself as one that is *contextual*. We can only deliberate on what we *ought* to say in virtue of our situation within the history of Being.

In the end, this does not really offer us that much by way of an analysis of the ethical. It is one thing to argue that ethics is only possible in the light of its necessary precondition, but it is quite another to conclude from this that this precondition (the thinking of Being) will somehow itself announce to us what is appropriate by way of reference to the context of the 'history of Being'. By way of an example, however, Heidegger stakes a claim with regard to the stage in this history at which he himself is writing:

> It is time to break the habit of overestimating philosophy and of thereby asking too much of it . . . The thinking that is to come is no longer philosophy, because it thinks more originally than metaphysics. However, the thinking that is to come can no longer, as Hegel demanded, set aside the name 'love of wisdom' and become wisdom itself in the form of absolute knowledge.   (p. 265)

So, Heidegger himself offers a diagnosis of how we *ought* to think in future. We must abandon the ideal of 'absolute knowledge', the idea that we can possess knowledge as autonomous thinking entities capable of mastering reality. We must replace that view with a humility in the face of thinking and Being. To this extent, Heidegger stakes a claim with regard to where we are in the history of Being: we are at the point where 'post-metaphysical' thought is now not only possible but *required* of us. But this itself, it seems, does not fit comfortably with Heidegger's own rejection of the view that we can construct an ethics directly out of the thinking of Being. For, in saying how we *ought* to think, has he not in fact himself implicitly propounded an ethics concerning what thought ought to do? Moreover, in drawing a distinction between the philosophical disciplines and an 'essential', non-disciplinary thought, has he not himself constructed an absolute opposition between thinking Being and the concrete social practices (the 'disciplines' and institutions, amongst which philosophy is but one) that make up the practical domain of human life? Such a turn to the 'essential' in effect negates the possibility of concrete and fruitful engagement with inevitable components of the social realm that comprise human existence, and hence, in Heideggerean terms, with the very context in which the thought of Being occurs.

2   Levinas: The Ethical Versus the Ontological

We might say that the 'Letter on Humanism' turns away from a problem that the text of *Being and Time* engages with in the most thought-provoking manner: the question of the Other. This question has in fact been taken up by a number of thinkers. Here, though, we shall consider the work of just two of them: Emmanuel Levinas (1906–96) and Jacques Derrida (1930–). Levinas's thought is deeply influenced by Heidegger's *Being and Time*, which is 'one of the finest books in the history of philosophy . . . One of the finest among four or five others'.[12] Levinas regards the phenomenological approach of this work as one that pays dividends with regard to the insights it yields, and he castigates the later Heidegger for abandoning it.[13] That said, instead of pursuing the project of fundamental ontology that Heidegger embarks upon in *Being and Time*, Levinas turns instead toward a mode of analysis that asserts the primacy of ethics over ontology. This is done by way of an articulation of what Levinas holds to be the essential and cognitively irreducible relation between the self (or 'I' of identity, or what he calls 'the same') and the 'other'. The Heidegger of *Being and Time* presents us with an elucidation of the nature of Dasein in terms of its 'pre-theoretical' understanding of Being and develops an analysis of the other through an ontological investigation of Dasein's existential composition that begins by asserting its individuated nature (the claim that the Being of every Dasein is in each and every case 'mine'). Levinas, in contrast, argues for an approach that places emphasis upon the metaphysical preconditions of all ontology, and such preconditions exceed the mere 'mineness' of Dasein's self-awareness. In this way, Heidegger's claim to the possibility of an overcoming of metaphysics through ontology is challenged by Levinas.

'Metaphysics', in Levinas's terms, is the tendency of thought to transcend the limits of its own particularity and seek out the other.[14] Metaphysics, Levinas tells us at the beginning of *Totality and Infinity*[15] (1961), 'is turned toward the "elsewhere" and the "otherwise" and the "other"' (p. 33). He argues that we are entities who are driven by a desire for the other. But such desire is not to be confused with the desire we might have to eat a sandwich, enjoy a good book, or go for a walk. Wanting things like these is a matter of finding something that one lacks, indulging in it, and thereby deriving satisfaction from it. We do not, in contrast, derive this kind of satisfaction from our encounter with the other, for, unlike a cheese sandwich, the other is not to be taken as a 'something' that I lack, the desire for which can be negated by a trip to the local delicatessen. In desiring the other I have a metaphysical desire that cannot be sated by treating it as a 'thing' or object: 'The metaphysical desire has another intention; it desires beyond everything that can complete it. It is like goodness – the Desired does not fulfil it, but deepens it' (p. 34). Why is such desire 'deepened' by the contemplation of its object? Primarily, because the metaphysically desired other can never be consumed in the way in which bread can be: I can never subsume the other within my own self-consciousness. The metaphysical desire for the other is not an instance of two different 'things', which exist apart from one another, being brought together in the manner in which the sandwich is consumed and digested by the eater. The other remains essentially 'indigestible' in that the desire for it expresses a relation 'with what is not given, [with something] of which there is no idea . . . Desire [in this sense] is desire for the absolutely other', i.e. for what is irreducibly *not* 'I'. This kind of wanting is 'metaphysical' because it implies a transcendence of our individual particularity, of our own sense of self, through the other. As such, Levinas claims, it is a desire for the infinite.

2.1   Self and other

In so far as we all desire the other, one might say that we are all 'metaphysicians'. But in desiring the infinite one thing immediately becomes clear: the relationship between the metaphysician and the other cannot be articulated in totalizing terms. Self and other do not constitute a relationship that makes up a unity, for infinity necessarily shatters the bonds of totality by overrunning it. By way of clarifying what is being argued here it is worth pondering what the terms 'self' and 'other' signify.

In Levinas's terms, the other is heterogeneous with regard to the self, it is defined in contrast to the 'I' and always remains incommensurable with it. 'To be I', in this sense, 'is to have identity as one's content' (Totality and Infinity, 36). This does *not* mean that the I possesses an essential core that remains always the same in the sense in which Descartes's conception of the I as individuated mental substance does. But, according to Levinas, what the I does do is continually 'recover' its identity through all the events in life that may happen to it. For example, a person may go through a chronic illness or a traumatic experience (cancer, or the violence of war, say). In going through such experiences, the person interprets their identity differently from before. In this way not only does their 'present' change ('I am [now] a sick/traumatized person'), but so does the significance of their past ('I was that person, now I am this'). Who they 'were' is something that is reinterpreted in the wake of what is happening to them now, it is rethought in terms of who they 'are'. And we might add that who they 'will be' is re-articulated through this, too. If I am chronically ill, the question 'Will I be anything at all in the near future?' becomes a defining one. At the same time, such a self-interpretation presupposes something enduring, what Levinas calls 'the primal identity, the primordial *work* of identification. The I [that] is identical in its very alterations. It represents them to itself and thinks them' (italics added). The 'work', which one could call the phenomenological process of the self-identification of the I *as* I, is what secures the incommensurability of the other. The I is that which remains 'the same', that which can never be other than the same. What, then, is the other? 'The absolutely other [*Autre*] is the Other [*Autrui*]' (p. 39). By this Levinas is claiming that the domain of the other is not something impersonal. What is absolutely other than the I is the 'You'. What we encounter in the world as radically or 'absolutely' other than us are other people, the 'Other' as an individual. Taken together, the I and the other do not form a unity or totality. I am related to the other – who is a stranger to me – in virtue of the fact that I have no control over them. He or she 'disturbs the being at home with oneself. Over him I have no power. He escapes my grasp by an essential dimension, even if I have him at my disposal. He is not wholly in my site' (p. 39). The Other, we might say, occupies a radically different space. The metaphysical desire for the other, then, turns out to hinge on the existence of the personal Other as a being who escapes the mastery of the self, but who is desired all the more for that. Fundamentally different, what both share is that they cannot be defined by way of 'genus'.[16]

2.2   *Ethics versus freedom: the priority of metaphysics over ontology*

Ultimately, the relation that inheres between the self and the other is one that is enacted through language, understood as 'conversation' or 'discourse'. In conversation, I speak with the Other, but this very activity ensures my continued distance from them. Conversation entails a continual recognition of the other as having 'a *right* over . . . [the] . . . egoism' of the self (p. 40). The self is not, therefore, presented in conversation with an 'object' in the form of the other, but with a relationship with something that cannot be totalized or contained by its egoism. To think in relation to the other means to engage in speaking. Since no totality can be deduced from this relation such speech remains essentially anti-systematic: 'It is not I who resist the system . . . it is the other' that overturns the unity of the same (the 'I think') by presenting it with what is incommensurable with it. In this way, the I is transcended by the self–other relation.

This transcendence, though, is not a form of 'negativity'. It is not something that proceeds by way of the removal of an already present, and hence primary, sense of self: it is not achieved by first positing the I and then negating it. Could we, perhaps, attempt to derive this metaphysical conception of transcendence from entities in the world that we are acquainted with? By way of analogy, we might try to derive the idea of perfection by noting the imperfect and finite 'things' in our world and negating the fact of their imperfection. This could give us an idea of the perfect as that which transcends the finitude of the imperfect. 'But', Levinas tells us, 'the negation of imperfections does not suffice for the conception of this alterity. Precisely perfection exceeds conception, overflows the concept; it designates distance: the idealization that makes it possible is a passage to the limit . . . a passage to the absolutely other' (p. 41). The other cannot be conceptualized through the act of negation. I do not derive the other from a negation of 'myself', for the other cannot be deduced from pre-existent concepts, nor, above all, from the supposed priority of the concept of the I. The other is that which already transcends the I, for it is and always remains at a distance from me. It is 'infinitely distant from my own reality'.

If the relationship of irreducible distance between the same and the other is an absolute as Levinas would have us believe, then it must take priority over not only concepts and representations but also all ontology, i.e. all relationships to 'things' which 'are'. For Levinas, the Western metaphysical tradition has concentrated on articulating the existence of entities in terms of their relation to the same, i.e. in relation to the identity of the subject. In doing so, ontology 'promotes freedom' (p. 42). By this, Levinas means that through an ontological understanding of the world, I, as thinking being, necessarily begin to elucidate my relationship with that world in terms of myself. In so doing, I am not 'alienated' by what I encounter being different from me. Freedom is posited in the sense of the freedom of 'the same' (the persisting identity of the self) to recuperate the world to itself: 'Here theory enters upon a course that renounces metaphysical desire, renounces the marvel of exteriority from which that Desire lives' (p. 42). Levinas, however, wishes to stress the primacy of this exteriority, the priority of that which always already escapes from conceptualization within the domain of the same. By paying 'respect' to the exteriority of the other we gain insight into the primacy of a metaphysical structure that is more essential and fundamental than the ontological relation to Being that Heidegger analyses in *Being and Time*. Turning toward an analysis of the other brings with it a 'calling into question of the same . . . We name this calling into question of my spontaneity by the presence of the Other ethics' (p. 43).

Ontology operates by establishing the ontological conditions of existence and, in doing so, effectively asserts the primacy of the spontaneous self. By way of example, if we recall Kant's work, what is most notable about his characterization of sub-jectivity is its *spontaneity*: it is the spontaneity of the subject that grounds human knowledge.[17] Likewise, for Levinas, Heideggerean ontology begins by affirming the freedom and spontaneity of the individuated subject that engages with a world of entities in terms of their relation to it. What Levinas terms 'the welcoming of the other by the same', in contrast, initiates an ethical relation because such welcoming necessarily brings with it a challenge to the autonomy and freedom of the I. In thinking the other I must think what is different from me, and in doing this I allow myself to be called into question. Levinas argues that this metaphysical transcen-dence of the same by the other is an ethical relation because the same must allow itself to be challenged by the other in the very recognition of him or her. This recognition is the consequence of an engagement with the other. As such, it is 'concretely produced', and this concrete engagement challenges the primacy of ontology that is characteristic of the Western philosophical tradition: 'Western philosophy has most often been an ontology: a reduction of the other to the same by the interposition of a middle and neutral term that ensures the comprehension of being.' Western philo-sophy pursues freedom, which is an ideal that is opposed to the ethical assertion of responsibility 'to an existent that refuses to give itself, the Other' (p. 45). The ideal of such freedom, Levinas argues, can be identified in Heidegger's thought. Freedom, which for Heidegger is understood as 'an obedience to Being', is that 'which pos-sesses man'. The essence of the human is regarded by Heidegger as being located in the primacy of the ontological relation with the existent. This relation consists in 'neutralizing' the other in order to understand it; it means reducing what tran-scends the same to what is compatible with it. And this reduction is, for Levinas, characterizable as the reduction of what is other to the status of a possession. Ontology transforms the existent into property. Thus, 'Heidegger, with the whole of Western history, takes the relation with the Other as enacted in the destiny of sedentary peoples, the possessors and builders of the earth. Possession is predomi-nantly the form in which the other becomes the same, by becoming mine' (p. 46).

We can see, in this last quotation, a parallel between Levinas's criticism of Western philosophy and Deleuze and Guattari's thought in *A Thousand Plateaus*. Both reject the predominance of the 'sedentary' form of metaphysics in favour of a 'nomadic' understanding of the other. But, where Deleuze and Guattari would have us remain locked in an ontology of becoming that transcends metaphysics, and as a result hold ethics to come down to no more than the assertion of pragmatic rules, Levinas asserts the transcendence of sedentary cultural forms in terms of metaphysics itself. '*Being* before the *existent*, ontology before metaphysics, is freedom . . . before justice . . . The terms must be reversed' (p. 47). The ontological reduction of the other to the same must be replaced by the recognition that the other precedes all ontology. This means, as it does for Adorno, abandoning 'first philosophy'. Such abandon-ment is not a turn away from the concept of truth, however. Rather, 'it goes unto being in its absolute exteriority, and accomplishes the very intention that animates the movement unto truth.' It does so by entering into discourse with the other, by recognizing him or her as a fact that challenges the hegemony of individual spon-taneity. Entering into a discourse with the other, engaging in conversation with them, pays homage to their priority: 'This "saying to the Other" – this relationship with the Other as interlocuter, this relation with an *existent* – precedes all ontology; it is the ultimate relation in Being. Ontology presupposes metaphysics' (p. 48).

2.3 The face

The other is always encountered by way of the face. 'The notion of the face . . . opens other perspectives' (*Totality and Infinity*, 51), for in recognizing the face of the individuated Other we necessarily affirm the possibility of alternative viewpoints. Whereas traditional ontology asserts immediacy to be grasped in the relation between thinking subject and pondered object (in the representation of a 'something' by individuated thought), Levinas argues that immediacy, properly understood, is only encountered in 'the face to face' relation (p. 52). But the same (the I) cannot take hold of the face, cannot grasp it in order to wrap a concept around it. The face is characterized by way of its resistance to being contained within a language of understanding and concepts. The face is the individuated (and hence personal) Other *par excellence*: 'The face resists my powers. In its epiphany, in expression, the sensible, still graspable, turns into total resistance to the grasp' (p. 197). In seeing the face of the Other I do not encounter something 'thing-like' that resists me in the way in which an immovable object resists me. The face is not hard, like 'the hardness of a rock' that challenges my power over it by being impossible to smash into pieces. Such resistance would still allow me to affirm that I have some power – just not enough to break the rock. The resistance of the face, in contrast, challenges 'my ability for power' (p. 198). In other words, the face of the Other places in question the very notion of *my* power by confronting me with someone else. 'This means concretely: the face speaks to me and thereby invites me to a relation incommensurate with a power exercised, be it enjoyment or knowledge.' My relation with the Other, in short, is not a relation with a 'thing', but a with a 'someone' over whom it is impossible to assert power, for they cannot be 'possessed' in the fashion in which things can be possessed. To be sure, we can seek to exercise power over others: we can seek to annihilate what, in the other, resists us. Humans can resort to murder as a means of annihilating the Other. But the annihilation of murder, Levinas argues, is not the same as possession: 'Murder exercises a power over what escapes power. It is still a power, for the face expresses itself in the sensible, but already impotency, because the face rends the sensible.' A person can only want to murder the Other, nothing else – one does not want to murder a tree. And this very fact pays testimony to the Other's transcendence. 'Killing', in this sense, is an act that negates the Other as a sensible being: they are no longer 'there' in the world of sensible experience. But murder does not negate the Other itself. For, what is opposed to the mastery of the self in the form of the Other is not some greater or lesser degree of power, but the metaphysical infinity of transcendence: 'This infinity, stronger than murder, already resists us in his face, is his face, is the primordial *expression*, is the first word: "you shall not commit murder"' (p. 199). It is for this reason that 'The epiphany of the face is ethical.' What transcends the desire for mastery that drives the same to commit murder is the recognition, already, that the 'absolutely *other*' threatens the very notions of mastery, possession and control that the murderer seeks to establish by the act of killing.

The face, Levinas is fond of reminding us, is 'nude'. Metaphorically speaking, we can say that a thing is 'naked' when it is unadorned – 'bare walls naked landscapes' (p. 74). In Heideggerean terms, we might say that the 'ready-to-hand' reveals the 'present-at-hand' when it is rendered 'naked' in this sense: the broken tool is a useless implement, whose nakedness reveals 'the surplus of its being over its finality'. The nudity of the face, however, announces itself in radically different terms. Such nakedness is possible because the Other speaks to me, it is a result of 'the work of language'. When the Other speaks to me I am presented by a naked face: 'The face has turned to me – and this is its very nudity. It *is* by itself and not by [way of] reference to a system' (p. 75). The nakedness of the face, then, is the very challenge to the same that is presented by the Other: a face turns to me to speak, and I am presented with it. This is a non-systematic presentation because any thematic reduction of relations in the form of a theory is only possible when the Other has already been recognized. I can, in other words, only systematize and construct theories because I am already in a relation with the Other (p. 201). The face over-turns systematic ontology by showing us that conversation or discourse with the Other is the necessary presupposition of all ontology.

This amounts to the contention that individuated self-consciousness, which grounds traditional ontology, is no longer to be taken as primary. The face speaks to me, and in this one realizes something essential about language. Language is not merely an act or 'gesture of behaviour', although it is also that. What is 'essential' in language is 'the coinciding of the revealer and the revealed in the face' (p. 67). Here, there is no 'borrowed light' – which is to say that I do not perceive the Other in virtue of my own linguistic and representational abilities. To this extent, the Other pertains to 'objectivity'. What is encountered in the speech of the Other is not merely an alternative perspective on the world but something that is a 'term of pure experience': 'The "objectivity" that is sought by the knowledge that is fully knowledge is realized beyond the objectivity of the object. What presents itself as independent of every subjective moment is the interlocuter, whose *way* consists in starting from himself, foreign and yet presenting himself to me.' The 'objectivity' of the Other represents the fact that coexistence is a presupposition of human life. For Levinas, this understanding of the Other is implicit in Heidegger's work. But Heidegger, in the last analysis, reduces the significance of the Being of the Other by articulating it in terms of Dasein's 'relationship with *being in general*'. Because of this, Heidegger understands inter-subjective relations in terms of a coexistence in which the '*we* [is] prior to the I and the other.' Against the first of these claims we have already seen that, for Levinas, the Being of entities rests upon the infinite transcendence of the other as an existent. With regard to the second, Levinas insists that Heidegger's prioritization of the 'we' renders the same–Other relation in terms of a 'neutral' conception of inter-subjectivity that cannot be accepted. 'The face to face both announces a society, and permits the maintaining of a separated I' (p. 68). Thus, the conception of an individuated, or 'separated', self is not challenged by the Heideggerean notion of the inter-subjective 'we', since the neutral term 'we' is taken to signify a collection of individuals. In contrast to such an approach, Levinas stresses the fundamentally linguistic basis of the self–other relation.

It is only by way of language that the relationship with the personal Other is realized. This, Levinas holds, is what is essential to the social domain. In the conversation or discourse of speech what is continually registered is the fundamentally incommensurable nature of the other: 'The other is maintained and confirmed in his heterogeneity as soon as one calls upon him, be it only to say to him that one cannot speak to him, to classify him as sick, to announce to him his death sentence; at the same time as grasped, wounded, outraged, he is "respected"' (p. 69). The other is respected in each of these cases in so far as he or she is always acknowledged as what is 'invoked', rather than being rendered something that is grasped or 'comprehended' through concepts. The respect we pay to the Other involves not regarding him or her[18] as a kind of object that can be categorized, but as someone that speaks. In speaking, someone expresses who they are in terms of a world that is already delineated and structured by language – 'by transcendence' (p. 70). Language is coterminous with transcendence because it embodies the relationship of the same with the other, with that which necessarily transcends individuated self-consciousness. In discourse with others I encounter them as the transcending of my individuality, I meet and acknowledge in them something 'absolutely foreign' (p. 73). The Other, to put it another way, is the voice of the 'stranger', of one who remains inextricably exterior to me, who is presented to me by way of the essential 'nakedness of the face' engaged in the uttering of speech (p. 74). In the acknowledgement of the Other, the individuated self finds itself as an essentially social entity: it is provoked to respond to what it cannot master, to what is not a mere 'thing' available for its personal use:

> To recognize the Other is . . . to come across him in a world of possessed things, but at the same time to establish, by gift, community and universality. Language is universal because it is the very passage from the individual to the general, because it offers things which are mine to the Other. To speak is to make the world common, to create commonplaces. Language does not refer to the generality of concepts, but lays the foundations for a possession in common. It abolishes the inalienable property of enjoyment. The world in discourse is no longer what it is in separation, in the being at home with oneself where everything is given to me; it is what I give: the communicable, the thought, the universal. (p. 76)

Language, Levinas is arguing, opens us on to the Other. In language we dwell in a shared world. This world is not characterized by way of our individual possession of it, but by the recognition that our lives are circumscribed by what we can neither possess nor master. Of course, this does not in itself allow us to construct an ontology of action. We can, to repeat the point, ignore the Other, or even murder them. But such acts already presuppose the ethical relation of recognition as fundamental to human existence. In this way it is not, as Heideggerean ontology strives to show, our relation to 'things' that is decisive, but the always already established relationship between the same and the other that is 'the ultimate fact' or 'ultimate situation' of human existence (pp. 77, 81).

Understood in this way, metaphysics is not, for Levinas, something that is abstract. On the contrary, metaphysics is concretely 'enacted in ethical relations' (p. 79). Although concrete, this relation nevertheless remains fundamentally undetermined in nature. It is not possible to reduce the relation between the same and the other to a systematic totality, for what is encountered in the other necessarily grounds, and thereby transcends, conceptualization in terms of a totality. The same–other relation is not to be understood in terms of action and reaction, but as essentially *relational*. In this sense, metaphysics is neither a grasping nor an optical representing of 'things', but human experience itself: it *is* 'the social relation' (p. 109). Metaphysics precedes all ontology because the social relation is the necessary precondition of all self-expression, of all understanding, of all identification of objects of experience.

2.4   The I as 'enjoyment'

We are not entities that live 'in' a world of things that we reflect upon and then use or dismiss as being either fit or unfit for our purposes. We 'live from' our world: 'We live from "good soup", air, light, spectacles, work, ideas, sleep, etc. . . . These are not objects of representations. We live from them' (*Totality and Infinity*, 110). 'Living from . . .' does not denote a means to an end; we do not live from the consumption of 'good soup' with a view to the purpose of living. There is in human life a quality about the things we live from that exceeds the merely utilitarian value we might place on them. Even tools, Levinas notes, are embellished, they are decorated in a manner that is designed to give the user an enjoyment in them that is nothing to do with the finality designated by their 'use'. Equally, survival is itself never a mere 'surviving'. Although we get hungry and we *need* to eat, ingestion is for us also an enjoyment: 'Nourishment, as a means of invigoration, is the transmutation of the other into the same, which is the essence of enjoyment' (p. 111). In a manner analogous to Hegel's analysis of consciousness in the *Phenomenology of Spirit*, the self grasps the world it lives from with a view to rendering it the same, to incorporating it. But, hunger, Levinas argues, is never a matter of the mere satisfaction of a bare need, since '*living from* . . . is not a simple becoming conscious of what fills life. These contents are lived: they fill life.' What we live from, therefore, constitutes living, and is hence not in any way coincidental to it. To put the matter another way: there is no such thing as a life that is 'bare', that is made up only of what is necessary, since life itself is composed of enjoyment and suffering. If reduced to its barest form, life would not be lived, for it would be 'a shadow', devoid of the enjoyment that affords it meaning. Thus, and against Sartre, Levinas can argue that 'Life is an existence that does not precede its essence. Its essence makes up its worth [*prix*]; and here value [*valeur*] constitutes being' (p. 112). What is characteristic of our existence is that we are creatures who *value* the world around us with a view to its enjoyments, and this at the same time constitutes our essence as living beings.

'Enjoyment', however, should not be taken to signify something that can be analysed as a kind of 'psychological state'. Understanding the significance of enjoyment cannot be achieved through drawing a line between the I that thinks and the pleasures it pursues, as if enjoyment were something separate from the I. Enjoyment is 'the very pulsation of the I', 'Subjectivity originates in the independence and sovereignty of enjoyment' (pp. 113, 114). Enjoyment is, therefore, incapable of being accounted for in terms of drives or dispositions on the part of an individual subject, for it makes the subject what it is. For this reason, 'living from . . .' does not imply a lack, since the needs that constitute the terrain of enjoyment give life its content: 'What we live from does not enslave us; we enjoy it' (p. 114). We depend upon what we need, but we also gain mastery over what is impersonally other than us by consuming it. It follows that in enjoyment what is impersonally other is exploited, and through this exploitation, through dwelling 'in what is not itself', the I gains its personal identity (p. 115).

Material needs are sated, and the recognition that they can be satisfied allows for the I to turn from what it needs to Desire. However, human need is not prior to Desire. As Levinas has already argued, it is the Desire for the (personal) Other that has priority over and above all other considerations in human life. It is only because I live in a world that is social, that is therefore constituted by the Desire for the Other, that I can have needs at all (p. 117). But this itself, he argues, can tell us something about the 'unicity of the I'. Having a 'personality', being a self, depends upon separation, upon being isolated from others: 'The I is not unique like the Eiffel Tower or the Mona Lisa. The unicity of the I does not merely consist in being found in one sample only, but in existing without having a genus, without being the individuation of a concept. The ipseity of the I [i.e. what we might call the 'personhood' of the person[19]] consists in remaining outside the distinction between individual and general' (pp. 117–18). The I is 'solitude' itself: that which cannot be accounted for in logical terms, in so far as no one's personality is ever an instance of a concept that precedes it. Who 'I' am as a person is not something that can be established by way of reference to a prior concept of which 'I' am an instance. The egoism of enjoyment is a happiness that is rooted in separation from others. Such happiness, which is derived from the pursuit of satisfactions, by the incorporation of what is impersonally other into the I, is a celebration of the 'terrestrial and celestial nourishments' of existence (p. 114). What gives nourishment is depended upon. Yet, in being assimilated by the same what is relied upon is also mastered. Thus, the I lives in a state that is one of 'mastery in this dependence'.

On the basis of this analysis, Levinas argues that the I, as enjoyment, is a 'withdrawal into oneself, an involution' (p. 118). Such egoism, in fact, breaks open totality, for the solitude of egotistical enjoyment cannot be expressed by way of a unified scheme. If the ipseity of the I is not an instance of a prior concept that defines it, then the solitude that is expressed through enjoyment cannot be conceptually articulated in terms of totality. There is no concept, no 'idea' that corresponds to the ipseity of the I, i.e. to the personhood of the person. The solitude of enjoyment exceeds all languages of definition. In turn, although the presence of the Other represents a challenge to this egoism it does 'not destroy its solitude' (p. 119). Even though the Other delimits the egoism of the self's desire for mastery, it does not allow for the construction of the identity of the same in terms of concepts. Again, therefore, the I *is* in such a manner that exceeds ontology, 'to exist in such a way as to be already beyond being, in happiness . . . For the I to be means . . . to enjoy something', not for it to be derivable from the ontological structure of existence (p. 120). In this way, enjoyment presents us with the 'notion of the separated person'. It follows that life is essentially lived *between* persons. This sense of 'between persons' constitutes the social relation, and the Other is confronted by way of the social relation: 'I have access to the alterity of the Other from the society I maintain with him, and not by quitting this relation to reflect on its terms' (p. 121). In short, social relations are given prior to all reflection, and the Other is for this reason not to be taken as a 'thing' that can be analysed down into determinate concepts that yield a definition of its essence. From this it follows that we are not 'representational' creatures, as traditional epistemology would have us believe (p. 128): it is neither intellect nor engagement with entities that characterizes us as what we are, but our separateness from others in virtue of our social character.

In the light of this Levinas argues that the individuality of the individual is 'enacted' through enjoyment (p. 147). It is the outcome of an irreducible process of 'auto-personification', in which, as self-enacted beings, we attain the state of being at home with ourselves by living from the world we depend upon as creatures endowed with sensibility. Only with the egoism of the I in place, with its potentiality for enjoyment, is the 'idea of Infinity' possible (p. 148). The metaphysical Desire for the Other, in other words, is only possible for a being that is already separated from others. However, neither the I of identity nor the Other of non-identity are dialectically produced, Hegelian style. Although a condition of possibility for the idea of Infinity, the egoism of the self is not the conceptual ground upon which the Other rests, for the social relation is always already composed of self and Other *in relation*, and the social relation is not a system. 'The whole of this work [*Totality and Infinity*] aims to show a relation with the other not only cutting across the logic of contradiction, where the other of A is the non-A, the negation of A, but also across dialectical logic, where the same dialectically participates in and is reconciled with the Other in the Unity of the system' (p. 150). The metaphysical Desire for the Other is not to be articulated in terms of a systematic, logical structure that aims to reconcile the two terms in a conceptually organized totality. The idea of infinity that is revealed in the face of the Other depends upon the separation of the social relation, but such separation is not itself determined in the first instance by the I of identity. Being at home with oneself is only possible in virtue of 'a first revelation of the Other' (p. 151), and to seek to comprehend the Other in terms of the priority of the I would amount to destroying its metaphysical transcendence.

2.5   Language as the teaching of the other

The Other inspires in the I the Desire for metaphysical transcendence, for what exceeds its internalized sense of enjoyment. In its Desire for the Other the I is thereby called into question by what is not pure enjoyment, by what escapes the possibility of satisfaction by way of incorporation in the manner in which food gives satisfaction by being ingested. As transcendence, the Other is not mere 'exteriority', in so far as it is not something that lies outside of the I. The Other 'approaches me not from the outside but from above' (*Totality and Infinity*, 171). The exteriority of the Other is, therefore, a transcendent being-other, alterity. It is an exteriority that lies 'above' me, that is situated in the dimension of unassailable 'height' rather than a matter of mere terrestrial distance. In turning to the Other we are no longer at home with ourselves alone, for we cannot master and thereby possess others, we cannot grasp them in the way we do 'things' that are external to us. The transcendence of the Other lies in the acknowledgement that it lies 'above' the I in a state of absolute separation that will not yield to mastery. This separateness is articulated, we have seen, by way of language. The I is called into question by language, which is none other than 'the manifestation of the Other in the face' (p. 171). In this the transcendence of the Other is, at the same time, the transcendence of language. The face of the Other speaks to us out of the transcendence of language, and this 'height' is designated by Levinas as 'teaching': 'This voice coming from another shore teaches transcendence itself.' By way of the speech of the Other I learn that they transcend me. In teaching one is addressed from 'above' by the Other. But what is taught is not some set of maxims or concepts. Teaching, in this sense, is not the pedagogical instruction given by a possessor of knowledge to the student. What is taught is 'the infinity of exteriority' of the Other, 'teaching is its very production'. In other words, what is taught is the transcendence of the I by the Other is the ethical itself.

Such teaching is not a form of violent imposition. The Other does not, through language, impose his or her will on me. But it does reveal violence. The Other teaches the I that it itself, in its pleasures and enjoyments, is potential violence: 'It discovers itself as violence, but thereby enters into a new dimension.' In such teaching I realize that others, too, are beings endowed with a freedom like mine. The infinite distance that separates the I and the Other is not bridged and reconciled by this teaching. The freedom of the Other is revealed as the shattering of the totality that makes one at home with oneself, its freedom is like mine, and consequently hostile to mine. From this I realize that the social relation is one in which I am situated by way of others who have different interests, with whom I am already in an ethical relation in virtue of their transcendence of my particularity. In this sense, the ethical realm is the realm of truth: 'For truth is neither in seeing nor in grasping, which are modes of enjoyment, sensibility, and possession; it is in transcendence, in which absolute exteriority presents itself in expressing itself, in a movement at each instant recovering and deciphering the very signs it emits' (p. 172). I neither simply 'see' nor 'grasp' the Other as a thing, I respond to its expression as language, for in language it speaks to me from the vantage-point of absolute alterity.

The face of the Other speaks, and in speaking it enacts transcendence. This transcendence is not, however, 'outside' the world that the I lives from. It comprises an essential condition of its possibility that places in question the possession that characterizes the enjoyment of the I. 'The relationship with the Other, transcendence, consists in speaking the world to the Other' (p. 173). As such, speech involves articulating the world through the recognition that others are there, too. Through speech the world is placed in common, it is shown to be shared, to be held in common. This itself presupposes 'a certain form of economic life' (p. 172). In order to be acknowledged as being shared and hence as something that can be held in common, the world must already be understood in terms of possessions, of a site in which I and others live: 'No human or interhuman relationship can be enacted outside of economy; no face can be approached with empty hands and a closed home.' Each of us has possessions in virtue of our being characterized by way of enjoyment, and dwells in a world that is characterized by economy. And through language what is affirmed is the generality of this possession, the placing 'in common

[of] a world hitherto mine' (p. 174) by offering it to the Other. Thus, Levinas argues, 'Language does not exteriorize a representation preexisting in me' but, instead, makes the world meaningful by showing that it can be rendered in common with the Other by offering it to him or her. Encountering the face of the Other, then, means encountering them as language. In this sense, I do not see another's face as a 'thing', but recognize it by way of the speech wherein their face is presented to me as a face. 'The "vision" of the face is inseparable from this offering [that] language is. To see the face is to speak of the world. Transcendence is not an optics, but the first ethical gesture.' In acknowledging the Other we do not comprehend their transcendence as a kind of 'representation' to which we can affix a concept. What we 'see' is a meaningful gesture, and it is this gesture that bestows the world to us by way of the Other's demand for recognition as that which transcends us.

The Other, in its own turn, can be neither seen nor touched, in the manner that objects of sensibility can be. Nor is it approachable by way of 'letting beings be' in order to disclose a fundamental relation to Being, as Heidegger would have it. The Other is solicited by language (p. 195). But, for Levinas, we must not understand language as something that derives from our individuated self-consciousness. Language 'comes to me from the Other and reverberates in consciousness by putting it in question' (p. 204). Language is not to be taken as something that is an 'activity' pursued by a thinking subject as it pursues its enjoyments. Language is the necessary condition of thought. As a necessary condition of thought language takes the form of a structure of signification that transcends all particularized thoughts, and so questions the freedom of the I (pp. 206–7). The sameness of the I is thereby challenged in its freedom by the structure of language, which bestows meaning by placing the I in question. 'Meaning', therefore, 'is the face of the Other, and all recourse to words takes place already within the primordial face to face of language' (p. 206). In language what we are presented with is the social realm, and this realm is one of 'obligation' (p. 207). The social, enacted as language, therefore announces the essentially ethical character of all human life. 'Ethical' here signifies an ought, an 'ethical exigency'[20] wherein the face of the Other is necessarily acknowledged as a condition of human possibility. This, as we have noted, does not of itself prevent the ontological fact of murder, of perpetrating violence against the Other. But, Levinas argues, what it does show us is the fact that in the very recognition of the face what we 'see' is itself a breaking open of 'being'.[21] The very humanity of the human stands against being. We might say that, for Levinas, humans 'stand out' over being precisely because they are ethical, because the relations between people rest upon the recognition of the ethical prohibition that forbids violence, even though such a prohibition cannot prevent it factually.

One thing is clear. Levinas's ethics is not a humanistic one in the Sartrean sense – the sense that, we have seen, the later Heidegger also rejects. The I is not the measure of all things. The transcendence inherent in the presentation of the face of the Other, and in language, is the measure of our humanity. Levinas's ethics is one that can be characterized in terms of alterity: it is an ethics of exteriority, an anti-humanism in so far as it is a humanism of the Other: the Other is the measure of the I, not *vice versa*. On such a view, we are necessarily responsible for each other: 'It is I who support the Other and am responsible for him. . . . My responsibility is untransferable, no one could replace me. In fact, it is a matter of saying the very identity of the human I starting from responsibility . . . I am I in the sole measure that I am responsible, a non-interchangeable I.'[22] So, the identity of the I arises from its responsibility to others – above all from the fact that *my* responsibility toward the Other cannot be transferred to either something or someone else. If the I is enjoyment, then even the possibility of enjoyment ultimately rests upon the facts that others are there, too. The ethical, it follows, constitutes the fundamental precondition of the social domain, in the form of the irreducible 'face to face' relationship between persons that makes human life possible. In this sense, we do not need to look 'beyond' the social to find the basis of the human essence. The face *shows* the human essence in and as speech.

What, though, are we being presented with by Levinas's arguments? Given his emphasis upon transcendence we might be tempted to regard his thinking as tending toward a theological standpoint. There is justification for this, since it is certainly true that Levinas regards God a signifying 'a putting of the Infinite into thought'[23] in a manner that transcends the identity of the 'I think' and challenges the ontological thematization characteristic of Western philosophical thought. Where the Christian tradition of rational theology tries to think God in terms of the existent, and conceptualizes the divine as an entity endowed with a determinate identity, Levinas (a Jew) regards God as that which challenges the finitude of the I.[24] God cannot be thought of as an entity. God, understood in this way, is neither a *someone* who speaks nor a 'thing'. 'God' signifies an infinity that transcends being. In this way, God and the ethical are conjoined: 'Ethics is not a moment of being; it is otherwise and better than being, the very possibility of the beyond. In this ethical reversal . . . God is drawn out of objectivity, presence and being. He is neither an object nor an interlocuter. His absolute remoteness, his transcendence, turns into my responsibility . . . for the other.'[25] The absence of God thus initiates the ethical, for God himself is not merely an 'Other', but is 'other otherwise'. God is that which transcends even the personal self–Other relation that determines the human and renders it possible. From this it is obvious that, for Levinas, God is not to be accounted for as a kind of divine agent, acting, as it were, 'behind the scenes' of the human web of existence. God is absent from life except as the idea of transcendence, and it is this absence which grounds the ethical.

We can clarify this by briefly reflecting upon Levinas's account of the I as enjoyment. The I, taken in this way, is a natural atheist. One could even say that he or she is, to coin a phrase, a 'mono-atheist': the world is characterized in terms of *my* needs, *my* enjoyments, *my* identity. Something analogous to this is reflected in Descartes's epistemology, where the 'I think', although ultimately resting upon the existence of God, is discovered first as an indubitable truth. The chronology of this account, its thematic ordering of terms, prioritizes the I as a matter of logical necessity. But, says Levinas, the fact of human separation signals the presence of an order that is not 'logical', of a logically absurd 'posteriority of the anterior' wherein the theoretical assertion of the 'I think' already embraces separation in spite of its claims to unity (*Totality and Infinity*, 54). As we have seen, it is this structure, the relation of transcendence, that sustains the I in its separateness. In thinking the Other we think the conditions of our separation from one another as an essential condition of our lives: 'The face to face is not a modality of coexistence . . . but is the primordial production of being', and on this 'production' the very possibility of our constructing and ordering concepts and ideas depends (p. 305). In this way, the Other is like God: it is an absence that calls to us, that invokes a response in us, and in doing so simultaneously appeals to and masters the egoism of the I. Like God, the Other is not a 'someone', it does not have an identity that is independent of its exteriority, but is identified essentially as 'Other' by way of its transcendence. It is this transcendence that both calls upon us and demands our response: 'The Other qua Other is situated in a dimension of height and of abasement – glorious abasement; he has the face of the poor, the stranger, the widow, and the orphan, and, at the same time, of the master called to invest and justify my freedom' (p. 251). Freedom, in this way, is only realized in the form of an adherence to the ethical. In other words, freedom is what is granted to us when we acknowledge the limits of our own interests.

There are a number of possible responses to Levinas's thought concerning ethics. We might wonder how it is that the face is recognized at all as a face. Are there (Kantian-style) transcendental preconditions that engender a face's being seen as such? Of course, this kind of objection rests upon precisely the kind of framework of presuppositions that Levinas is seeking to throw into question. However, instead of pursuing such objections, I shall confine myself here to the discussion of Levinas offered by Derrida. There are two reasons for this. First, although there may be room for objecting to aspects of Derrida's discussion of Levinas, it is nevertheless the case that he is highly sensitive and receptive to the tenor of Levinas's thinking. Second, a brief account of Derrida's response to Levinas can serve as a helpful means of situating some of the central concerns of Derrida's own thinking. Such an account also necessitates a consideration of questions concerning the nature of method, the political, and the ethical as they occur within Derrida's thought. At the same time, an adequate understanding of the nature of the debate between Levinas and Derrida requires some discussion of Derrida's own work. Thus, we will need to talk about deconstruction, about certain important notions that Derrida has discussed (such as the trace and *différance*), and about structuralism, prior to a consideration of Derrida's response to Levinas.

3   Derrida, Deconstruction and the Question of Ethics

Jacques Derrida, whose name is inextricably associated with deconstruction, must be numbered amongst the most controversial of post-war European thinkers. There are a number of reasons for this. There is, for instance, the matter of Derrida's relationship to the institution of Anglo-American analytic philosophy, which was marked most famously by his dispute in the late 1970s with the American philosopher, John Searle. In an essay entitled 'Signature, Event, Context' Derrida offered an account of the English philosopher J. L. Austin's (1911–60) theory of 'speech acts'.[26] Searle wrote a piece ('Reiterating the Differences') criticizing Derrida's analysis of Austin, and Derrida in turn responded with an essay ('Limited Inc.') that irritated Searle. This seems to be because Derrida was arguing that Searle had not really grasped the point he was making about Austin, but did so in a manner that comprehensively cited and yet at the same time (at least from Searle's point of view) distorted the intentional meaning of Searle's own arguments by recontextualizing them. The significance of Derrida's gesture derives from the fact that Austin's work makes a great deal of the role both of intentionality and literal language in securing the meaning of words. But, Derrida argues, neither pure intentionality nor the 'literal' meaning of words plays a fundamental role in securing the generation of meaning. In addition to such matters we must also pay attention to questions about the context of utterances, and this is linked to what Derrida terms 'iterability' – a complex notion to which we shall return in due course. I do not propose here to consider in detail the Derrida–Searle dispute, although I will in fact shortly turn to some of Derrida's comments in connection with this as a means of clarifying his philosophy. One thing that can be said is that the dispute has contributed in its own small way to fostering the continued Analytic–Continental division within philosophy that I discussed briefly in the introduction to this volume.[27]

Derrida's name is controversial for a number of other reasons that are worth mentioning here. Foremost amongst these is that he is a thinker who has sought to challenge a number of what he argues to be deeply rooted presuppositions that dominate the practice of philosophical enquiry. It is this challenge, or rather the importance attributed to it by some of Derrida's readers, that in its own turn led in the late 1970s and early 1980s to his being taken up in the first instance by a readership that one would not immediately define as 'philosophical', at least not in the institutional sense that is associated with this word. In the English-speaking world, the readers who initially responded positively to Derrida's work sprang largely from the Literature departments of universities in the United States and Britain. There are a number of possible explanations for this. We might, for instance, suspect that this readership perhaps saw in Derrida's writings a possible avenue for challenging the dominant position that philosophy departments tended to claim for their subject within the study of the humanities in the university system. To express the matter crudely, one might say that whereas the study of literature, for example, ultimately depends upon the prior production of fictional works, which the literary critic then analyses with a view to unpacking their metaphorical structure, ambiguities of meaning and the like, the study of philosophy has in general put questions of the nature of fiction safely to one side and got on with the business of enquiring into the nature of knowledge, truth, the nature of existence, ethics, etc. Putting it rather differently, it might be argued that, with some notable exceptions,[28] philosophers have not usually worried too much about certain 'literary' aspects of language use, such as metaphor. Rather, they have tended to the view that literal language can be analysed as a means of arriving at precise and reliable accounts of the issues at hand, and that metaphor can itself be comprehended through literal paraphrase or structural analysis. In this manner, it might be contended that the discipline of philosophy has frequently lodged a claim to predominance among the humanities. To the extent that a form of challenge to philosophy could be mounted by way of it, there is good reason to suspect that the burgeoning of the kind of critical theory[29] associated with literature departments, which pays great attention to political, gender and race issues in relation to literary texts, owes much to the influence of certain readings of Derrida's work. Equally, Derrida's work is also conjoined with the phenomenon of structuralism, which itself gave rise to a form of literary criticism in the 1970s.[30] Again, therefore, there is good reason to suspect that Derrida's reception on the part of the literary academic community might have been further enhanced by this fact. Let us, however, leave the question of academic divisions to one side and instead consider Derrida's work in its philosophical context. By adopting this approach we shall be able to see how his writings relate to the philosophical questions that we have so far examined, and this will lead us back to the question of ethics. Since I have already mentioned it, let us begin with the phenomenon of structuralism.

3.1   Structuralism

Although associated in one of its forms with a variety of literary criticism, the methodology that goes under the name of structuralism has in fact been employed in a wide range of fields. There is, for example, the structural anthropology of Claude Levi-Strauss (1908–), and structuralist approaches have also been developed within the field of the social sciences. Likewise, thinkers such as the French philosopher Louis Althusser (1918–90) developed a structuralist version of Marxism in the 1960s.[31] Althusser's importance in relation to Derrida should not be underestimated. Not only was Althusser an immensely influential figure within the French academic scene of the 1960s, but as 'caïman' at the Ecole Normale Supérieure (rue d'Ulm), he supervised Derrida in preparation for his *agrégation*. Given these circumstances, it is unsurprising that Derrida's work, like that of other near contemporaries on the French scene,[32] has its own very particular involvement with structuralism. However, while influenced by many of the central tenets of structuralism, Derrida's thought springs from the questioning of some of its central presuppositions.

Although the term was coined by the Russian formalist theorist Roman Jakobson (1896–1982), structuralism is generally traced back to the writings of the Swiss linguist, Ferdinand de Saussure (1857–1913). Saussure's most famous work, the *Course in General Linguistics* (1916), which was compiled from students' notes taken from lectures given between 1907 and 1911, seeks to construct what he regards as a scientific account of the process of signification, i.e. how words present meaning. He terms this science 'semiotics', or the science of signs. On the Saussurean conception, all language (the definition of which includes forms of communication other than simply spoken language, i.e. all kinds of signs) is susceptible to being analysed in terms of a structural system of relations. In turn, Saussure argues that the meaning of any individual word is determined by this structural relation, not by way of any direct referential function that the word might have. According to this view, we do not arrive at an understanding of what a word or any other sign means by way of what it refers to. A sign is held to possess a meaning as a direct consequence of its relationship to the other words with which it is associated. To put the matter bluntly, meaning is regarded as resulting from the *difference* that pertains to signs, and this difference is secured first and foremost by way of reference to their relation to one another. Additionally, Saussure contends that language in general can be articulated in terms of one fundamental distinction: *langue* and *parole*. Within this model, *langue* constitutes the fundamentally *structural* element of language. *Langue* is the structurally organized network of possible meanings that have to be in place at any given time if a speaker is to utter a sentence. *Parole*, in contrast, is a term that denotes the use of these elements as they are actualized within any individual utterance (i.e. speech).

One notion that is central to structuralism is that of binary opposition. This effectively states that all meaning is ultimately determined by a relationship of opposition that inheres between different signs (good/bad, light/dark, etc.), and this oppositional structure exerts a determining force on the constitution of meaning. For a thinker like Jakobson this relationship of opposition makes up the fundamental structure of all language. This notion, which is not strictly speaking Saussure's, led to the development of critical approaches associated with structuralist literary criticism. What marks out the structuralist project, be it that of the textual analyst, of the structural anthropology of Claude Levi-Strauss, or the structural Marxism of Althusser, is a commitment to the view that it is possible to decode with scientific validity the organization of meanings which are to be found in written works or social relations alike. This amounts to a commitment to the view that it is possible to construct an objective and universal account of meaning that can, in turn, be used to reveal the particular meanings hidden within texts or social relations and codes. Structuralism, therefore, seeks above all to elucidate the objective conditions that constitute all linguistic and social relations. As such, structuralism claims to be regarded as an objective science. The emphasis on structure has led many exponents of structuralism to take a critical stance toward humanism. The main reason for this is not difficult to grasp: if meaning is a matter of nothing more than the causal relationship between signs that pertains within any given structure, then issues of human agency, of individual or shared interests, of community, and so forth, are susceptible to being either ignored or accounted for within the confines of the structural-causal framework of analysis that the structuralist adopts. A number of criticisms of the structuralist approach are possible. We might be tempted to accuse the structuralist approach of producing a reductive account of the notion of agency, in so far as subjectivity might well be a rather more complex matter than the mere result of structural forces. Equally, the adequacy of the structural metaphor might be questioned in terms of its applicability to the process of the generation of meaning. Is meaning, after all, the result of a 'process', or is there something rather more complex at work here?

3.2   Derrida and the limits of structuralist thought

For Derrida, too, there are problems with the structuralist enterprise. His criticisms of structuralism in fact in some ways allow him to be counted amongst those who are called 'poststructuralist',[33] although this is not a term that is necessarily helpful in understanding Derrida's work. In the first instance, it is possible to mount an attack upon the purported 'objectivity' of structuralism's methods. This point, amongst others, is made by Derrida in his essay 'Force and Signification', which aims at both decoding the significance of structuralism and questioning its central presuppositions.[34] According to Derrida, structuralism can be understood as springing from 'an anxiety about language – which can only be an anxiety of language, within language itself' (p. 3). This form of anxiety, however, is no mere historical accident; it cannot be reduced in significance to a sign of its own times. The structuralist enterprise, Derrida claims, presents us with the insight that we must turn toward the analysis of language itself as a means of uncovering the 'origin of history . . . [of] . . . historicity itself' (p. 4). Structuralism, however, is not synonymous with this anxiety. For, structuralism can, in principle, be subjected to the critical scrutiny of the historian of ideas. If such criticism were to be offered at some time in the future what might be concluded? Perhaps, Derrida muses, the pursuits of the structuralist will come to be regarded 'as a relaxation, if not a lapse, of the attention given to *force*, which is the tension of force itself. *Form* fascinates when one no longer has the force to understand force from within itself. That is, to create. That is why literary criticism is structuralist in every age' (pp. 4–5). Structuralism can be defined as the privileging of the formal conditions governing meaning over the creative conditions that give rise to it. The attention to form, as a kind of 'movement of diminished ardor', defines what must always remain essential to the structuralist enterprise. But there is more. For, Derrida argues, what the 'structural consciousness' also attains is the exposure of its own constituted nature. The structuralist insight both seeks to convey the objective totality that goes to make up the structure of meaning, and yet at the same time exposes its own limitations in the very act of doing so. It is a 'reflection of the accomplished, the constituted, the constructed. Historical, eschatological, and crepuscular by its very situation' (p. 5). This kind of reflection presents us with a totality that can be all the more easily perceived, in the sense in which one can survey and analyse the structure of a building without paying any attention to those who might live or work in it. The formal elements of the building, its structure, are thereby exposed in the form of a whole that can be interpreted independently of the lives of those who may be situated within it. By the negation of force, structuralism offers us an insight into the constituted and constituting conditions that operate in the production of meaning and history. Derrida himself, by way of clarification, offers us the metaphor of a deserted city to illustrate this point:

> Thus, the relief and design of structures appears more clearly when content, which is the living energy of meaning, is neutralized. Somewhat like the architecture of an uninhabited or deserted city, reduced to its skeleton by some catastrophe of nature or art. A city no longer inhabited, not simply left behind, but haunted by meaning and culture.

Meaning is rendered as something ghostly by the structuralist perspective. The disengagement of the living force of meaning that structuralism must enact in order to reveal the objective conditions that its aspirations toward the status of a science demand thereby produces an uncanny result. But what is at stake here? What does the demand for this kind of objectivity imply? According to Derrida, we can conclude that this itself shows structuralism to be determined by something that it cannot account for, something that in fact is the precondition of the kind of illumination and insight that the structuralist viewpoint offers us. In illuminating the structural and hence formal component of meaning to us, the structuralist model also at the same time conceals the force that makes this illumination possible.

This notion of a simultaneous unveiling and covering up (a theme that we might note has its precursor in Heidegger's analysis of the significance of traditional metaphysics in the opening pages of *Being and Time*) is central to Derrida's account of the structuralist enterprise. However, the notion of force that is at stake within the context of Derrida's discussion should not be confused with the creative force of an expressive individualism. 'Force' here does not imply an expressive overflowing, still less a mode of intentionality. Force, as Derrida wishes to consider it, cannot be *thought*, in the sense of being conceptualized. It is not the thought of force (i.e. its conceptualizable aspect) that is at stake here, but force itself understood as 'the other of language without which language would not be what it is' (p. 27). Force, in other words, is for Derrida something that produces meaning as language. But it is not itself purely 'linguistic' in nature. Nor is force merely 'empirical', i.e. the product of social and historical factors – hence Derrida's argument that an analysis of structuralism must bring with it reflections on the nature of historicity itself, the condition of possibility of the historical, which is force. In fact, what is at issue here is in part a matter of ontology. Structuralism presupposes that it can offer us an illumination of the formal conditions of the production of meaning presented within texts (literary or otherwise) or other social forms. But in order to do this these formal conditions must be conceptualized as *fixed*. A structure is always a form and a form is always frozen. Because of this, structuralism must ultimately be indebted to a traditional ontological mode of understanding. This understanding is in fact concealed in the very act of the structuralist writer's revealing the formal conditions of meaning that inhabit the structure of a written work or cultural practice.

Although the object of Derrida's interest in 'Force and Signification' is the French writer 'Jean Rousset's fine book: *Forme et Signification*' ('Force and Signification', 6), an analogous point can be made by way of reference to the Saussurean conception of *langue*. In conceptualizing language primarily in terms of structure, as *langue*, Saussure must assume that it is possible to take a kind of 'snapshot' of those formal conditions that govern the nature of meaning and in doing this reveal what is essential about it. But the very notion of meaning as being wholly structural and formal in nature ignores the fact that meaning also changes. In so far as it does change, meaning is not 'in itself' structural. In metaphysical terms, we could say that the structuralist account presupposes the very thing that Nietzsche castigates when he attacks 'metaphysical philosophy': it presupposes that stability is both an ontological norm and a defining feature of objectivity. Derrida's point is a similar one. The structuralist conception of meaning requires that the totality of a structure can be revealed. But the possibility that such a totality can be revealed is not something that can be shown to be the case. We can, indeed, envisage ourselves gazing at the world of human existence from the structuralist point of view: we can imagine a city devoid of its inhabitants, so that the city's formal pattern is revealed all the more clearly to us. But cities, of course, are not quite like that. What makes a city a city is the fact that it exhibits signs of life, that it changes: parts are added, parts are demolished as a result of various human acts or natural catastrophes, etc. Any particular representation of a city's structure necessarily construes a moment in its history as a unity, which it is not. In the same way, meaning is not a structural totality. In order for words and signs to make sense it may be true that they must exist in some kind of structural relation to one another. But this relation is not given to us, and no more is it given to the structuralist analyst, as a unified whole. In short, the word 'meaning' is not equivalent to the word 'structure'.

Something else follows on from the structuralist belief that its gaze is capable of surveying a totality. It is this: in order to conceptualize something as a totality one must, at the same time, commit oneself to the view that one can also grasp the organizing principle that governs the structure of that totality, and grasp it in a very particular manner: 'the notion of structure refers only to space, geometric or morphological space, the order of forms and sites. Structure is first the structure of an organic or artificial work, the internal unity of an assemblage, a *construction*: a work is governed by a unifying principle, the *architecture* that is built and made visible in a location' (p. 15). Structuralism, like Cartesianism, is transfixed by an architectural metaphor. This means that it must always articulate the problem of meaning in terms of spatial concepts: architectures, constructions that occupy locations in space. It is the power of this metaphor that makes structuralism susceptible to 'confusing meaning with its geometric, morphological, or, in the best of cases, cinematic model', and it thereby 'risks being interested in the figure itself to the detriment of the play going on within it metaphorically' (p. 16). Structuralist thought, Derrida is arguing, is seized by a metaphor when it takes the substitution of the image or the formal pattern (e.g. 'geometry' or 'morphology') to be equivalent to the metaphorical 'play' that is an essential component in the generation of meaning. The cinematic model is the 'best of cases' here because with it at least some acknowledgement of the fluidity inherent in the production of meaning, of the play of force, is implicitly acknowledged. Derrida is arguing that we need to be suspicious of the claim that the word 'meaning' can be equated with the metaphor implied by the word 'structure'. The point, for Derrida, is that meaning is at work *when metaphor operates*, when the substitution of one word for another occurs. But this substitution, this *movement of metaphor*, is not something inherently structural, for, necessarily, what is fluid is not fixed or frozen in form. What Derrida terms 'force', or the 'play' inherent in meaning, 'is the other of language' (p. 27) in so far as it is the case that language indeed announces itself to us as a kind of structure. But this structure has as its precondition that which escapes the limits imposed by any concept that seeks to encompass a structural totality. One does not approach the question of force and meaning by thinking it as a *concept*, which would be to reduce it to something that can be decided upon once and for all, and in so doing to enmesh it within the formalized mode of thinking that takes structure to be the defining feature of reality. To do this would be to remain within the guiding metaphorical tendency within Western metaphysics that asserts the primacy of form over force. Such a move is characteristic of the Western tradition of metaphysics because it is this tradition, Derrida contends, that thinks in a manner that privileges structure. By way of support for this argument we need, perhaps, only to think of the work that the foundational metaphor does for Descartes's epistemology, or likewise of the formalized conception of the transcendental subject that Kant presents in the first *Critique*.

Privileging structure is for Derrida a characteristic of the Western metaphysical tradition not merely in so far as it allows us to talk about the 'foundations' of knowledge, etc., but also because the structural metaphor foregrounds the role of the image in thought. The Western tradition, Derrida argues, cleaves to the representational notion of thought: thought as image, as the equivalence of image to truth. Again, such a mode of conceptualization tends to ignore the problem of force. If we were to seek to *think force* by presenting it as a structural concept, as a form, then what this implies is that we must, at the same time, seek to throw light upon force, to *illuminate* it. But understanding force in terms of form alone, as something that can be grasped within the metaphorical imagery of structure, is precisely to fail to grasp it: '*To comprehend* the structure of a becoming, the form of a force, is to lose meaning by finding it . . . The meaning of meaning is Apollonian by virtue of everything that can be seen' (p. 28). In other words, meaning, if taken as force, is becoming. But attempting to condense a becoming into a structure is immediately to lose what makes a becoming what it is. Put simply, *force cannot be seen*: it is not susceptible to being articulated as that which can have light thrown upon it, as something that can be envisaged within the language of spaces that the structural mode of thinking requires in order to function. The Apollonian element that Derrida alludes to, which is in fact a reference to a thesis presented by Nietzsche in *The Birth of Tragedy*,[35] is always already a matter of form. But meaning, as we have seen, is for Derrida not simply a question of form. Meaning, we might say, is not simply about the relations that inhere between words situated within a structural totality. It is something that also involves a becoming that is distinctly non-structural. It is this becoming that escapes the structural metaphor, and which any analysis of meaning that highlights the role that structure plays must cover up at the very moment that this metaphor is deployed.

The question of metaphor turns out to be one of Derrida's central concerns not only in 'Force and Signification' but elsewhere.[36] If, for him, the structural metaphor conceals an unacknowledged force of becoming upon which it depends, it also pays testimony to a central presupposition of European philosophical thought. We have already alluded to this presupposition in relation to the role of the representational image within philosophical discourse. This presupposition establishes a metaphorical relationship that is itself the basis of metaphysics: it is 'the metaphor of darkness and light . . . [that is] . . . the founding metaphor of Western philosophy as metaphysics' (p. 27). This metaphor is a 'founding' one in at least two senses. First, it is a 'photological' metaphor, and as such it privileges the notion of the representational image as the production of light, where 'light' is equivalent to 'truth'. Western philosophy, in other words, is a way of thinking that envisages truth as a matter of the throwing of light upon a world composed of entities in order to reveal them as they are. The light in which the world is thereby bathed is the light of representational thought. Second, the photological metaphor is a founding one in the sense that 'it is a metaphor.' The Western metaphysical tradition, then, is anchored in a metaphorically determined understanding that legitimates its own particular mode of thought. This mode of thought is what Derrida calls a 'heliocentric metaphysics', a metaphysics in which force is sundered by the power of the representational image, in which intensity gives way to the primacy of representation. Structuralism presents us with a paradigm case of this metaphysics in so far as it is a 'tributary' of this stream of thought. We are, Derrida holds, faced with a tradition that shies away from thinking in terms of intensities and forces, a tradition that must cover them up in order to reveal them, for 'How can force or weakness be understood in terms of light and dark?' (p. 27). More follows from the adherence to the founding metaphor of European metaphysics. Above all, perhaps, we can single out the belief that transparency and singularity are of the greatest value in thought. In other words and speaking metaphorically, what is true must be both 'transparent', 'clear', a product of light, and at the same time 'univocal', i.e. one not many. Thus, heliocentric metaphysics offers us an all embracing ontology: an account of truth as transparency, of truth as the product of the light of reason that is thrown onto the realm of Being in order to illuminate it.

What, though, is Derrida's position with regard to this metaphysics of meaning? The first thing to note is that Derrida does not in any way propose its abandonment. The appropriate critical response to this metaphysics does not of itself legitimate the embracing of an ontology of pure becoming, which a thinker like Deleuze pursues. One does not, in other words, aim at leaving metaphysics behind. True, we 'must', says Derrida, aim at attaining some kind of 'emancipation' from this metaphysics. But we cannot be emancipated from metaphysics in the sense of entering into a line of thought that would fly out of it, for this 'would be meaningless and deprive us of the light of meaning' (p. 28). This is because the history of thought is, for us, the history of Western metaphysics. We cannot abandon this history without at the same time abandoning the possibility of meaningful discourse that it has bestowed upon us. Instead, what we can and *must* do is resist this metaphysics from a standpoint that is situated firmly within it and which acknowledges that fact as the condition of its possibility. It is the pursuit of this project that characterizes what Derrida calls the 'deconstruction' of metaphysics. Deconstruction, in its simplest terms, may be described as a turn away from the structuralist mode of thought that Derrida holds to be characteristic of Western metaphysics. This metaphysical understanding is a mode of thinking that, in order to *think* of structure at all, must also maintain its commitment to a purely theoretical and disembodied conception of enquiry, to a model of thought conceived of as the roving gaze of an incorporeal spectator floating above the structure of the existent, of Being. From the standpoint of deconstruction, however, such a perspective is always open to question, for all enquiry occurs in the context of the structure it inhabits and from which there is no easy means of escape. In this, Derrida is taking up some of the lessons of Heidegger's criticism of metaphysics, as well as his argument that thinking occurs essentially *in* and *as* its world. However, in its own turn, Heidegger's emphasis on the role of Being, his claim that the presence of Being is essential to all thought, is also subjected to Derridean criticism.

It should be clear by now why I have chosen to begin a discussion of Derrida by referring to his essay 'Force and Signification'. Derrida's comments on structuralism offer us a path that leads into his approach to the *practice* of philosophical thought. Moreover, there is an ethical position at stake from the outset with regard to Derrida's discussion of Western metaphysics. This ethics shows itself at the conclusion of 'Force and Signification', which is marked by a kind of prescription, an ought: we *must*, Derrida tells us, seek to criticize metaphysics from within its own domain. As we shall see, the nature of this 'must' is not to be taken simply as a matter of mere compulsion, in the sense that one 'must' eat in order to survive. True, if the history of metaphysics is in any sense *our history* then if we are to criticize metaphysics we must do so from within its own domain, for that is where we are situated. But there is also an 'ought' contained within this kind of talk. If we must criticize metaphysics at all it is because we *ought* to do so, it is because we are in some sense ethically obliged to engage in this kind of criticism. Deconstruction is the enactment of this ethical imperative, and as such it rests upon a conception of the ethical. What kind of conception this is we will discover in due course. The discussion of this ethics will finally lead us back to Levinas. For the moment, however, let us provisionally note that what Derrida is proposing under the rubric of 'deconstruction' is a taking leave of an ontology of Being, a critical departure from the tradition of Western metaphysics, of which structuralism is a paradigm case. Yet, as we will see, this taking leave remains in many ways faithful to that metaphysical tradition.

3.3 The question of metaphor is a question of cultures

According to Derrida's conception, as we have seen, what is termed 'heliocentrism' is a language that is founded on the metaphors of light and darkness. In such a model, 'light' is taken as a metaphor for 'truth' and 'darkness' as a metaphor for 'error' or 'untruth'. This heliocentric language is one that, Derrida argues, has grounded Western philosophical discourse. We might say, then, that this language essentially characterizes philosophical discourse as it is practised within the European tradition. The import of this analysis 'comes to light' (as one might put it if one is speaking within this discourse) in a wide range of philosophical contexts. For instance, when Aristotle writes of metaphor in his *Poetics*, he defines it as a process of substitution wherein something is given a name that belongs to something else. For Derrida, such a definition can be taken in two ways. On the one hand, this definition of metaphor is just that: it is a philosophical thesis that puts forward a claim about the nature of metaphor. On the other hand, though, 'it is also a philosophical discourse whose entire surface is worked by a metaphorics.'[37] The definition of metaphor that Aristotle offers is only possible because it takes place within a discourse that itself is riven with metaphor. In line with his argument concerning the heliocentric nature of metaphysics, Derrida's point here is that metaphor is a necessary component within *any* philosophical discourse. If this is the case, then the very act of offering a definition of metaphor within philosophical discourse must itself rest upon the metaphorical workings that are at play in the language that is being used to define metaphor as such. In order for a definition to be offered, the play of metaphor within language must be a condition of possibility for the definition's being constructed in the first place. But, as Derrida argues with regard to heliocentrism, this metaphorics remains hidden within philosophical discourse.[38] In turn, a series of oppositions can be (and indeed have been) constructed within philosophical language that in equal measure depend upon and suppress the role that metaphor plays in philosophy. Above all, this suppression occurs at the level of the analysis of the nature of truth and meaning. Thus, Derrida argues, metaphor, which is an essential component of the everyday use of language, is traditionally separated off from the use of literal or fact-stating language that philosophy relies upon in order to elucidate concepts of truth and meaning (a case in point is the example of speech act theory, cited in section 3 above, which takes the literal meaning of words to be primary). If truth is taken to be what is said in literal language, in a language that purportedly refers in unproblematic fashion to how things are, then it must be the case that this language functions in a manner that is different in kind from the way in which metaphorical language functions.

On such a view, literal language is not prey to the kind of substitution wherein one word is used to stand in for another word, as occurs with metaphor. A literal meaning is, in this case, always taken to be the *proper* meaning of a word, and this propriety signifies the consonance between a word and that to which it refers. Derrida's point, however, is that this privileging of literal language ultimately relies upon the metaphorical propensity that is inherent in everyday language, and it is this everyday aspect of language that a philosophy which privileges the literal must suppress in order to construct the notion of the literal as the true. Thus, 'meaning proper', so to speak, is taken to be equivalent to the articulation of the literal relations that inhere between language and the world of sensory experience, while metaphor is relegated to a secondary role in so far as it is taken to be something that is rendered possible in the light of the fact that the capacity of words to refer to things (literal language) is already secured.

> Metaphor . . . is determined by philosophy as a provisional loss of meaning, an economy of the proper without irreparable damage . . . a history with its sights set on . . . the circular reappropriation of literal, proper meaning. This is why the philosophical evaluation of metaphor has always been ambiguous: metaphor is dangerous and foreign . . . but it is in complicity with what it endangers, is necessary to it in the extent to which the de-tour is a re-turn guided by the function of resemblance . . . under the law of the same.[39]

Western philosophy has generally taken metaphor to be conceptualizable within the framework or 'economy' of literal language. This privileging of literal language pays testimony to the fact that truth is taken as the equivalence between word and thing, i.e. truth is regarded as the true *representation* of something by a word. Yet, metaphor is, at the same time, necessary to this conception. The reason for this is that in order to fix the literal meaning of a word or phrase we must first presuppose the 'movement of meaning', i.e. the process of metaphorical substitution that is supposed to be subservient to the fixing of literal meaning.

Derrida's point is that metaphor is not some mere accident within what he calls 'the text of philosophy'.[40] Rather, metaphor is essential to this text. What is at stake here is the relationship between philosophical talk and everyday language and the extent to which philosophers would like to distance what they say from the vicissitudes and ambiguities of this everyday, metaphor-ridden language. If, however, this assertion of distance is questionable, that is, if philosophers must always already find themselves caught up in so-called natural language in order to philosophize at all, then we are obliged to consider in a critical manner the implications of 'the usage of natural language *as* philosophical language'.[41] We are, in other words, obliged to consider that philosophical concepts are not purely 'philosophical', but are essentially contaminated by the mode of everyday speech. Foremost amongst these implications is a cultural and historical matter. This is because the privileging of the literal over the metaphorical occurs within the *Western* metaphysical tradition: 'Metaphysics – the white mythology which reassembles and reflects the culture of the West: the white man takes his own mythology, Indo-European mythology, his own *logos* [i.e. discourse], that is, the *mythos* of his idiom, for the universal form of that [which] he must still wish to call Reason.'[42] Where we can argue that metaphor does not have *a* history as such, in so far as metaphor is a feature common to the languages of all cultures, the *concept of metaphor* does have a history that is culturally specific.[43] The history of the *concept* of metaphor is the history of the culture that typifies Western metaphysical discourse. This is the heliocentric discourse which equates universal Reason with 'natural light' (for instance, the 'clear and distinct ideas' of Descartes's epistemology, which sets the 'light of Reason' as the standard of certainty and truth). This discourse has displayed a tendency to regard the languages of other cultures as primarily figurative, as metaphorical rather than rational – and in this way it has tended to regard other cultures as being divorced from the discourse of the true.[44] Derrida's reading of heliocentric metaphysics thus takes us from the domain of the 'philosophical' text into a domain of historico-cultural (and hence political) relations. A critical analysis of heliocentric thinking, then, necessitates a critical analysis of the historical and cultural dimension of philosophical language and concepts.

3.4 Heliocentrism is a phonocentrism

If the culture of heliocentrism places metaphor at one step from the truth attainable by way of literal language it can also be characterized in other ways. Perhaps the most significant amongst these ways is linked with what Derrida refers to in 'Force and Signification' as the notion of 'acoustics' (p. 27). Acoustics, of course, is a word that concerns sound. Here, more specifically, the acoustical concerns the role allotted to the spoken utterance within philosophical discourse. In so far as heliocentrism prioritizes the role of form over force it likewise places emphasis upon the role of the speaker (or, we could say, the subject: a formally characterizable entity who is in possession of specifiable attributes like intentionality, will, dispositions, rationality, etc.) in the production and securing of meaning. In Derridean terms, meaning is taken within heliocentric metaphysics as something that can be equated with the living presence of the speaker who 'uses' language intentionally. Heliocentric metaphysics, therefore, is also a 'metaphysics of presence', since it holds that the proper meaning of words is ultimately linked to the intentions, and hence living presence, of a speaker/subject. On this view, the Western metaphysical tradition is not simply dominated by a hierarchical metaphorics of light versus dark or truth versus error. It is also a tradition that takes truth to be a matter that essentially concerns the expression of a speaker's true intentions by way of language.

We could turn to the example of structural linguistics once more to illustrate this point, and in particular to Derrida's account of Saussurean linguistics as it is presented in *Of Grammatology* (1967).[45] Saussure offers a theory that not only privileges form over force and literal over metaphorical language. In addition, the Saussurean account privileges the notion of 'speech' over 'writing' in its determination of the nature of meaning. Again, Derrida holds that this is a view that typifies the Western metaphysical tradition and, as with the structuralism of Rousset in the essay 'Force and Signification', Saussure's linguistics has for him the status of a paradigm instance of Western metaphysical thinking. On the kind of view that characterizes this tradition, Derrida claims, 'writing' is always regarded as a 'supplement', that is a kind of unnecessary or derivative and accidental side effect of living speech. What the Saussurean account of the nature of language and meaning does, according to Derrida, is to engage in 'the historico–metaphysical reduction of writing to the rank of an instrument enslaved to a full and originally spoken language' (*Of Grammotology*, 29). Writing becomes regarded as the mere adjunct of speech when it comes to the analysis of meaning, whereas speech, in contrast, bears all the defining features that characterize authenticity, originality, etc. As such, speech grounds the concept of truth. If we were to turn to the example of Plato's dialogues, truth, Derrida could argue, is presented by Plato as a matter that can only be arrived at through the exchange of speech that occurs between *living* interlocuters who have the characteristics of will, intentionality, etc. (in the *Gorgias*, for instance, between the figures Socrates and Gorgias).[46] In the living exchange of the dialogue what is at stake is truth, and truth is arrived at by each interlocuter subjecting their views to the interrogation of the other. In such a situation there is no room for error, for each speaker can ensure their intended meaning is communicated by answering the questions of the other speaker, by correcting misunderstandings, etc. The dialogue is a form that holds the priority of living speech, of psycho-acoustics, to be a defining characteristic of all language. On such a model, language is a *vehicle* of thought. Much is presupposed by this view – for instance, a division between thought and language, and the contention that language is a kind of neutral 'material' that can be manipulated by the living speaker in order to communicate his or her beliefs, intentions, and so on. Acoustics, as 'that which ties sense to sound, the "thought-sound"' (p. 36) presupposes meaning to be essentially a matter of intentions: it is a 'phonocentrism' – the privileging of the spoken over the written. Derrida also refers to this as a 'logocentrism': a discourse which holds that living discourse (*logos*) grounds sense or meaning: 'the sense of being as presence . . . logocentrism . . . [is the] . . . *epoch* of full speech' (p. 43). 'Logocentrism' is therefore a term that Derrida uses to signify the 'metaphysics of phonetic writing . . . which was fundamentally – for enigmatic yet essential reasons that are inaccessible to a simple historical relativism – nothing but the most original and powerful ethnocentrism' (p. 3).

Recalling the arguments put forward in 'Force and Signification' we can note once more that, for Derrida, the stakes of the metaphysical tradition are essentially linked to the question of culture, to the view that one culture has priority with regard to establishing the nature of meaning and hence truth. The 'phoneticization of writing', that is, the rendering of the significance of writing in terms of living speech, marks this cultural epoch. Likewise, we could add that no simple historical relativism will suffice to articulate the nature of this epoch, for that would presuppose that we can be liberated entirely from it, which we cannot be. However, the main point to grasp here is that the Derridean account of Western metaphysics is ultimately staking some very large claims. Above all, Derrida's contention is that the metaphysical tradition which takes living speech to be a defining feature of truth has dominated philosophical thought since its inception, and has a lineage that can be traced from Plato to Hegel, and even from the pre-Socratic thinkers to the work of Heidegger.[47] Amongst other things, Derrida is therefore providing a critical account of '*the history of* (the only) *metaphysics*, which has . . . always assigned the origin of truth in general to the logos', i.e. to the discourse presented in the form of the living presence of 'full' speech. It is this metaphysics which can be defined as the *one and only* metaphysics that has thought of truth as linked essentially to the presence of a living speaker, that has opposed the concept of speech to that of 'writing'.

3.5 Speech and writing

According to the Western metaphysical tradition, writing is best regarded as something that is parasitic: a non-essential element in the production and determination of meaning and truth, and a mere 'vehicle' for thought. From this it is clear that for Derrida the key philosophical problem is 'the problem of language' (*Of Grammatology*, 6), at least in so far as the Western tradition has always comprehended the meaning of language as a matter that exclusively concerns intentionality. However, the metaphysical privileging of living speech over writing is no mere accident of history; it is not some contingent matter. This is because the priority that has been given to 'acoustics', Derrida argues, does not depend upon the existence of some kind of freely made 'choice' that could have been avoided if only some other option had been selected. This priority 'responds to a moment of *economy* (let us say of the "life" of "history" or of "being as self-relationship")' (p. 7). There is, in other words, an economy of relations of force that has had a decisive role in constituting the metaphysics of opposition that is a defining feature of heliocentrism/phonocentrism, in so far as it thinks by way of the oppositional structure inherent within terms like 'light-dark', 'truth-error', etc. This oppositional thinking, Derrida tells us, 'has even produced the idea of the world, the idea of world-origin, that arises from the difference between the worldly and the non-worldly, the outside and the inside, identity and non-identity, universal and non-universal, transcendental and empirical, etc.' (p. 8). The 'world', as a philosophical *concept*, is already determined in a manner that endows it with significance by an *economy of meaning* that is founded upon opposition. It is this economy that tends to 'confine writing to a secondary and instrumental function' (p. 8). Against this, Derrida's point is that what has been designated by the term 'writing' is *not* secondary. Writing, as he will redefine it in *Of Grammatology* and elsewhere, has an equal or even primoridal role in the production of meaning and also philosophical discourse. The text of *Of Grammatology* thus allots itself the task of announcing the 'death of speech' as it has been traditionally understood, i.e. speech as the foundation of meaning. For, Derrida argues, 'the concept of writing exceeds and comprehends that of language.' This is because language is always already, in a very specific sense, writing (p. 37).

What, we might ask, is Derrida seeking to do? First, he is obviously challenging the metaphysical view implicit within Cartesianism: the view that meaning stems from a self-reflective mind that can be isolated from its physical or historical context.

In this regard, at least, Derrida has much in common with many other thinkers (Hegel, Nietzsche, Horkheimer, or Adorno, to name but a few). However, Derrida's challenge is articulated at a very specific level: 'Now we tend to say "writing" . . . to designate not only physical gestures of literal pictographic or ideographic inscription, but also the totality of what makes it possible' (p. 9). 'Writing', in other words, is used by Derrida to designate the *condition of possibility of meaning*. There is a move in Derrida's argument that pays testimony to a certain kind of 'Kantianism': he is presenting us with a conditions of possibility argument. However, the condition of possibility that makes spoken language possible is not a formal *a priori* condition in the sense in which Kant elucidated the notion in the *Critique of Pure Reason*. Rather, the condition of the possibility of formalizable conceptual thinking, Derrida is arguing, rests upon the metaphorical 'play' that is an inherent feature of the production of meaning. This, then, is a move that is designed to both undercut and demonstrate the limitations of the phonocentric tradition of the West. According to phonocentrism, the voice is ultimately wedded to the mind such that thought expresses itself 'naturally' *through* speech (p. 11). Hegel, for example, 'demonstrates very clearly the strange privilege of sound in idealization' (p. 12). Even Heidegger, a thinker who openly challenges Western metaphysics, remains trapped within this model in so far as he thinks of Being as presence. Hence, the Derridean introduction of writing as an essential precondition of speech questions the purportedly 'natural' status of the relation that is assumed to inhere between thought and language. Language, when it is no longer considered merely as 'speech', does not find its essential precondition in the intentions of a speaker, in their presence. Speech itself is rooted in the possibility of inscription. This condition of possibility is in turn articulated by Derrida in terms of what he variously calls the 'trace', the logic of the 'supplement', or 'differance'.

3.6   The trace and differance

The trace, the supplement, differance: none of these 'words' yields a simple definition. Indeed, given Derrida's project, we are perhaps not entitled to expect him to provide a simple or formal definition of the 'movement' of meaning that is alluded to by these terms. How, after all, could what makes meaning possible be defined as such and thereby given a meaning? That said, in *Of Grammatology* Derrida does offer the following observation concerning the trace: it is '*the absolute origin of sense in general. The trace is the differance* which opens appearance and signification . . . *no concept of metaphysics can describe it*' (p. 65). Discussing the trace, therefore, takes us at least to the limit of metaphysical discourse – albeit not outside it. Meaning, we can say, is founded upon this movement of differance. And it is differance which is 'the origin of presence itself' (p. 63). 'Differance' conveys an essential ambiguity and 'undecidability' that is inherent in the production of meaning.[48] Meaning is not a matter that merely concerns so-called 'literal' language. Rather, meaning is produced by a process of simultaneous differing and deferring. The substitution of an 'a' for an 'e', which transforms 'différence' (meaning to differ, in a spatial sense) into 'différance' (meaning to defer or delay, on the level of temporality – but also to be distinct) cannot be detected when spoken. It is hence a means of indicating the limitations of prioritizing spoken language over written inscription. We can say that differance, which Derrida tells us is 'literally neither a word nor a concept',[49] pays testimony to the concern with force that is highlighted in 'Force and Signification'. Meaning involves 'movement', and this movement never comes to a final resting-place in so far as its condition of possibility is deferral, non-presence, etc.

The trace is a movement of differance that constitutes the condition of possibility of thinking. Without the trace there is no sense, no signification, no speaker, no thought as such. Yet, at the same time, the trace is none of these. Rather, it indicates a fundamental possibility of repetition (what, in the essay on Austin's speech act theory, Derrida calls 'iterability') that is inherent in the production of meaning. This is a possibility that cannot be derived from the notions of consciousness or presence, or from their purported opposites (unconsciousness or absence).[50] The trace has nothing to do with speech or the oppositional logic upon which the metaphysical account of meaning as residing in living speech rests.

The trace, in fact, is 'irreducible' (*Of Grammatology*, 70). It is neither an object of empirical experience (we cannot 'encounter' the trace as a thing-like entity), nor is it a formal *a priori* structure. As the *'origin of sense in general'*, however, we can say that the word 'trace' indicates for Derrida an 'arche-phenomenon' which itself gives rise to phenomenality, i.e. to a sensible 'world' that is composed of entities. This occurs through the movement of differance. In turn, this movement is 'the formation of form. But it is *on the other hand* the being-imprinted of the imprint' (p. 63). What we are faced with is something analogous to what Derrida discusses under the name of 'force' in relation to structuralism. The trace is not 'opposed' to anything, since it is a term that does not signify a determinate concept. But it is that 'which must be thought before the opposition of nature and culture, animality and humanity, etc., [and] belongs to the very movement of signification' (p. 70). This being the case, the trace is open to being interpreted as a kind of 'arche-writing': it is the already inscribed condition of possibility of living speech that opens up any possible relationship that thought can have with what is other than it. The trace, we might say, is what allows meaning to be articulated as structure. It allows us to speak of the human and the non-human, of the living and its other, of what is 'inside' (the self-reflexive moment in which we say 'I think') and what is 'outside' (the phenomenal world of experience, other cultures). To put the matter another way: if language involves a process of signification, that is, if language involves the putting of names to 'things', then the trace is the very process of *signification* that makes this possible. In this sense, 'signification is a priori written, whether inscribed or not, in one form or another, in a "sensible" and "spatial" element that is called "exterior".' The trace, therefore, indicates that meaning itself is, in a very particular sense, always already *written before it can be spoken.*

3.7 *Deconstructing Rousseau's* Essay on the Origins of Language

'Writing', in this sense, does not have to be literally 'inscribed', i.e. it is not necessary to think of writing as the mere putting into written form of something that has already been thought, spoken, and hence lived. Indeed, Derrida argues, although

Western metaphysics can be essentially characterized by way of its regarding writing as a merely 'parasitic' activity that rests upon the dispositions, intentions, etc. of living subjects, it has in fact always *needed* writing in order to define itself in this way. One example of this discussed in *Of Grammatology* is the theory proposed by the philosopher Jean-Jacques Rousseau (1712–78) in his *Essay on the Origins of Language*. In this text, and in a manner that is characteristic of much of his thinking, we find Rousseau arguing for the view that human language first arose out of the instincts and dispositions of primitive humans. For Rousseau, a cry is first always a cry of pain, and as such it is a direct expression of an authentic and natural inner feeling. According to Rousseau there was originally a 'natural' language, and it was only on the basis of this natural language that a more complex and abstract linguistic competence (including metaphorical language) was rendered possible. Speaking like Derrida, we can say that 'natural language', on Rousseau's view, is an authentic language of unmediated self-presence. Only once this was in place, along with more abstract linguistic ability, was writing finally possible. But writing itself, for Rousseau, betrays something rather sinister. For writing only intervenes in human life when the personal social bond that binds people together dissolves and is replaced by the impersonal and inauthentic relation that characterizes civil society. If we were to turn to another of Rousseau's works, the *Discourse on Inequality*,[51] we find that civil society, which is characterizable in terms of the rule of law in order to protect the institution of private property, is regarded as the harbinger of an era in which the natural happiness that is associated with life enjoyed both in a 'state of nature' and in the more 'primitive', tribal forms of society that gave way to it is replaced by a mode of human existence that is both artificial and unjust. The freedom that accompanies the collective life-style of purportedly primitive peoples is, for Rousseau, undercut by the instituting of property ownership, and this gives rise to a society in which people are no longer able to enjoy their natural freedom. Law, the formal and *written* legislation that ensures the rights of property ownership, turns out not to have the function of protecting all who are subject to it, but only ensures the rights of the minority who are already the possessors of goods. Writing, therefore, is not merely parasitic upon living speech, it is also an essential and defining characteristic of a corrupt form of social organization: of Western, or Northern, civilization.

Derrida's point, however, is that Rousseau's account in fact always presupposes writing in order to get off the ground in the first place. In chapter 10 of the *Essay* Rousseau draws a distinction between languages of the South and languages of the North in a manner that reflects his distinction between primitive/natural and civilized/unnatural societies. Primitives, who are Southerners, are defined as natural and passionate people; their speech is 'lively, sonorous, accented, eloquent'.[52] Northern speech, in contrast, is one that involves 'emphatic articulation'; their language is 'dull, harsh, articulated, shrill, monotonous'. So, Derrida notes, we are presented by Rousseau with a distinction between 'accent' (South) and 'articulation' (North). Of these, the Southern propensity to accent is linked to their capacity for natural expression. The word 'accent' implies the role of the voice of the Southerner as an unmediated expression of their inner feeling. 'Articulation', in contrast, is an unnatural and artificial characteristic: it implies a knowing ability to use speech and the predominance of grammar and other artificial aspects of language are essential to it. In turn, Northern culture is *not* to be regarded as one of natural expression, for within this culture what was once the foundation of natural expression (the voice) has been subverted by the use of writing, which institutes an artificial relation between people: living speech is replaced by dead writing. Thus, Derrida notes, 'Writing is at the North: cold, necessitious, reasoning, turned toward death' (p. 226). Articulation is a harbinger of the dominance of writing. Moreover, once underway, this 'fall' from the innocence of unmediated speech increases continually, for the more articulated language is the more rigorous and forceful (the more rational) it becomes. Writing, according to Rousseau, usurps natural language. Living speech has been invaded by dead writing, by a language that is fragmented into parts, that has become punctuated, subjected to 'rules' of grammar and presentation. But, says Derrida, the point about Rousseau's argument is that he cannot himself denigrate writing without at the same time invoking it, above all without invoking writing in such a way that it becomes essential to his conception of language. In describing the way in which natural speech is invaded by writing Rousseau *shows* us that the origin of language must be found not in speech but in writing itself. This is because language, as Rousseau defines it, would not be 'language' at all if it were not also situated in relation to writing. Rousseau wishes to persuade us of one thing, but he ends up showing us something else. Articulation, the ability to use speech, presupposes something more than simple passions, for when one is articulate one already has an ability that transcends the mere expression of immediate feeling. If one is able to 'articulate' this is because language is never simply a matter of the voice expressing a feeling; it is also already a matter of language being broken up into sounds and words, etc. In order to engage in speech one must first have the power of articulation at one's disposal. But this power is *not* to be subsumed within the characteristics that define living speech. On the contrary, Derrida argues,

> *Articulation is the becoming-writing of language.* Rousseau, *who would like to say* that this becoming-writing *comes upon the origin unexpectedly*, takes it as his premise, and according to it *describes in fact* the way in which that *becoming-writing encroaches upon the origin*, and arises from the origin. The becoming-writing of language is the becoming-language of language. He *declares* what he *wishes to say*, that is to say that articulation and writing are a post-originary malady of language: he says or *describes* that which he *does not wish to say*: articulation and therefore the space of writing operate at the origin of language. (p. 229)

The above argument is typical of Derrida's deconstructive approach. Rousseau wishes to tell us one thing, but he shows us the contrary to be the case. The hierarchy of terms that Rousseau must resort to, which valorizes what is 'natural' and denigrates what is 'unnatural', is itself shown to be dependent upon the whole of its range. What is natural could not be defined as being 'natural' at all without what is 'unnatural'. Derrida thereby shows us that the 'inferior' term in Rousseau's discourse is *at the same time essential to it*. What is taken by Rousseau to be a mere supplement (writing) turns out to be a condition of possibility for his talking about language at all. As such, writing, too, lies at the very origin of language.

A deconstructive reading, then, shows how a hierarchy of terms turns out to depend as much upon the purportedly 'inferior' term as the valorized one. By way of another example one could take Derrida's reading of the role of the 'frame' in Kant's *Critique of Aesthetic Judgement*. Here, Kant allots the frame a traditional role in aesthetics: a frame (like a frame around a painting) is merely an addition or supplement to an artwork and has no bearing upon its intrinsic aesthetic unity or integrity. A frame is just one example of *parerga*. Other *parerga* include things like the clothes that adorn statues: again, the clothes are mere adornments that purportedly have nothing to do with the aesthetic unity of the statue, which is a representation of the human form. A *parergon*, then, serves to divide what is 'outside' from what is 'inside', to draw a distinction between the artwork and where it is situated. But, Derrida notes, '[t]his delimitation of the center and the integrity of the representation, of its inside and its outside, might already seem strange . . . Where does a *parergon* begin and end . . . ?'[53] Through Derrida's reading the *parergon* is brought to the centre, invading the supposed autonomy of the aesthetic object. Instead of simply framing the pre-established unity of the work of art, the *parergon* becomes a necessary part of it, disturbing the field of the work's autonomy to the extent that the assumed dominance of the one over the other is rendered questionable. For Kant, the *parergon* in its ideal form would remain invisible, and its degeneration would be signified at the point at which it imposes some 'external' affect of attraction on the viewer of the artwork:

> [W]hat is called *ornamentation* (*parerga*), i.e. what is only an adjunct, and not an intrinsic constituent in the complete representation of the object, in augmenting the delight of taste does so only by means of its form. Thus it is with the frames of pictures or the drapery of statues, or the colonnades of palaces. But if the ornamentation does not itself enter into the composition of the beautiful form – if it is introduced like a gold frame merely to win approval for the picture by means of its charm – it is then called *finery* and takes away from the genuine beauty.[54]

Derrida, however, is intent on demonstrating how Kant 'imports' a specific analytic mode, 'a table . . . [or] . . . *border* into the analytic of aesthetic judgement' from the *Critique of Pure Reason*.[55] The autonomy that ought, in principle, to define Kant's own discourse on aesthetics in the third *Critique* is itself surrounded by a frame (that of the first *Critique*) that invades it. In turn, the third *Critique's* autonomy becomes fissured. The analytical frame of the *Critique of Pure Reason*, which concerns the nature of knowledge but *not* of the aesthetics of taste, instead of being regarded as little more than an undesirable addition to the aesthetic object discussed by the *Critique of Aesthetic Judgement*, reveals itself as a necessary constituent in the formal structure of the aesthetic phenomenon. What is on his own terms supposedly extrinsic to matters of taste and aesthetic evaluation (namely, logic and reason) is surreptitiously introduced by Kant in order to classify aesthetic judgements. As a result, Derrida argues, 'a *logical* frame is transposed and forced in to be imposed on a *nonlogical* structure, a structure which no longer essentially concerns a relation to the object as object of knowledge.'[56] As with Rousseau's *Essay*, then, Derrida seeks to show how concepts and terms that ought to have nothing to do with the object at hand are in fact essential to it. Kant's aesthetic discourse is deconstructed by showing how the formal conditions of rationality, which ought on Kant's own account to have nothing to do with the aesthetic, are in fact constitutive of it.

From the above readings of Rousseau and Kant it is clear that, for Derrida, deconstruction involves the critical placing in question of hierarchies of value. There is, one might say, an inherent *overturning* of values inherent in deconstruction – but this is so only in a limited sense. At first glance, we might be tempted to argue that deconstruction involves nothing more than the wholesale unravelling of conceptual orders as they present themselves within Western metaphysical discourse. As such, deconstruction would concern itself with nothing more than the destruction of metaphysical thought. In one particular sense, of course, deconstruction does do this, in so far as every deconstructive reading is a form of critical engagement with the dominant presuppositions of Western metaphysical discourse. In the 'Parergon' essay Kant's formalism, a feature shared by him with the structuralist enterprise, is targeted – and this, we have already seen in 'Force and Signification' is characteristic of Western philosophical discourse. But, in the same way in which Heidegger, in *Being and Time*, proposes the 'destruction' of Western metaphysics as an actualization of what is already contained within that tradition (its 'radicalization', if you like) so Derrida, too, takes a similar approach to this issue. This is a matter that will cause us to return to the question of the ethical, and in particular to the thought of Levinas. However, it may be useful here to offer some further thoughts on the nature of deconstruction as a prelude to these matters.

Deconstruction has been taken to signify many things. Most obvious amongst them and, I would argue, most obviously *mistaken*, is the view that deconstruction is no more than a kind of strategic intervention, a strategy. On such a conception, deconstruction would be a form of critical debunking of the values implicit within any theory. A deconstructive reading would, on this view, set out to criticize a dominant set of values (such as the prioritizing of speech over writing, the West over the East, or of the human over the animal, etc.) in the name of an alternative standpoint that defines itself by way of its being antithetical to these values. We might describe this as the 'This is how the world looks from here' approach. The problem with such a view, however, is that it involves both a pure instrumentalism and a form of empiricism. In other words, a deconstructive reading would simply be in place to serve the purposes of a particular perspective and would amount to little more than a mere 'tool' of empirically determined perspectives. In turn, we would end up with readings of philosophical and other problems that take a 'methodological' approach of invoking difference or the trace in order to destabilize the hierarchy of meaning within particular texts as if such terms were there simply to serve the purposes of that criticism. As such, deconstruction would have nothing whatsoever to do with ethics. At best, we would be presented with a deconstruction that is exclusively concerned with questions of power, and hence with a certain and rather narrow conception of politics.

Why, then, is such a view of deconstruction questionable? First, we could say that the reasons that one might offer for providing a deconstructive analysis could only ever be a matter of contingency. This, however, is an untenable view if we are to take seriously Derrida's claim in *Of Grammatology* and elsewhere that issues of differance, the trace, the logic of supplementarity, or of iterability, are never merely 'contingent' matters. It is worth recalling that what is called 'history', Derrida tells us, is linked essentially to the development of Western metaphysics (i.e. to the increasing power of European culture), and there is nothing 'accidental' in this. Nor is there any simple means of escape from this metaphysical discourse. Deconstruction, in other words, does not purport to stand 'outside' metaphysics, but springs from elements inherent within the metaphysical tradition itself. One essential component of this tradition, moreover, is the kind of discourse that concerns ethics, and Derrida's view of deconstruction is linked in a fundamental way to this problem. We can see this in two important respects. First, in the context of Derrida's discussion of the thought of Levinas. Second, in relation to Derrida's comments concerning that infamous exchange with John Searle in the late 1970s, which are to be found in the 'Afterword' to the volume *Limited Inc.* (1988).[57] Let us begin with the second of these.

3.8   Deconstruction and ethics

The 'Afterword' to *Limited Inc.* has a subtitle that is significant: 'Towards an Ethic of Discussion'. From this we can infer that in this piece Derrida wishes to offer some observations concerning the rights and wrongs that both arise out of, and ought, to govern discussion.[58] In other words, Derrida is immediately staking a claim that there *are* right ways and wrong ways of conducting oneself when one engages in critical debate. Derrida's 'Afterword' is important for other reasons, though – above all, because here he offers some observations concerning the nature of deconstruction, including addressing the issue of its aims. Equally significant, in this essay Derrida also affirms his relation to the Western metaphysical tradition, albeit in a very particular way.

What, to reiterate the question, is deconstruction? Derrida tells us at least one thing: he tells us what it is *not*. Deconstruction is not, he argues, a form of relativism – it does not involve affirming the view that anything goes, that all questions concerning the nature of truth or value are pointless questions. Moreover, deconstruction is not a form of 'skepticism, empiricism, even nihilism' as some of its critics have argued (p. 137). It is not a scepticism because it does not assert the absolute impossibility of knowledge. It is not an empiricism because it does not assert the priority of (even socially mediated) 'experience' over and above all else. It is not a nihilism because it does not argue for the destruction of all ethical values. At the same time, deconstruction spurns absolutism in so far as it operates 'without claiming any absolute overview'. As such, the word 'deconstruction' does not denote a unified methodological approach to philosophical problems. It is not, in other words, a 'method' that can be applied. It is better taken as a form of critical engagement that arises from the context in which it finds itself situated. It is not enough, in other words, to simply invoke a word like 'differance' in order to perform a deconstructive analysis of a philosophical or other kind of text, for that would be converting differance to a methodological principle that is contextually autonomous. The adequacy of such principles is precisely what is in question from the Derridean standpoint. To the extent that there is no methodology of deconstruction there is therefore 'no one, single deconstruction' (p. 141). Deconstruction, we can say, involves a kind of pluralism. Because of this pluralism deconstruction is not inherently 'political', if by the term 'political' one means that it always involves the advocacy of one particular politics over all others (for example, the contention that all political issues are issues of power and nothing else). No determinate political agenda can follow from deconstruction. The politics of any deconstructive reading depends upon the *context* in which it is articulated.

The notion of context is central to Derrida's claims concerning the nature of deconstruction. If we can talk in any manner at all about questions concerning, for instance, scientific objectivity or truth, this is because what is referred to by these words has arisen 'only within a context which is extremely vast, old, powerfully established, stabilized or rooted in a network of conventions (for instance, those of language)' (p. 136). It is within the context of such conventions that terms like 'objectivity' and 'truth' have taken on a specific meaning and value and, Derrida says, 'imposed' themselves. That they have been generated in this way 'does not in the slightest discredit them', for effectively the context in which such notions arose is a limitless one in so far as we cannot adopt any perspective that would place us outside this context. Meaning, in turn, is rooted in the incessant contextual slippage that is at play within history, and the role of deconstruction is to attempt to 'to take this limitless context into account, to pay the sharpest and broadest attention possible to context, and thus to an incessant movement of recontextualisation'. Again, we may recall here the point Derrida makes in 'Force and Signification' concerning the role of force within the 'movement' of metaphor. Deconstruction is an attempt to show that the concepts at our disposal are inherently context-related, yet at the same time governed by absolute conditions that make the ultimate determination of meaning irreducible to any *particular* context. Derrida's account of his own relationship with the Western metaphysical tradition is significant in respect of this. For, he tells us, not only is there no simple means of escape from that tradition, but we should not, he argues, undervalue the importance of tradition. Indeed, traditions, Derrida tells us, should be the object of 'jealous conservation' (p. 141).

We can note, therefore, that neither metaphysics in itself, nor the values that pertain to the metaphysical tradition, are ever actually abandoned by Derridean deconstruction: 'it does not renounce (it neither can *nor ought to do so*) the "values" that are dominant in this context' (p. 137, italics added). Deconstruction does *not* abandon notions about which, from *Of Grammatology* onwards, Derrida is critical. On the contrary, it actively requires them in order to be what it is. Such a requirement, though, is not one rooted in mere necessity – it is not a 'must' in the sense of compulsion that is at stake here. In other words, the deconstructionist is not simply compelled to acknowledge notions of truth, value, etc. In addition, there is an ethical requirement that these be acknowledged. The deconstructionist *ought* to recognize the importance of the value of truth, of the value of illumination over and above obfuscation (to speak within the terminology of heliocentrism). If this is the case, then deconstruction ought, in some sense, to conserve these values even as it opens them up to criticism:

[L]et it be said in passing how surprised I have often been, how amused or discouraged, depending on my humour, by the use or abuse of the following argument: Since the deconstructionist (which is to say, isn't it, the skeptic-relativist-nihilist!) is supposed not to believe in truth, stability, or the unity of meaning, in intention or 'meaning-to-say', how can he demand of us that we read *him* with pertinence, precision, rigor? . . . The answer is simple enough: this definition of the deconstructionist is *false* (that's right: false, not true) and feeble; it supposes a bad (that's right: bad, not good) and feeble reading of numerous texts, first of all mine . . . [T]he value of truth (and all those values associated with it) is never contested or destroyed in my writings, but only reinscribed in more powerful, larger, more stratified contexts . . . [W]ithin interpretative contexts (that is, within relations of force that are always differential – for example socio-political-institutional – but even beyond these determinations) that are relatively stable, sometimes apparently almost unshakeable, it should be possible to invoke rules of competence, criteria of discussion and of consensus, good faith, lucidity, rigor, criticism, and pedagogy.   (p. 146)

Derrida's writings, in so far as they are of necessity situated within the conventions that govern Western discourse, remain faithful to it. This compulsion, however, is not of itself a bad thing. The fact that Derrida's writings acknowledge this compulsion means that they embrace an ethical imperative and recognize the value of doing so. We can only make sense so long as we speak (and also write and read) with good faith, i.e. so long as we take the conventions that determine the value of truth as being valuable precisely in so far as they govern our own speech, writing and reading. Derrida may be adopting a position that seeks continually to draw our attention to the role of metaphor, of force, differance, etc. in the production of meaning. But at the same time he insists that we must acknowledge the priority of convention in determining the ethical regulation of speech and writing.

It likewise becomes clear from the 'Afterword' that Derrida conceives of the nature of his deconstructive analysis of Western metaphysics, and above all of the notions of the trace, of differance, of the *parergon*, of supplementarity, etc., as being presented within a philosophical discourse that owes a great deal to Kant's example. Deconstruction, he tells us, organizes its 'theoretical space' in a ' "quasi"-transcendental manner' (p. 127). The problems with which Derrida's deconstructive readings occupy themselves cannot be reduced in their significance to the context of their production. There may be nothing 'outside' the context, but the nature of context itself is enigmatic and approachable only from a perspective that does not seek to reduce the notion of context itself to something determinate, but rather acknowledges its essential undecidability. Derrida may spurn the idea of creating a 'metalanguage', yet at the same time he is seeking to allude to an *a priori* structure of possibility that inevitably pervades the construction of meaning. The question of this structure of possibility is not an empirical issue, since it is not a matter that can be reduced to any particular time or place, to any given form of experience – indeed, it is not 'given' by way of any mode of unmediated experience (p. 119). Nor, however, does this structure of possibility that Derrida alludes to spring forth ready-made in the shape of a Kantian formalism composed of the pure intuitions of time and space. This should come as no surprise, since we have noted that on Derrida's view no structure is ever given in a manner that can be elucidated independently of context: there are no 'pure intuitions' just as there is no pure meaning irrespective of context. What we are faced with, rather, is an irreducible and enigmatic relation between the two: context 'determines' meaning, but the nature of context itself is never completely decidable.[59] For this reason, meaning itself is ultimately irreducible and involves an essential undecidability.

We can note from his advocacy of a quasi-transcendentalism that Derrida's relationship to the classical philosophical tradition is one that seeks to keep in play what he regards as its most important insights, for example the 'all or nothing' logic that is employed in conceptual analysis: 'not only do I find this logic strong, and, in conceptual language and analysis, *an absolute must*, it must (and this "it must" translates the faithfulness of my love for philosophy) be sustained against all empirical confusion' (p. 122). To this extent, Derrida remains a self-avowed 'classical philosopher' (p. 125, cf. also p. 130). Returning to the issue of ethics and politics, however, it is clear that ethico-political questions are, for Derrida, implied within every theoretical formulation (p. 135). This, we might say, is because all theories are constructed within a context, and all human contexts are composed of interests. To this extent we can never escape from the problem of ethics, or from the interrelation between ethics and politics. The two are linked, therefore, but at the same time the one cannot be reduced to the other, for what is 'political through and through . . . is not only political' (p. 136). Ethics is essentially linked to the conventions and practices (the ways of doing things) that go to make up any particular context, but it is not simply reducible to this dimension. Rather than being simply overturned by it, the notion of what we can call here 'right understanding' (which allows Derrida to draw the distinction between false, not true, and bad, not good, readings of his own writings) is precisely what is at stake within any deconstructive reading. Such right understanding is constantly threatened by the very tension between meaning and context that Derrida seeks to elucidate in much of his work. Thus, good faith, lucidity, rigour, etc., are all characterizable as 'positive values'. But such values are, by their very nature 'contextual, essentially limited, unstable, and endangered' (p. 147). It is for this reason that 'the essential and irreducible possibility of *mis*-understanding or of "*in*felicity" must be taken into account in the description of those values said to be positive.' Deconstruction, we can infer, pays attention to the essential instability and undecidability that is an ever present (and hence an *a priori*) condition of all meaning. Context is both a necessary, though not sufficient, condition of meaning, and it is the very instability of context, its irreducible unpredictability in so far as there is no *one* context, that bestows upon meaning the particular and inherent instability that is peculiar to it. There is, in other words, an inherent *tension* within the notion of context itself: it both yields meaning, and is a condition of its reiteration and its transformation. This movement, this instability and undecidability is what Derrida tries to capture when he writes of the trace, the supplement, differance, or iterability.

In turn, if we follow Derrida's argument one stage further, it is clear that there is within the notion of contextual undecidability itself a kind of 'unconditionality' that remains independent of any particular context (p. 152). The very word 'unconditionality' is significant here, for 'I use [it] not by accident to recall the character of the categorical imperative in its Kantian form.' Kant's categorical imperative, to recall, states that one ought to do the right thing irrespective of the particular context in which one is situated. It states that when faced with a moral dilemma one ought to act in such a way that it could consistently be willed to become a universal law (i.e. 'Do unto others as you would have them do unto you'). In formulating this, Kant draws the distinction between a purely instrumental conception of action ('If you want such and such a thing, then do such and such an action') and an ethical one. The injunction not to kill, for instance, is a good example of how the categorical imperative works: not killing is ethical requirement that ought to be acknowledged independently of what one may want.[60] Derrida's conception of deconstruction involves affirming this kind of unconditionality, i.e. it affirms an ethical mode of thought as being implicit to the nature of deconstruction. Unconditional affirmation, in this sense is something that arises independently of any particular context and 'from an injunction, a law, a responsibility, that transcends this or that determination of a given context' (p. 152). Such unconditionality, Derrida argues, appears as soon as any context is opened up, and it must be articulated within that context in terms of the strategic, political or ethical issues that arise within it. The question of unconditionality thus concerns the limit of any particular context and also 'defines the injunction that prescribes deconstructing' (p. 153). In other words, the unconditionality that transcends contextual specificity is a kind of '*ought*': it is an ethical imperative, and this imperative is what drives deconstruction to engage in critique.[61] What we have here, then, is a Derridean conception of the ethical. And it is one that allows him to take a stand – to state unconditionally, for example, that apartheid is wrong (p. 152), or that 'good faith', 'rigour', etc., *ought* to be a condition of intellectual engagement and debate. It is because such things are endangered, unstable, etc., that Derrida values them. Also, it is because of this that the project of a work like *Of Grammatology* can be summarized as setting out to show that the presupposition that meaning is already secured by intentionality and hence the presence of the speaker is a misguided one: 'To make enigmatic what one thinks one understands by the words "proximity", "immediacy", "presence" . . . is my final intention in this book' (*Of Grammatology*, 70). In so far as deconstruction places in question key philosophical presuppositions concerning the fixing of meaning it performs an inherently *ethical* role.

3.9   Derrida contra Levinas

What, then, of Levinas in relation to this? We can begin by noting that Levinas is the subject of a long piece by Derrida included in *Writing and Difference*, 'Violence and Metaphysics: An Essay on the Thought of Emmanuel Levinas'.[62] In this essay Derrida both expresses an admiration for Levinas and at the same time engages in a criticism of his conception of ethics as transcendence. What is it, though, that divides Derrida from Levinas? This question can be approached in relation to *Of Grammatology*, where Levinas's work is alluded to in the context of Derrida's conception of the trace and, above all, terms of the response of these two thinkers to the work of Heidegger. What is at stake in the notion of the trace is, Derrida claims, something that is linked to Levinas's 'critique of ontology' (*Of Grammatology*, 70). But it is linked to Levinas's critique in a manner that is 'reconciled' to 'a Heideggerean intention'. If Derrida seeks by way of the trace to make enigmatic notions that, he feels, have all too often been accepted within the metaphysical tradition as if they were unproblematic (i.e. presence, immediacy, etc.) he nevertheless believes that this is only possible if it is done in a manner that remains faithful to the metaphysical tradition in some important ways. Like Heidegger, Derrida aims, in effect, to mobilize this tradition against itself, to undermine the Western tradition from within and thereby to radicalize it. Levinas, in contrast, seeks to question the entire metaphysical tradition with a view to overcoming it by leaving it behind him. Levinas takes Heidegger's attack on metaphysics one step further, arguing that constructing a fundamental ontology on the basis of entities is the first and defining mistake of the European tradition, and that the conceptual and logical relations that inhere within such a view must be exposed in their insufficiency. The question of the difference between Levinas and Derrida thus resolves itself into the question of the relation between the 'outside' and 'inside' of the Western tradition – whether it has an 'outside' at all. For Derrida, the outside 'is' the inside (*Of Grammatology*, 44ff). Therefore, there is no question of breaking free of the inside, for there is nowhere else to go, no radically exterior 'place' that is available to thought.

Derrida's essay 'Violence and Metaphysics' develops this point, and it does so right from the outset. So, Derrida begins the essay by ruminating on the fate of philosophy – on the heritage of the philosophical tradition as it is inherited from Kant, Hegel, Marx, Nietzsche, and Heidegger, all of whom dwell, in one way or another, on the *end* of philosophy. The word 'end' as it is used here has two senses: on the one hand it concerns the purposes of philosophizing, on the other it concerns the demise of philosophy.[63] A numer of issues arise from this: What is the relation between philosophy and history? What is the future of philosophy? Will philosophy die? Such questions, Derrida says, are ones that, although not necessarily 'philosophical questions' in the usual sense, are 'the only questions today capable of founding the community, within the world, of those who are still called philosophers' ('Violence and Metaphysics', 79). As such, philosophy can be defined as 'the community of the question' concerning the very possibility of philosophizing (p. 80). Once again, then, we can note the Kantian aspect of Derrida's approach: philosophy is characterized in terms of its aiming to think its own condition of possibility, its own *a priori*. If we were to object that questions of this sort are nonsensical, that in asking philosophy to account for itself in this way we are asking for what cannot be accounted for, Derrida has an answer: 'The impossible . . . has occurred: there is a history of the question' (p. 80). It is philosophy's ability to ask the question of its own possibility that makes it what it is. And what philosophy is, in this regard, is a mode of thought that is fundamentally bound by an ethic, by an 'ought': philosophy *ought* to address this issue about itself. This may sound rather grand, but one in fact needs to be modest about the matter: 'A community of the question about the possibility of the question. This is very little – almost nothing – but within it, today, is sheltered and encapsulated an unbreachable dignity and *duty* of decision. An unbreachable *responsibility*' (p. 80, italics added). 'Duty' and 'responsibility' are what characterize philosophy today. Philosophy, for Derrida, takes its place in the world first and foremost as an ethical mode of thought: it concerns the relationship between thinkers (philosophers) and the limits of what they can think. Their duty is to pay attention to these limits. Paying attention to these limits, refusing to think in terms of an already secure future for philosophical thought, is the *duty* of philosophy itself and of those who practice it. This is the end of philosophy in the two senses already mentioned.

The central point about such an ethics is that it is always mediated by the metaphysical tradition. If philosophy has an ethical duty to ponder its own limits this is because of a movement that is essentially intrinsic to it – even if philosophers have not always recognized this fact. According to Derrida, Levinas is a thinker who both alludes to this limit and at the same time ignores the condition of his being able to allude to it. In so far as Levinas's 'great book, *Totality and Infinity*' ('Violence and Metaphysics', 84) points to the essential problem of philosophical discourse, which is its entrapment within the Greek ontological tradition, his is a mode of thought that 'can make us tremble . . . this thought . . . no longer seeks to be a thought of Being and phenomenality . . . this thought summons us to a dislocation of the Greek logos [of Greek philosophy], to a dislocation of our identity, and perhaps of identity in general' (p. 82). For Derrida, then, Levinas propels us into thinking the limits of Western metaphysical and ontological discourse. If Heidegger identifies European thought as a tradition that has its roots in Ancient Greek ontology and argues for the internal transformation of this tradition, Levinas summons us to question the very presuppositions of this tradition. Levinas must, it follows, oppose this tradition with something, and it is what Levinas opposes to the Western tradition that Derrida finds questionable. Levinas's is 'a thought which . . . by remaining faithful to the immediate, but buried nudity of experience itself, seeks to liberate itself from the Greek domination of the Same and the One'. We need not rehearse Levinas's arguments in detail again to grasp Derrida's point: Levinas seeks to liberate thought from the Greek metaphysical tradition, from the tradition which thinks of experience in terms of the relation between the self and objects in its world. Yet, Derrida notes, Levinas nevertheless seeks to define his own thought as metaphysics, which is 'a Greek notion': the ethical relationship in general is asserted as being self-supporting, as requiring no further foundation (p. 83). This being so, is it not the case, Derrida asks, that Levinas's thought can be questioned in a number of ways? Let us have a look at these ways, taking them in reverse order so to speak, by starting with the last of Derrida's observations: that the term 'metaphysics' is itself always already a Greek one.

Levinas seeks to articulate a pure form of exteriority in the shape of the relation between the Same and the Other:

> Ethics, in Levinas's sense, is an Ethics without law and without concept, which maintains its nonviolent purity only before being determined as concepts and laws. This is not an objection: let us not forget that Levinas does not seek to propose laws or moral rules . . . but rather the essence of the ethical relation in general . . . But why does Levinas return to categories he seemed to have rejected previously in attempting this very difficult passage beyond the debate . . . ?' (p. 111)

Levinas's thought does not, it follows, offer a *theory* of ethics: it is not a theory about the nature of right and wrong. Rather, it is 'an Ethics of Ethics'. How though would any particular, practical morality arise from this? Only, perhaps, by this Ethics of Ethics 'negating and forgetting itself'. If Levinas is driven to articulate this meta-ethics, however, then he ends up doing so in terms that are essentially Greek: by invoking the notions of 'metaphysics' and 'transcendence'. For Derrida, what can be gleaned from this is the fact that Levinas's thought is driven by a peculiar kind of *necessity*, a necessity imposed upon it by the very ontological tradition he castigates: 'does it [Greek philosophy] hide . . . some indestructible and unforseeable resource of the Greek logos? Some unlimited power of envelopment, by which he who attempts to repel it would always already be *overtaken?*' (pp. 111–12). What, we might ask, is the 'power of envelopment' that Derrida speaks of here, a power which entraps all who seek to escape it? It is, in fact, something that is linked to none other than the problem of metaphor, in which we have already seen Derrida has a great interest. The problem of metaphor here is the problem of the power of the *metaphorics* of Western philosophical discourse within which, Derrida argues, even as he seeks to overcome it, Levinas remains trapped. If, then, the Other for Levinas is to be understood as that which is radically *exterior*, that which transcends the same and the rule of self-identity, he must still, *in the act of articulating this* (in his very *language*), effectively acknowledge the necessity and envelopment of the tradition he is questioning. What must be acknowledged is that 'it is necessary [for Levinas] to state infinity's *excess* over totality *in* the language of totality; that it is necessary [for him] to state the other in the language of the Same' (p. 112). Thus, Derrida argues that in seeking to *think* exteriority in the form of the Other Levinas must remain situated within the metaphorical workings that govern the philosophical language of Western/ Greek discourse, for the very notion of an 'Inside-Outside structure' is generated by that tradition, as is the 'spatial metaphor' that this structure implies.

If Levinas aims at finding a non-violent means of expressing the transcendence of the ethical, for Derrida such violence *has already occurred*, for it is interspersed within the very language that Levinas must resort to in order to argue his case.[64] Likewise, Levinas's emphasis on the face of the Other succumbs, Derrida argues, to this same point. If the face of the Other does not reside somewhere that is irreducibly *outside* the same, then 'The entire Metaphysics of the Face would collapse' (p. 115). Here, too, there is an inherent violence functioning as a condition of the face of the Other being opened up to the self (the same). In so far as the heliocentric metaphysical tradition throws light upon the world by way of its unconscious employment of the metaphorics of light and dark, this necessarily involves a kind of originary violence being enacted in relation to the Other in order for it to announce itself. In turn, if Levinas would illuminate the Other for us, if he would *show* the ethical in this way, then this, too, involves opposing heliocentrism (light) with light: 'If the movement of metaphysical transcendence is history, it is still violent for . . . history is violence. Metaphysics is *economy*: violence against violence, light against light: philosophy (in general)' (p. 117). Here we can see a reassertion of the Derridean view that light itself (the light of philosophical discourse) embodies an ethics that should not be ignored, and cannot be escaped from so easily. The ethical, it follows, is for Derrida located not '*outside*' philosophy (whatever kind of non-place that might be) but within the tradition that is philosophy.

Derrida's other main point against Levinas is that the metaphysics of the face embodies an empiricism. This is because the experience of the 'nudity of the face' (to recall Levinas's phrase) is, Derrida argues, presented by Levinas as an unmediated mode of experience (pp. 82–3). If the Western metaphysical tradition is bounded by a metaphorics of 'outside' and 'inside', it is also bounded by the ontology this implies. The logic of this ontological distinction invades even the discourse of empiricism: 'As Hegel says somewhere, empiricism always forgets, at very least, that it employs the words to be. Empiricism is thinking *by* metaphor without thinking the metaphor *as such*' (p. 139). If we apply this point to Levinas, then we would say that he employs a metaphysical language haunted by metaphor but refuses to acknowledge the metaphoricity inherent within that language itself. In this sense, for Derrida, Levinas presupposes the very preconception of Being that he castigates Heidegger for cleaving to in order to ground the project of fundamental ontology. Levinas's articulation of 'Ethico-metaphysical transcendence therefore presupposes ontological transcendence' (p. 141). What, then, has Levinas achieved with regard to the empiricism of which Derrida speaks? According to Derrida, he has effectively radicalized 'the aim which has more or less secretly animated all philosophical gestures which have been called *empiricism* in the history of philosophy. He does so with an audacity, a profundity, and a resoluteness never before attained. By taking this project to its end, he totally renews empiricism, and inverses it by revealing it to itself as metaphysics' (p. 151). Empiricism, Derrida notes, has been designated as a non-philosophy since Plato, but Levinas's rethinking of it effectively 'contests the resolution and coherence of the logos (philosophy) at its root, instead of letting itself be questioned by the logos' (p. 152). To, put the matter rather differently, in Levinas 'experience' reasserts its right to challenge the philosopheme of identity that underpins classical epistemology and ontology.

But this achievement, Derrida claims, does not amount to an escape from the Greek ontological heritage. All thinking, as we have already noted, is inexorably trapped within this heritage: 'It was a Greek who once said "If one has to philosophize, one has to philosophize; if one does not have to philosophize, one still has to philosophize (to say it and to think it). One always has to philosophize"' (p. 152). We can note, then, that Derrida's criticism of Levinas is not an unreserved one, for it is full of a kind of admiration. Yet, Levinas's promulgation of the ethical as the transcendence of the same by the Other is, for Derrida, something that remains questionable. This should come as no surprise, since philosophy, on a Derridean conception of it, gains its dignity from the recognition that it is bound, by its own internal logic, to a duty to ask about the condition of its own possibility. Deconstruction itself pays testimony to this duty, and it is a duty that Levinas's thought questions in the most radical manner.

We need not end here. For Levinas has a response to these objections. This response is to be found in the essay 'God and Philosophy'.[65] Levinas, I think, needs to be given his due, so let us conclude this discussion by briefly noting some of his thoughts on the matter. That Levinas's essay is a reply to Derrida is evident from the opening sentence: ' "Not to philosophize is still to philosophize". The philosophical discourse of the West claims the amplitude of an all-encompassing structure or of an ultimate comprehension. It compels every other discourse to justify itself before philosophy' (p. 167). Levinas, of course, will dispute this Derridean point (the point with which 'Violence and Metaphysics' concluded). First, Levinas argues, if it is the case that philosophical discourse is as all encompassing as Derrida implies, then it should be able to 'include God, of whom the Bible speaks – if this God does have a meaning'. We should recall here that for Levinas God signifies 'a putting of the Infinite into thought' (p. 174) in such a way that it transcends the identity of the 'I think'. In so far as it does this, thought of God challenges the ontological thematization characteristic of Western philosophical thought. Equally, in so far as God is a transcending of the same, he also transcends the philosophy of identity that characterizes the ontology of Western philosophical discourse. However, Levinas argues, philosophy, if it is to discuss God, will necessarily recuperate him to the notion of Being 'as an *entity* par excellence' (p. 168). In other words, the transcendence that is thought in the form of God is destroyed by conceptualizing the divine as an entity. Thinking about God, the God of the Bible, is one mode of thought that philosophy must master by recuperating it to itself – the metaphysical ontology of Being. Equally, from a philosophical standpoint one could also dismiss the God of the Bible as nonsensical: one could say that such a God cannot be thought at all in a meaningful way. However, the point of both such approaches to the question of the divine is that philosophy, in staking its claim to master another kind of discourse, reveals itself to be an imperialism of meaning. Philosophy, to put the matter simply, thereby presupposes that all meaning is quantifiable in philosophical terms. 'The problem thus posed . . . is whether the meaning that is equivalent to the *esse* of being, that is, the meaning which is meaning in philosophy, is not already a restriction of meaning.' In other words, meaning, in Levinas's view, is *not* exclusively philosophical. The encounter of the Same with the transcendence of the Other is not strictly reducible to the philosopheme of meaning that Derrida presupposes it to be. Moreover, this encounter may be an 'empirical event', but this does not mean that we know what the 'empirical' means in this case: 'the empirical event of obligation to another is something we cannot remain indifferent to' but at the same time 'it is impossible to fix limits or measure the extreme urgency of this responsibility' (p. 80). The relation of transcendence has a meaning that is not itself quantifiable in purely philosophical terms. This is because this kind of responsibility does not derive from a pre-given structure or metaphorics, as Derrida claims. To say that it does would be to say that a pre-given structure of meaning (the said) is always present whenever one speaks to others (the saying): 'In addressing the Other in language one *gives* to them' (p. 183). But, Levinas argues, 'saying' has to be differentiated from 'the said'. The said may be conceptual, it may fix identities, etc. But saying does not of itself do so, nor can it be shown that it does in an *a priori* fashion, as Derrida's approach implies: 'Saying opens me to the other before saying what is said, before the said uttered in this sincerity forms a screen between me and the other.' 'Saying', in this sense, is never something that can be decided upon in advance in the way in which the said can be. In so far as language occurs within the domain of saying it 'loses its superfluous and strange function of doubling up thought and being'. Saying, then, does not operate according to a pre-established relation between speakers that are already conceived of as *entities*, that are already thought of as thing-like. Saying already pays testimony to a responsibility that binds speakers together in a mutual relation that *precedes* what is said.

How does saying, then, relate to experience – to the kind of 'empiricism' that Derrida talks about in relation to Levinas? Saying, to be sure, signifies, but it is 'a way of signifying prior to all experience . . . it does not testify to a prior experience [of the face of the Other], but to the Infinite which is not accessible to the unity of apperception,[66] [but which is, rather] non-appearing and disproportionate to the present' (p. 183). We can conclude that Levinas has some objections to Derrida's reading of him as an 'empiricist', if the sense of 'empiricism' means asserting the purely pre-given immediacy of empirical experience over all else. In so far as it transcends all conceptual schemes by signifying in a manner that transcends all particular subjective experience and thereby confronts us with the Other, the 'empirical event' of ethical responsibility precedes experience as its non-formalizable condition of possibility. There is, for Levinas, a level of meaning that transcends the bounds of philosophical discourse. And he can, in turn, serve the following rejoinder to Derrida: '*Not to philosophize would not be "to philosophize still"* . . . There is a meaning testified to in interjections and outcries, before being disclosed in propositions, and meaning that signifies as a command, like an order that one signifies. Its manifestation in a theme already devolves from its signifying as ordering; ethical signification signifies not *for* a consciousness which thematizes, but *to* a subjectivity, wholly an obedience, obeying with an obedience that precedes understanding' (p. 186).

Rather than add any further criticisms of Levinas's views we will leave Derrida's observations to stand, taking them as thought-provoking questions that require further reflection rather than resolution. With regard to Derrida, however, some points may be made by way of a conclusion. To begin with, we can note that Derrida's conception of the ethics of deconstructive criticism, like much of his work, stands or falls with the trace and difference. In so far as the trace is *'the differance which opens appearance and signification . . . no concept of metaphysics can describe it'* (*Of Grammatology*, 65), surely difference, too, does *not* operate solely in the classically oriented manner that is, on Derrida's own reading of Levinas, characteristic of Western metaphysical discourse. Rather, the movement of difference that marks the trace, which is paradoxically an origin that is not an origin, produces the conceptual differentiation that is characteristic of all contexts. The opening of context, in this sense, is not necessarily determined by the power of philosophical discourse. As has been noted by Peter Dews,[67] Derrida's position is marked by a dual resistance, on the one hand to classical foundationalism and, on the other, to any final abandonment of a transcendental perspective (which is retained in the form of a modified '"quasi"-transcendentalism'). Derrida, as we have seen, argues that his conception of deconstruction does not embrace a form of nihilism, that is, it does not entail an abandonment of the problematics of ethical value, and this is evidenced in his retention of a mode of transcendental argument. Yet, at the same time, the critical potential of deconstruction must nevertheless operate on the cusp of such a nihilism, and hence be constantly prey to falling into it. Difference, in other words, announces itself as a kind of displaced (non)origin of meaning that is, in its own turn, reliant upon the historical precedent of nihilism. This 'nihilism' is something that the writings of Nietzsche both identify and codify under that name.[68] In its emphasis upon the suspension of terms, upon undecidability, the Derridean postulation of difference represents an attempt to resist the solidification of concepts into mere analogues of empirical experience – hence Derrida's criticisms of Levinas. However, even though difference is regarded by Derrida as being strictly unconditioned by either purely conceptual or experiential determining factors, it nevertheless exerts its own peculiar *necessity*: '*différance* maintains our relationship with that which we necessarily misconstrue, and which exceeds the alternative of presence and absence.'[69] In this sense, even as difference is construed to operate in terms of a 'play' or 'movement' of undecidable components, there is a mode of necessity at work within it. Speaking like Adorno, we can argue that whether or not it is the authentically first, whether or not it must function as the 'unnameable'[70] that makes play possible, is perhaps significant in relation to this. For, in invoking necessity the Derridean postulation of difference falls within a domain analogous to other foundationalist positions which, along with Kant, assert that 'a proposition which in being thought is thought as *necessary*' is, in some sense, legitimate *a priori*.[71] Although for Derrida this necessity has now become an *a priori* necessity of a mode of regulation that emphasizes *misunderstanding* (which, after all, is the problem of 'iterability' as Derrida defines it) – and even if the legitimacy that grounds this is itself a kind of delegitimation of authorized meaning in so far as it is 'an enigmatic relation of the same to the other'[72] – the principle of necessity nevertheless remains intact. But what kind of necessity is this? Surely, a necessity that is unhooked from any decidable relation is a mode of the absolute identity that thinkers like Adorno and Levinas criticize in their respective ways. Likewise, even as difference teeters on the verge of collapsing into the absolute identity of the Same which defines the very notion of pure origination that Derrida spurns, it is at the same time not immune from the danger of a spontaneous reduction to an empirical contingency. How else are we to interpret the following?: '[Difference is] untranslatable: you have in English to "defer", or "delay", "postpone"; but differing in the sense of being distinct is also part of it, and the two don't go together directly into English. And this highlights the indissociability of what is said, and the language, untranslatability. There is a difficulty in isolating the sense independently of the language.'[73] If, as Derrida here asserts, difference is strictly untranslatable and therefore exceeds the grasp of other language formations – even those in close cultural proximity – it might be possible to consider it as little more than a by-product of a certain cultural (i.e. French-linguistic) determination. If so, the empirical context of the articulation of difference itself would outstrip and subvert such claims to a reformulated retention of the transcendental perspective that would guarantee Derrida's critique of Western metaphysics immunity from the accusation of being rooted in contingency.

Perhaps it is this kind of problem that has led Derrida, in the 'Afterword' to *Limited Inc.* for example, to emphasize the view that the undecidability and play of difference are not to be confused with an originary indeterminacy. As such, difference would render the determination of meaning in any particular context 'possible and necessary'.[74] In this way, Derrida can argue, difference ought not to be construed as being either identical with determinacy or its opposite (i.e. as an absolute indeterminacy), since this would in either case render it subject to the dominion of a logic of identity. In asserting the value of non-identity in this way, however, Derrida seems to be moving toward a variant of the positions advocated by Adorno and by Levinas. Difference, since 'it "is" in *itself* nothing', is not to be confused with any noumenal realm of relations absolutely detached from the phenomenal world of concrete experience. Nevertheless, it is to be inferred, like the Kantian *noumenon*,[75] from the realms of conceptual and empirical determination alike, albeit in such a way as to resist codification within the logic of relations that offers Kant grounds for the postulation of things-in-themselves. Again, however, Derrida appears here to be on the verge of propounding a notion of mediation that falls within the categories of classical semiology that he wishes especially to resist. If undecidability (the movement or play of differance) is ultimately determined by the limits of contextual applicability,[76] it is itself mediated by contextual forces as the condition of its possibility. Thus, identity becomes the precondition of non-identity's being postulated at all. Since, however, Derrida does not feel compelled to work this problem through in terms of, for example, the dialectical interplay between identity and non-identity, the empirical and transcendental polarities that underpin differance return to haunt it, and so render it an abstract and unmediated idealism.

This is not to underestimate Derrida's contribution to a critique of transcendental modes of analysis – nor his insight into the problem of metaphor in philosophical language. Certainly, a movement away from concepts of origination in order to give a turn to non-identity is not, I think, to be gainsaid. Much of what is interesting and valuable in the thought of Nietzsche, the Frankfurt School, or Levinas is due to the fact that they attempt something similar. But such a turn is only a viable proposition if one is prepared to take history itself not as something that is 'opened' by differance, but as an open-ended mode of concrete experience that is not determined in advance by the categories of the Western tradition. Like Heidegger and Levinas, Derrida seeks to think the limits of this tradition, and the ethics of deconstruction springs from this engagement. But it is not clear that the kind of ethical commitment that Derrida derives from philosophy's self-reflection upon its own conditions of possibility can fulfil the requirements he makes of it. As Levinas argues, philosophical meaning is not the *only* kind of meaning.

4   Anti-humanism and Ethics

Whatever the differences that separate Levinas from Derrida it is clear that both thinkers offer us reflections on the nature of ethics that engage with the problem outlined by Heidegger's reaction to Sartrean existentialism in the 'Letter on Humanism'. If the development of epistemology from Descartes to the Frankfurt School marks a move away from notions of 'immediate experience' and a de-contextualized conception of subjectivity in favour of a conception of knowledge that stresses its socially mediated aspect, so too the accounts of the ethical that Levinas and Derrida present spurn the purportedly primary role of subjectivity in such matters. If Levinas embraces an empiricism, as Derrida points out, it is an essential aspect of this empiricism that it articulates the nature of the ethical not in terms of the immediate self-awareness of the subjective ego, but by way of an encounter with what is Other as a mode of transcendence. So, too, Derrida offers us reflections on the nature of ethics that devolve from the role that writing (in its extended sense), metaphorics, contextuality, and the philosophical tradition play in determining the nature of the ethical relation. In this regard, Levinas and Derrida are thinkers who represent a move further away from the Cartesian tradition of epistemology that was outlined in chapter 1, above. Whether one agrees or disagrees with Levinas or Derrida, an important point emerges from our encounter with them: philosophical questions are by no means always only 'philosophical' in nature. Philosophical questions – whether concerning problems of ontology or matters of language and metaphor – also have connotations that are necessarily cultural, ethical, and political. Whatever their differences with regard to Heidegger, or indeed with one another, Levinas and Derrida share with Heidegger a common strand of anti-humanism that embraces a move away from the subject as the benchmark standard for enquiry into philosophical problems. Of course, of the thinkers we have discussed it is not only Heidegger who stands as the initiator of this move, but also in important respects Hegel and Nietzsche. Thus, the Hegelian dialectical analysis of history in terms of the development of Spirit effectively devolves priority away from the subject and into an objective unfolding dialectic of Spirit that grounds notions of subjectivity. Equally, Nietzsche, who is by no means an Hegelian but who nevertheless advocates a certain 'Hegelianism' with regard to questions about the nature of reality (i.e. an attitude that stresses becoming over being), also regards the subject as something constituted by historical conditions and as an untenable foundation upon which to base an account of the nature of knowledge. Whereas Levinas and Derrida in their respective ways initiate discussion about the nature of ethics from an anti-humanist perspective, Heidegger's work remains significantly quiet about this matter. With the advantage of historical hindsight we might be tempted to say that there is good reason for this. For Heidegger, as we have already briefly mentioned at the end of chapter 3, is a thinker whose own personal history is compromised by an entanglement within the ethical and political morass of Nazism. What, though, of the political ramifications of anti-humanism? This is one question that will be addressed in the next chapter.

Notes

1 Varieties of this approach are most famously associated with thinkers like Jeremy Bentham (1748–1832) and John Stuart Mill (1806–73).

2 In the twentieth century a number of variants on the basic utilitarian methodology have been developed as a way out of such a problem. I do not propose to discuss these here, however.

3 Immanuel Kant, *Groundwork of the Metaphysic of Morals*, tr. H. J. Paton (London: Hutchinson University Library, 1972), p. 67.

4 Plato, *Theaetetus*, tr. M. J. Levett, revised Myles Burnyeat (Indianapolis: Hackett, 1992), 152 a.

5 Jean-Paul Sartre, *Existentialism and Humanism*, tr. Philip Mairet (London: Methuen, 1980). All further references are given in the text with page number.

6 It should be added that Sartre's *Being and Nothingness* (1943), tr. Hazel E. Barnes (London: Routledge, 1996), suggests a rather more antagonistic relationship between individuals than is implied here (in part derived from Sartre's reading of the master/slave dialectic discussed by Hegel in the *Phenomenology of Spirit*). This is coupled with an account of subjectivity that concentrates on the role that 'nothingness' plays in its constitution. It is an account that has a somewhat Kantian aspect, in that Sartre argues that human freedom is constituted by the negativity of 'nothingness': 'what determines me is like a hollow in the middle of what I shall call my empirical plenitude' (p. 177).

However, in this work, too, Sartre embraces an approach that cleaves to a humanistic philosophy of consciousness, in that he holds that human beings make themselves what they are through the activity of living.

7   Sartre, *Being and Nothingness*. Central to Sartre's analysis is an account of the 'pre-reflective cogito'. He is critical of Descartes's argument that the 'I think' typifies the consciousness of thought. For Sartre, the claim 'I think, therefore I am' rests upon a more fundamental state of consciousness which exists prior to the act of reflection upon it, since 'Strictly speaking, no fact of consciousness is this consciousness' (p. 100). In this sense, the 'I' of the 'I think' is always transcended by an impersonal pre-reflective consciousness that overflows it. It is in this sense that the notion of consciousness forms the fundamental basis for Sartre's articulation of the nature of human existence.

8   Heidegger, 'Letter on Humanism', in *Martin Heidegger: Basic Writings*, ed. David Farrell Krell (London: Routledge, 1993), pp. 217–65. All further references are given in the text with page number.

9   Another example of the contrast between Heidegger and Sartre is furnished by the following passage from Sartre's *Being and Nothingness*: 'A geological plication, a storm do not destroy – or at least they do not destroy *directly*; they merely modify the distribution of masses of beings. There is no less after the storm than before. There is *something else* . . . there must be a witness who can retain the past in some manner and compare it to the present in the form of *no longer* . . . In order for destruction to exist, there must be first a relation of man to being . . . It is necessary to recognize that destruction is an essentially human thing and that it is man who destroys his cities through the agencies of earthquakes or directly, who destroys his ships through the agencies of cyclones or directly' (p. 9). What Sartre means is that only humans are able to recognize cities, ships, etc., as things that can continue to exist or be destroyed. In this sense, it is *me* who 'destroy' them, not the world of empirical events.

10   See *Martin Heidegger: Basic Writings*, pp. 93–110.

11   *Being and Time*, p. 255. See chapter 3, section 1.15.

12   Emmanuel Levinas, *Ethics and Infinity: Conversations with Philippe Nemo*, tr. Richard A. Cohen (Pittsburgh: Duquesne University Press, 1985), p. 37.

13   What disappoints Levinas about the later Heidegger's work is 'the disappearance in it of phenomenology properly speaking' (Ibid., p. 42).

14   Levinas's discussion of the other covers both the personal and impersonal connotations of the word. Thus, following Alphonso Lingis's translation of *Totality and Infinity*, Levinas talks of the 'you', the 'Other' ('*autrui*') and the 'other' ('*autre*').

15   Emmanuel Levinas, *Totality and Infinity*, tr. Alphonso Lingis (Pittsburgh: Duquesne University Press, 1998). All references are given in the text with page number.

16   Levinas thus transposes Heidegger's analysis of Being as transcending all notions of genus on to the self-other relation.

17   See, Chapter 1, section 4.13.

18   One should note that the question of Levinas and gender has been raised by some of his readers. Amongst them, Luce Irigaray has argued that Levinas views woman as nothing more than as a negative image of man rather than as being truly Other. Jacques Derrida has also developed a similar line of argument. For discussion of this issue see Colin Davis, *Levinas: An Introduction* (Cambridge: Polity Press, 1996), p. 140. See also, Tina Chanter, 'Reading Hegel as a Mediating Master: Lacan and Levinas', *Levinas and Lacan: The Missed Encounter*, ed. Sarah Harasym (New York: State University of New York Press, 1998). See also essays by Derrida, Irigaray and others in *Re-Reading Levinas*, ed. Simon Critchley and Robert Bernasconi (London: Athlone Press, 1991). For a brief discussion of Irigaray see chapter 5, below.

19 *Ipse*: Latin for 'self'.

20 *Ethics and Infinity*, p. 87.

21 What Levinas refers to in *Ethics and Infinity* as 'a rupture of being' (p. 87).

22 Ibid., pp. 100–1.

23 Emmanuel Levinas, 'God and Philosophy', in *The Levinas Reader*, ed. Seán Hand (Oxford: Blackwell, 1996), p. 174.

24 A contrast could therefore be made between the Levinasian understanding of God and the reading of the Hebraic semiotic offered by Deleuze and Guattari (discussed in chapter 3).

25 'God and Philosophy', *The Levinas Reader*, p. 179.

26 See J. L. Austin, *How to do Things with Words* (1955) (Oxford: Oxford University Press, 1975). By way of the shortest possible summary, we can say that Austin developed his theories in the 1950s, and his ideas have been taken up and developed by a range of people working in different disciplines (for example, philosophers, linguists, literary theorists, and psychologists). The main thing to grasp concerning speech act theory is that Austin holds that we can formulate distinctions between different kinds of words according to the different functions they perform. Hence, he argues that the activity of uttering words, although a complex matter, is susceptible to being analysed by way of the functions of particular types of word. Austin then provides an analysis that concentrates on everyday language use, and argues that the most fitting language to be analysed is that which is used in *as direct and literal a manner as possible*. By way of an aside, it is worth noting that one of the purposes of Austin's theory is to demonstrate the limitations of a positivistic account of meaning. We have already discussed positivism in the context of Adorno and Horkheimer's thought, so all we need to do here is recall that such a theory argues for the view that all meaningful sentences or propositions are ultimately to be understood as descriptions of states of affairs (what are called 'constative utterances'). This being the case, positivism holds, it follows that all sentences are either true or false. The point for Austin is that this is a *reductive* account of meaning. It is a reductive account because some linguistic expressions convey meanings that are neither true nor false but are nevertheless meaningful. Such expressions Austin calls 'performative utterances'. Performatives are the kinds of utterances that people use when they do things like make promises, issue warnings, declare things, etc. (e.g. 'I promise I'll give you my ticket for the game', 'Look out!', 'I name this ship HMS Pinafore'). Performatives, it follows, do not pertain to truth conditions. This is because a promise, for example, is neither true nor false: it is either kept or broken. Performatives, it follows, are conventional, in other words they are either appropriate or inappropriate.

Austin, though, does not rest content with the constative/performative distinction outlined above. Rather, he then blurs the distinction by seeking to demonstrate that constatives can have a performative status, and *vice versa*. On this view, *all* utterances are susceptible to being defined as speech acts, since any utterance that makes a statement concerning a matter of fact can be recast in the form 'I hereby assert that . . .'. In other words, all propositions can be viewed as speech acts. Searle, in his own turn, has sought to develop Austin's work by articulating a model that stipulates the rules specific to different kinds of speech act. Thus, for Searle, a promise can be further characterized as of necessity involving some future action. In addition, a promise must concern something that the person who is promising would not simply do if they did not make a promise, and must also account for the intentions of the one who makes the promise. (See John Searle, *Speech Acts* (Cambridge: Cambridge University Press, 1969)).

27 For a brief and perceptive discussion of Derrida and Searle see Christopher Norris, *Derrida* (London: Fontana, 1987), pp. 177ff.

28 By way of example, Nietzsche is without doubt a 'literary' philosopher – and was hardly considered a philosopher at all in some quarters in good measure because of this (see P. Sedgwick, 'Nietzsche as Literature/Nietzsche as German Literature', *Journal of Nietzsche Studies*, 13, Spring 1997, pp. 53–71). Likewise, although I have chosen not to discuss his work in this volume, the nineteenth-century Danish philosopher and theologian Sören Kierkegaard (1813–55) might be cited as another example of a 'literary philosopher'. Thus, Kierkegaard's *Either/Or*, edited by the pseudonymous 'Victor Eremita', includes the diary of 'Johannes Climacus', the ruminations of a man intent on seducing a young woman through the exploitation of social conventions. The diary itself is, we are told, a transcription of the original made by one 'A', a friend of Johannes. What the reader is thereby presented with is a profusion of authorial layers whereby the reader is continually distanced from the purportedly original author of the text. Kierkegaard's philosophy, which ultimately aims at persuading the reader of virtues of an anti-institutional Christian faith, is thereby presented in the most 'literary' of fashions (see *Either/Or*, tr. Howard V. Hong and Edna H. Hong (Princeton, N.J.: Princeton University Press, 1987)). For a discussion of this text see Dennis A. Foster, *Confession and Complicity in Narrative* (Cambridge: Cambridge University Press, 1987).

29 It should be noted that 'critical theory' in this sense is not to be confused with the critical theory developed by members of the Frankfurt School (discussed in chapter 2, above).

30 For an introduction to structuralist critical analysis see T. Hawkes, *Structuralism and Semiotics* (London: Methuen, 1977).

31 For a discussion of Althusser see chapter 5.

32 For instance, Jean-François Lyotard and Michel Foucault, both of whose work is discussed in chapter 5, below.

33 Poststructuralism is a movement that covers fields as diverse as cultural theory, literary criticism, political theory, and sociology. Poststructuralism emerged from a reaction against perceived weaknesses in structuralist theory – particularly the claims to 'scientific' status that structuralists made for their theories. This rejection of scientific methodology is paradigmatic, since poststructuralists argue that it is not possible for any theory to claim objective status. In other words, no theory can claim the right to being regarded as a 'master narrative' or 'metalanguage' that exists independently of the context in which it is situated. In place of one single master narrative (such as is offered by the Marxist account of socio-historical development) the poststructuralist advocates a pluralism on all fronts, whether 'methodological', or in matters of ethics, politics, etc. Some aspects of this are evident in Derrida's work, although his maintaining of a modified form of transcendentalism does not fit in well with the views generally associated with poststructuralism. Of recent thinkers, some of the writings of French philosopher Jean-François Lyotard might be called poststructuralist – although his name is more usually associated with the term 'postmodernism' (see the discussion of him in chapter 5). For a detailed discussion of poststructuralism see Richard Harland, *Superstructuralism* (London: Methuen, 1987), or Robert Young, *Untying the Text: a post-structuralist reader* (London: Routledge & Kegan Paul, 1981).

34 Jacques Derrida, 'Force and Signification', in *Writing and Difference* (1967), tr. Alan Bass (London: Routledge & Kegan Paul, 1978). All further references are given in the text with page number.

35 *The Birth of Tragedy* (1872) was Nietzsche's first book. In this work Nietzsche offers what at the time was regarded as a shockingly original interpretation of the significance of Greek culture, and principally the Greek tragic form of art, as the sublimated expression

of the inherent violence of Greek cultural life. Nietzsche introduces the aesthetic categories of the 'Apollinian' (or 'Apollonian', depending upon your preferred spelling – though Nietzsche himself uses the term '*Apollinisch*') and the 'Dionysian' as fundamental to a reading of the significance of Greek tragedy. The Apollinian represents a formally imposed limitation placed on artistic expression and is, in Walter Kaufmann's words, 'the form-giving force, which reached its consummation in Greek culture' (Kaufmann, *Nietzsche: Philosopher, Psychologist, Antichrist* (Princeton: Princeton University Press, 1974), p. 128). In contrast, the Dionysian represents violent and chaotic forces of becoming. Nietzsche argues that these violent forces were sublimated through the Apollinian element to engender the production of the Ancient Greek tragic form. Contrary to some interpretations that have been offered of *The Birth of Tragedy*, Nietzsche does not in fact privilege the Dionysian over the Apollinian. The two are locked in a reciprocal relationship: the form-giving power of the Apollinian is only rendered possible by virtue of the chaotic force of Dionysian becoming, but the latter in its own turn is only rendered presentable by way of the Apollinian process of 'structuration'. In *The Birth of Tragedy* Wagner's music is invoked as a contemporary expression of this aesthetic synthesis, and thereby represents a possible avenue for the rejuvenation of contemporary German culture, and with it the possibility of a cultural achievement akin to that attained by the Greeks. Nietzsche was, however, to become disenchanted with Wagner within a few years – the text of *Human, All-Too-Human* (1878) marks the break with Wagner.

36 See, for example, Derrida's essay 'White Mythology', in *Margins of Philosophy* (1972), tr. Alan Bass (London: Harvester Wheatsheaf, 1982), pp. 209–71.

37 Derrida, 'White Mythology', pp. 232–3.

38 In his analysis of Aristotle, Derrida goes on to argue that Aristotelian philosophical language is permeated by the metaphorics that characterizes heliocentrism (see 'White Mythology', pp. 248 ff).

39 'White Mythology', p. 270.

40 Ibid., p. 209.

41 Ibid.

42 Ibid., p. 213.

43 Ibid., p. 264.

44 See 'White Mythology', pp. 266–7 for the discussion of Descartes. The problem of other cultures is alluded to by Derrida in the context of texts like Rousseau's *Essay on the Origin of Language*: 'And "the genius of the Oriental languages" is to be "vital and figurative"' ('White Mythology', p. 269).

45 Jacques Derrida, *Of Grammotology*, tr. Gayatri Chakravorty Spivak (Baltimore: Johns Hopkins University Press, 1976). All further references are given in the text with page number.

46 See Plato, *Gorgias*, tr. Donald J. Zayl (Indianapolis: Hackett, 1987).

47 Thus, Heidegger regards Being as a determing presence that constitutes the horizon, and hence meaning, of Dasein's Being-in-the-world. See chapter 3.

48 See Derrida's essay 'Différance', in *Margins of Philosophy*, pp. 3–27.

49 Ibid., p. 3.

50 See Jacques Derrida, *Speech and Phenomena and Other Essays on Husserl's Theory of Signs*, tr. David B. Allison (Evanston, Ill.: Northwestern University Press, 1973), p. 88.

51 See, Jean-Jacques Rousseau, *A Discourse on Inequality*, tr. Maurice Cranston (Harmondsworth: Penguin, 1984).

52 Passages from the *Essay on the Origins of Language* are all quoted from *Of Grammatology*, p. 225.

53   Jacques Derrida, 'Parergon', in *The Truth in Painting*, tr. Geoff Bennington and Ian McLeod (Chicago & London: University of Chicago Press, 1987), pp. 17–147, p. 57.

54   Immanuel Kant, *Critique of Aesthetic Judgement*, tr. James Creed Meredith (Oxford: Clarendon Press, 1911), p. 68.

55   Derrida, *The Truth in Painting*, p. 69.

56   Ibid.

57   Jacques Derrida, *Limited Inc.*, ed. Gerald Graff (Evanston, Ill.: Northwestern University Press, 1988). All further references are given in the text with page number.

58   Since *Limited Inc.* contains the essay on Austin mentioned at the beginning of our discussion of Derrida ('Signature, Event, Context'), a synopsis of John Searle's reply, and Derrida's notorious riposte to that piece, we can note that the ethics of discussion in question concerns not least the rights and wrongs of academic exchange.

59   How, after all, could it be? For, in order for this to be the case one would need to have a perspective that transcends all notions of context in order to decide upon the nature of contextuality in an exhaustive manner, i.e. to attribute the word 'context' a specific and thus determinate sense. Derrida's point is that contexts are always, by their very nature, undecidable because of this.

60   See Immanuel Kant, *Critique of Practical Reason*, tr. Lewis White Beck (New York: Garland, 1976).

61   Derrida notes in this connection that he has usually rejected putting matters in this way (i.e. resorting to the language of the categorical imperative) because such a form of presentation is intrinsically linked to the key philosophical presuppositions that his writings set out to deconstruct.

62   See *Writing and Difference*, pp. 79–153. All further references are given in the text with page number.

63   Thus, we can note, Hegel thought of philosophy as something that would cease to be necessary when the stage of Absolute Spirit is arrived at; Nietzsche dwells frequently on the 'prejudices of philosophers', arguing that the goal of the classical tradition, in the shape of platonism, must be abandoned. Likewise, for Marx, the end of philosophy is to change the world, not merely to describe it, and in changing it successfully philosophy must pass away. Finally, the later Heidegger, we have already seen, thinks of 'genuine thought' about Being as something that must be bought at the cost of ceasing to think in terms of the constituent disciplines that make up philosophy in its academic guise (recall that, for Heidegger, the Greeks did not call genuine thinking 'philosophy').

64   See also Derrida's discussion of Levi-Strauss in *Of Grammatology* for another version of this argument.

65   Immanuel Levinas, 'God and Philosophy' (1978), in *The Levinas Reader*, ed. Seán Hand (Oxford: Blackwell, 1989), pp. 166–89. All further references are given in the text with page number.

66   I.e. the transcendental unity of the self that must, according to Kant, serve as the formal precondition of the possibility of experience (see chapter 1).

67   See Peter Dews, 'Nietzsche and the Critique of *Ursprungsphilosophie*', in *Exceedingly Nietzsche*, ed. David Farrell Krell and David Wood (London: Routledge, 1988).

68   See, for example, the opening sections to *The Will to Power*, tr. Walter Kaufmann and R. J. Hollingdale (New York: Vintage, 1968).

69   *Margins of Philosophy*, p. 20.

70   Ibid., p. 26.

71   Immanuel Kant, *Critique of Pure Reason*, tr. Norman Kemp Smith (London: Macmillan, 1989), B3.

72 Jacques Derrida in discussion with Raoul Mortley, in *French Philosophers in Conversation*, ed. Raoul Mortley (London: Routledge, 1991), p. 99.
73 Ibid., p. 100.
74 *Limited Inc.*, p. 136.
75 See Kant, *Critique of Pure Reason*, A236–60/B295–315.
76 In other words, 'there is nothing outside the context' (*Limited Inc.*, 136).

5

Politics, Ideology, Power and Justice: Althusser, Foucault and Nietzsche, Lyotard

I have already said that Hegel and Nietzsche make their own distinctive contributions to arguments about the nature of ethics and politics, and of the relation between the two. Their respective influences (upon figures like Levinas[1] and Derrida,[2] but not only upon them, as we will see) are sufficiently great to make any simple summary of them impossible. That said, there is an important strand in Nietzsche's work that has been developed by other thinkers associated with poststructuralism and also with postmodernism (a term I shall return to below) that warrants discussion in the present chapter. This strand concerns the possible political ramifications of Nietzsche's analysis of the nature of morality within the framework of his theory of the 'will to power'. This kind of approach has been further developed by thinkers such as Michel Foucault (1926–84), to whom we will come in due course. Before this, however, an aspect of the Hegelian-Marxist heritage will be addressed, albeit indirectly, by way of a discussion of a variant of Marxist theory put forward by the French structural Marxist Louis Althusser (1918–90).[3]

We have seen that for Derrida any philosophical theory has 'ethico-political' ramifications. In other words, there are no theories that are not embedded in contexts, and all contexts have ethical and political aspects. What, though, does one mean by the term 'politics'? Above all, we can ask in the light of this, what is involved in the articulation of 'political *theory*' in general? If all theories are political in their implication, then what kind of status are we to attribute to a theory that itself offers us an account of politics in overt terms? This is a difficult question, and there is no clear answer to it. However, one thing that relates directly to the issues we have already encountered by way of the discussion of the anti-humanist position can serve as a means of entry into this problem. Anti-humanism, we have noted, is a form of thinking that stresses the constructed nature of concepts and categories that are taken for granted within the epistemological tradition associated with thinkers such as Descartes and Locke. Additionally, the anti-humanist thesis, which holds that individual self-consciousness is a questionable starting point for the construction of any theory (be it a theory of knowledge or ethics), also has its particular point to make with regard to conceptions of politics that stress the role of the individual in the political process. A key tradition of political thought that does this is liberalism, and so it would seem obvious to lay out the groundwork for discussion of the anti-humanist legacy in its political register by first offering some account of liberalism. This done, we can contrast the liberal approach to politics and to issues of political legitimacy (that is, issues of right as opposed to power), with the anti-humanism inherent within Althusser's conception of Marxism, the Nietzschean/Foucaultian power theory, and the postmodernist account of politics offered by Jean-François Lyotard.

1   Liberalism and the Justification of Political Right

'Liberalism' is one of those words whose meaning is not easy to define because of the very diversity of approaches of the thinkers associated with it. One thing, however, is clear: liberalism constitutes one of the key traditions within political philosophy. Moreover, however diverse its possible meanings, liberal thinkers do share certain common features. They have, for example, a concern for individual liberty, and thereby embrace both a particular conception of the individual as a political agent and a particular understanding of the nature of political freedom that stems from this. We can begin to arrive at some account of the meaning of 'liberalism' by reflecting on some of the thinkers who have been associated with it. These thinkers include John Locke (whose empiricist epistemology was briefly discussed in chapter 1), the economists Adam Smith (1723–90) and Thomas Malthus (1766–1834), and the philosopher John Stuart Mill (1806–73). There are also more recent exponents of liberalism.[4] However, here we will look at the work of Locke and Mill as a means of arriving at an understanding of the liberal tradition.

Locke's work can with justification be said to stand at or near the historical origins of liberalism. Indeed, his work exhibits many of the features that we have already noted as being characteristic of the liberal tradition. Locke's *Two Treatises of Government* (1690)[5] seek to show that an analysis of the nature of political power involves the consideration of certain attributes common to all human beings. This, for Locke, involves accounting for human nature in terms of the characteristics that individuals have independently of the social context in which they may live. Locke seeks to offer an analysis of human beings in their 'natural state', or what he calls the 'state of nature' – a notion in fact found in the work of one of Locke's predecessors, Thomas Hobbes (1588–1679).[6] The 'state of nature' is one that, for Locke, predates any form of social relationship that may inhere between individuals as they exist within society – or what, after the analysis presented by Hegel in the *Philosophy of Right*, has come to be called 'civil society'.[7] The key function of Locke's conception of the state of nature is to allow him to claim that certain fundamental principles exist both naturally and independently of the realm of civil society. Indeed, such principles actually serve to ground civil society. These principles are *freedom of action* and *equality of right*. Individuals in the state of nature are free by way of right, for the freedom is endowed by natural law. No individual, Locke claims, has the right to transgress another individual's basic freedom. Locke's justification for this view is presented through an appeal to the conception of natural law, and can, he argues, be derived from the authority of human reason, which is 'the common rule and measure God hath given to mankind'.[8] We can already note a central feature of Locke's liberalism. Locke's political theory begins with the *individual*, i.e. with a conception of the self as a rational agent, and the notion of the individual that is presented is definable in a manner that is independent of socio-political relationships. Equally, Locke's conception of rationality is central to his understanding of political freedom, or liberty: it is from a rational point of view that all individuals have the *right* to protect themselves and also to claim damages from another party should they suffer a wrong at their hands. From the above it is evident that Locke's liberalism endorses a particular conception of the human individual: the individual is to be conceived of in a way that divorces questions about the nature of human subjectivity from modes of social organization. It is this divorcing of the individual and the social that forms the basis of Locke's entire political discourse.

How, then, are we to characterize the individual as such? According to Locke, every individual is definable as a self-interested party. This being the case, one thing is needed for the proper administration of the relations between individuals in civil society: some kind of regulative framework is necessary for the impartial administration of the rights that each individual has. It is this argument that constitutes a good portion of the Lockean justification for the existence of government. Government exists in order to arbitrate between the disputes that necessarily arise between individuals, even when they are situated in a state of nature. Government, in turn, is *instituted* as a means of providing this arbitration, and rests upon the structure of civil society, which is constituted by way of a voluntary contract.[9] The central point of this argument is to present us with a persuasive case for holding that legitimate government devolves from the active and free consent of those who are subject to it. Locke's central principle of government, it follows, is that individuals are only subject to the political power of government in so far as they have agreed to leave the state of nature, enter into civil society and in this way become civil agents.

But matters do not stop with this. Locke defines the transition that marks the transformation of the individual from a being in the state of nature into a civil agent in another important manner. Locke argues that civil society is derived from one foundational principle that resides in natural law. This principle, it follows, exists *first* in the state of nature, and its doing so is what subsequently legitimizes a key component of the social relation. This is the individual's right to the possession both of their own body and of what is produced by way of it, i.e. the products of their labour. Locke's argument, presented in sections 25–30 of the Second Treatise, may be summarized in eight steps. (1) All humans existing in the state of nature possess a God-given right to preserve their own lives. (2) In the state of nature the earth (i.e. the land and its resources) is something that is in the first instance held in common by all human beings. (3) Since the earth is held in common, the natural products of the earth (such as the fruit that grows naturally on a tree) belong in equal measure to everybody, in so far as they are available to anybody who cares to collect them. (4) Because these natural products are available for collection, or appropriation, there must therefore be some manner in which they can be appropriated and, by way of this, become the property of those who appropriate them. (5) There is one instance of property that all individuals do actually already possess, namely their own physical bodies. (6) In so far as a person owns their own body, then what is either made or produced by their labour belongs exclusively to them. (7) If one appropriates something that is first of all in the state of nature then this must be the result of one's own labour. (8) Consequently, the investment of one's labour makes what one has taken from the state of nature one's private property. Once this stage has been arrived at, Locke argues, it is possible to claim that no other persons have the right to take possession of what is now yours. This is because any goods that are appropriated from the state of nature in the above manner become as a direct result of this appropriation a matter of 'private right'. Such private right is a God-given matter, in so far as God would hardly have placed the world of nature at the disposal of humanity were it not to be taken advantage of in this way.

In consequence there is, Locke maintains, a 'law of reason', what he also calls 'an original law of nature', that legitimates the individual ownership of property. It is this law that effectively forms the justification for civil society.[10] Since such possession is justified, then it can be further argued that the legitimate role of government is the protection of the rights of both individuals and of their property, i.e. of an individual's own person and of the fruits of their labour. Such a view appears to justify the unrestrained appropriation of goods from the state of nature. But Locke adds a limitation to such appropriation. In the state of nature, at least, one can only justifiably possess what one can *use*, e.g. I cannot take more fruit from the apple tree than I can eat before it goes to waste. This limitation, though, is short-lived when it comes to civil society. For, civil society is characterized by the invention of a non-perishable good in the form of *money*. The limitation Locke sets on the appropriation of goods is thereby rendered irrelevant to society because I can, for example, possess a large amount of property in the form of land and exchange the goods that this land produces for money. Such goods do not, therefore, go to waste, since they are used or consumed by others. This move in Locke's argument finally justifies the unequal distribution of goods in the form of private property. Moreover, he argues that since all people use money, in doing so they in effect agree 'to the disproportionate and unequal possession of the earth'.[11] The main thing to note here is that Locke is thereby claiming that political freedom or liberty is no guarantee of social equality. In fact, the move from the state of nature to civil society brings with it a necessary inequality, because some people will be more productive than others, and will hence end up being wealthier.

Having very briefly summarized Locke's argument we can now note some features of liberalism present within it. Foremost is a concern for the individual. Above all, the individual is characterized in terms of their right to property ownership, which derives in the first instance from their being the sole legitimate possessors of their own body. Even more significant, we can note that such a right is essential to the definition of legitimate government, since it is the role of law and government to protect the individual and their property alike. 'Freedom', it follows, is characterized in the light of this as the freedom to pursue one's own goals without being subject to interference from others, so long as such goals do not impinge upon their freedom (this is often referred to as 'freedom from . . .' or 'negative liberty').[12] We can note that the role of government, and hence the state, is articulated by Locke in terms of the model we have outlined. Any form of government ought to be based on consent and ought to serve the interests of the civil agents who live under its dominion. Consequently, government can only aspire to a very limited role with regard to the lives of the individuals it is there to serve. Government cannot, for instance, impose codes of behaviour upon individuals. All government can legitimately do is arbitrate between the competing interests of individuals in civil society, making sure that they do not infringe each other's basic liberties. This conception of the relationship between the individual, society and government is characteristic of the liberal tradition in general; and in effect it holds that the consideration of individual liberty must take priority over all other social concerns (such as the need for equality).

Stated in these broad terms, these characteristics are common to many liberal thinkers. By way of illustration, we can turn to the example of John Stuart Mill, whose classic work, *On Liberty* (1859) sets out to examine and elucidate 'the nature and limits of the power that can be legitimately exercised by society over the individual'.[13] For Mill, the relationship between social power and individual freedom can be best understood within the context of the social 'struggle between liberty and authority' (p. 59). This tension between freedom and authority is, Mill notes, not a new one. The ancient states of Greece and Rome, and also earlier periods of English history, are marked by it. However, modern society presents us with a different problem. Modern society is the fruit of a process of historical development that has effectively redefined both the nature and terms of this struggle. In earlier civil societies, struggles over authority occurred between subjects and rulers. As such, political struggle primarily concerned fixing limits to the power of monarchs or aristocratic rulers. However, Mill argues, the development of the modern social provisions that were required to satisfy a 'new demand for elective and temporary rulers' (p. 60) led to the construction of institutions intended to serve representative democracy. The nature of such institutions raises a new problem concerning liberty. For, a society where the ideal of popular democracy is realized concretely is necessarily also open to the creation of a new kind of collective and authoritarian tyranny (pp. 61, 63). This tyranny is what Mill famously calls the 'tyranny of the majority', the political condition in which 'society itself is the tyrant' (pp. 62, 63).

According to Mill, this problem is to be comprehended as generating a conflict between two distinctive kinds of interest. On the one hand, there are individual interests; and on the other, there are those of society. Thus, we have a conflict between what Mill terms 'collective opinion' and 'individual independence' (p. 63). For Mill, the individual is to be regarded as an independent being, whose status as such is 'of right, absolute' (p. 69). To clarify Mill's point, we can say that an individual exhibits abilities (reflection, choice, etc.) and also desires and purposes. Taken in unison such features allow for us to regard the individual as a being that possesses interests. If a diversity of individuals is present in a society, then we can conclude that this society will also contain a diversity of interests. A society like this is the kind of society that Mill regards as being the most progressive: 'A people, it appears, may be progressive for a certain length of time, and then stop: when does it stop? When it ceases to possess individuality' (p. 136). Moreover, individuals are also capable of possessing interests that are 'anti-social' in the sense that they may conflict with the norms (i.e. rules of behaviour) that regulate social life. The individual subject's relative autonomy with regard to collective norms means that this kind of conflict is always possible. Since this is so, Mill argues, there is a necessary conflict between collective forms of social organization and the individual, and hence specific, interests that are present within such social formations. This kind of conflict is a necessary outcome of the fact that individuals can and do make choices. Opposed to such freedom of choice are the normative regulations of custom: 'He who does anything because it is the custom makes no choice' (p. 122). The 'tyranny of the majority' is in this way identified by Mill with the force of the collective will of society. Such tyranny is realized in the form of the normative codes of behaviour that form the context within which individuals live, and which also serve to govern the behaviour of individual agents.

We might respond to Mill by noting that his account of the individual is somewhat problematic. For one thing, one might object that he over-emphasizes the issue of autonomy, and in doing so creates a distinction between self-regarding and other-regarding actions which is unworkable.[14] Against this view, we could argue that it is very difficult to secure a criterion that justifies our separating an individual's self-regarding actions from the (other-regarding) public consequences such actions may have. This is simply because even the most private of self-regarding actions are liable to produce consequences that affect others. However, let us leave this and a number of other possible objections to Mill's thesis to one side in order to try and arrive at some general notion of liberalism in light of the work of Locke and Mill.

As with Locke, there is also for Mill an inherent tension between the spheres of individual liberty and governmental authority. Like Locke, Mill regards the individual as an independent being endowed with a right to liberty that springs directly from this independence.[15] Locke and Mill also share in common the view that individual rights and liberties can be preserved by way of the conception of minimal interference on the part of government or popular opinion. Both take 'freedom' to mean the liberty of individuals to act according to their own desires, providing that such actions do not infringe the liberties of others (again, then, we are talking about the advocacy of 'freedom from . . .', rather than 'freedom to . . .').

Locke and Mill take rather different routes in order to arrive at their respective defences of individual liberty. From this we can note that liberalism is not to be defined in terms of the use of a particular methodology that tells us how to conceive of the most desirable form of social order. So, where Locke turns to the state of nature, and therefore a model that subtracts the social context from the individual as a means of arriving at an account of principles of right and liberty, Mill does not. As a matter of fact, Mill regards the individual in a more socially embedded manner, and sees the esteeming of individuality in modern European society as the direct result of social and historical development. That said, Mill remains committed to viewing individual rights and liberties as being of primary importance in accounting for what goes to make the most desirable form of society. In any case, the question of Mill's brand of liberalism is something to which we will return. What we can note here is that Locke and Mill both make a firm distinction between the public and private spheres. We can say that for a liberal what individuals decide to do with their own goods is no one else's concern (and certainly not an affair of government) so long as it does not affect other people's rights. This emphasis upon the individual as the fundamental 'unit' of political discourse is characteristic of liberalism in general. Speaking metaphysically, we might say that in general a liberal is someone who is committed to an ontological conception of the individual in so far as they regard the individual as an irreducible entity, one that transcends the socio-historical boundaries that separate different cultures – even if, as with Mill, the individual is produced by specific historical processes.

From what we have noted already concerning Marx's analysis of society[16] it is fairly clear that any Marxist analysis will offer us a very different view from the liberal one not only of the political sphere but also of the individual. Whereas a classical liberal like Locke or Mill would take the individual as an entity endowed with a personal 'sovereignty', to use Mill's word, that can be articulated independently of the social and historical conditions that characterize any particular society, Marxists would argue that this is simply not the case. For it is not individuated self-consciousness that determines the nature of historical change, but material conditions, and these material conditions are at the same time in the last instance characterizable in material/economic terms. The Marxist variant of Hegel's historical and dialectical understanding of human social development would in this way immediately take issue with the liberal account of the self. Whereas the liberal would see the self as functionally independent of the social order, a Marxist analysis would turn precisely upon socio-economic conditions that serve to constitute the identity of those who are individuated within any political order. So, when Marx discusses the capitalist or the landlord in the text of *Capital*, they are not to be identified primarily by way of their individuality, but as 'personifications of economic categories, embodiments of particular class-relations and class interests'.[17] We should note two things from this quotation. The first is that Marx explicitly defines *interests* as being central to any analysis of the social processes that underlie political structures (the base-superstructure distinction). These interests, moreover, are *antagonistic*. The second point to note is that the 'individual' capitalist is rendered a kind of *metaphor* by Marx's analysis, a 'personification' of objective social forces. Individuals are depersonalized by way of this personification. It is as such personifications that they have social and historical significance. If individuals are mere personifications of impersonal social forces, and these forces are themselves indicative of the presence of antagonistic interests, it would follow that an analysis of the nature of politics ought *not* to start with a conception of the individual that is independent of the social context in which he or she might be situated. The individual cannot be identified as such independently of the social antagonisms of economic and class interests from which they spring. It is in his appreciation of the force of this kind of metaphor that Althusser's conception of Marxist theory takes its leave from the more broadly 'humanistic' variants of Marxism that, we have seen, are advocated by thinkers associated with the Frankfurt School. Moreover, it is likewise in the light of this kind of metaphor that Althusser develops a conception of the ideological forces governing social relations that questions not only the humanism implicit within classical liberalism, but by implication the very notion of a 'political theory' upon which the expression of a liberal politics rests.

2 Althusser, Ideology and State Power

Althusser first came to prominence in the 1960s with the publication of a series of articles in which he expounded his combination of structuralism and Marxism, and likewise presented his criticisms of the humanism of traditional Marxist thought. Althusser's structural Marxism puts forward a revised view of the role of economic determinacy with regard to the ideological, political, legislative, and cultural structures present within capitalist social orders. He seeks to displace the perceived emphasis in much of Marx's work upon a classical model of political economy which, coupled with an empiricist model for the analysis of social relations, had been taken as providing the basis for the purportedly 'scientific' status of Marx's conclusions. For Althusser, each of these structures (ideological, political, etc.) possesses a relative autonomy within the larger network of social relations that constitute capitalist society. Capitalist society is a totality, but it is also a structure that does not have a centre of organization. It is because of this that rather than advocating a direct determinacy according to which the economic base dictates the superstructure (the model of classical Marxism), Althusser views capitalist society as a network of interrelated structures.[18] The autonomy of these structures is, however, seen as relative rather than absolute since, in the last instance, economic factors exert a causal influence over the structure as a whole. In turn, the traditional Marxist conception of 'society', in the sense of an empirically verifiable whole, is replaced within Althusser's account by the concept of the 'mode of production'. The capitalist mode of production is marked by particular features, e.g. the commodification of goods, the notions of exchange and surplus value, the organization of labour. Modes of production, in turn, evolve through history, and Marxism, on this account, becomes the historical analysis of the development of modes of production in their immanent relationship to the various social, political, cultural, ideological, and legislative structures that make up the social totality. Marx is thereby credited by Althusser with developing a new theoretical articulation of social relations which, due to the economic and scientific paradigms at his disposal, he could not himself fully articulate. In turn, Althusser's work proposes replacing the traditional Marxist conception of science as a form of empirical analysis with a model which, instead of grounding itself in procedures of observation and verification, stresses the internal consistency of a theory as providing compelling proof of its validity. For Althusser, what Marxist theory states need not correspond to an immediately verifiable social reality. The veracity of Marxist analysis is shown in the internal consistency of the premises that underpin that analysis. The conception of modes of production is then supplemented by Althusser with a reformulation of the meaning and significance of ideology in the shape of his theory of ideological state apparatuses, a conception again developed in order to fill what he contended were gaps in traditional Marxist theory. It is to a discussion of this theory that we will turn shortly.

Prior to this discussion it is worth noting that Althusser espouses the view (already at least implicit within the quotation from Marx, above) that individuals do not in any sense exist independently of the constitution of economic and social structures. It is this view that lies at the heart of Althusser's anti-humanism. Whereas more traditional Marxists would argue that human beings are ultimately the authors of their own destinies, Althusser's contention is that individuals are themselves essentially an expression of the relations which inhere within the historically determined structures which make up the capitalist mode of production.[19] Analysing this mode of production is central to Althusser's Marxist project, for through such a mode of analysis we can reveal not only the coercive nature of state power but also the ways in which it exerts its influence over society as a whole.

2.1   The question of the reproduction of the conditions of production

Near the beginning of his essay 'Ideology and Ideological State Apparatuses' Althusser makes the following comment: 'As Marx said, every child knows that a social formation which did not reproduce the conditions of production at the same time as it produced would not last a year. The ultimate condition of production is therefore the reproduction of the conditions of production.'[20] From this we can note that Althusser begins by arguing that it is a necessary condition of any form of social organization that it is able to reproduce the conditions which ensure its continued existence. The 'conditions of production' are those elements which, in for example a modern industrial society, allow for the production of goods; they are such conditions as make the production of goods possible and without which such production would be impossible. Keeping with the example of modern industrial society, any industrial social formation that did not at the same time ensure that these conditions were also reproduced would simply cease to exist. This being the case, we need to ask a further question: 'What, then, is *the reproduction of the conditions of production?*' Althusser notes that this is a question that takes us into volume two of Marx's *Capital.* It is, he adds, an issue both 'very familiar . . . and uniquely ignored' within Marxist theory. Everyday life and consciousness are so permeated by the structure of *production* which goes to make up modern industrial societies that 'it is extremely hard, not to say almost impossible, to raise oneself to the *point of view of reproduction.*' In short, asking questions about the reproduction of the conditions of production in modern societies means asking questions that are difficult to elucidate with the necessary clarity, because society itself is structured according to the very logic that governs these conditions. However, Althusser tries to outline the issue he has raised in the following way:

> [A]ssuming that every social formation arises from a dominant mode of production, I can say that the process of production sets to work the existing productive forces in and under definite relations of production. It follows that, in order to exist, every social formation must reproduce the conditions of its production at the same time as it produces, and in order to be able to produce. It must therefore reproduce: 1. The productive forces, 2. The existing relations of production.   (p. 124)

So Althusser is presenting us with a model which is purporting to describe both the nature of societies and how they function. This model holds that (1) all societies are essentially definable as *structures* and (2) the 'design' of any of these structures would in each instance be the direct consequence of the 'dominant' mode of the production of goods present in that particular society. This dominant mode of production must replicate itself in order to survive, and what allows this process of replication to take place is the process that Althusser calls the 'reproduction of the conditions of production'. However, developing an analysis of what this involves requires Althusser to offer some account of a broader range of Marxist concepts concerning the production of goods in capitalist society.

Even if they are not a Marxist, anyone who is knowledgeable about economics, Althusser says, recognizes that Marx had a point when he stressed the fundamental importance of 'the reproduction of the means of production' in modern societies. For example, every year the owner of a factory (a capitalist) must estimate accurately what will be 'used up or worn out in production' (p. 124). What will be used up would include such things as the raw materials needed by the factory, while things such as factory buildings, machinery, etc., will be subject to wear and tear. In consequence, both raw materials and machinery will need to be replaced. The material needed for production to take place must be constantly replenished. However, what is at stake here should not be understood merely at the level of the factory or company which is involved in one kind of production of goods (say, a factory that makes woollen yarn). As Althusser puts it, 'thanks to . . . Marx . . . we know that the reproduction of the material conditions of production cannot be thought at the level of the firm [or company], because it does not exist at that level in its real conditions' (p. 124). These 'real conditions' consist in a web of relations that stretch beyond the confines of the firm that makes wool yarn. The manufacturer of wool yarn has to get more raw materials, more machines, etc. But the capitalist yarn producer does not produce these things for their own use, other capitalists do it for them. Think of three capitalists, X, Y, and Z, says Althusser. X is the manufacturer of wool yarn, Y is a sheep farmer, Z is a machine manufacturer. X buys wool off Y and machinery off Z in order to make yarn. There is, it follows, a connection between X, Y and Z, and together they form a series of links in a chain that extends beyond them, for both Y and Z must also replace what is necessary for them to continue to produce wool or machinery, respectively. There is a structural 'mechanism' of production in place that takes on global proportions.

So far, something is missing from this account which needs to be added: the 'reproduction of labour power' (p. 125). Whereas the reproduction of the means of production (raw materials, machinery, etc.) takes place within the firm or company, the reproduction of labour occurs elsewhere. Of course, in order for the capitalist system to thrive, a continued supply of labour must be ensured just as much as a supply of raw materials needs to be. This is achieved 'by giving labour power the material means with which to reproduce itself: by wages' (p. 126). Wages, therefore, 'represents only that part of the value produced by the expenditure of labour power that is indispensable for its reproduction'; in other words, wages are paid only in order that the labour force has the wherewithal to feed, clothe and shelter itself.

It is not sufficient just to ensure that labour power has what is necessary to survive. Labour must also have the required competence for the tasks it needs to perform in the factory and elsewhere. The types of skill, Althusser notes, are determined 'according to the requirements of socio-technical division of labour, its different "jobs" and "posts"' (p. 127). This is another way of saying that if you work in a factory, for example, you have a particular job allotted to you and in order to carry out that job successfully you need to have certain abilities, certain kinds of 'know-how'. Here we arrive at the central issue that Althusser is going to address in his essay: 'How is this reproduction of the (diversified) skills of labour power provided for in a capitalist regime?' The question here concerns not merely the notion of how those 'skills' appropriate to a given job are to be acquired by a labourer. The issue is also a matter of the provision of a diversity of different skills, since the different jobs necessary to the successful functioning of a factory require different abilities on the part of those who do them. Althusser's immediate point in the wake of this is to hold that the 'reproduction of the skills of labour power' is generally not something that is provided for within the framework of the firm which produces goods. It is 'achieved more and more outside production: by the capitalist education system, and by other instances and institutions'. Children at school learn a variety of skills. But, they do not all learn the same things. Although all children usually learn reading, writing and arithmetic they all 'go varying distances in their studies'. Besides these basic skills, school also teaches children the rudiments of good social behaviour, 'rules for morality, civic and professional conscience, which actually means rules of respect for the socio-technical division of labour and ultimately the rules of the order established by class domination'. Children not only learn different basic skills, but also how to behave correctly within the system of production.

What this means, according to Althusser, is that the school is an institution of the state, and has a similar function to other state institutions like the army or the church or the police. Like these other state institutions, the school functions in such a way as to 'ensure *subjection to the ruling ideology* or the mastery of its "practice" ' (p. 128). Thus, the reproduction of labour power depends upon the construction of a labour force that accepts its role within capitalist society. This means that labour must be subjected to the 'ruling ideology' of capitalist society and it is through this form of subjection that '*provision is made for the reproduction of the skills of labour power*'. If we accept this view, then what we are accepting is the fundamental importance of *ideology* to the functioning of capitalist economy and society. Ideology, taken in this way, is a reality of social life. Having got this far, Althusser notes that he has supplied us with an account of the way in which the productive forces in society are maintained (namely, through the 'means of production on the one hand, and of labour power on the other'). But he has not taken up his original question concerning the '*reproduction of the relations of production*'. This he will do next, via a preliminary analysis of the issue 'what is a society?'

2.2 *The nature of society*

'Marx conceived the structure of every society as constituted by "levels" or "instances" articulated by a specific determination: the *infrastructure*, or economic base . . . and the *superstructure*, which itself contains two "levels" or "instances": the politico–legal (law and the state) and ideology (the different ideologies, religious, ethical, legal, political, etc.)' ('Ideology and Ideological State Apparatuses', 129). On a Marxist account, then, society consists of both economic relations of production (which, taken together, make up a unity), and a web of legal/political and ideological relationships. This conception of society (that is, of society as consisting of both an infrastructure and a superstructure) is, Althusser notes, a metaphorical representation. What we have here is a 'spatial metaphor', and this metaphor implies that the superstructure 'rests' (so to speak) on the base structure (or infrastructure) and depends upon it. In the 'last instance', in other words, the structure of society is determined by the economic base (pp. 129–30). The notion of 'in the last instance' is important here. It implies that 'the "floors" of the superstructure are clearly endowed with different indices of effectivity.' In simpler language, the superstructure is delimited by the base, but the superstructure is composed of levels which will exert their own influence autonomously, even if the base is in the last instance decisive with regard to them. Althusser is saying that each level of the superstructure will have particular characteristics that are specific to it. In turn, the Marxist approach has been to conclude two things from this. First, there is 'a "relative autonomy" of the superstructure with respect to the base'; and second, 'there is a "reciprocal action" of the superstructure on the base' (p. 130). So, even if the superstructure rests upon the base structure, the superstructure nevertheless operates in a manner that is not wholly determined by the base and the superstructure exerts its own specific influence on the base. The great advantage of this metaphor, Althusser argues, is that it exposes the importance of the base structure as a necessary condition of the superstructure (so that the totality which makes up society is in the last analysis determined by the base), while at the same time showing that there must be a kind of 'effectivity' (that is, a kind of 'causality', for want of a better term) that is specific to the superstructure and which the base structure does not possess. It is for this reason that the superstructure has both relative autonomy with regard to the base, and can therefore also exert its own particular influence over the base.

However, Althusser maintains that there is a problem with the metaphor that Marx coined: it is only a metaphor and because of this 'it remains descriptive.' What Althusser means is that the basic problem with the model is that it only offers us a kind of 'description' (an 'image', so to speak) of society. What it does not do is offer something more theoretically substantial; it doesn't *explain* what it describes. Althusser does not want to abandon this metaphor, merely to 'go beyond it'. He wishes to embrace Marx's insight by agreeing with the basic model offered within the metaphor. However, this metaphor is to serve only as a starting point for further *theoretical* considerations: 'I am not going beyond it in order to reject it as outworn. I simply want to attempt to think what it gives us in the form of a description' (pp. 130–1). Thinking about the superstructure means, in Althusserean terms, thinking through the metaphor that Marx has given us *'on the basis of reproduction'* (that is, in relation to the topic first mooted at the opening of the essay: the *reproduction of the conditions of production*) (p. 131). By thinking in this way, Althusser tells us, we will find that there are many issues implicit within the Marxist metaphor that can be both addressed and answered, and these are issues that would hitherto have remained enigmatic or unnoticed. As a means of broaching his claim for the theoretical primacy of reproduction, Althusser first offers a schematic account of the Marxist conception of the state.

2.3   The state

The state, according to 'Marxist tradition',[21] is first and foremost a 'repressive apparatus' which serves the function of repressing the working class so as to defend the interests of the ruling class ('Ideology and Ideological State Apparatuses', 131). The state, it follows, is first and foremost a *tool* which serves the interests of a particular class. This apparatus consists of *both* the structure of law and its administration (police, courts, prisons, etc.) and more overtly repressive things like the army. This apparatus provides a definition of the state and its 'basic "function"' (its primary role). However, Althusser argues, even this account of the state is still 'partly descriptive' (p. 132). What, then, does 'descriptive' mean here, and why is this reason for Althusser to be critical of what Marxist theory has so far achieved?

First, Althusser tells us that he is, in fact, all in favour of 'descriptive theories'. All properly scientific breakthroughs that have happened with regard to theory must first pass through a 'descriptive' phase as a prelude to their full-blown theoretical phase. That there is a seeming conflict when one conjoins the words 'descriptive' and 'theory' serves, for Althusser, his purpose of arguing that the 'descriptive' phase of a theory is only a transitional one. This contradiction tells us that a theory must move beyond being a mere description if one is to realize its full theoretical potential. Claiming that the Marxist 'theory' of the state is still 'descriptive' means first that Althusser is in agreement with the description/theory but, second, he wishes to elaborate it further and hence move beyond it. So, the Marxist 'descriptive theory' of the state can be deemed 'correct', in so far as it accurately reflects the fact that the state is a repressive apparatus that serves the interests of a ruling class. Althusser thinks that one can find many facts to show that this theory of the state is correct. But if one does not refine one's 'descriptive theory' into a more full-blown theory, then one would be condemned to a future which involved no more than the mere collection of further, trivial facts (the train-spotter approach to theory). It is for this reason that Althusser argues we need to refine the Marxist theory of the state: 'I think it is indispensable to *add* something to classical definition of the State as a State apparatus' (p. 134).

Althusser remains a classical Marxist, at least to the extent that he holds the state to be solely an apparatus of political repression on the part of the ruling class. He likewise holds that all political struggles are class struggles that are centred on the aim of possessing the state and monopolizing state power. Equally, therefore, Althusser endorses the Marxist distinction between 'state power' and 'state apparatuses'. State apparatuses may survive changes of state power (e.g. a *coup d'état* involves a transfer of state power, but the apparatus of the state can remain intact and work perfectly well under the new regime). State power is what is fought over in political class struggles, and in the Marxist's view the aim of the proletariat is to take hold of state power so as to destroy the existing bourgeois state apparatus, then replace it with a proletariat apparatus and, finally, to destroy the state and its apparatus altogether (p. 135). All of this Althusser is happy to agree with. Why is he so keen to show what a traditional Marxist he is? The answer is because he is about to do something that is nothing to do with traditional Marxism: he is going to introduce something new, but it is going to take the form of an amplification of the existing 'descriptive theory' of the state.

2.4   *Ideological State Apparatuses*

What, then, is to be added to the Marxist theory of the state? 'In order to advance the theory of the State it is indispensable to take into account not only the distinction between *State power* and *State apparatus*, but also another reality which is clearly on the side of the (repressive) State apparatus, but must not be confused with it. I shall call this reality by its concepts: *the ideological State apparatuses*' ('Ideology and Ideological State Apparatuses', 136). Ideological State Apparatuses are not to be confused with the state apparatuses already alluded to in classical Marxist theory (i.e. an apparatus which includes the courts, prisons, police, government, administration). These apparatuses Althusser now calls 'Repressive State Apparatuses', and taken together with Ideological State Apparatuses, he says, they form the State Apparatus. *One* key distinction between the Repressive State Apparatuses and Ideological State Apparatuses is that the Repressive State Apparatuses operate through 'violence': all Repressive State Apparatuses are, in one way or another, violent (even 'administrative' repression is a form of violence). Ideological State Apparatuses are different: 'I shall call Ideological State Apparatuses a certain number of realities which present them-selves to the immediate observer in the form of distinct and specialised institutions.' So, Ideological State Apparatuses are, first and foremost, 'institutional' structures. Althusser then offers us a list of Ideological State Apparatuses: educational (the private and state schools system), family, legal, political (the party political system), trade-union, communications (press, radio, television), and cultural (literature, arts, sports, etc.). Again, there is an immediate contrast with the State Apparatus: the latter is a single entity, there is only one State Apparatus; Ideological State Apparatuses, in contrast, are multiple, there are many of them and they come in different varieties. Equally, whereas the State Apparatus is an exclusively public structure, Ideological State Apparatuses are predominantly private. For example, newspapers, independent schools, radio stations, families, etc. are private, i.e. they are not funded by the state, nor are they directly run by the state. Indeed, since the public/private distinction is viewed by Marxism as a product of 'bourgeois law' even this shows something important about Ideological State Apparatuses. For, the state is neither a public nor private institution but is 'the precondition for any distinction between public and private'.

Actually, for Althusser it is irrelevant as to whether Ideological State Apparatuses are public or private: 'What matters is how they function' (p. 138) for it is this that distinguishes them from the '(Repressive) State Apparatus' (police, administration, courts, etc.). Whereas the State Apparatus ultimately functions primarily through *repression* and only secondarily by way of ideology,[22] Ideological State Apparatuses are *predominantly ideological* and repressive only in a secondary sense.[23] In the case of Ideological State Apparatuses, such repression is often concealed: the film censor, the methods of punishment used in schools, etc. are all, Althusser says, examples of such forms of repression.

Ideological State Apparatuses ' "function" massively and predominantly by ideology, [and] what unifies their diversity is precisely this functioning' since the ideology is always going to be that of the ruling class (p. 139). Althusser then stakes a large claim concerning the significance of Ideological State Apparatuses and the importance of his own theory: '*no class can hold power over a long period without at the same time exercising its hegemony over and in the State Ideological Apparatuses.*' Both control of and the exercise of power through the Ideological State Apparatuses is a precondition of any ruling class remaining in power. If this is the case, then Ideological State Apparatuses may also be not only at stake within any class struggle, but the sites upon which class struggles take place (p. 140). They are sites of such struggle because whereas the ruling class may well be able to hold a tight rein on the State Apparatus this may not be as easy to achieve with regard to Ideological State Apparatuses. In Ideological State Apparatuses 'the resistance of the exploited classes is able to find means and occasions to express itself there' – either because at this level the contradictions inherent in the ideology of the ruling class are more liable to be evident, or because by 'conquering combat positions in them in struggle' the interests of the exploited classes are able to be voiced. We are left with some questions: 'what exactly is the extent of the role of Ideological State Apparatuses? What is their importance based on?' (p. 141). These questions boil down to one single question: what is the function of Ideological State Apparatuses?

2.5   Securing the reproduction of the conditions of production

Althusser can at last return to his opening question: how does capitalist society secure the *reproduction of the relations of production?* First, one can reply to this question by stating that the reproduction of the relations of production is secured and ensured by the 'legal-political and ideological superstructure' ('Ideology and Ideological State Apparatuses', 141). This response, we may recall, remains for Althusser trapped at the level of a mere 'description'. But he can now add that 'for the most part, it is secured by the exercise of State power in the State apparatuses, on the one hand the (Repressive) State Apparatus, on the other the Ideological State Apparatus.' Again, the contrast can be drawn between Repressive State Apparatuses and Ideological State Apparatuses:

1   All State Apparatuses share in common the fact that they function by means of repression and ideology: but the Repressive State Apparatus operates by way of repression, whereas Ideological State Apparatuses mostly work by ideology;
2   whereas the Repressive State Apparatus is a unity whose parts (courts, police, army, etc.) are organized according to the demands of class struggle by the ruling class, the Ideological State Apparatuses 'are multiple, distinct, "relatively autonomous" and capable of providing an objective field to contradictions which express . . . the effects of the clashes between the capitalist class struggle and the proletarian class struggle' (pp. 141–2);
3   whereas the unity of the Repressive State Apparatus is the result of an organized leadership which represents the interests of its own class enacting the politics of that class through the state, Ideological State Apparatuses gain what unity they have from the ruling ideology of capitalist society.

On the basis of this model, Althusser can argue that the reproduction of the relations of production is achieved through the state apparatus, complete with its instruments of repression if need be, 'securing . . . the *political conditions* of the reproduction of relations of production' (p. 142, italics added). This involves 'above all' securing the conditions necessary for the functioning of Ideological State Apparatuses. It is Ideological State Apparatuses which 'largely secure the reproduction specifically of the relations of production, behind a "shield" provided by the repressive State apparatus'. The increased predominance of Ideological State Apparatuses is a historical development. In the feudal system of the medieval period, for example, Ideological State Apparatuses were less predominant and less diversified in their forms. In this period, the Church performed many of the functions that now are carried out by different Ideological State Apparatuses, as did the family and the political system, and early 'guilds' of master craftsmen (p. 143). In the modern context, however, there is one Ideological State Apparatus that has taken on an increasingly important role: 'the *educational ideological apparatus*' (p. 145). This Ideological State Apparatus has taken on many of the functions that were allotted to the Church in the medieval system. Why is this the case? And in what ways does the educational Ideological State Apparatus function? This is how Althusser lays out his case. All Ideological State Apparatuses contribute to the reproduction of the relations of production. Each does so in a manner 'proper to it' (p. 146), e.g. the political Ideological State Apparatus by 'subjecting individuals' to the ideology of the state's political form – be it democratic/capitalist/liberal, fascist, etc.; or the communications Ideological State Apparatus by dosing citizens with the ideology of the state through radio, television or press. All these Ideological State Apparatuses work in a kind of 'harmony'. Althusser then offers us another metaphor: 'This concert is dominated by a single score, occasionally disturbed by contradictions' (p. 146).[24] However, within this 'concert', one Ideological State Apparatus performs the 'dominant role': the educational Ideological State Apparatus, 'the School'. The school functions by taking all infants at a specified age, and inculcating into them a basic minimum of ' "know-how" wrapped in the ruling ideology' (p. 147). It then filters off an appropriate number of children at different ages: at around 16 the majority are 'ejected "into production" ': the working class. Another, smaller, batch are kept on until they are rendered suitable for clerical and administrative work. Finally, 'A last portion reaches the summit, either to fall into intellectual semi-employment, or to provide, as well as the "intellectuals of the collective labourer", the agents of exploitation (capitalists, managers), the agents of repression (soldiers, policemen, politicians, administrators, etc.) and the professional ideologists (priests of all sorts . . .).' Whatever the specifics that one might object to, Althusser's point is clear. The educational Ideological State Apparatus has the ideological function of reproducing the conditions of production. Each 'ejection' of children from the educational Ideological State Apparatus into the market place takes place in such a way that each individual is equipped with the skills necessary for the social function they are expected to perform. By doing so, the educational Ideological State Apparatus provides for the reproduction of the conditions of production, and it does so in a concealed way: the school is supposed to be an ideology-free zone, somewhere that is 'purged of ideology' (p. 148). Althusser's contention, of course, is that this is simply not the case.

2.6   *Ideology and history*

Althusser then goes on to provide a more detailed account of the nature of ideology, above all in relation to the claim put forward by Marx that 'ideology has no history.'[25] Why does Marx make this claim? Because, as Althusser notes, for Marx ideology is 'conceived as a pure illusion, a pure dream, i.e. as nothingness' ('Ideology and Ideological State Apparatuses', 150). Ideology 'is for Marx an imaginary assemblage (*bricolage*), a pure dream, empty and vain, constituted by the "days' residues" from the only full and positive reality, that of the concrete history of material individuals materially producing their existence' (p. 151). Ideology cannot have a history because it is the illusory product of real historical relations. While Althusser is happy to defend this view in one sense, there is another sense in which he believes it is flawed. While it is true that ideology is the illusory product of concrete social relations and therefore cannot have a history, nevertheless particular 'ideolog*ies have a history of their own*' (p. 151).

Althusser introduces Freud into his analysis at this point. If ideology is a dream, then like the Freudian 'unconscious' it is 'eternal'. By 'eternal', Althusser means 'not transcendent to all (temporal) history, but omnipresent, trans-historical and therefore immutable in form throughout the extent of history' (p. 152). In other words, as long as there is history, there will be ideology, because ideology is one of the conditions of history. But if ideology is a condition of history it cannot itself be 'historical'. Like Freud's conception of the unconscious,[26] ideology is therefore eternal. Althusser's contention is that there is no 'history' of ideology, for ideology is an ever present element of all social formations.

2.7   *Ideology is false consciousness, and has material existence*

Ideology may not have a history, but it does have a function, as we have seen. Althusser now turns to further explicate this function. What ideology does is to provide individuals within any society with a false representation of 'their real conditions of existence' ('Ideology and Ideological State Apparatuses', 153). Ideology creates false consciousness in the individual. This representational mode of thought, it follows, is a kind of unconscious force that structures the relation between the individual and society. As such, ideology conceals 'the reality of the world behind . . . [an] . . . imaginary representation of that world'. We might ask, straight away, is Althusser thus posing a disjunction between appearance and reality – the very disjunction that is so vehemently opposed by thinkers like Nietzsche and Heidegger? The answer is, 'Yes'. However, Althusser's account will itself destabilize this very notion even in its articulation. 'Reality' here signifies the concrete conditions that inhere in the relations of production in capitalist society. These relations of production are necessary for a capitalist (or indeed any other) economy to function. What ideology does is distort this relation by representing it in terms that do not correspond to its genuine structure. This imaginary relation, which produces false consciousness on the part of all who are constituted within it as individuals, has an existence that is, Althusser maintains, 'material'. Ideology is not something analogous to Descartes's conception of 'mind', which is different in kind from the material properties that characterize physical bodies. Rather, ideology is in a specific sense physical. Paraphrasing Aristotle, Althusser can say that ' "matter is discussed in many senses" '[27] and it is obviously the case that ideology does not have the kind of material existence that a stone has. The materiality of ideology relates to the fact that it is a concrete fact of life, it is lived by individuals. Individuals live in an environment, and this environment, Althusser argues, is always one that can be understood in terms of *'practices'*. In enacting practices we observe rituals, e.g. we greet one another in certain way when meeting on the street, we knock at someone's door before entering, etc. Such practices 'are governed by the *rituals* in which these practices are inscribed, within the *material existence of an ideological apparatus*' (p. 158). If we think of a single person, then we can say that he or she has ideas or beliefs. These ideas or beliefs have material existence to the extent that they are enacted in that person's life. By being so enacted such ideas and beliefs are, of course, rendered in terms of the governing rituals that define particular practices. In turn, since these rituals are themselves inscribed within the framework of ideological apparatuses, it follows that they have a materiality. Equally, then ideology itself has materiality. This being the case, we can, Althusser argues, dispose of a word like 'ideas'. There are no ideas as such, because all ideas are in fact inscribed within 'practices governed by rituals defined in the last instance by an ideological apparatus' (p. 159). We can, however, retain words like 'subject', 'consciousness', 'belief', and 'action'. However, if we turn to the notion of the subject, we shall discover something else that is important.

2.8   The subject

All practices, we have seen, are for Althusser inherently ideological. Ideology, equally, concerns only subjects (selves) living in the concrete environment of a society. It operates both by way of them and for them. Ideology, in short, makes a subject the kind of thing that it is. This forms the basic premise of Althusser's 'central thesis'. This thesis states that *subjectivity is itself an ideological construction*: 'the category of the subject (which may function under other names: e.g., as the soul in Plato, as God, etc.) is the constitutive category of all ideology, whatever its determination (regional or class) and whatever its historical date – since ideology has no history' ('Ideology and Ideological State Apparatuses', 160). This is another way of saying that the very notion of the subject, of the self, is not a natural term, but is rendered what it is as a consequence of power. There is, of course, a paradox present with Althusser's argument. If we are all constituted as what we are by ideology, then what is it that allows us to note this in the first place? His answer is that a 'scientific . . . discourse on ideology' is one that dispenses with the subject and maintains its objectivity by way of its scientific status. This amounts to claiming that there is a kind of knowledge that exceeds subjectivity, but is produced from within it. We realize that we are constituted as who we are by ideology, and in accepting this fact we also acknowledge the need to try and 'outline a discourse that tries to break with ideology' (p. 162). Althusser is arguing that we need to recognize that when in everyday life we are addressed by others we are in effect being constituted by their addressing us as subjects as soon as we acknowledge that their speech is addressed to us. Acknowledging the common practices that go to make up the social domain, it follows, enlists us as subjects: a person who is hailed in the street will turn around in answer to the call of another, and 'By this mere one-hundred-and-eighty-degree physical inversion, he becomes a *subject*.' Ideology, it follows, is not merely external to the historical formation of societies in that it has no history. At the same time, it is present within them in the form of the notion of subjectivity to which everyone adheres whenever they respond to being addressed by others. Ideology, in other words, '*interpellates concrete individuals as concrete subjects*'. To this extent, ideology constitutes the fabric of everyday life. This is true even before birth. A child is awaited, and when it arrives will already have a name waiting for it to which it will learn to answer (pp. 164–5). In this way we actually enlist ourselves as subjects within ideology. It is this form of enlistment, this answering to the call of others that, for Althusser, secures the reproduction of the conditions of production. We know where we 'ought' to be within the social structure. We learn to answer the call that summons us to the workplace, etc. Althusser's central achievement here has been to decentre the subject from political discourse by drawing it into the centre of his theory. The subject is that according to which we are all constituted as civil and social beings. Yet, in articulating this very fact Althusser points to the possibility that subjectivity itself is constituted by way of relations of power, by ideology. An Althusserian version of Marxist analysis ultimately rejects the kind of humanism that is associated with more traditional Marxist forms of enquiry. The human subject is *not* the object of political freedom, nor therefore of political emancipation.

One could argue from this that Althusser highlights a key problem with liberal political discourse as we have outlined it. If the subject is central to a liberal politics, is it not the case that Althusser's critique of the subject effectively shows that the very freedom that the liberal takes as being desirable is itself an illusion, one that rests upon the ideological construction of subjective identity? Whether such an abandonment of the subject actually overcomes liberalism, is however, quite another matter, as we shall see in relation to Lyotard's post-Marxist politics. That we can talk here of a post-Marxism is, in fact, central to this last point. For, in so far as Althusser offers us a conception of ideology that is totalizing, is it not the case that any aspiration to 'scientific' status is thereby immediately rendered suspect? Given that scientific enquiry, even in its Althusserian/structuralist sense, is nevertheless always inextricably entwined within a network of social practices, does it not follow that the Marxist view, far from being a scientific analysis of ideology becomes, on its own terms, merely another interpellation within the field of ideology in general? Moreover, to transform all political discussion, and the condition of its possibility (i.e. the subject) into nothing more than ideology is perhaps self-defeating. For, surely there is nothing left on Althusser's account to save from political oppression, no purpose for Marxist analysis, if subjectivity is itself ideological. In its criticism of the notion of subjectivity, Althusser's significant contribution here is to echo, in a Marxist register, some themes that have already been suggested by the work of those within the Nietzschean/Heideggerean tradition. We can note that Althusser's work, too, embraces the anti-humanist thesis wholeheartedly. In doing so he overturns the constitutive role that the subject might be thought to play in social, political and historical relations and events. This critique of the subject, coupled with a critique of so-called 'value-free' institutions (i.e. Ideological State Apparatuses), means that Althusser ultimately argues for a totalizing conception of society. All society is permeated by ideology to the extent that it is not to be located merely in relation to the false consciousness of individual subjects, but within and *as* the notion of the subject itself. It is a variant on this kind of approach, albeit cleansed of its structuralist and Marxist components, that opens the way for a thinker like Michel Foucault.[28] Foucault does not cleave to Althusser's Marxist understanding of society but pursues a Nietzschean path, one that we can now turn to in greater detail: the Nietzschean philosophy of power. We will do so first by way of a preliminary account of some of Foucault's ideas, and then a more sustained analysis of Nietzsche's own interpretation of the implications of his power theory.

3 Politics, Subjectivity and Power: A Nietzschean Perspective (Foucault)

Foucault's work is in fact the product of a complex variety of interests – as well as Nietzsche, the work of Georges Bataille, of Maurice Blanchot, of Heidegger, and in his later period the writings of Adorno are all of importance to him in various ways. Foucault, like a significant number of the French intellectuals of his generation, finds established perspectives and methods of enquiry (as epitomized especially by the humanism of existentialism, Marxism, and phenomenology) wanting. He turns, instead, to such thinkers as Nietzsche, especially using the latter's conceptions of genealogy and power to develop his own approach. That said, Foucault nevertheless included Marx, alongside Nietzsche and Freud, as one of the 'masters of suspicion' who sowed the seeds of doubt concerning the validity of earlier, humanistic discourses of European culture, with their ideal of a value-free objective methodology of scientific investigation and its accompanying faith in the political and ethical possibilities of an emancipatory reason.

Foucault's works cover a wide range of topics, including the construction of concepts of mental illness, the analysis of systems of discipline and punishment, of sexuality and subjectivity, the relationship between forms of knowledge and discourses of power. Frequently, his enquiries take the form of a close analysis of the historical development of these notions. Through such meticulous historical accounts Foucault aims to reveal the structure of interests and hidden presuppositions which underlie discourses dealing with these topics. As a consequence, it is difficult to label Foucault's work as belonging to any particular discipline of academic enquiry. He has, to be sure, philosophical concerns (principally in relation to questions of knowledge). But his concerns might be more correctly described as all falling within the realm of politics. Overall, it might be more accurate to describe his approach as 'interdisciplinary', as crossing the boundaries that frequently demarcate different lines of analytical enquiry according to the subject-matter at hand. Foucault's intellectual development can be roughly summarized as occurring in two stages. First, in the late 1960s, his work deploys an 'archaeological' and historical mode of investigation, through which he sought to uncover the genesis of the human sciences, the development of notions of reason and unreason, and the historical development of the modern episteme.[29] Second, Foucault's later work displays a turn toward a Nietzschean-inspired 'genealogical' method of investigation which seeks to supplement the earlier historical analyses by revealing the underlying power relations in discourses of knowledge. The political implications of this later approach are what I will consider in what follows. Let me say at once that I do not, therefore, propose to offer here an exhaustive account of Foucault's thought. Rather, what I do offer is a brief resumé of Foucault's conception of power. Then I will comment on some claims that have been made concerning the politics that might accompany this view, making particular reference to Nietzsche's own views concerning the implications of his power theory.

3.1   Power

Foucault follows Althusser in one important respect. Like Althusser he believes that the subject is primarily a political notion that must be subjected to rigorous criticism. Equally, like Althusser, Foucault is no humanist, and holds that an elucidation of the dominant practices within any form of social organization is essential to its being subjected to critique. However, whereas Althusser's thought cleaves to the dual strands of structuralism[30] and Marxism in an attempt to resolve the apparent inconsistencies of capitalist society by rendering them within the meta-narrative of dialectical materialism, Foucault spurns any such attempt. Foucault's turn to Nietzsche is at the same time a turn away from a Marxist form of analysis. In place of that model, Foucault offers an account of the political ramifications of discourses of knowledge that takes all knowledge forms to be definable in terms of their relation to power. Indeed, for Foucault, the words 'power' and 'knowledge' are closely related, for the two terms necessarily invoke each other.[31]

Even the possibility, offered by Althusser, of a critique of ideology is, within the parameters of Foucault's conception of the confluence of power/knowledge, a delusion. If we were to offer an account of the nature of ideology such as Althusser proposes then it would be necessary to posit at least the possibility of a perspective that is emancipated from the power relations implicit within them. For Foucault, however, this is simply not possible. Given the presence of power, which permeates societies, even the notion of ideology becomes questionable.[32] 'The notion of ideology', he says, 'appears to me to be difficult to make use of, for three reasons'. These reasons are that ideology (1) 'always stands in virtual opposition to something else which is supposed to count as truth'; (2) is a concept that always refers us back to 'something of the order of a subject' – and Foucault, even more than Althusser, believes that the subject itself must be criticized; (3) 'stands in a secondary position relative to something which functions as its infrastructure, as its material, economic determinant, etc.'.[33] Of Foucault's reasons for this, the first is perhaps the most telling. Ideology-talk presupposes truth-talk, and Foucault is a thinker who has little time for the concept of a disinterested, objective 'truth'. Foucault's suspicion of truth arises from the fact that he regards social relations as being determined solely in terms of power, i.e. that all social relations are relations of power. The suspicion of truth-talk is directly linked to the power/knowledge thesis: in so far as all knowledge claims have overtones of power relations inherent within them so, too, truth-talk must partake of the same relation to power. To put the matter another way, for Foucault 'knowledge' is something that occurs only in the nexus of power relations. Knowledge, in this sense, is a relative term. There is no external standpoint from which one could envisage viewing the totality of human relations and interests with a view to judging them objectively, so all knowledge is in its very nature situated.

In line with this and with his rejection of Marxist critique, Foucault also abandons any pretensions to offering an all-encompassing account of history and society. In its place he proposes a series of more discrete analyses of particular knowledge forms. Thus, Foucault's writings on madness and psychiatry, on medicine, on punishment, on sexuality, all ultimately concentrate upon elucidating the particular power relations involved in different knowledge forms of the modern era by way of an analysis of their respective histories.[34] This is not to say that such works were necessarily written with this aim in mind. Indeed, it is only with the benefit of hindsight that Foucault himself realizes that what he was doing in some of his earlier work can be accounted for in terms of power: 'When I think back now, I ask myself what else was it that I was talking about in *Madness and Civilization* or *The Birth of the Clinic*, but power? Yet I'm perfectly aware that I scarcely ever used the word and never had such a field of analyses at my disposal.'[35] We might ask why is it that Foucault did not have the requisite field of analysis ready to hand? His answer is 'because of the political situation we found ourselves in', which was one in which 'the mechanics of power in themselves were never analyzed.'[36] We can interpret this, amongst others things, as Foucault saying that he was blocked from his insight into the nature of power by his own early adherence to Marxist thought. Looking exclusively at issues of class domination, as Marxists do, is to adopt a limiting perspective when it comes to revealing the 'concrete nature of power'. His own overcoming of the limitations of this kind of thinking is a matter, Foucault tells us, linked to the student uprisings in Paris in 1968.[37] At such a moment the struggle with power revealed power itself in its concrete light, illuminating the fact that all political struggle takes place 'in the fine meshes of the web of power', rather than in the context of an all-embracing narrative of historical development. We can note in passing the significance of this last metaphor: power is analogous to a 'web', it is something that captures and entraps individuated subjects by defining them as such. Subjects, in other words, only discover themselves as what they are (i.e. as subjects) in the very act of attempting to *resist* power. By doing so, power shows itself to be constitutive of social relations and of individual subjectivity alike. In this way, power creates its own resistances by constituting subject positions that are antithetical to it in the very activity of one party seeking to dominate another. We can also note from this that Foucault's thematization of power occurs within the context of politics. For, power is matter of the constitution and differentiation of competing interests and this occurs as a socio-political phenomenon. Power itself arises from the struggles that occur at the political level, and these struggles make subjects what they are. Yet, since power is constitutive of subjectivity, by the same token it also creates resistances in the shape of the subjects it constitutes.

Foucault's conception of politics, in turn, is one that concentrates upon the notion of resistance to power. But since resistance only occurs within specific contexts, politics itself is always a kind of practical engagement within particular social relations. 'Politics', therefore, is not a word that signifies a unified whole, but is always a 'micropolitics' – a view that can be contrasted with the Marxist conception of politics as a global political struggle against ruling–class ideologies. It follows that power is revealed not by way of a general and abstract thesis, but through the process of a meticulous historical analysis of particular forms of discourse in their specific contexts. Such histories themselves are analysed by Foucault as domains of practices. The concrete exercise of power over subjects, and hence their being defined as such, is regarded by him as the chief aim of such practices. If we take the example of the question of punishment, Foucault argues that the prison can be understood as a means of policing the behaviour of individuals, and by way of that process constituting them as subjects:

> People tend to suppose that the prison was a kind of refuse dump for criminals, a dump whose disadvantages became apparent during use, giving rise to the conviction that the prisons must be reformed and made into means of transforming individuals. But this is not true: such texts, programmes and statements of intention were there from the beginning. The prison was meant to be an instrument comparable with – and no less perfect than – the school, the barracks, or the hospital, acting with precision upon its individual subjects.[38]

Whether or not such an aim was successful (and Foucault contends it was not), the point is that power is exercised in order to *subject* the criminal, in every sense of the word. Not only is the criminal subjected to the power of the prison's regime, but at the same time in being defined as such he or she is identified and thereby rendered an individuated subject or self. Likewise, in seeking to 'transform' individuals the prison is already located within the framework of a kind of 'knowledge' of them. The aim of forms of knowledge, it follows, includes constituting subjectivity as such through the exercise of power. In this respect the act of definition is itself an expression of power – be it the definition of the 'criminal type', the 'insane', of 'sexuality', etc. In all of these instances, the exerting of power over the body serves both to define subjectivity and thereby to shape and so police social order. At its most overt and bloody there is the public execution of the criminal.[39] Such an execution demonstrates power over the criminal's body and the expression of this power over the body determines their identity as such.

However, regimes of power are not definable simply by way of such explicit power over the body. The fact that there was an increasing abandonment of public executions in Western society from the eighteenth century does not, for Foucault, indicate a weakening of power. It tells us, rather, that modern societies are not so much policed by force (by the police, the army, and hence by the kind of Repressive State Apparatuses that Althusser alludes to), as by more hidden forms of coercion. So, increasingly 'humane' practices pay testimony to the fact that the inflicting of pain is no longer required, not that we have become more humane. This is because power over the body can be attained more efficiently if a subject is constituted in such a way that he or she is the subject of knowledge. This, Foucault argues, is the aim of the kinds of knowledge that he details in his histories of criminality and sexuality. The modern criminal is above all a subject of the discourses of knowledge present within modern penal systems: 'A whole set of assessing, diagnostic, prognostic, normative judgements concerning the criminal have become lodged in the framework of penal judgement . . . Small scale systems and parallel judges have multiplied around the principal judgement: psychiatric or psychological experts, magistrates concerned with the implementation of sentences [etc.].'[40] The psychologist's knowledge of the criminal's mental condition plays its part in determining the criminal's sentence. Thus, the psychologist's knowledge exerts power over the criminal, whose identity is thereby determined by power expressed as knowledge.

However, for Foucault power 'as such' does not exist, it is not to be described in terms of characteristics that exist independently of the context in which power struggles occur. All expressions of power are particularized and local in their nature. Modern society, it follows, cannot be accounted for in terms of a unified conception of power, but rather (to return to Foucault's own metaphor) in terms of a 'web' of localized relations of power (i.e. at the 'micro-' rather than the 'macro-' level). In turn, the Marxist vision of overthrowing the power of the dominant class in favour of the utopian ideal of attaining a society unfettered by power relations can be rejected. In its place we have a localized politics of resistance, one that seeks to liberate the body from subjectivity. One reason for this is that power is both multiple and ubiquitous. Another reason is that 'power' does not of itself denote something merely negative, but also something 'productive'.[41] The very fact that power is multiple means that its productivity is not to be conceived solely in terms of repression, domination, etc. For example, power is productive of discourses of truth, but these discourses are themselves open to being questioned and rearticulated in alternative forms. What is at stake when this is done is not so much truth itself, 'but the political, economic, institutional regime of the production of truth'.[42] Foucault thus advocates a politics that aims at 'constituting a new politics of truth': 'The political question, to sum up, is not error, illusion, alienated consciousness or ideology; it is truth itself. Hence the importance of Nietzsche.'

3.2 *Genealogy*

The 'importance of Nietzsche' in fact announces itself in two distinctive registers within Foucault's thought. On the one hand, there is the issue of the relation between discourses of truth and power. On the other, there is the question of 'genealogy'. Foucault's histories are an extrapolation of the model offered by Nietzsche in his account of the origins of morality in *On the Genealogy of Morals*.[43]

In Nietzsche, the term 'genealogy' principally relates to the analysis of forms of ethical discourse. In *On the Genealogy of Morals* Nietzsche argues that morality and the meaning of moral language (i.e. of the meaning attributed to words like 'good', 'evil' and 'bad') is not to be interpreted in terms of ideas of 'usefulness' or 'altruism' – a view he attributes to 'English psychologists', amongst others. Instead, Nietzsche argues that ethical systems can best be understood by way of reference to their 'genealogy'. Ethical systems are the products of socio-historical processes. Moral language, for Nietzsche, cannot be properly accounted for by way of reference to a disinterested conception of notions of 'good', 'bad', etc., but is itself an expression of particularized interests. The word 'good' has, he argues, two different roots of derivation. These two roots signify the presence of very different social perspectives, and therefore they also represent two different (and indeed competing) modes of evaluation. On the one hand, Nietzsche tells us, 'good', in its original sense, expressed the viewpoint of the noble or aristocratic classes that inhabited the ancient world. In this context, that is, speaking like a noble, 'good' meant 'beloved of God' and was used by the noble class to refer to themselves. As such, the word 'good' expressed the nobles' affirmation of their own identity. Against the backdrop of this initial self-affirmation the nobles' use of the word 'bad' expressed something secondary. By calling someone 'bad' the nobles indicated they were socially inferior (commoners, plebeians). What Nietzsche calls 'noble-' or 'master-morality' is a form of ethical discourse that takes as its premise the affirmation of the identity of the noble: the noble bestows values in virtue of first affirming themselves. On the other hand, there is another sense to the word 'good' that, Nietzsche maintains, arises as a *secondary* phenomenon out of the initial attribution of the word 'evil'. This is done by the slave, who uses the word 'evil' to allude to his or her noble oppressors and in virtue of this act subsequently posits themselves as 'good'. This is the form of evaluation that is characteristic of what Nietzsche calls 'slave morality'. Whereas self-affirmation is the creative evaluatory act of the noble, the slaves' 'creative deed' is a negative act. Slave morality, which Nietzsche argues is the morality of the Hebrew and Christian traditions alike, is a morality of '*ressentiment*'. The slave resents the master's power over them, and posits values accordingly.[44] What is notable here is that values are interpreted as arising from socially specific domains composed of competing interests. They need not be interpreted by way of reference to human individuals, or values that transcend the social context in which they arise.

For Foucault, as for Nietzsche, the word 'genealogy' indicates a form of historical analysis that proceeds by way of accounting for social, political, ethical and other forms of discourse without making reference to the notion of human *agency*:

> One has to dispense with the constituent subject, to get rid of the subject itself, that's to say, to arrive at an analysis of the subject within a historical framework. And this is what I call genealogy, that is, a form of history that can account for the constitution of knowledge, discourses, domains of objects, etc., without having to make reference to a subject which is either transcendental in relation to a field of events or runs in its empty sameness throughout the course of history.[45]

Genealogy, for Foucault, is the historical analysis of forms of knowledge, practices, etc., that operates without making any reference to the notion of a subjectivity that would exist independently of the historical context in which such knowledge forms, practices, etc., were located. It is 'gray, meticulous, and patiently documentary' and 'must record the singularity of events outside of any monotonous finality'.[46] Genealogy, it follows, embodies an open-ended form of analysis. It spurns any attempt to reduce the significance of its subject-matter to a determinate meaning that may be found outside of its specific context – for instance, in relation to a notion of subjectivity that is a-historical.

In this, as in his formulation of the power thesis, Foucault follows more or less closely what he considers to be Nietzsche's example. What, though, is at stake within such an example? Does the kind of politics of resistance Foucault advocates follow from his adoption of a power theory? Given the fact that Foucault advocates the view that power is multiple, it follows that his politics likewise entails the advocacy of a pluralism. This pluralism is, at first glance, one far distanced from the liberal ideal of a pluralism of individuals pursuing their own goals within the domain of civil society, and *may* be characterized as an anti-authoritarianism. Despite his importance to Foucault, Nietzsche's own politics, however, are not pluralistic in this sense. Does the advocacy of a power theory entail the kind of micro-politics of resistance that Foucault embraces, or does it entail something else?

Others have followed Foucault in his contention that Nietzsche's thought needs to be made overtly political[47] – a view that was not generally held within the earlier tradition of post-war Nietzsche criticism.[48] In order to arrive at an idea of what is at stake here we should perhaps start by recapitulating Foucault's position as we have already outlined it. First, 'power' is a term that is to be taken in a non-substantive sense. As such, power is always specific: it denotes relations of 'force', not some kind of essential property that is possessed and manipulated by dominant interests within a society. This entails the abandonment of both liberal and Marxist conceptions of power, i.e. power conceived of as a matter of individual agency, or as an expression of the interests of a ruling elite. In turn, social relations come to be viewed within this model in terms according to which every social being (individual agent) is what he or she is as a result of the influence of power. The social realm becomes a web of power relations, the structure of which can be elucidated by way of articulating the relations of force present within that structure. 'Power' denotes something intrinsic to any society. This means that power can be neither read into nor subtracted from the structure of social relations in a manner that posits it as being different in kind from them, since power is an *a priori* necessary condition of the existence of all societies. The second point we can note is that the relations of force that characterize modern society also constitute the domains of subjectivity present within it. This being the case, subjectivity may be interpreted as a product of power, not as the independent ground of human agency itself. Agents, it follows, do not produce power, nor do they simply manipulate it like a tool: they are made what they are by it. Of these two points, the first refers us to Nietzsche's philosophy of 'will to power'. This, in short, is his contention that everything can, if only in principle, be interpreted in terms of struggles for dominance between contending drives.[49] The second of these points (Foucault's conception of the subject) refers us to Nietzsche's critique of subjectivity.[50] If we take these two points seriously, then it will follow that we ought to be thinking differently from either the liberal or Marxist traditions when it comes to addressing issues concerning the identity and status of political agents or notions of political legitimacy. We can say that the issue of political legitimacy, understood as the key problematic of traditional political theory, is subverted. In its place there is the different kind of question: what is at stake within discourses of truth (which includes discourses about the nature of politics)?

In more traditional language, we can say that what occurs here is the turning away from *de jure* questions (i.e. questions concerning matters of political right and the nature of legitimate political authority) toward an instrumental conception of the political. In other words, what might be traditionally considered a *de jure* issue concerning political legitimacy is transformed into a *de facto* one (i.e. a question concerning matters of fact). One can, it follows, argue that the main consequence of Foucault's 'Nietzschean' discourse is to recast traditionally framed *de jure* questions about the nature of political right in general into a matter of *de facto* instances. Theories about the conditions that power ought to observe in order to be legitimately exercised are subverted by an empirically oriented analysis of what power determines to be the case.

Foucault's reading of Nietzsche can be taken as amounting to the claim that Nietzsche's insight into the nature of power may be put to work in relation to questions of politics in a productive manner. However, what are we to make of the side to Nietzsche's thought that appears to be distanced by this Foucaultean reading of him? This is a question that relates to what one might call the 'aristocratic Nietzsche', that is, the aspect of Nietzsche's thought that argues for the following view: 'Every enhancement of the type "man" has so far been the work of an aristocratic society – and it will be so again and again – a society that believes in the long ladder of an order of rank and differences in value between man and man, and that needs slavery in some sense or other' (*Beyond Good and Evil*, section 257).

3.3   Modernity as a crisis of values

We could, of course, seek to overcome the 'aristocratic Nietzsche' with the following kind of argument: Nietzsche's philosophy of power is one matter, but the matter of his own 'aristocratic' views (particularly in relation to democracy and order of rank) is another and quite unrelated issue.[51] But this kind of argument can be contested. First, in order to understand Nietzsche's politics, we need to note the context within which Nietzsche articulates his views. It is a context that Nietzsche and Foucault share. We can call this context 'modernity'. Where Foucault interprets modernity as being characterized in terms of a process in which subjects are increasingly policed by discourses of knowledge, Nietzsche approaches the matter with a rather different emphasis. For Nietzsche, modernity is a context that pays testimony to a crisis of values, above all concerning the validity of Christian values. Most famously, this crisis is spelled out in terms of the 'death of God', the 'greatest modern event'.[52] The magnitude of this event concerns the fact that not only the *metaphysics* (i.e. belief in God) but also the *values* of Christianity have become 'unbelievable' – something that occurs at the hands of modern science. The modern era is marked by a denuding of belief in the moral certainties that accompanied Christianity and with this an accompanying scepticism concerning the politics that may be generated out of such values – for Christian values are, for Nietzsche, also democratic values. What is the significance of such a decline in the validity of these ethical and political ideals? Above all, Nietzsche argues, Christian beliefs gave structure to the world, and in this way they provided the yardstick for determining good and bad. Nietzsche's account of the rise and fall of Christian values needs, however, to be situated within the framework of the master–slave struggle that is outlined in the *Genealogy*. For, with the victory of Christianity over noble (Roman) values what was achieved was the overturning of the morality of the Ancient world.[53] There are two consequences of this victory of the 'slave revolt in morality' (*Genealogy*, first essay, section 10). First, there is the establishment of a belief in the divinity of truth.[54] Second, the steady growth in the power of this belief sows the seeds for the destruction of Christianity at its own hands, for it generates what Nietzsche terms the 'will to truth'.[55] Modernity is, in consequence, a crisis of order with regard to the nature of values and social hierarchy. But, even though this crisis opens up the difficult question of the nature of value, understood above all in terms of an issue concerning what we can term the 'order of rank' in modern society, it does not follow that it negates it. In fact, in Nietzsche's terms one can argue that the question of rank (understood as the question of what values are to predominate within the modern context) is a defining feature of what modernity is. This question concerns what will become of modernity since the modern era is one in which a crisis of value serves to make issues of authority and rank all the more urgently in need of our attention. This is because modernity, on his view, signifies the opening of new possibilities concerning not merely how things are now, but how they *ought* to be in the future (a question that is linked to the Nietzschean view of philosophy as a legislative practice).[56] We can call this a 'political' question since it concerns the kinds of interests that *ought* to predominate within society. And Nietzsche's conception of politics is rooted in the noble ideal.

3.4   Power and hierarchy

Nietzsche's politics does not have a contingent role in relation to what we have discussed above concerning modernity. We can note already, on the basis of Nietzsche's analysis in *On the Genealogy of Morals* (cited above: essay one, sections 9–10),[57] that the rise and fall of Christian metaphysics and morality is elucidated in a manner that emphasizes a thematics of struggle between the competing interests of the noble and the slave. This struggle is made possible only by virtue of the existence of a hierarchy of competing interests, of aristocratic versus slave morality. The notion of a hierarchy of interests in this way underpins Nietzsche's account of the genealogy of Christian morality. Without the existence of hierarchy there can be no struggle. In turn, this account is itself linked to Nietzsche's power theory (the will to power). And Nietzsche's conception of the will to power is inextricably entangled with his contention concerning the necessity of hierarchical structures, as exemplified by what he calls the 'noble type'. Given that the noble is a form of legislative being, the noble form of moral discourse is one that has a definite connection with Nietzsche's conception of the 'legislative' value which pertains to 'genuine' philosophy. As such, Nietzsche's conception of the noble type has a central role in his re-articulation of the nature and role of the subject as it is presented in the *Genealogy*.

Nietzsche is perfectly aware that his claims concerning the importance of aristocratic value systems will be deeply offensive to those equipped with modern ears. Indeed, the very fact that we are repelled by noble morality reveals its true significance: 'noble morality . . . is not the morality of "modern ideas" and therefore is hard to empathize with today, also hard to dig up and uncover' (*Beyond Good and Evil*, section 260). This is, at least in part, because the violent nature of noble value systems distresses minds that foster 'humanitarian illusions'. But, Nietzsche tells us, echoing a theme from *Thus Spoke Zarathustra* that is to reappear in *Twilight of the Idols*,[58] 'truth is hard' (*Beyond Good and Evil*, section 257). When confronted with this alien mode of evaluation, we moderns will display a tendency to resist and reject it out of hand. However, Nietzsche's own understanding of noble morality, and of its significance, is directly linked with his conception of will to power.

How, then, are Nietzsche's politics conjoined with his power theory? First, let us recall that Nietzsche's elucidation of a power theory is, he tells us, a consequence of the demands placed upon him by 'the conscience of method'; and Nietzsche is a thinker who, in spite of appearances, is keen to stress that 'the most valuable insights are methods' (*The Will to Power*, section 469). The conscience of method requires us 'Not to assume several kinds of causality until the experiment of making do with a single one has been pushed to its limit . . .' (*Beyond Good and Evil*, section 36) – even if that leads us to absurdity.[59] Nietzsche, then, follows the dictates of this 'moral of method', and it leads him to develop a viewpoint that analyses all phenomena (organic and inorganic alike) in terms of contending forces.[60] Method also requires that these forces be conceptualized in terms of a single principle. This principle Nietzsche calls 'the will'.[61] Although the word 'will' does not for Nietzsche denote an individuated subject (or agent), it nevertheless refers to intentional states: each force pushes against other forces, seeking to subordinate them to itself in a continual struggle for power. Each is therefore bound to all the others in an agonistic relationship (i.e. one of competition and struggle). This point made, Nietzsche can now interpret 'all mechanical occurrences' as 'will force, effects of will' (*Beyond Good and Evil*, section 36). The '*one* basic form of the will' that is common to all such mechanical occurrences is the ' "will to power" and nothing else –'. Of course, we might object to this reduction of the behaviour of even physical phenomena to matters of the 'will' in this extended sense, arguing that it is merely one possible interpretation of such phenomena. If we do this, then 'well, so much the better' (*Beyond Good and Evil*, section 22). But, whatever the limitations of such a view it is, Nietzsche argues, not to be numbered amongst the 'bad modes of interpretation' that try and interpret the world in terms of physical laws. Such bad ways of interpretation contradict the principle of method by constructing a multiplicity of 'laws' to account for the divergent behaviour of different phenomena. If we were to accept that the kind of interpretation Nietzsche offers has some credence, then he can also try to persuade us to accept the view that 'life itself is will to power' (*Beyond Good and Evil*, section 13). In a world conceived in this manner 'every power draws its ultimate consequences at every moment' (*Beyond Good and Evil*, section 22). In other words, we are faced with a world that is organized by way of the constant tensions that exist between contending forces, one in which 'the tyranically inconsiderate and relentless enforcement of claims of power' hold sway.

If the world, and hence life itself, is '*the will to power – and nothing else besides!*' (*The Will to Power*, section 1067), then human communities and individuals are in equal measure expressions of this fact. We have now arrived at the basic hypothesis which grounds the analysis Nietzsche offers in the *Genealogy*.[62] Power, on this view, constitutes what the world is. As such, power also constitutes what human society is. If we were to seek to interpret human societies without reference to the power thesis we would, Nietzsche argues, be guilty of ignoring the fundamental aspect of human existence. Human life may be composed of pleasures, pains, moral sentiments, etc., but 'there are higher problems than all problems of pleasure, pain, and pity; and every philosophy that stops with them is a naïveté' (*Beyond Good and Evil*, section 225). If we are committed to the view that all societies are analysable in terms of relations of power this does not, and indeed cannot, allow us to claim at the same time that social relationships exist as relationships between equals. Society, on Nietzsche's view, is established according to the dictates of power. In this sense society is to be regarded as a realm of contending forces, of different degrees of force that produce different degrees of social stratification. The assertion of the necessity of differences of force in all relations, it follows, forms the basis for Nietzsche's contention that hierarchy will necessarily be a constituent feature of all aspects of life. This is because the necessity of there being different degrees of power ensures that there will always be an imbalance of power, that 'exploitation' will be a permanent feature of human life. ' "Exploitation" does not belong to a corrupt or imperfect and primitive society: it belongs to the essence of what lives, as a basic organic function; it is a consequence of the will to power, which is after all the will of life' (*Beyond Good and Evil*, section 259).

We can see from this that it is Nietzsche's power theory (i.e. a theory that allows him to assert power relations to be constitutive of all social relations) which also provides him with the *justification* for holding that all human societies will be composed of orders of domination and subjugation. In so far as life is will to power, so both society and the subject, as living expressions of power, can be understood in terms of the hierarchy of struggles which arise as a consequence of their constituted natures. Any attempt to deny that hierarchy is necessary to social life is, on this view, a denial of the very constitutive nature of the will to power. To deny the necessity of hierarchy one must also deny that exploitation and stratification necessarily follow from the immanence of power. To interpret Nietzsche's hierarchical attitude as a merely personal aberration, as something that has accrued to the power theory simply by way of some subjective or historical contingency, is to ignore the point which devolves from accepting the theory itself. To argue that 'exploitation' is wrong would be to adopt a moral standpoint that cannot be inferred from the hypothesis of the will to power itself. A moral standpoint of this kind would need to invoke some additional principle, one that is derived independently from the methodology of power that Nietzsche elucidates. In short, it would mean constructing ethical propositions from a standpoint capable of transcending the world of power relations, rather than being an expression of power, which is what Nietzsche contends all ethical views embody. In the socio-political realm, the subject matter in question is humanity, and the question of subjectivity needs to be explored within the context of a discussion of humanity.

3.5 The normative subject and the sovereign individual

For Nietzsche, humans are at once the most problematic and interesting instances of the will to power. In humanity, nature set itself a 'paradoxical task': 'To breed an animal *with the right to make promises* – . . .' (*Genealogy*, second essay, section 1). In Nietzsche's view, it is the human ability to make a promise that defines what we are. But in order that we could make a promise at all, humanity first had to be made to think of itself itself in terms of prescriptive norms, i.e. in terms of rules which prohibit certain actions: 'Man himself must first of all have become *calculable, regular, necessary*, even in his image of himself, if he is to stand security for *his own future*, which is what one who promises does!' The means to such self-understanding, Nietzsche argues, is society and morality. These attain this end by imposing conditions and rules wherein individuals are both constituted and their behaviour regulated. This is by no means a straightforward process, for it requires that the opposing force of forgetfulness, which is 'an active and in the strictest sense positive faculty of repression', be overcome through the construction of memory. Memory is 'no mere passive inability to rid oneself of an impression', it is 'an active desire not to rid oneself, a desire for the continuance of something desired once, a real *memory of the will*. . . .' This 'memory of the will' was, Nietzsche maintains, quite literally burned and battered into individuals in the form of punishments, on the basis of the principle that through such 'procedures one finally remembers five or six "I will not's," in regard to which one had given one's *promise* so as to participate in the advantages of society' (*Genealogy*, second essay, section 3). Memory, it follows, is a necessary precondition for social existence. Through memory the rules which constitute the social bond are observed. Only in this fashion is human society rendered possible.

However, all this, it turns out, produces another kind of subject. For, the 'ripest fruit' of this process is 'the *sovereign individual*', an 'emancipated' being who transcends these conditions, who overcomes the force of custom to become an 'autonomous and supramoral' instance of the human species (*Genealogy*, second essay, section 2). Thus, for Nietzsche, the ramifications of an ability to make a promise do not stop at the level of providing us with an analysis of social relations in general. The social realm can itself become the precondition for the constitution of autonomous individuals who are able to make their own promises as free beings. The autonomy of such free beings allows them to transcend the normative rules which govern the social world, for they have the right to 'stand security' for themselves, and this is tantamount to 'the *right to affirm oneself*' (*Genealogy*, second essay, section 3). Such self-affirmation is the positive expression of power, for sovereign beings of this kind are themselves *productive*. The creation of these individuals does not, however, take the form of a new regulative norm for humanity as a whole. To put it another way, we are not, for Nietzsche, talking about a universal ideal toward which humanity as a whole should strive, for Nietzsche is *not* claiming that the human race in general ought to be able to partake of this kind of sovereign subjectivity. In fact, the contrary is the case: sovereign individuals are by their very nature exceptions to the rule. They must be exceptions to the rule, for they transcend the conditions that make them possible, and these conditions must continue to exist if such individuals are to be possible.

In order to appreciate fully the nature of these claims we can note the following three points: (1) for Nietzsche, society and the sovereign individual who is capable of rising above its normative structure of prescriptive rules are both expressions of the will to power; (2) Nietzsche's power theory itself justifies his division of forms of subjectivity into what may be termed 'normative' and 'supra-normative' types. Of these, the normative type represents humanity *en masse*, whereas the supra-normative type is able to stand apart from that mass as an autonomous being. From this it follows that (3) humanity as a whole can never be conceptualized in terms of the supra-normative model, for humanity in this sense could not, and indeed does not, even exist.

That the first of these points holds does not, I think, require further demonstration. We need merely recall that the will to power is a monistic principle, and hence applies to life in all its possible forms. As for the second point, we have seen that the normative conception of subjectivity that Nietzsche develops denotes an achievement of human societies. In order to thrive, which for Nietzsche means at the same time increasing its power, a society must impose prescriptions (in the form of 'thou shalt not . . .') upon its members. These prescriptions both regulate and at the same time constitute the normative subject. The normative subject is, it follows, an expression of the power relations that inhere within any social order. Only then do we have the conditions under which the supra-normative subject can arise. The supra-normative subject, as a 'sovereign individual', internalizes the exterior conditions of social order and, by doing so, negates them with regard to their own subjectivity. When the sovereign individual makes a promise, however, it is no longer a promise given to society that he or she will observe its rules and regulations. Rather, it is a promise that marks the birth of a supra-moral, subjective form of autonomy understood as the freedom of self-affirmation. In short, 'I will not . . .' becomes 'I will . . .'

Finally, any attempt to argue that the possibility of becoming a sovereign individual is open to humanity as a whole defies a principle devolved from the will to power itself. This principle asserts that human development cannot be understood in terms of a single, universal goal. There is, for Nietzsche, no such goal, because ' "Mankind" does not advance, it does not even exist' (*The Will to Power*, section 90). In simple terms, no single account of human history or of the development of humanity as a whole is possible, since such an account lacks a referent (i.e. there is no human essence – as is presupposed, for example, by the political principles of liberty and equality) about which it could be said that one society conforms to, or will conform to, better than any other. Humanity is to be considered as 'an inextricable multiplicity of ascending and descending life-processes . . . the strata are twisted and entwined together' (*The Will to Power*, section 339). It follows that there is no single point in history at which it would it be possible to separate one human type from another, for the enmeshed complex of forces that as a whole constitute the will to power must always take on a multiplicity of forms. Different societies, one might say, have different norms and therefore create different manifestations of the normative subject. The sovereign individual is just one of the possible extrapolations that may be derived from this. Understood from the perspective of social interaction, such a conception of individuality will arise only within the context of a rigidly regulated social order that is already composed of normative subjects. Given that, for Nietzsche, 'The will to power can manifest itself only against resistances; therefore it seeks that which resists it' (*The Will to Power*, section 656), we can also argue that the supra-normative subject, which is an expression of the will to power, can only exist within the context of a society that has its share of regulated and regularized individuals.[63] The rule is a necessary precondition of the existence of exceptions to the rule. So, one kind of human being is impossible without the other: the transcendence of morality achieved by the sovereign individual is only possible because there will always be other people who are incapable of transcending the norms that regulate society. That society can be regarded by Nietzsche as a kind of means to an end in this way does not entitle us to infer from this fact that the goal of society is the *universal* attainment of the sovereign individual. In so far as any society has a 'purpose' it is limited to the preservation of its own power against the backdrop of a world in a constant state of flux, which is again the world conceived of as will to power, 'a monster of energy, without beginning, without end; a firm iron magnitude of force that does not grow bigger or smaller . . . a household without expenses or losses . . . a becoming that knows no satiety, no disgust, no weariness' (*The Will to Power*, section 1067). Within such a conception continual change means either that power is increasing or decreasing within any particular locality and relative to the whole. But the immanence of such becoming also means that there cannot be an even distribution of power, for all forces are engaged in an eternal struggle against one another.

It is the framework of a philosophy of power that *legitimates* the claim Nietzsche stakes concerning the inevitability of hierarchical and exploitative social structures. For the world conceived in terms of power is one that consists of dominating and subjugated drives enmeshed in relations of struggle. Hierarchy is, in this way, entailed by the power theory, for all talk of power needs slaves just as much as it needs masters: 'The will to power specializes as will to nourishment, to property, to tools, to servants (those who obey), and masters: the body as an example. – The stronger will directs the weaker' (*The Will to Power*, section 658). Nietzsche's conception of the sovereign individual, in turn, manifests itself as an expression of this tension between the subjugated and the subjugator, for resistance is only possible when subjugation is a realized fact:

> The degree of resistance that must continually be overcome in order to remain on top is the measure of freedom, whether for individuals or for societies – freedom understood, that is, as positive power, as will to power. According to this concept, the highest form of individual freedom, of sovereignty, would in all probability emerge not five steps from its opposite, where the danger of slavery hangs over existence like a hundred swords of Damocles . . .   (*The Will to Power*, section 770)

If the 'stronger will directs' it does so because it subjects weaker forces to its own particular intentional structure, which is none other than an expression of the 'intention to increase power' (*The Will to Power*, section 663). Such a will to domination of necessity transforms other forces, and thus other subject positions, by rendering them its tools. Relationships, in this way, are always fundamentally instrumental: 'Slavery and division of labor: the higher type possible only through the subjugation of the lower, so that it becomes a function' (*The Will to Power*, section 660). Subjugation, it follows, is a necessary condition for the expression of the will to power realized as the freedom of the sovereign individual.

The emancipated individual's freedom brings human performativity (the ability to make promises) to its fruition as individual autonomy: 'Value is the highest quantum of power that a man is able to incorporate – a man: not mankind! . . . mankind is merely the experimental material, a tremendous surplus of failures: a field of ruins' (*The Will to Power*, section 713). Such expressions of power necessitate the articulation of values and, above all and prior to this, their *creation*. The sovereign individual is thus an aesthetically conceived form of sublimated subjectivity. Individuals that measure up to this supra-normative model define themselves by way of their ability to create their own values. And creative ability of this kind defines their autonomy. In the realm of values this creativity is expressed through the power to legislate. The latter is the genuine task of philosophy, the task of the 'new philosophers' (*Beyond Good and Evil*, section 211).

Nietzsche's 'new philosophers' are 'philosophers of the future' in two senses. First, they are themselves expressions of the legislative aspect of the will to power. As such, they cannot be conceptualized by way of reference to the values dominant in a democratic era, that is, in terms of the discourse of modernity: ' "The will to power" is so hated in democratic ages that their entire psychology seems directed toward belittling and defaming it' (*The Will to Power*, section 751). Second, such philosophers will be future legislators, they will legislate concerning the future itself, and they will do so because they are embodiments of the aristocratic view that Nietzsche favours:

> But where may I look with any kind of hope for my kind of philosopher himself, at the least for my need of new philosophers? In that direction where a noble mode of thought is dominant, such as believes in slavery and in many degrees of bondage as the precondition of every higher kind of culture, where a creative mode of thought dominates . . . a mode of thought that prescribes laws for the future. . . . (*The Will to Power*, section 464)

In other words, for Nietzsche, it is the noble mode of evaluation that instantiates the supra-moral reality of a world conceived of as a totality of power relations. In so far as the noble type seeks to subjugate others he or she only acts according to the conception of will to power as life and society, for it 'is part of the concept of the living that it must grow – that it must extend its power and consequently incorporate alien forces . . . aggressive and defensive egoism are not matters of choice . . . but the fatality of life itself' (*The Will to Power*, section 728). From this we can conclude that the creative expression of power, which is an essential feature of it, requires that there exist those who are subjected to the power of others. It requires we accept the view that society will be stratified and unjust, since the concept of 'legislation' would have no content were it not for those subjected to it. It is for this reason that Nietzsche decries a democratic mode of social organization.

We can note, above all, that this view is in keeping with Nietzsche's power theory. Indeed, it is derived from it. It is not a dispensable element of his thought that bears scant relation to the philosophy of power. Subjects are themselves merely expressions of this principle of power, which tells us that 'Life is not the adaptation of inner circumstances to outer ones, but will to power, which, working from within, incorporates and subdues more and more of that which is "outside" ' (*The Will to Power*, section 681), and no values, no human existence, can be articulated in terms of power without this conclusion being drawn. Avoiding such a conclusion would require that power be redefined in such a way that its constitutive force would be negated. It is the fact that power is constitutive of identities that gives rise to hierarchies, 'an order of rank and division of labour' are 'the conditions that make possible the whole and its parts' (*The Will to Power*, section 492). In Nietzsche's view, hierarchies are the necessary accompaniment to acknowledging power as constitutive of the social and subjective domains alike – they are not coincidental to power but derive from it. This amounts to claiming, as Foucault does, that there is no means of escaping from the affects of power. And if this is the case, then questions of hierarchy and of the legislative aspect of forms of thinking must remain an important issue for us when seeking to appreciate the implications of any discourse that seeks to articulate human relations solely in terms of power.

3.6   The limitations of a politics of power

Of course, we need not take Nietzsche's own politics uncritically. But what we do need to consider is the question of the relationship between the kind of view that Nietzsche develops, the kind of politics that Foucault advocates, and philosophies of power. For, being critical of Nietzsche's politics means also being critical of the kind of philosophy that Foucault, too, adopts in the wake of Nietzsche's thinking. We need here to acknowledge the possibility that the analysis of social relations exclusively in terms of power, whilst it may provide insights into the drawbacks inherent within traditional political theory (be it liberal or Marxist) is itself beset with problems. It is perhaps too easy an option to conclude that elucidating the domains of society and subjectivity alike in terms of power serves only those with an interest in extolling an avant-garde politics of dissent such as Foucault seeks to pursue.[64] This is a politics that aims to express the interests of oppressed subjects, that seeks, for example, to give voice to the perspective of madness by 'letting madness speak for itself'.[65] We may object that to attempt such a thing is itself a deeply problematic enterprise. But more than this, from within the structure of a philosophy of power it is also an exercise that cannot be legitimated. The brutal question is: why give voice to the oppressed at all? If, as Nietzsche argues, oppression is a necessary consequence of power, is itself needed in order that power may be productive, then no such requirement exists. We could, of course, counter such an objection with Foucault's contention that power creates its own resistances, that resistance is a necessary condition of power relations as such. But, again, it does not follow from this that the dissenting voice of the subject of power either *will* or *ought* to be heard. Nor does it follow that such dissent will achieve anything even at the level of a micro-politics. One reason for this is that, as Nietzsche too argues, power *needs* resistance in order to be what it is. But it is the fact that such resistances can also be absorbed and incorporated that constitutes an essential aspect of the dynamic of power as such. Nietzsche, like Foucault, argues that power is productive, since normative power on the Nietzschean view can be productive of sovereign individuals. But it does not follow from this that the dissent that can arise out of power relations is itself productive of a resistance to hierarchies of power. Contrary to this view,

Nietzsche's work demonstrates that a hierarchical politics may equally arise and receive its justification from the philosophy of power.

This aspect of Nietzsche's thought is not an adjunct to, but springs directly from the hypothesis of power taken to its most rigorous, supra-moral limits. To put the matter another way: claiming that power is essentially constitutive of societies means accepting that 'exploitation' (in whatever form it may take, and that includes sub-jection) is an inevitable outcome of power itself, since in so far as power is productive it is also productive of exploitation. In turn, we can note that even though Foucault advocates a 'liberation' from subjectivity as a means of decentering power relations, it does not follow from this that his thought can rule out elitism. For, such a form of liberation is not equivalent to contesting hierarchy itself. It is to Nietzsche's credit, perhaps, that he does not turn away from this fact, but presents it to us face on. We might ask, therefore, what kind of politics a politics of resistance rooted in a philos-ophy of power would be? Certainly, it need not be an anarchistic anti-political philosophy of the kind that Foucault's thought implies. Providing an analysis of the nature of power in these terms need not of necessity bring with it a radical politics of liberation of the feminine, of the prisoner, or of the insane. For, by way of a philosophy of power one abandons all interest in the ethico-political aspect of the relations that define the social realm. Let us, then, leave aside the most obvious objection to any power theory of this kind: namely that, on its own terms, it is itself a product of power, and hence something contingent upon the vicissitudes of history. Even if this does not pose an insurmountable problem, the fact that a Nietzschean politics *cannot be ruled out on the basis of it* ought to cause us to wonder whether or not adopting this kind of view is not regressively authoritarian in its implications.

4   Lyotard: A Postmodern Politics

If a philosophy of power has its limitations in relation to politics we might well ask what other possible avenues are open to be explored? One possible route is linked to the writings of French philosopher, Jean-François Lyotard (1925–97). Like Derrida and Foucault, Lyotard is thinker who is associated with poststructuralism. He is also a thinker who stresses the role of interests in knowledge forms and in politics. However, Lyotard is no straightforward 'power philosopher' – at least not in such later works as *The Differend: Phrases in Dispute* (1983), a text we will look at in more detail below. More particularly, Lyotard's name is most commonly linked with the word 'postmodernism', since he is perhaps best known for his book *The Postmodern Condition: A Report on Knowledge* (1979). What the word 'postmodern' means is not, in fact, entirely clear, since it has been used in a wide range of contexts: architecture, the arts, literature, and philosophy. Certainly, for some commentators it has links with the thought of both Nietzsche and Heidegger and, like the work of Foucault, embraces an abandonment of the project of Enlightenment that is pursued by thinkers like Kant and Hegel.[66]

Lyotard's *The Postmodern Condition* offers one of the more overtly philosophical accounts of the postmodern. What Lyotard presents is an analysis of the postmodern as marking the end of 'grand narratives' of politics and history (e.g. that of Marxism). Within the postmodern framework, grand narratives are replaced by 'little narratives'. This, Lyotard argues, is a direct consequence of modern technologies. Technology transforms knowledge: 'We can predict that anything in the constituted body of knowledge that is not translatable in this way will be abandoned . . . the direction of new research will be dictated by the possibility of its eventual results being translatable into computer language.'[67] Thought, then, becomes subject to 'the hegemony of computers', and the thinking subject is displaced by the inherently machine-like tendencies of modern technology. What Lyotard calls 'postmodernism' fits into this scenario in that it embodies a critique of the subject, for whom knowledge, under the conditions dictated by technology, becomes externalized. Knowledge, thus transformed, becomes linked to exchange value and the play of exterior forces. Lyotard defines the postmodern in relation to the immanent consequences of technical/scientific knowledge forms, but also in connection with alternative 'narrative knowledge' forms (p. 7). Scientific knowledge, Lyotard claims, is not a 'totality', but exists in relation to a larger domain of narrative forms of knowledge, which it has a tendency to exclude. These latter, however, form the basis of social cohesion. Science requires one discursive practice in order to function, which relies on the assumed existence of criteria of evidence (the empirical level), and the belief that an empirical referent cannot provide two contradictory proofs. This, for Lyotard, is science's 'metaphysical' assumption, which it cannot itself prove. On the social level, however, this assumption, in excluding other knowledge forms, has the effect of splitting science off from the social order, and the relationship between knowledge and society 'becomes one of mutual exteriority' (pp. 24, 25). This, in turn, demonstrates that it is not possible to judge the validity of scientific claims by reference to narrative knowledge claims, or vice versa. Questions of legitimation stem from this tension, in so far as the development of 'postmodern science' (p. 60) has demonstrated the futility of trying to construct grand narratives which seek to describe the totality of experience. Experience thus exceeds the limits of cognitive grasp. Postmodernism steps in at this point as a pragmatic response to the problem of legitimation. A postmodern view embraces a pluralistic approach, in that it attempts to provide alternative narratives, but nevertheless spurns the pretension to universal knowledge claims.

The kind of fragmentation Lyotard alludes to is, he says, a consequence of science itself. Lyotard notes that, in the same way that Nietzsche's diagnosis of European nihilism turned on the idea of science as having reached the point of realizing that it itself did not match up to its own criteria for truth, so, too, the search for legitimation, which defines all knowledge forms, has a natural tendency to arrive at the point of delegitimation (p. 39). In other words, knowledge always finds itself to be rooted in unprovable assumptions. Hence the possibility of error is encoded into the project of knowledge as one of its constituent conditions. Thus, Lyotard concludes that the destruction of grand narratives is a result inherent in the search for knowledge itself. What he terms 'postmodern scientific knowledge' (p. 54) is therefore an immanent condition of all knowledge. And it is for this reason that grand narratives are, in consequence, best replaced by 'little narrative[s]' oriented toward 'a multiplicity of finite meta-arguments' (pp. 60, 66).

Lyotard also offers a further clarification of the postmodern in an essay appended to *The Postmodern Condition*, 'Answering the Question: What is Postmodernism?' Here Lyotard argues that we can understand the postmodern by way of an elucidation of Kant's presentation of the 'sublime' in his *Critique of Judgment* (the third *Critique*).[68] According to Kant, the sublime is a feeling that is aroused in a spectator when their intellect is presented with something that defies conceptualization. The sublime moment is encountered when we are faced with, for example, an object of such enormity that it defies conceptualization. The sublime, therefore, is that which 'is sublime in comparison with which everything else is small'.[69] Because of this, Kant concludes that the sublime moment involves our aesthetic rather than our cognitive or empirical mental abilities. To put it simply: it expresses a feeling. Extrapolating from this conception, Lyotard argues that the postmodern may be characterized as a form of expression that aims to present new ways of presenting the sublime feeling. Hence, postmodernism represents an avant-garde aesthetic discourse, one that tries to overcome the limitations of traditional modes of thought by seeking out new ways of describing and interpreting experience. Notably, Lyotard claims that postmodernity is not to be taken in a historically periodizing sense. We do not move out of the modern era 'into' a postmodern one. For, modernism can itself be characterized as a form of response to a range of issues that are already postmodern in nature. In Lyotard's view, modernism can be described in terms of nostalgia for a lost sense of unity. In turn, modernism develops an aesthetic discourse that emphasizes fragmentation as a result of this nostalgia.[70] Postmodernism, too, is a response to this sense of a lack of unity. But rather than lamenting this lack, the postmodernist rejoices in it.[71]

Lyotard also uses other terms to characterize postmodern experimentalism. It can be called a form of 'paganism', or more recently a 'rewriting' of modernity.[72] Of these two, the notion of rewriting modernity is spelled out in the following manner: 'I have myself used the term "postmodern". It was a slightly provocative way of placing (or displacing) into the limelight the debate about knowledge. Postmodernity is not a new age, but the rewriting of some of the features claimed by modernity, and first of all modernity's claim to ground its legitimacy on the project of liberating humanity as a whole through science and technology.'[73] What Lyotard is arguing here is that he wishes to distance his own account from the kind of postmodernism that is prevalent 'on the market of contemporary ideologies', as a form of resistance to contemporary socio-political forms. We can conclude two things from this. The first is that Lyotard wishes, in his later works, to distance himself from the common usage to which the word 'postmodern' has become subject. The second thing is that the project of rewriting modernity is to be taken in political terms: it is an attempt to question the Enlightenment belief that humanity can liberated through recourse to technological and scientific forms of knowledge. Thus, for Lyotard, as for Foucault, the political consequences of forms of knowledge are of utmost importance. Whereas Foucault cleaves to a philosophy of power as a means of articulating resistance to these developments, Lyotard does not. To be sure, social antagonism and issues of power relations are an important feature of our understanding of the political for Lyotard. But the political realm need not be accounted for solely in terms of power.

To be sure, this last claim is not strictly true of Lyotard's earlier works – of texts such as *Libidinal Economy*.[74] In works such as this, Lyotard explores the political ramifications of a philosophy of the will as counter to what he considers to be the barrenness of Marxist theory. However, along with Marxism, this, too, is a project of which Lyotard is to become increasingly suspicious, as is witnessed in the collection dialogues with Jean-Loup Thébaud, *Just Gaming*. Here, having defined postmodernism in terms of a form of pagan judgement that occurs 'without criteria', as 'a power to invent criteria' that 'bears the name of a certain philosophical tradition, namely Nietzsche's: the will to power',[75] Lyotard suddenly rejects this point of view. When later in the dialogues Thébaud reminds Lyotard of this kind of philosophy, Lyotard responds by saying that it is a question that is 'not worth returning to'. Why? Because 'the point of view of the will, what does it mean in politics? That is the heart of the matter . . . I am almost tempted to say now that this philosophy of the will . . . has become a sort of purgatory' through which one must pass in order to get somewhere better.[76] One reason for Lyotard's reservations concerning the political implications of a philosophy of the will is that it implies a conception of politics contained within both Hegelianism and Althusserian and other forms of Marxism alike. But, at the same time, it invokes a Nietzschean philosophy. This is a philosophy that, in Thébaud's words, 'yields a world that imposes its law upon another, or else it can go as far as saying – and then the unification can be total – that it is the will that produces both worlds, as in Nietzsche.' All realms of experience, in other words, become productions of power, and in this manner are unified according to the narrative that asserts the immanence of power. Lyotard agrees with this. As well as being critical of the Hegelian and Marxist viewpoints, what is needed is an approach to politics that overcomes this form of Nietzscheanism, since, Lyotard argues, 'a philosophy of the will cannot be passed, as such, for a political philosophy.'[77] The reason for this is that any philosophy of the will, any philosophy that seeks to comprehend to totality of social relations in terms of power and nothing else, embraces a monism that reduces all differences between subjects and perspectives to matters that concern only 'ratios of velocities' (Thébaud). Such a reduction, Lyotard argues, 'is quite broadly a politics of capital', in so far as the logic of capitalism means that it has no interest in addressing questions of justice as they present themselves at the political level. This is an important point, because 'in so far as one is a political thinker', Lyotard says, 'one cannot do without justice.'[78] Lyotard's use of the word 'justice' does not denote something unified, here. It is multiple. There are many kinds of justice that can be defined according to the specific contexts in which ethical questions are raised. Justice is a matter that can only be defined 'in relation to the rules specific to each game'. The notion of the 'game' is important here. For, it marks Lyotard's rethinking of the implications of Ludwig Wittgenstein's (1889–1951) later philosophy of language for our conception of politics.

In the *Philosophical Investigations*, Wittgenstein develops an approach to language and meaning that is couched in terms of the notion of 'language games'. One can, in crude terms, grasp what Wittgenstein is doing by way of the following question: how is it that words have meaning? One possible answer, and a common one, is to say that words mean what they do because we use them to denote objects in the world. Imagine a teacher instructing a child in the meaning of words. The teacher points to an object and names it (what is called 'ostensive definition'). The child repeats the name. Hence, the meaning of the word is secured by way of reference to the thing that is named through the act of ostensive definition. One problem with this view concerns how it is that the meaning of pointing to the object itself is secured in the first place. For, in order for the child to know that a certain word denotes a certain thing he or she must already understand that the act of pointing is a way of indicating an object. In other words, resorting to pointing in order to establish how the meaning of words is secured is insufficient, for pointing itself has a meaning that cannot be defined in this way. Wittgenstein proposes an alternative way of conceptualizing meaning. Think, he says, of the process of learning the meaning of words as being akin to 'one of those games by means of which children learn their native language.'[79] Children learn by playing games. A game is composed of rules. If a child is engaged in learning the meaning of words by repeating them after the teacher, then the child is acting according to a set of rules and conventions wherein he or she repeats the words of the teacher. This is what Wittgenstein terms a 'language game'. Language games are composed of gestures, rules, etc. All of these taken together constitute a structure of conventions. These conventions are in place in order to serve the purpose of the game. On this view, the meaning of a word, at least in many if not all instances, is 'to be defined thus: the meaning of a word is its use in the language [game].'[80] In turn, there are many different kinds of language game, and different language games represent instances of different 'forms of life': 'the term "language game" is meant to bring into prominence the fact that the *speaking* of language is part of an activity, or of a form of life.'[81]

Lyotard develops his own philosophy of language in the wake of Wittgenstein in his book *The Differend: Phrases in Dispute*.[82] This is a work that has one feature in common not only with Lyotard's other books, but also with the thinking of figures like Nietzsche, Heidegger, Althusser and Foucault. Like them, Lyotard is no humanist, for he does not believe that there is an originating subject that can be posited as existing outside the different language games that constitute the realms of human life. As Lyotard puts it elsewhere, 'the first task' in elucidating a philosophy of language 'is that of overcoming this humanist obstacle . . . Humanity is not the user of language, nor even its guardian; there is no more one subject than one language.'[83] Such a view also entails criticizing Wittgenstein, too, in so far as he remained trapped within this conception by assuming that meaning is a matter of use, i.e. that there is a subject who 'uses' language and is hence external to it (*The Differend*, section 122). At the same time the question of language is for Lyotard a political issue. For *The Differend* is a work that has as one of its central concerns the project of addressing one key question about the nature of politics. We can phrase the question in the following terms: in what way, or ways, are we to understand the meaning of the word 'politics'? This is a question that is posed in the context of Lyotard's development of a linguistic conventionalism derived principally from his reading of Wittgenstein. And it is to an account of this that we must turn first in order to appreciate the conception of politics that Lyotard advocates.[84]

4.1   *Lyotard's conventionalist account of language*

Lyotard argues that we can understand languages as operating in two registers. These are what he calls 'phrases'[85] and 'genres'. The word 'phrase', for Lyotard, can be applied to any kind of utterance. Thus, 'Hello', 'He knocked at the door', 'What is the time?', 'Ouch!' are, for Lyotard, all examples of phrases. We might say, therefore, that the phrase is the basic 'unit' of language. All phrases are composed of what Lyotard calls 'instances'. There are four instances pertaining to every phrase. Every phrase has an addressor, an addressee, a sense, and a referent (*The Differend*, section 25). In order to function, that is in order for it to have meaning, it is not necessary for a phrase to have a designated addressor or addressee, a determined sense, or a designated referent. In other words, a phrase need not be spoken by a named speaker, nor need it be addressed to a specific person. Equally, phrases do not have to encapsulate a specific meaning, nor need they be about something in particular in order to be phrases. We might say, then, that taken on their own terms (if this were possible) phrases are empty bits of language. However, no phrase can be taken as such, since every phrase presents what Lyotard calls a 'phrase universe'. What kind of phrase universe is presented by a particular phrase is a matter that concerns how each of the four instances that constitute any phrase are situated, and hence function, in relation to one another (section 28). We can illustrate this point by noting that there are, on Lyotard's conception, numerous and different kinds of phrases. Thus, there are cognitive phrases, aesthetic phrases, ethical and political phrases, etc. Each of these kinds of phrase Lyotard characterizes by way of their belonging to different 'phrase regimens', or regimes. There are, then, different ways of speaking according to the kind of phrase at hand. A cognitive phrase concerns how things are, i.e. what is the case. An example of an aesthetic phrase would be 'What a pretty flower!' In so far as phrases belong to different regimens they are heterogeneous. This means that it is not possible to translate one phrase directly into another (section 178). Thus 'What a pretty flower!' cannot, on this view, be recast in cognitive terms, for it involves an aesthetic judgement concerning the flower (that it is pretty), and this kind of judgement is not pertinent to the use of cognitive phrases.

Genres of discourse can be contrasted with regimens. Whereas a phrase operates by way of presenting us with a phrase universe that is determined according to the manner in which each of the four instances is situated, genres supply us with the rules for linking phrases together. Above all, genres are, Lyotard says, defined by the fact that the rules they supply stipulate ways of linking phrases according to particular purposes (section 179ff). Again, we can illustrate this by way of the notions of the cognitive and the aesthetic. The cognitive genre has as its purpose the description of the material world. Scientific language, therefore, is cognitive. The cognitive genre stipulates a way of linking phrases with the purpose of stating what is true and what is false, what is or is not the case. The aesthetic genre, in contrast, is a way of speaking that concerns aesthetic judgement. As with phrase regimens, genres are incommensurable with one another. It is not appropriate to respond to the phrase 'What a pretty flower!' by discoursing on the chemical composition of the flower, or upon the wave-length of the light that it reflects in order to be the colour it is. One cannot, in short, *prove* or *disprove* that the flower is pretty by resorting to cognitive discourse. For what is at stake in aesthetic talk is not something that can be validated in this way. It is therefore impossible to validate any genre of discourse by way of reference to rules that are external to it. This is another way of saying that there is no meta-language available to which we can resort in order to *judge* different genres.[86]

To further illustrate this point, we can say that in the same way as the cognitive phrase regimen is merely one regimen amongst others, so the cognitive genre is merely one amongst many genres. Lyotard is thus effectively claiming that we cannot arrive at a final conception of truth, a final judgement concerning the nature of reality, even by way of scientific language. For not all language is scientific or can be accounted for in such terms. Any genre's legitimacy is, it follows, solely a matter of the internal consistency of the rules that pertain to that particular genre. On the basis of this claim, Lyotard can then argue that one cannot legitimate the way in which phrases are linked from a position external to the particular genre in which a phrase is at any moment situated.

Phrase regimens are different from genres, therefore, because they do not offer any rules for the linking of phrases. Regimens are non-teleological, that is, they do not of themselves pertain to a purpose. All that regimens do is provide the 'rules of formation' wherein a phrase can be characterized as being concerned with matters of fact (cognitive), questions of taste (aesthetic), right and wrong (ethical), etc. As such, the rules of formation cannot prescribe which phrase from which regimen ought next to be linked onto a preceding phrase. Lyotard's analysis, then, draws a distinction between regimens and genres in terms of contingency and necessity. That phrases *are* linked together is necessary. But the question of how they *ought* to be linked together is a contingent matter (section 136). What we have here is, in fact, a version of the old philosophical argument which states that one cannot legitimately derive an 'ought' from an 'is'. For it is, Lyotard argues, impossible to assert legitimately from a standpoint external to, for example, the cognitive genre that one ought to link on to a cognitive phrase with another phrase compatible with the rules of the cognitive genre. The validity of one genre, in other words, cannot be secured by means that are independent of that genre and its purposes. What we are faced with is an argument reminiscent of *The Postmodern Condition*: it is impossible to establish the legitimacy of any genre by way of a meta-narrative.

4.2 Differends

What Lyotard's account does try to make room for, however, is a consideration of those instances of phrases that cannot be voiced within the framework of a given genre. Phrases of this kind would be the phrases of what can be designated 'victims'. A victim, on this view, is someone who is silenced by the rules that constitute a genre, who cannot articulate their interests in so far as such interests are not recognized within the confines of a particular genre. Phrases of this type Lyotard calls 'differends'. Hence, a differend can be characterized as an instance wherein someone suffers 'a damage accompanied by the loss of means to prove the damage' (*The Differend*, section 7). Possible examples of differends are legion. They include the victims of the Nazi death camps. Lyotard also provides the example of a French citizen who is a Martinican. The French Martinican is a person who cannot, as a French citizen, complain about any possible wrongs they may suffer as a result of being a citizen. The reason for this is that the genre of French law, which is the only genre within which a complaint of this kind could be stated, itself prevents the possibility of the complaint being made. One cannot complain in law about the wrongs one may suffer as a consequence of one's legal status. The victim thus has a complaint that is silenced. A differend is therefore primarily characterized in linguistic terms: it is 'the unstable state and instant of language wherein something which must be put into phrases cannot yet be' (section 22). By arguing that phrases of this kind must be phrased, that, in other words, there is a kind of ethical imperative that transcends the limits of genres, Lyotard's text presents us with a statement of ethico-political concern. For such an ethical imperative is, on Lyotard's view, the proper goal of culture. 'Culture', Lyotard tells us, has come to mean 'the putting into circulation of information rather than the work that needs to be done in order to arrive at presenting what is not presentable under the circumstances' (section 260). Thus, *The Differend* establishes its own stakes in terms of the need to voice differends. From this, we may conclude that Lyotard conceives of politics as involving the realization of a cultural ideal voiced as far back as 1962, in the essay 'Dead Letter'. According to that essay, 'Culture is lending an ear to what strives to be said, culture is giving a voice to those who do not have a voice and who seek one.'[87] So, in Lyotard's view, genuine cultural activity is both an ethical and a political pursuit.

4.3   The political

What, though, does a phrase like 'political pursuit' mean in this context? One thing is clear from the account Lyotard offers in *The Differend*. This is that we would be wrong in assuming 'politics' to be a form of human interaction that is definable in terms of purposes. Put in his own terms, we can say that politics is not a genre of discourse. For, on this view, the political realm is to be conceived of as a kind of space within which different, heterogeneous and hence also competing discourses meet:

> Were politics a genre and were that genre to pretend to that supreme status, its vanity would be quickly revealed. Politics, however, is the threat of the differend. It is not a genre, it is the multiplicity of genres, the diversity of ends, and par excellence the question of linkage . . . It is, if you will, the state of language, but it is not *a* language. Politics consists in the fact that language is not a language, but phrases. . . .   (section 190)

Politics is not a genre since it is, in its very nature, pluralistic, it is a multiplicity. Lyotard's justification for this view springs from his Wittgensteinean-inspired understanding of the nature of language. The fact is that there is no 'Language' (with a capital 'L') as such. Language itself, we might say, is not something to be grasped linguistically. It is not susceptible to being *conceptualized* in this way, for that would be to situate it within a genre of discourse: the genre that tells us what language is. Rather, there are only phrases, and phrases are discrete, discontinuous, and heterogeneous. The problem is that although politics is not a genre, it 'always gives rise to misunderstandings because it takes place as a genre' (section 199). Hence, Lyotard draws a distinction between what language 'is' (i.e. phrases) and the necessity that there be events of language, that phrases must be linked by way of genres. It is this necessity that gives rise to the mistaken belief that politics is a genre. One can only say this ungrammatically, but it needs to be said: politics is not a genre, it is phrases. Lyotard, then, is committed to offering an account of the political sphere that is obliged to maintain this distinction. This is a distinction between (1) the general state of language, which consists of a plurality of phrases that cannot be exhausted by any single generic account of them; and (2) the fact that, substantively speaking, politics necessarily 'takes place' as a genre. As a result, we can note that the issue of how to link phrases is, for Lyotard, an issue of ethico-political import.

Nevertheless, the question of linking cannot be subsumed under any answer that is offered, as of necessity it must be, from within any single genre. This claim is made by Lyotard on the basis of his agreeing with 'Russell's aporia'.[88] This aporia tells us that any attempt within one genre to offer a universal solution to the multiplicity of questions inevitably posed by all other genres of discourse founders. It founders because either 'this genre is part of the set of genres, and what is at stake in it is but one among others, and therefore its answer is not supreme . . . Or else, it is not part of the set of genres, and therefore does not encompass all that is at stake . . .' (section 189). The political level is, of course, the level at which the linkage of phrases by different and therefore competing genres is played out in terms of the pursuit of a diversity of potentially incompatible ends. As such, there is no one genre that is capable of supplying an all-inclusive and hence universally valid means of choosing one single genre or set of genres over and above any others. This being the case, there can be no question of offering a universally legitimate account of the nature of politics. We cannot, in other words, advocate any one system of social relations over and above another. This is because the stakes of that genre will necessarily conflict with both the stakes of other genres and the diversity of phrases that constitute language.

From this it follows that advocating a purportedly 'universal' solution to specific social ills (for example, promoting revolution as a means of overcoming the injustices of capitalist society) is unacceptable. This is because even if a revolution were to succeed in so far as it righted old wrongs, it would *at the same time* create new ones. Thus, Lyotard argues, even 'supposing the change [i.e. the revolution] took place, it is impossible that the judgments of the new tribunal would not create new wrongs, since they would regulate (or think they were regulating) differends as though they were litigations' (section 197).[89] Hence, the predominance of a new 'revolutionary' genre would merely serve to create new wrongs, since it would legitimate the universal application of a rule that would not be applicable to everyone. What, therefore, is a politician to do? One thing is for sure. Although we may not be able to say what politicians ought to do for the greater good, we can perhaps say what they ought not to have in mind when they act. They cannot justifiably be said to 'have the good at stake, but they ought to have the lesser evil'. For to pursue the greater good would mean treating the political realm as if it were a genre, as if the multiplicity of phrases that makes it what it is could be reconciled. This, in turn, would necessarily create new wrongs, and therefore new differends, i.e. those who lack the means even to assert their status as victims. How, then, might we interpret the notion of the political realm as it is presented within Lyotard's account?

4.4   A return to liberalism?

Lyotard's view entails a commitment to the standpoint that no single genre is suitable for deliberating upon political questions, because pursuing such a project will generate differends. There is, therefore, an ethical dimension to this account of the political. Lyotard must also be committed to claiming that although they are inevitable, it is wrong to create differends. Justice is a matter of observing 'the justice of multiplicity'.[90] Hence, for Lyotard the recognition that politics is not to do with the establishing of tribunals in order to settle disputes between competing modes of life derives from the view that respecting multiplicity is itself just. Such multiplicity is expressed through the diversity of actual phrases that are linked and in relation to future possible phrases alike. What we can call 'society' is, therefore, this very multiplicity of phrases. And 'politics' is a word that signifies this variety: 'The social is implicated in the universe of a phrase and the political in its mode of linking' (*The Differend*, section 198). Hence, people are already implicated within the social world simply because they are linguistic beings. It is this fact that makes them subjects, and allows us to talk of one another in terms of our interests. Equally, therefore, everyone is also always and already implicated in politics, since politics is above all the question of how one ought to link phrases together. This being the case, the political realm, properly regarded, can be interpreted as a space of possibility. Such a space offers an unlimited potential for linking phrases together in different possible ways. It is for this reason that politics itself cannot be resorted to in order to supply a rule that can tell us how phrases ought to be linked. In short, Lyotard is committed to the view that one cannot legislate about the goal of politics. For, it is impossible to provide a universal rule concerning the purpose of that which is itself a plurality of purposes. Attempting to resolve disputes between contending purposes is impossible, since the activity of solving disputes will, practically speaking, be an endless task. This is because language is to be understood as being composed of phrases, not of genres. From this it follows that any act of linking a particular phrase with another phrase according to a rule supplied from one genre cannot of itself exclude the possibility of other modes of linkage, of other genres being asserted. This, we can note, follows directly from the principle, noted earlier, which states that 'To link is necessary, but a particular linkage is not' (section 136).

But what are we to make of this? What of the implications of this kind of pluralism? One thing seems evident. Lyotard's view brings with it a commitment to a conception of the nature of politics that has more than passing resemblance to the brand of classical liberalism that we have already encountered in the brief discussion of Mill's *On Liberty*. For, Mill, likewise, has a view of society that extols the virtues of pluralism. True, we could point to the fact that Mill argues the case for an individualism that Lyotard would find repugnant. But, that said, Mill's conception of the individual (unlike Locke's) is, as we have already noted, a historical one. But this is not really the point. Rather, the point is that both thinkers argue for the view that plurality, a diversity of interests, is the sign of a better society. Just as, in Lyotard's case, politics must concern maximizing the range of possible ends that may be pursued within any particular social context,[91] so for a thinker like Mill the diversity and antagonism inherent within 'political life' is what allows us to define it in its truest sense:

> Unless opinions favourable to democracy and to aristocracy, to property and to equality, to cooperation and to competition, to luxury and to abstinence, to sociality and individuality, to liberty and discipline, and all the other standing antagonisms of practical life, are expressed with equal freedom and enforced and defended with equal talent and energy, there is no chance of both elements obtaining their due. Truth, in the great practical concerns of life, is so much a question of the reconciling and combining of opposites that . . . it has to be made by the rough process of struggle between combatants fighting under hostile banners.[92]

In other words, for Mill just as for Lyotard there is no final means of reconciling disputes between competing modes of life, simply because disputes of this kind are a necessary condition of social existence.

The fact is that one can extrapolate from Mill's liberalism a view of politics that is uncannily similar to Lyotard's. For Mill endorses the view that politics *is* an engagement in disputes over what kinds of rules are appropriate in particular contexts consisting of individual agents pursuing particular goals. Lyotard would, I have already said, object that, on his account, individual agency (and hence subjectivity) is inseparable from the fact that there are phrases: 'A "subject" is situated in a universe presented by a phrase' (section 119). Hence, he would argue, we cannot defend the view that subjects are distinct from the conditions they inhabit. For, their identities are constructed both within and by the context of these conditions – we are what we are because we exist within phrase universes. There is, therefore, no concept of the self that would not derive from the fact that there are phrases and genres. A cursory analysis of Mill's view of the self, as exemplified in both his account of the problem of liberty in terms of a dichotomy between individuality and authority, and his rigidly held distinction between the public and private spheres,[93] might conclude that he falls foul of such an objection. But Mill does not in fact maintain that individuality is an a-historical ontological category. Societies can, he admits, exist in which there is no 'individuality' in the sense in which he uses the word. Mill's point is that cultivating individuality is a necessary condition for a healthy culture, that is a culture in which human diversity is celebrated.[94]

Let us, though, grant that there might be some credence to this criticism. Even so, Lyotard remains committed to some of Mill's central contentions concerning liberty. For example, when Mill argues that 'different persons also require different conditions for their spiritual development',[95] he is effectively telling us that the heterogeneity of differing and competing modes of social existence is a good thing. Is there really much difference between this and Lyotard asserting the incommensurability of different genres, and celebrating the plurality that devolves from it? Likewise, Mill argues that 'the liberty of the individual must be thus far limited; he must not make himself a nuisance to other people',[96] leads to two conclusions, both of which may be re-phrased in Lyotard's terms. First, no single goal (genre) ought to dominate over all others. Second, that individuality itself presupposes a diversity of subject positions (or in Lyotard's language, individual cases of phrases), each of which needs to be given its due. So, however we might want to think about the nature of the subject (classical liberal or Lyotardean), it is still the case that the principle of 'lesser evil' that Lyotard promotes as a guiding political principle is one which implicitly rejects the majoritarian approach to political life which is also the target of Mill's critique of the 'tyranny of the majority'. This, in turn, leads to similar conclusions concerning the nature of politics and culture, alike. We should recall here (in relation to the essay 'Dead Letter', mentioned above) that Lyotard's view concerning genuine cultural activity is couched in terms of an ethical and political pursuit. This view, too, parallels some aspects of Mill's position.[97]

Whether the nature of politics is regarded as an issue concerning the practical limits of normative power that may be exercised over the individual (Mill), or the necessary conditions that govern language and the political implications that may be derived from that (Lyotard), what we encounter here is a common set of presuppositions. Lyotard's attitude to the word 'postmodernism' may have become somewhat jaundiced, in so far as he now regards the word as being linked with contemporary capitalism. Thus, in *The Differend* Lyotard now presents the postmodern project by way of the ambivalent metaphor of an old man picking his way through the various political and aesthetic detritus of a failed modernism.[98] Whatever one may make of the problem of postmodernism in relation to this, one thing is clear: the project of *The Differend* still situates itself within a framework of presuppositions shared in common by Mill's modernist liberalism. Of course, we need not object to Lyotard's claim that liberalism is a political philosophy that can serve the ends of capitalism.[99] But from this one need not necessarily endorse the view that liberalism is itself *identical* with the genre of capital (i.e. the genre of the pursuit of profit). As Mill's text shows us, liberal thought shares with Lyotard's a concern with preserving the irreconcilable conflicts that must arise between differing modes of life.

Equally, one might also point out that even Lyotard's anti-humanism does not offer a ready means of escape from Mill's key contention. This is simply because the issue of political diversity and the question of whether or not there are subjects who 'use' a language (rather than subjects of a language, as Lyotard would maintain) are matters of a different order. Even if we were to accept that subjectivity is constituted by language, the question of what a subject is must always remain a metaphysical question. As such, we cannot escape from the problem posed by the liberal conception of political freedom by simply objecting to the notion of the self that liberals might endorse. In Lyotard's own terms, the reason for this can be put thus: the subject that is presented within one phrase or genre cannot be used to secure a definition of other modes of subjectivity as they will be presented within other kinds of phrases or genres. So, we could, perhaps, try to derive a particular account of politics from a specific notion of the subject. This being done, then it will follow that a specific set of political concerns may well centre on debates about the nature of subjectivity. But even then, this must remain a metaphysical matter rather than a specifically 'political' one. And it must remain so unless it could be shown that there is a necessary connection between the genre of metaphysical enquiry and the constant state of heterogeneity and antagonism that Lyotard himself asserts to exist between phrases and genres of discourse. But, even a claim like this is a metaphysical one; one made, in this instance, with a view to proving a point about what politics is. Hence, the political connection here can only be shown by presupposing the authority of metaphysical investigation (which is a genre of discourse). This would mean that we are, once again, engaged in constructing the sort of meta-discourse that Lyotard himself rejects.

We can argue, then, that the question of the nature of politics, for Mill and Lyotard alike, cannot be phrased as 'What is the *purpose* of politics?' Both argue that politics is realized in the struggle between conflicting purposes. Hence, and in spite of his anti-humanism, Lyotard's conception of politics cannot escape from the concern underlying Mill's advocacy of individual liberty. This is the concern that argues for the view that particular cases (whether it be 'individuals' or 'phrases') when they are subsumed under a general rule will be endangered in that they may become the victims of a wrong. Lyotard, it follows, cannot avoid the charge of providing a justification for the liberalism he rejects. This may be a liberalism that is re-cast in postmodernist form, but it is a liberalism nonetheless. Moreover, we should perhaps ask the question as to whether Lyotard's own conception of politics may fall prey to his own objection that politics is treated as if it were a genre. Like Mill, Lyotard is committed to the claim that in matters of politics diversity *ought* to be pursued as a matter of principle. What, though, is this if it is not treating the arena of politics as if it were a genre?

4.5   *Two criticisms of postmodern thought*

Are we, then, left wondering whether an abandonment of the cherished ideals of liberalism leads itself to the paradoxical endorsement of . . . *liberalism*? If this is so, then what of Lyotard's criticism of capitalism as the hegemony of the economic genre over all others (*The Differend*, sections 250–3)? Doubtless, those in favour of the classical liberal outlook would point to the economic genre as one in which a diversity of interests are pursued and identities realized, and hence as also being capable of fostering the very diversity that Lyotard values. This is simply because it is possible to argue that the *consequences* of the economic genre need not be linked intrinsically to its *purposes*, as Lyotard would necessarily have us believe if his criticism of this genre is to hold water. One needs only to turn to the theories of a thinker like Adam Smith to reflect upon this. As Smith argues in *The Wealth of Nations*, the outcome of the pursuit of profit is not exhaustively analysable in terms of its explicit purposes. The pursuit of profit, Smith maintains, even if it is driven by entrepreneurial greed, produces as its consequence greater general wealth within civil society, and thereby provides the conditions under which social diversity and hence political liberty thrive.[100]

Is it perhaps not the case that, in abandoning a conception of a universal rationality such as Kant endorses, Lyotard also effectively abandons the ethical domain he so values? Certainly, this kind of claim would be accepted by contemporary Frankfurt School thinker, Jürgen Habermas, (1929–). Habermas is himself one of Lyotard's targets in *The Postmodern Condition*. Here, Lyotard claims that Habermas argues for 'orienting our treatment of the problem of legitimation in the direction of a search for a universal consensus' (p. 65). From our discussion of Lyotard's position it is clear why he would reject such a 'meta-discourse'. Habermas, though, has himself criticized thinkers like Lyotard and Foucault (whom, along with Derrida, he identifies as 'young conservatives') for abandoning 'the project of modernity'.[101] Such a project, according to Habermas, is one that aimed at applying the values of scientific objectivity, universal morality and law as they had developed according to the rules of their own 'inner logic' to the everyday social realm. The attempt may not have been successful, but that of itself is no reason to give up on the Enlightenment project as, Habermas argues, thinkers like Nietzsche, Heidegger, Foucault, Derrida,[102] and Lyotard have done. Rather, we need to learn from the mistakes of the project of modernity. Thus, Habermas cleaves to what he regards as the Enlightenment ideal of a rationality that is capable of criticizing contemporary systems of belief. This has led Habermas to formulate his theory of 'communicative action'. One of Habermas's key contentions here is that all statements can always be judged according to four 'validity claims'. Thus, in uttering a statement or making any other kind of speech act a speaker necessarily adheres to four conditions. These are that what he or she says (1) is meaningful (i.e. that it can be understood), (2) is true, in terms of in its grounding assumptions about the world, (3) is sincere (i.e. that he or she is being truthful and can hence be trusted) and (4) is thereby open to being challenged by others should any of the first three conditions not be fulfilled.[103] Although it is true that in practice these conditions cannot be satisfied, Habermas maintains that they nevertheless constitute the basis for envisaging a regulative ideal of communication, which he calls the 'ideal speech situation'. This, he says, functions as a necessary presupposition, and hence is also a necessary condition, of all communication. According to this conception, the distortions that intervene between individual speakers may be inevitable (a speaker, X, may be more powerful or wealthy than another speaker, Y, for example), but we can still aspire to the regulative ideal of undistorted communication. For Habermas, the construction of this ideal is in keeping with the Enlightenment project. An ideal speech situation is *necessarily* presupposed by all communication not in spite of but 'because convictions are formed and confirmed in a medium that is not "pure" and removed from the world of appearances in the style of Platonic Ideas.'[104] The reason for this is that the very recognition of this kind of 'impurity' is itself only possible if we have an ideal of communication that falls short of it. Thus, Habermas argues, it is possible to maintain some conception of a form of Enlightenment critique that aspires to a validity that is not reducible to the internal consistency of genres and their rules of linking. To give up on this ideal is to abandon the Enlightenment path before it has come to its proper fruition, for modernity is, Habermas contends, an as yet 'unfinished project'.

In similar vein, Karl-Otto Apel (1921–) has sought, by way of a critical engagement with the legacies of Kant, Heidegger and Wittgenstein, to develop an approach that is distanced from the sceptical attitudes to traditional accounts of the nature of rationality, subjectivity and ethics adopted by French postmodernists and poststructuralists. Such a project involves elucidating the 'normative presuppositions of philosophical discourse' that all members of the philosophical community must ascribe to in common if they do not want to get themselves caught in the snare of a 'performative contradiction'. Apel argues that philosophers strive to achieve consensus on the validity of their own validity claims in principle with all (ideally, with all possible) partners in the discourse. They do so with the help of arguments, that is to say, by way of convincing, but not persuading, not to speak of other strategic ways of using language such as bribing or threatening. (They may no doubt expect and accept in the interest of their practical arguments that there will be actual dissent. But, in spite of Lyotard, they cannot strive for dissent by way of arguing. Rather, in the case of dissent, they at least have to strive for a consensus on the reasons for the dissent, provided they continue to argue at all.)[105]

Philosophers must, in short, acknowledge that there are certain assumptions that they share with one another. If philosophy involves the construction of arguments, then it must also follow that there is a need to recognize (implicitly or explicitly) that there are norms that make any argument worthy of our attention. Philosophical argument, in other words, is not to be reduced to a matter of mere 'persuasion', which it would be if it were simply a matter of emphasizing dissensus, as Lyotard is wont to do.

That said, in *The Differend* Lyotard reserves a special place for the genre of philosophical enquiry: 'Philosophical discourse has as its rule to discover its rule: its *a priori* is what it has at stake' (section 98). This, in effect, amounts to the claim that philosophical discourse is open-ended, since it does not operate according to a rule that is *known*. Thus, with regard to phrases situated within the philosophical genre, Lyotard can also claim that 'the rule for their concatenation remains to be found' (section 180). The problem with this, though, is that it effectively collapses the fundamental distinction to which Lyotard resorts in order to specify different genres, and so distinguish them from one another. If the rule that governs philosophy is yet to be found, is it not the case that it bears an uncanny resemblance to politics? Politics, we may recall, 'takes place' as a genre, but is not really one. Equally, it seems that philosophy in Lyotard's terms 'takes place' as a genre, but might turn out to not be one at all. This is simply because Lyotard cannot rule out the possibility that there might be no *a priori* of the philosophical genre at all. However, even if there turned out to be such an *a priori*, it is nevertheless the case that, pragmatically speaking, this cannot for the moment be shown to be the case. If it cannot be shown to be the case, then we might, with equal validity, argue that philosophy is 'like' politics, at least in so far as it could be describable as a realm of competing interests. Equally, if philosophy were this, then would we not be licensed in suspecting it to embody particularized interests, ones far removed from the lofty goal of searching out its own *a prioricity*?

5   What Kind of Language is Philosophical Language? (Irigaray and Le Doeuff)

The kind of terrain that is marked out by this last question could take us in a number if different directions, since it concerns the kind of norms that dominate within philosophy itself. One possible avenue for reflection of this sort is the one that has been explored by feminist thinkers. Amongst these, Luce Irigaray (1932–) rejects the rational discourse that philosophy traditionally, at least, aspires to. Instead, Irigaray has argued for the construction of an *écriture féminine* (a feminine writing) that would be suitable for the purpose of women representing their own interests. This kind of writing would be different in kind from the kind of language associated with a male-dominated reason and the discourses of knowledge associated with it. Amongst Irigaray's writings, *Speculum of the Other Woman* (1974) argues that the ideas dominant within psychoanalytic theory must be questioned. Irigaray's key contention here is that psychoanalysis is dominated by male (or patriarchal) language, and is hence unable to articulate female interests, for it necessarily distorts such interests. Recalling Levinas's articulation of the Other as being of a radically different order than the Same, Irigaray seeks to resituate this notion within the context of woman as Other. She thus argues for the view that the representationalist paradigm of traditional philosophical language is placed in question by the empirical fact of female existence. Male-oriented language is thus the defining feature of philosophical discourse, and indeed of other discourses about knowledge. Thus, for Irigaray, if we turn to the sciences we can ask the question as to whether the kind of knowledge they produce is objective and thus value-free. This, she argues, is simply not the case, since 'Any knowledge is produced by subjects in a given historical context. Even if it tends towards objectivity . . . science is the manifestation of certain choices, certain exclusions, essentially because of the sex of the scientists.'[106] Even though epistemology may have moved toward the view that the subject's standpoint is important in terms of the selection of objects examined, and so the kind of knowledge that is produced, this has still not really been developed to the point of 'interpreting the subject's sex'. Indeed, the question of a gendered subject has been generally ignored by the philosophical tradition (as well as in the sciences, in sociology, and in psychoanalysis). Thus, for example, the kind of critique of the subject that is pursued by advocates of deconstruction can, on Irigaray's view, be situated within the context of a male-dominated historical framework. This has led to important issues about the nature of identity being ignored. 'Philosophers take a keen interest in the deconstruction of ontology, in the ante- and the post-, but little interest in the constitution of a new, rationally founded identity.' The reason for this is that the presupposition of a male-oriented conception of the self has predominated, and this has led to a state wherein 'men are struggling with the absolute that they have created.'[107] The proper establishment of an ethical and political basis for a more just mode of civil association is, on Irigaray's view, linked to the need to articulate a 'triple dialectic . . . one for the male subject, one for the female subject, and one for their relationship as a couple or in a community.'[108] This means challenging the existing linguistic norms and practices which operate within society by way of rethinking the notion of civil identity in such a way that the status of women is respected within the civil realm. However, it is clear that the kind of account Irigaray offers can be criticized for presupposing an all-too-totalizing conception of the feminine. Speaking like Lyotard we could argue that the view that there are forms of discourse specific to men and women at the same time implies a heterogeneity that renders it impossible to reconcile the interests of the two, while at the same time ignoring the possibility that language itself is neither exclusively 'male' or 'female'.

Although she expresses admiration for Irigaray's work, Michèle Le Doeuff, (1948–) takes a rather different view. It may be true that the metaphysical tradition 'founds the duality of masculine rationality and feminine disorder'. However, this need not of itself mean that the traditional philosophical enterprise should be abandoned. 'Today it is possible to think of rationality otherwise than in a hegemonic mode.' Le Doeuff argues that Marx's thought already offers the possibility of an overcoming of this masculine conception of reason: 'This struggle was begun by historical materialism, in so far as this is a rationalism that renounces the idea of the omnipotence of knowledge.' On this basis, it is possible to 'trace a new form of philosophy' that seeks to mediate between the ' "philosophical" and the "feminine" '.[109] Hence, where Irigaray argues that the philosophical tradition (above all in relation to its conception of rationality) is essentially patriarchal, Le Doeuff holds that it is possible to articulate an open-ended approach to questions of reason from within philosophy itself. 'I have heard it said, a little too often for my liking, that rationality is a masculine thing, so that women trying to disengage themselves from the colonialist grip of the patriarchy should, urgently and once and for all, throw rationality into the bin.'[110] But, rationality is not so easily definable, for there are many forms of it. Indeed, Le Doeuff suggests, it may well be the case 'that rationality works in any case, in exile from itself and for better or worse'.[111] On the bad side, this may mean that philosophers have said some very stupid things about women and femininity.[112] On the good side, however, there is the possibility of a rationality that is not oriented toward such a reductivism. This kind of rationality is possible for philosophy, Le Doeuff argues, because philosophy is itself an open form of discourse. Even though the institutional framework within which philosophy is usually practised is sexist, in that it has a tendency to exclude women, this need not be the case with regard to the kinds of problem that philosophy concerns itself with.

Le Doeuff's exploration of what she terms the 'philosophical imaginary' underlies this last claim. Philosophy is, for Le Doeuff, primarily an abstract enterprise, and it is this tendency to over-value abstraction that she criticizes. For philosophical language is not merely abstract and conceptual, it is also riven with imagery. It is this imagery that constitutes the level of the philosophical imaginary. Philosophy may state that it has broken from myth, fable and poetry. Yet, from Plato to the present philosophical texts are laden with 'statues that breathe the scent of roses, comedies, tragedies, architects, foundations, dwellings, doors and windows, sand, navigators, various musical instruments, islands, clocks, horses, donkeys and even a lion, representatives of every craft and trade, scenes of sea and storm, forests and trees: in short, a whole pictorial world sufficient to decorate even the driest "History of Philosophy" '.[113] Are such images merely decorative? No, says Le Doeuff, such images in fact have a definite relation to conceptual thought. For one thing, 'imagery copes with problems posed by the theoretical enterprise itself', even as the philosopher who uses them is tempted to deny what is really going on.[114]

One of Le Doeuff's examples of the philosophical use of imagery is Kant's in the first *Critique*. In book II, chapter 3 of the 'Transcendental Analytic' Kant tells us that he has now surveyed 'the territory of pure understanding'. This territory is an 'island' surrounded by stormy oceans and other dangers. Before he takes us on a journey on to these seas Kant proposes an examination of the 'map' of the island.

Two questions may be asked about it. First, are we happy with it; and second, by what title deed are we in possession of this island. The understanding, in its pure form, is thus represented by way of the island image. And this allows Kant, in turn, to resort to a language of 'mapping' and 'possession' with regard to it. According to Le Doeuff, Kant's use of this imagery marks a moment at which the integrity of his own philosophical enterprise is sundered. For, 'Images are the means by which every philosophy can engage in straightforward dogmatization, and decree "that's the way it is" without fear of counter argument, since it is understood the reader will by-pass such "illustrations" – a convention which enables the image to do its work all the more effectively.'[115] The image of an island surrounded by stormy seas tells us that we ought to accept the view that there is nowhere else to go that is habitable. Kant's imagery implies that we ought to be compelled to accept his model of the understanding on pain of being left somewhere inhospitable if we do not (in that the 'island' of pure understanding stands amidst a dangerous environment). Thus, the openness that characterizes philosophical reflection is endangered by the imagery that philosophers are tempted to use. One cannot subject Kant's image to the kind of critical analysis appropriate to the abstract conceptual thought that goes to make up the bulk of the *Critique*. Thus, this kind of analysis is suspended and we are compelled by Kant's image. Images of this kind, Le Doeuff argues, are neither mere illustrations nor *parerga* (i.e. frames or borders) of the philosophical texts that resort to them. Rather, they compel by being what they are. As such, what such images are is never a matter of 'mere metaphor'. Rather, images of this kind serve to structure philosophical discourse. This, of itself, is not an entirely bad thing, for the effect of philosophical imagery is double-edged. At moments where they resort to imagery philosophical texts situate themselves concretely and thereby become open to criticism. The 'historical singularity of the Kantian island' allows Kant to try and impose his view upon us. Yet, at the same time, 'it reinstates everything which the work tends to empty or to disavow, it cancels the renunciations demanded by the theory ... making apparent the troubles of the system.'[116] In short, Kant is driven to introduce a concrete language into the *Critique* that he has been at pains to exclude from it. What is purportedly 'abstract' becomes concrete and hence limited. From this kind of example, Le Doeuff argues that we can conclude that 'imagery and knowledge form, dialectically, a common system.'[117] It is this dialectical structure of philosophical thought that constitutes philosophy's self-critical possibilities. And, it follows, such possibilities can, on this view, be drawn upon as a means of questioning the practice of philosophy as it has developed historically and thereby challenging the sexism that is present within that history. In this way, likewise, one can also argue that philosophy has the potential to pose a political challenge to the values that predominate within contemporary society. Equally, on this basis we might, with good reason, advocate a kind of rationalism that is also a pluralism – a discourse of reason that is self-critical concerning its own rights and duties. At the same time, however, is it not necessary to be wary of the advocacy of pluralism for pluralism's sake? Certainly, on the basis of Le Doeuff's view we do not need to reject the kind of rational critique to which philosophy has traditionally aspired.

Le Doeuff's arguments can be used as a means of carrying us full circle. For, here we come back to where we started. This, to recall, was with the question of the nature of reason, and its espousal by thinkers such as Descartes, Kant and Hegel. As Le Doeuff maintains, there is a good case for the view that the rationality to which philosophy aspires offers the potential for resistance to dogmatism. This is because the nature of the rationality that is at stake here is not a foregone conclusion, and it is this that makes the continued reflection upon rationality and philosophy worthwhile. Only if we were to adhere to this kind of view would it make sense to think of philosophy in the way that Lyotard does, i.e. as an enquiry that is essentially self-critical, as one that is devoted to uncovering its own presuppositions. In this sense, philosophy must, as Le Doeuff argues, also realize itself concretely within historical contexts. Philosophers, too, need to negotiate the social world. That they negotiate it with the purpose of questioning received assumptions is surely of value, since this itself entails that philosophy risks itself whenever and wherever it thinks. In risking itself, philosophical reflection thereby offers the possibility of criticizing the conditions that dominate within society. This, I would argue, does not mean simply embracing an unrestrained pluralism. It is not sufficient to valorize multiplicity for multiplicity's sake. The consequences of doing so, in Lyotard's case, lead to a paradoxical *legitimation* of the logic of liberal thought, a logic of which he himself is critical, and perhaps with good reason. For, as Horkheimer argues, the reduction of rationality to a mere instrumentalism that is characteristic of modern capitalist society should invite us to reflect upon its limitations just as much as we need to reflect upon the shortcomings of the Enlightenment project of developing an emancipatory reason. However, Lyotard, in offering us a philosophy of language that concentrates upon the notion of purposes as a means of defining genres, is perhaps himself not immune to endorsing the very instrumentalism of which, we have seen, Horkheimer speaks. Philosophers necessarily negotiate the social world they inhabit, and such negotiation entails recognizing the limits of both that world and philosophy itself as a prelude to criticizing it. In this sense, there is perhaps *a* purpose for philosophy. When we philosophize we need to aim at adopting the viewpoint that a stranger is obliged to when faced with the inevitable misunderstandings encountered as a result of being in a foreign place. It is a matter, perhaps, of discovering that one is not 'at home' where one felt most at home. Acknowledgement of this is something that involves recognition of a point that is, perhaps, analogous to Levinas's claim against Derrida: not *all* meaning is intrinsically 'philosophical' in nature. This fact, perhaps, should be numbered amongst philosophy's *a prioris*.

Notes

1   For some account of Levinas's relation to Nietzsche see John Llewelyn, *Emmanuel Levinas: A Geneaology of Ethics* (London: Routledge, 1995). With regard to Hegel, Levinas is an avowed anti-Hegelian – a position which, according to Derrida, gives rise to its own distinctive problems (see Jacques Derrida, *Writing and Difference*, tr. Alan Bass (London: Routledge & Kegan Paul, 1978), pp. 117–20).

2   Derrida's relationship to Nietzsche is a complex one, and I do not intend to do justice to it here. Suffice it to say that Derrida reads Nietzsche in a variety of ways depending upon context. Nietzsche is, for example, regarded by Derrida as one of those thinkers in whose writings *différance* 'appears almost by name' (*Margins of Philosophy*, tr. Alan

Bass (London: Harvester Wheatsheaf, 1982), p. 17). This is because Nietzsche's texts are seen by Derrida as actively plotting the limitations of conscious (and therefore conceptual and intentional) thought in relation to a larger domain of unconscious forces. The ethico-political ramifications of Nietzsche's thought, principally in relation to the usurpation of Nietzsche's name by Nazism, have been discussed by Derrida in his essay 'Otobiographies', see *The Ear of the Other*, ed. Christie McDonald, tr. Peggy Kamuf and Avital Ronell (Lincoln & London: University of Nebraska Press, 1988).

3   In this connection let us recall here only that Marx's work is based upon a critical development of Hegel's conception of the dialectic (see the brief account of Marxism that serves as a preface to the discussion of Horkheimer and Adorno in chapter 2).

4   Perhaps the most famous of recent exponents is the American philosopher John Rawls. See his *A Theory of Justice* (Oxford: Clarendon Press, 1972). Rawls follows both Locke and Mill in arguing that political authority is legitimate only in so far as it stems from the aim of protecting individual interests, and that these interests can be articulated by way of a rational framework. In Rawls's work, this framework is legitimated via a heuristic device called the 'original position'. This envisages a group of individuals placed behind a 'veil of ignorance', the 'veil' ensures that no individual knows where he or she will end up in society, i.e. wealthy or poor. Placed behind this veil these individuals must now choose the ground-rules according to which society is to operate with regard to how wealth and income are to be distributed. Rawls's argument is that, deprived of any knowledge concerning how wealthy one will end up after the veil has been lifted, any rational and self-interested individual will choose a social arrangement that minimizes the hardship they would endure should they find themselves on the lower rung of the social ladder. Thus, by way of the device of the original position, Rawls claims that the basic social norms that would make a just social order can be discovered and legitimized. Legitimacy, it follows, springs from the force of free and rational choice. Also, the work of F. A. Hayek has been very influential, especially in the UK in the 1980s. See, for example, his *The Constitution of Liberty* (London: Routledge & Kegan Paul, 1960). Hayek adopts a rather different view from Rawls in emphasizing the negative conception of liberty as being fundamental to individual freedom. Following Adam Smith, such freedom ultimately concerns the pursuit of individual wealth and, says Hayek, such pursuit has the benefit of creating greater overall wealth. Thus, individual freedom is to be valued over and above other notions, such as equality.

5   John Locke, *Two Treatises of Government*, ed. P. Laslett (Cambridge: Cambridge University Press, 1988).

6   See, Thomas Hobbes, *Leviathan* (1651), ed. R. Tuck (Cambridge: Cambridge University Press, 1994).

7   See G. W. F. Hegel, *Elements of the Philosophy of Right* (1821), ed. Alan Wood, tr. H. B. Nisbett (Cambridge: Cambridge University Press, 1991). In using the term 'civil society' Hegel was referring to the social realm of market exchange, or what is called the 'market economy'. This concept is derived from works such as Adam Smith's *Wealth of Nations* (1776). In civil society civil agents (individuals) pursue financial wealth. For Hegel, civil society is contrasted with the realm of the family, whose members are bound together by way of mutual affection (the bonds of love). As opposed to the family, civil society is a realm in which individuals pursue their private ends. In doing so each individual regards others primarily as means for the satisfaction of their own subjective needs. Thus, the relationship between individuals in civil society is essentially an instrumental one.

8   Locke, *Two Treatises of Government*, Second Treatise, section 11.

9   Ibid., sections 13–14.

10   Ibid., section 30.

11   Ibid., section 50.

12   For a discussion of this see Isaiah Berlin's essay 'Two Concepts of Liberty', in *Four Essays on Liberty* (Oxford: Oxford University Press, 1969).

13   John Stuart Mill, *On Liberty* (Harmondsworth: Penguin, 1984), p. 59. All further references are given in the text with page number.

14   For example, Mill claims that 'In the part which merely concerns himself . . . over his own body and mind, the individual is sovereign' (p. 69).

15   Thus, Mill says of the individual that 'his independence is, of right, absolute', (p. 69).

16   That is, in chapter 2, at the opening of the discussion of Horkheimer and Adorno.

17   Karl Marx, *Capital*, ed. David McLellan, tr. Samuel Moore and Edward Aveling (Oxford: Oxford University Press, 1995), p. 5.

18   Althusser's understanding of how we are to interpret the elements within this structure is indebted in some respects to his appreciation of the writings of Spinoza. For Althusser, Spinoza offers a key means of interpreting the significance of the elements that, taken together, constitute the social whole. Above all, this is to be done by way of reference to the whole not the parts. Society, according to Althusser, can be understood as a structure. If this is the case, then, he asks, how are we to interpret the manner in which the elements that exist in this structure are determined? This is a problem because resorting to the structural model means that traditional notions of causality are rendered useless. Althusser puts it this way: 'it becomes impossible to think . . . [the determination of the elements] . . . in the category of the global expressive causality of a universal inner essence immanent in its phenomenon' (Louis Althusser and Étienne Balibar, *Reading Capital* (1968), tr. Ben Brewster (London: NLB, 1970), p. 187). To put it another way: if all individual parts are situated within a whole that endows them with their identities, then it does not make sense to think of these parts as each possessing some universal power of 'causality'. How, therefore, are we to think of causality? The thinker to solve this quandry, Althusser contends, is Spinoza. This is because Spinoza holds that all individuated parts need to be grasped in terms of the whole (see also chapter 3 note 30). This whole Spinoza calls 'God or Nature', and it is composed of one substance. All individuated parts are modalities of this one substance. Althusser argues that Spinoza's view 'implies that the structure is immanent in its effects, a cause immanent in its effects' in that '*the whole existence of the structure consists of its effects* . . . [and] . . . is nothing outside its effects' (ibid., p. 189). From this it follows that the logical necessity that governs the whole also governs and thereby determines the nature of the parts. In this way, the individual elements that we find within any social context gain their identity from the fact that society is a structural whole. No other form of causality is required in order to explain the behaviour of any of the individuated elements that we find within a society. It is interesting to compare Althusser's use of this notion with Deleuze's. Both take the Spinozist account to imply that traditional notions of subjectivity can be questioned. At the same time, these two thinkers generate very different implications from the Spinozist view: on the one hand, Althusser takes the Spinozist thought to imply the necessity of a unity (the structural whole), whereas Deleuze regards this as questioning the very notion of such a unity. All bodies may be composed of one substance, but it does not follow from this that the effects of a body are determinable in this manner, for the totality in question is not a structure.

19   For Althusser's presentation of his conception of Marxist theory see his *For Marx* (1959), tr. Ben Brewster (London: New Left Books, 1969). For a general introduction to Althusser's thought and its influence, see E. Kaplan and M. Sprinker, *The Althusserian*

Legacy (London: Verso, 1993), and S. Smith, *Reading Althusser: An Essay on Structural Marxism* (Ithaca, NY: Cornell University Press, 1984).

20   Louis Althusser, 'Ideology and Ideological State Apparatuses (Notes towards an Investigation)', in *Lenin and Philosophy and other essays*, tr. Ben Brewster (London: NLB, 1971), pp. 123–73, p. 123. All further references are given in the text with page number.

21   And it is worth noting that Althusser is very aware of the role of *tradition* as being significant here: he is self-reflexive about the importance of received interpretations of Marx.

22   'There is no such thing as a purely repressive apparatus' which means that ideology must always already be involved in there somewhere: the police have beliefs which ensure their internal cohesion, even though they are fundamentally repressive in function (p. 138).

23   Although, again, 'There is no such thing as a purely ideological apparatus' – which means that repression always accompanies ideology (ibid.).

24   We should perhaps note in passing that in spite of his pretensions to a 'theoretical' elucidation of Marx's base-superstructure metaphor, Althusser ends up here producing yet another metaphor of his own in order to describe the manner in which Ideological State Apparatuses are unified. This, of course, is a musical and 'orchestral' metaphor. Could it be, as Derrida would doubtless note, that metaphor returns here to haunt Althusser's scheme, so rendering the possibility of a 'cleansed' and purely theoretical elucidation of the Marxist metaphor impossible?

25   A comment culled from Marx and Engels's *The German Ideology*, see vol. 1, ch. 1, 'Feuerbach', tr. W. Lough, in Karl Marx and Frederick Engels, *Collected Works*, vol. 5, 1845–1847 (London: Lawrence and Wishart, 1976), pp. 36–7.

26   According to Freud the unconscious may be defined as a process of mediation that intercedes between the perceptions generated by our senses and our processes of conscious thinking. As such, the unconscious is takes priority over consciousness. It is a realm in which opposites can coexist quite happily. Since the unconscious always intercedes between sense perceptions and conscious thought it cannot have, in any true sense, a 'history' in the manner in which different conscious episodes in an individual's or a culture's life can do. It is, in this limited sense, 'eternal'.

27   The allusion is to Aristotle's *Metaphysics*, Book IV, 1003a, line 34, where Aristotle is discussing being.

28   Foucault, we should remind ourselves here, knew Althusser personally.

29   A phrase by which Foucault alludes to the dominant mode of thinking about knowledge in the modern period.

30   That is, in so far as he both regards an objective science in the structuralist sense as being possible, and in his use of a structural metaphor to envisage the nature of society.

31   See, for example, Michel Foucault, *Discipline and Punish* (Harmondsworth: Penguin, 1979), p. 27.

32   We can also note, in this connection, that Foucault shares something in common with Deleuze and Guattari, for whom the notion of ideology is completely redundant (see chapter 3).

33   Michel Foucault, 'Truth and Power', in *Power/Knowledge: Selected Interviews and Other Writings 1972–1977*, ed. Colin Gordon, tr. Colin Gordon et al. (London: Harvester Wheatsheaf, 1980), p. 118.

34   See, for example, Foucault's books: *Madness and Civilization* (New York: Pantheon, 1965), *The Birth of the Clinic: An Archaeology of Medical Perception* (New York: Pantheon, 1973), *Discipline and Punish: The Birth of the Prison* (New York: Pantheon, 1977), *The History of Sexuality*, 3 vols, (New York: Pantheon, 1978, 1985, 1986).

35 'Truth and Power', in *Power/Knowledge*, p. 115.

36 Ibid., p. 116.

37 For discussion of this see Peter Starr, *Logics of Failed Revolt: French Theory After May '68* (Stanford, Cal.: Stanford University Press, 1995).

38 'Prison Talk', in *Power/Knowledge*, pp. 39–40.

39 See the opening of *Discipline and Punish*, where Foucault presents an excruciatingly detailed eye-witness account of the execution of a man for the attempted regicide of Louis XV.

40 *Discipline and Punish*, pp. 19–21.

41 Although earlier texts like *Discipline and Punish* generally take 'power' to be a negative term, i.e. as signifying something repressive, even there Foucault asserts that in so far as power is also productive of social reality it is also positive (cf. p. 194).

42 See, 'Truth and Power', in *Power/Knowledge*, p. 133.

43 Friedrich Nietzsche, *On the Geneaology of Morals*, tr. Walter Kaufmann, in *Basic Writings of Nietzsche* (New York: Modern Library, 1968). The substance of Nietzsche's argument is spelled out in the first essay of the *Genealogy*: 'Good and Bad/Good and Evil'. All further references to the *Genealogy* are given in the text with essay and section number.

44 We can note that Nietzsche's development of the genealogical method has its roots in his earlier works, such as *Human, All-Too-Human* (a text discussed in chapter 2). The opening sections of *Human, All-Too-Human* argue that it is possible to outline a 'chemistry' of religious and moral 'sensations' and values. Thus, values (moral 'sensations') can be interpreted by way of a causal and historical account of their origins.

45 Michel Foucault, 'Truth and Power', in *Power/Knowledge*, p. 117.

46 Michel Foucault, 'Nietzsche, Genealogy, History', in *Language, Counter-Memory, Practice*, ed. Donald F. Bouchard, tr. Donald F. Bouchard and Sherry Simon (Oxford: Blackwell, 1977), pp. 139–64, p. 139.

47 See, for example, Keith Ansell Pearson, 'The Significance of Michel Foucault's Reading of Nietzsche: Power, the Subject, and Political Theory', in *Nietzsche Studien*, vol. 20, 1991, pp. 267–84; also reprinted in *Nietzsche: A Critical Reader*, ed. Peter Sedgwick (Oxford: Blackwell, 1995). See also Mark Warren, *Nietzsche and Political Thought* (Cambridge, Mass.: MIT Press, 1988). Both argue, following Foucault, that Nietzsche's aristocratic politics can be divorced from his theory of the will to power.

48 Let us rest content with the example of Walter Kaufmann's classic study, *Nietzsche: Philosopher, Psychologist, Antichrist* (Princeton: Princeton University Press, 1974), first published in 1950. Kaufmann argues that the 'leitmotif of Nietzsche's life and thought – [is] the theme of the anti-political individual who seeks perfection far from the modern world' (p. 418). Doubtless, given the appropriation of Nietzsche's work by Nazi academics, Kaufmann's aim in marginalizing the political implications of Nietzsche's thought was to make it more approachable during a time when any rumination on Nietzsche's value for political thinking seemed to entail unpleasant and uncomfortable associations.

49 See Friedrich Nietzsche, *The Will to Power*, tr. Walter Kaufmann and R. J. Hollingdale (New York: Vintage Books, 1968). Section 1067 offers what must be Nietzsche's most famous and extreme presentation of this view (it is cited in the main text, below). All further references to *The Will to Power* are given in the text with section number.

50 As exemplified by his assertion that the ego is a fiction added to the deed after the fact as a convenient means of explaining it, rather than an actual cause of actions as many philosophers have hitherto believed. A discussion of this is already offered in chapter 2, above. But see also in connection Nietzsche's comments in *Beyond Good and Evil*,

tr. Walter Kaufmann, in *Basic Writings of Nietzsche*, sections 16, and 17, and *The Will to Power*, sections 480, 484, 485. All further references to *Beyond Good and Evil* are given in the text with section number.

51   This point of view is advocated by both Mark Warren and Keith Ansell Pearson (see n. 47 above).

52   Friedrich Nietzsche, *The Gay Science*, tr. Walter Kaufmann (New York: Vintage, 1974). See section 125 for the presentation of the death of God. For Nietzsche's elucidation of its significance as the 'greatest modern event', see section 344.

53   See, for example, *On the Genealogy of Morals*, first essay, section 9.

54   See *The Gay Science*, section 344.

55   See the *Genealogy*, second essay, section 27: the '*will to truth* . . . this *remnant* of an ideal is . . . not so much its remnant as its kernel . . . – it is the awe-inspiring *catastrophe* of two thousand years of training in truthfulness that finally forbids itself the *lie involved in the belief in God.*'

56   See, in connection, *Beyond Good and Evil*, section 211, where Nietzsche defines '*genuine philosophers*' as '*commanders and legislators*' in that their knowing is a form of will to power.

57   See also *Beyond Good and Evil*, section 260.

58   See Friedrich Nietzsche, *Twilight of the Idols*, tr. Walter Kaufmann, in *The Portable Nietzsche* (London: Chatto & Windus, 1971), which concludes with a quotation from *Thus Spoke Zarathustra*, III, 'On old and New Tablets', section 29: ' "Why so hard?" the kitchen coal once said to the diamond. "After all, are we not close kin?" Why so soft? O my brothers, thus I ask you . . . if your hardness does not wish to flash and cut and cut through, how can you one day create with me? For all creators are hard. And it must seem blessedness to you to impress your hand on millennia as on wax. . . .' This can be compared with the legislative and creative conception of 'genuine' philosophy that Nietzsche extolls in *Beyond Good and Evil*.

59   Pursuing a methodology to the point of absurdity, after all, tells us something about it: it tells us about the method's limitations.

60   We can note here a connection with the project outlined in the opening sections of *Human, All-Too-Human*, which pursues the methodology of accounting for 'moral sensations' in terms of drives.

61   This is a notion that is present within Nietzsche's earliest philosophy, primarily as a consequence of his early adherence to the work of Arthur Schopenhauer (1788–1860). Schopenhauer, an avowed anti-Hegelian, attempted a development of the philosophy of Kant, above all in its attempt to explore the limits of various forms of philosophical explanation (see *On the Fourfold Root of the Principle of Sufficient Reason*, (1813, tr. E. F. Payne (La Salle, Ill.: Open Court, 1974)). In his *magnum opus*, *The World as Will and Representation* (1818, tr. E. F. Payne, 2 vols (New York: Dover Publications, 1969/1966)), Schopenhauer took the Kantian distinction between phenomenal and noumenal realms and argued that the self can be interpreted in the light of this. Thus, the self is both a phenomenon (it appears in the world as an entity that can be perceived – in the form of persons) and has a noumenal aspect: in itself the self is taken as an expression of will. Schopenhauer's philosophy is usually given the name 'pessimism', for it adopts the view that the renunciation of the will is the only viable means of avoiding suffering in life. In this regard there are links with the tradition of Buddhist thought, in which Schopenhauer was well versed. Although indebted to Schopenhauer's work, Nietzsche's conception of the will is rather different. For one thing, in Nietzsche's view there is no individuated, noumenal subject to be found lurking beneath or behind the realm of phenomenal experience (see chapter 2).

62   This analysis is also prefigured in *Beyond Good and Evil* (sections 257ff.).

63 Or, to use one of Nietzsche's terms, in the context of the 'herd'.

64 We could, of course, also call this an 'anti-politics' in so far as Foucault, like Nietzsche, spurns the modern liberal consensus concerning the nature of the political. But such an 'anti-politics' remains a politics to the extent that it is bound by the context of modernity: one cannot oppose politics without at the same time being political.

65 These are Jacques Derrida's words – see 'Cogito and the History of Madness', in *Writing and Difference*, tr. Alan Bass (London: Routledge & Kegan Paul, 1978), p. 33. This is an essay that is critical of Foucault's project, largely because Derrida contends that the demand that one be able to step outside rational discourse in order to allow madness to show itself is highly problematic, for 'madness' is constituted within this discourse. This is not an entirely accurate criticism of Foucault, to the extent that he himself makes this very point.

66 See Anthony Giddens, *The Consequences of Modernity* (Cambridge: Polity Press, 1990) for some discussion of this. Equally, some writers have sought to analyse postmodernity in terms of social and economic developments within late capitalist society. See David Harvey, *The Condition of Postmodernity: An Enquiry into the Origins of Cultural Change* (Oxford: Blackwell, 1989). According to Harvey, the postmodern era is marked by a shift away from a localized mode of production (the factory) toward a more decentered model. Thus, a diversity of sources are organized in such a manner that the factory ceases to be the centre of production (parts of, say, a car are made in a variety of locales and then transported to one site in order to be assembled). According to Harvey, this can be interpreted as a development of the same logic of capitalist production that Marx outlined in *Capital*. For another account of the postmodern that makes this kind of connection see Fredric Jameson, *Postmodernism, or, The Cultural Logic of Late Capitalism* (London: Verso, 1991).

67 Jean-François Lyotard, *The Postmodern Condition: A Report on Knowledge*, tr. Geoff Bennington (Manchester: Manchester University Press, 1989), p. 4. All further references are given in the text with page number.

68 See Immanuel Kant, *The Critique of Judgement*, tr. Werner S. Pluhar (Indianapolis: Hackett, 1987), sections 18ff.

69 Ibid., section 25.

70 Lyotard is thinking here of 'modernism' in the sense that relates to the arts and literature. For example, the works of a novelist such as James Joyce are 'modernist' in this sense.

71 Thus, Lyotard compares the modernist 'fragment' with the experimental form of the postmodern 'essay'. Here his characterization of the essay bears comparison with the view outlined by Adorno in 'The Essay as Form' (see chapter 2 above).

72 See, for example, Jean-François Lyotard and Jean-Loup Thébaud, *Just Gaming*, tr. Wlad Godzich, with an Afterword by Samuel Weber, tr. Brian Massumi (Manchester: Manchester University Press, 1985), pp. 15ff. See also, Lyotard's essay 'Rewriting Modernity', in *The Inhuman: Reflections on Time*, tr. Geoff Bennington and Rachel Bowlby (Cambridge: Polity Press, 1991).

73 Lyotard, 'Rewriting Modernity', in *The Inhuman*, p. 34.

74 In this work (published in 1974) Lyotard seeks to challenge the philosophical methodology of Marxist theory by way of a turn to the Freudian notion of the libido. This notion has its links with the Nietzschean conception of will to power, for the libido is to be understood in terms of an energetics of force. See *Libidinal Economy*, tr. Iain Hamilton Grant (Bloomington: Indiana University Press, 1993).

75 *Just Gaming*, pp. 16–17.

76 Ibid., p. 89.

77 Ibid., p. 90.

78   Ibid., pp. 90–1.
79   Ludwig Wittgenstein, *Philosophical Investigations*, tr. G. E. M. Anscombe (Oxford: Blackwell, 1996), para. 7. The *Philosophical Investigations* were written between 1945 and 1949, and published after Wittgenstein's death.
80   Ibid., para. 43.
81   Ibid., para. 23.
82   Jean-François Lyotard, *The Differend: Phrases in Dispute*, tr. Georges Van Den Abeele (Manchester: Manchester University Press, 1988). All further references are given in the text with section number.
83   Jean-François Lyotard, *Political Writings*, tr. Bill Readings and Kevin Paul Geiman (Minneapolis: University of Minnesota Press, 1993), p. 21.
84   I have already presented a version of the following account of Lyotard and the political in 'Politics as Antagonism and Diversity: Mill and Lyotard', in *Varieties of Victorianism: The Uses of a Past*, ed. Gary Day (Basingstoke: Macmillan Press Ltd., 1998).
85   Georges Van Den Abeele's rendering of Lyotard's use of the French *'phrase'* as 'phrase' is perhaps not entirely germane, in so far as *'phrase'* might more correctly be translated as 'sentence'. However, the English 'phrase' serves well enough, and I will retain it in the following discussion.
86   We should add, in passing, that for Lyotard it is the function of 'proper names' (which he treats of in the sense adopted by the American philosopher Saul Kripke – see his *Naming and Necessity* (Harvard: Harvard University Press, 1980)) to allow phrases from different regimens to be linked together. 'Proper names', in this context, include not only names like 'Vienna' or 'Peter', but any name that serves as a 'rigid designator'. By this, Lyotard means that such names are 'empty'. Names are 'rigid' in so far as they do not change between contexts, but they are empty in that their content is determined by the current phrase in which they are situated, e.g. 'Kant the author of the first *Critique*'; 'I baptize thee Immanuel Kant', etc. As such, a name has no determinate sense (see *The Differend*, sections 54, 61, 62, 66–77).
87   Lyotard, *Political Writings*, p. 33.
88   'Russell' as in Bertrand Russell, one of the most famous of analytic philosophers.
89   From this one could argue that Lyotard shares with other French ex-radicals, like Foucault, a post-1968 disenchantment with a radical politics of revolution.
90   Lyotard, *Just Gaming*, p. 91.
91   And we should recall here that Lyotard claims it is a condition of the existence of phrases that they are inherently social (193).
92   Mill, *On Liberty*, pp. 110–11.
93   See *On Liberty*, pp. 59, 71.
94   See ibid., p. 120.
95   Ibid.
96   Ibid., p. 119.
97   See ibid., pp. 127ff. Although Mill's argument is often couched in terms of the threat of mediocrity, it is nevertheless the case that he endorses the view that the development of new practices and competences (in Lyotard's terminology, new genres) is culturally beneficial: 'There is always a need of persons not only to discover new truths and point out what were once truths are true no longer, but also to commence new practices and set the example of more enlightened conduct and better taste and sense in human life' (p. 129).
98   See *The Differend*, section 182, where Lyotard characterizes postmodernism as 'the pastime of an old man who scrounges in the garbage-heap of finality looking for leftovers', as a genre fitting for 'a certain [type of] humanity. A genre. (A bad parody of Nietzsche.

Why?)' In other words, this is not a Nietzscheanism, it is not a politics of power, of the will to power.

99   See Lyotard, *Political Writings*, p. 11.
100 See Adam Smith, *An Enquiry into the Nature and Causes of the Wealth of Nations*, ed. W. B. Todd (Oxford: Clarendon, 1976).
101 See Jürgen Habermas, 'Modernity versus Postmodernity', tr. Seyla Benhabib, in *New German Critique*, 22 (Winter 1981), p. 9.
102 In fact, Derrida rejects Habermas's attribution of such a view to him. See, the 'Afterword' to *Limited Inc.*, ed. Gerald Graff (Evanston, Ill.: Northwestern University Press, 1988).
103 See Jürgen Habermas, *The Theory of Communicative Action*, vol. 1: *Reason and the Rationalisation of Society*, and vol. 2: *Lifeworld and System: A Critique of Functionalist Reason*, tr. Thomas McCarthy (Cambridge: Polity Press, 1984 and 1987).
104 Jürgen Habermas, 'The Entwinement of Myth and Enlightenment: Max Horkheimer and Theodor Adorno', in *The Philosophical Discourse of Modernity*, tr. Fredrick Lawrence (Cambridge: Polity Press, 1994), p. 130.
105 Karl-Otto Apel, 'Regulative Ideas or Truth Happening?', tr. Dale Snow, in *From a Transcendental-Semiotic Point of View*, ed. Marianna Papastephanou (Manchester: Manchester University Press, 1998), p. 206.
106 Luce Irigaray, *Thinking the Difference: For a Peaceful Revolution*, tr. Karin Montin (London: The Athlone Press, 1994), p. 31.
107 Ibid., pp. 32, 33.
108 Ibid., p. 39.
109 Michèle Le Doeuff, *The Philosophical Imaginary*, tr. Colin Gordon (London: Athlone Press, 1989), pp. 117, 118.
110 Michèle Le Doeuff, *Hipparchia's Choice*, tr. Trista Selous (Oxford: Blackwell, 1991), p. 23.
111 Ibid., p. 51.
112 And indeed, they have. Witness Nietzsche's many ill-informed comments about women. For example, 'When a woman has scholarly inclinations there is usually something wrong with her sexually' (*Beyond Good and Evil*, section 144).
113 Le Doeuff, *The Philosophical Imaginary*, p. 1.
114 Ibid., p. 5.
115 Ibid., p. 12.
116 Ibid., p. 17.
117 Ibid., p. 19.

Afterword: 'Hell Fire!'

What, then, of the purposes of philosophy? Is philosophy, as Plato argued, a discipline defined by way of a specific purpose? Although they might differ with regard to what that purpose is, Plato and Lyotard have, at least, this belief in common: that philosophy is a 'craft'[1] or a 'genre', and is hence definable in terms of the purpose proper to it. Certainly, we can say what areas can legitimately be considered within the framework of such a purpose. The chapters of this book deal with these areas: the problem of what we know and the conditions of such knowledge; the nature of reason and experience; questions of meaning; ontological issues; the problems of ethics and of politics. All these concerns remain proper to philosophy. We can, in any case, say what is *not* proper to philosophical enquiry. The philosopher does not seek to please but to challenge. Since philosophy is, like those who practice it, part of life, such a purpose announces itself in the context of lives that are lived. As such, philosophers are as much a subject of their context as anyone else. Philosophers, too, must negotiate with a world that is not entirely their own, with a world that is, at times, obstinately *un*philosophical. And this is all for the good. As Michael Oakeshott puts it in *Experience and its Modes* (1933), a life that consisted of philosophy and nothing else 'would, indeed, be at once febrile and insipid and not to be endured'.[2] Following Kant, we need to accept that there are limits to philosophical reasoning; and it is only because there are such limits that one can comment upon the world in a manner that is worthy of being called 'philosophical'.

In his poem, 'Wittgenstein',[3] the Welsh writer Eirian Davies relates the following tale about the philosopher. During the Second World War, Davies and Wittgenstein resided at the same lodgings. 'Once' Davies tells us in a note explaining the background to the poem, 'near my home in Nantgaredig, Carmarthenshire, he was arrested by the Home Guard, as they thought he was an enemy agent.' According to Davies, three local men, who were farmers acting 'under the authority of their [Home Guard] uniform', jumped 'with bared teeth' upon Wittgenstein as he was about to cross over a bridge. Perhaps not surprisingly, when faced with this situation, Wittgenstein, the great philosopher of language, responded in the most unphilosophical of fashions: 'All you said was "Hell Fire!" ["Uffern dân!"].'[4] As Davies presents it, Wittgenstein, trying 'to reason wildly under the onslaught of phrases', fighting 'against the destructive rape of language on the minds of the fools' who accosted him, is ultimately placed in a position wherein his language and reason are rendered impotent. He, the philosopher, is suddenly not at home in a place where he thought he was at home. He seeks to negotiate with others, but he cannot. He has a foreign accent; he does not speak like they do. Speaking like Lyotard, we could say that what we have here is an instance of the incommensurability of heterogeneous genres of discourse. The philosopher, trying 'to cross over in friendship' to those on the other side of the bridge is rendered their victim when they seize hold of him. His language is stifled by their actions. Yet, the actions of these men, Davies also tells us, pay testimony to their own 'hurt': 'They were unable to understand you, and that hurt them like the teasing of a knife on the heart's meat', for 'they came nowhere near to know the language you spoke. Its meaning was lost to them.' Like the expression 'Hell Fire!', brute actions, too, are an expression of an inability to communicate with others. Taken together, the philosopher's expletive and the soldiers' actions offer an intimation of the limits of rational discourse. The 'bridge' of the narrative is, of course, a metaphor for these limits. A bridge is that across which one must pass in order to reach and communicate with others. But, at the same time, a bridge also serves to separate them from one another. The metaphor itself, as Le Doeuff would say, sets a kind of limit to the aims of communication even before it has been attempted.

'Why', Davies asks us in a manner that alludes to the only work that Wittgenstein published during his lifetime, the *Tractatus*, 'isn't the language of bridges comprehensible to men? The word a name and the name a meaningful object?' Why, in other words, do the aspirations of philosophical reason always fall short of practice, and thus of the conventions and habits, the presuppositions, fears and purposes that go to make the world of human relations what it is? Doubtless, the later Wittgenstein, the Wittgenstein of the *Philosophical Investigations*, would not seek to offer an answer to such a question: 'my reasons will soon give out. And then I shall act, without reasons'; 'When someone whom I am afraid of orders me . . . I act quickly, with perfect certainty, and the lack of reasons does not trouble me.'[5] And yet, when accosted by 'Harri Weun-hir, with his pitchfork warm from the hay' and his two comrades, the 'blue-eyed weakling from Vienna' is troubled precisely by their lack of understanding of his attempts to reason with them. He is swallowed up within a context that cannot be negotiated, and all that is left of his reasoning is an expletive. Davies's poem, too, does not seek to offer an answer to the question it poses, for it is not easy to explain why the 'language of bridges' is inaccessible. He can only end the poem with three questions and the expletive itself: 'An incomplete picture? Incorrect grammar? An ambiguous word? Hell Fire!' Philosophy cannot offer a complete picture of the world. Indeed, the very notion of 'picturing', of *representing* the world, which is so essential to Descartes's project and forms the point of departure for Hume's empiricism, is precisely what is placed in question by most of the thinkers we have discussed in this book. Philosophers do not merely 'picture' the world of human experience, they negotiate it – albeit sometimes badly. Equally, they are also thereby obliged to speak with an 'incorrect grammar' and perhaps with an accent that separates them from their context. And it is, indeed, in the uttering or formulation of an 'ambiguous word' that they fall short of their own aspirations. But this, of itself, does not invalidate the philosophical project. On the contrary, it makes the activity of philosophizing all the more interesting.

Notes

1   See Plato, *Gorgias*, tr. Donald J. Zayl (Indianapolis: Hackett, 1987), 449dff.
2   Michael Oakeshott, *Experience and its Modes* (Cambridge: Cambridge University Press, 1991), p. 3. Interestingly, Oakeshott's book develops a viewpoint that has similarities with Lyotard's approach, in that he seeks to analyse incommensurable realms of experience, arguing that they must be separated according to their specific character: 'confusion . . . is itself the most fatal of all errors, and . . . it occurs whenever argument or inference passes from one world of experience to another' (p. 5).
3   Eirian Davies, 'Wittgenstein', in *Cerddi '75*, ed. Derec Llwyd Morgan (Llandysul: Gwasg Gomer, 1975). I am indebted to my father-in-law, Bryan Martin Davies, for both drawing my attention to this poem and translating it from the Welsh.
4   Given the situation, we could perhaps render Davies's Welsh phrase, 'Uffern dân!' (literally 'Hell Fire!') as something akin to the English expression 'Bloody Hell!'
5   Wittgenstein, *Philosophical Investigations*, paras 211, 212.

Further Reading

1 Knowledge, Reason and Experience: Descartes, Locke, Hume and Kant

Beck, Lewis White, *Essays on Kant and Hume* (New Haven and London: Yale University Press, 1978).

Bennett, Jonathan, *Kant's Analytic* (Cambridge: Cambridge University Press, 1966).

Bennett, Jonathan, *Locke, Berkeley, Hume* (Oxford: Clarendon Press, 1971).

Chadwick, Ruth F. and Cazeaux, Clive (eds) *Immanuel Kant: Critical Assessments* (London: Routledge, 1992).

Cottingham, John, *Descartes* (New York: Blackwell, 1986).

Cottingham, John, *The Rationalists* (Oxford: Oxford University Press, 1988).

Cottingham, John (ed.), *The Cambridge Companion to Descartes* (Cambridge: Cambridge University Press, 1992).

Dancy, Jonathan and Sosa, Ernest (eds), *A Companion to Epistemology* (Oxford: Blackwell, 1992).

Deleuze, Gilles, *Empiricism and Subjectivity: An Essay on Hume's Theory of Human Nature*, tr. Constantin V. Boundas (New York: Colombia University Press, 1991).

Deleuze, Gilles, *Kant's Critical Philosophy: The Doctrine of the Faculties*, tr. Hugh Tomlinson and Barbara Habberjam (London: Athlone Press, 1994).

Norton, David (ed.), *The Cambridge Companion to Hume* (Cambridge: Cambridge University Press, 1994).

Pippin, Robert B., *Kant's Theory of Form: An Essay on the Critique of Pure Reason* (New Haven: Yale University Press, 1982).

Priest, Stephen, *The British Empiricists: Hobbes to Ayer* (London: Penguin, 1990).

2 Knowledge, History and Society: Hegel, Nietzsche, Horkheimer and Adorno

Benhabib, Seyla, Bonss, Wolfgang and McCole, John (eds), *On Max Horkheimer: New Perspectives* (Cambridge, Mass.: MIT Press, 1993).

Bottomore, Tom, *The Frankfurt School* (Chichester: Ellis Horwood, 1984).

Bowie, Andrew, *Aesthetics and Subjectivity: From Kant to Nietzsche* (Manchester: Manchester University Press, 1990).

Harris, H. S., *Hegel: Phenomenology and System* (Indianapolis: Hackett, 1995).

Held, David, *Introduction to Critical Theory: Horkheimer to Habermas* (London: Hutchinson, 1980).

Jay, Martin, *Adorno* (London: Fontana, 1984).

Jay, Martin, *The Dialectical Imagination: A History of the Frankfurt School and the Institute of Social Research, 1923–1950* (Berkeley: University of California Press, 1996).

Kaufmann, Walter, *Nietzsche: Philosopher, Psychologist, Antichrist* (Princeton, NJ: Princeton University Press, 1974).

Kim, Jaegwon and Sosa, Ernest, *A Companion to Metaphysics* (Oxford: Blackwell, 1994).

Kofman, Sarah, *Nietzsche and Metaphor*, tr. Duncan Large (London: Athlone Press, 1993).

Krell, David Farrell and Wood, David, *Exceedingly Nietzsche: Aspects of Contemporary Nietzsche Interpretation* (London: Routledge, 1988).

Magnus, Berndt and Higgins, Kathleen M. (eds), *The Cambridge Companion to Nietzsche* (Cambridge: Cambridge University Press, 1996).

Plant, Raymond, *Hegel* (London: Phoenix, 1997).

Rose, Gillian, *The Melancholy Science: An Introduction to the Thought of Theodor W. Adorno* (London: Macmillan, 1978).

Schacht, Richard, *Nietzsche* (London: Routledge & Kegan Paul, 1983).

Schacht, Richard, *Making Sense of Nietzsche: Reflections Timely and Untimely* (Urbana: University of Illinois Press, 1995).

Schrift, Alan, *Nietzsche and the Question of Interpretation* (London: Routledge, 1990).

Schrift, Alan, *Nietzsche's French Legacy* (London: Routledge, 1995).

Sedgwick, Peter (ed.), *Nietzsche: A Critical Reader* (Oxford: Blackwell, 1995).

Taylor, Charles, *Hegel* (Cambridge: Cambridge University Press, 1975).

3   Two Ontologies: Heidegger, Deleuze and Guattari

Bogue, Ronald, *Deleuze and Guattari* (London: Routledge, 1989).

Boundas, Constantin, V. and Olkowsi, Dorothea (eds), *Gilles Deleuze and the Theater of Philosophy* (New York: Routledge, 1994).

Dallmayr, Fred R., *Life-World, Modernity and Critique: Paths Between Heidegger and the Frankfurt School* (Cambridge: Polity Press, 1991).

Dreyfus, Hubert L. and Hall, Harrison (eds), *Heidegger: A Critical Reader* (Oxford: Blackwell, 1992).

Gadamer, Hans Georg, *Heidegger's Ways*, tr. John W. Stanley (Albany: State University of New York Press, 1994).

Grossmann, Reinhardt, *The Existence of the World: An Introduction to Ontology* (London: Routledge, 1992).

Guignon, Charles B. (ed.), *The Cambridge Companion to Heidegger* (Cambridge: Cambridge University Press, 1993).

Hodge, Joanna, *Heidegger and Ethics* (London: Routledge, 1995).

Marks, John, *Gilles Deleuze: Vitalism and Multiplicity* (London: Pluto Press, 1998).

Mulhall, Stephen, *Heidegger and Being and Time* (London: Routledge, 1996).

Patton, Paul (ed.), *Deleuze: A Critical Reader* (Oxford: Blackwell, 1996).

Sadler, Ted, *Heidegger and Aristotle: The Question of Being* (London: Athlone Press, 1996).

4 Anti-humanism and the Problem of Ethics: Levinas and Derrida

Bennington, Geoffrey and Derrida, Jacques, *Jacques Derrida* (Chicago: University of Chicago Press, 1993).

Bernasconi, Robert and Critchley, Simon (eds), *Re-Reading Levinas* (London: Athlone Press, 1991).

Critchley, Simon, *Ethics – Politics – Subjectivity: Essays on Derrida, Levinas and Contemporary French Thought* (London: Verso, 1999).

Critchley, Simon, *The Ethics of Deconstruction: Derrida and Levinas* (Edinburgh: Edinburgh University Press, 1999).

Danto, Arthur C., *Sartre* (London: Fontana, 1975).

Davies, Tony, *Humanism* (London: Routledge, 1997).

Gasché, Rodolphe, *Inventions of Difference: On Jacques Derrida* (Cambridge, Mass.: Harvard University Press, 1994).

Harland, Richard, *Superstructuralism* (London: Methuen, 1987).

Llewelyn, John, *Emmanuel Levinas: The Genealogy of Ethics* (London: Routledge, 1995).

McCulloch, Gregory, *Using Sartre: An Analytical Introduction to Early Sartrean Themes* (London: Routledge, 1994).

Norris, Christopher, *Derrida* (London: Fontana Press, 1987).

Wood, David (ed.), *Derrida: A Critical Reader* (Oxford: Blackwell, 1992).

5 Politics, Ideology, Power and Justice: Althusser, Foucault and Nietzsche, Lyotard

Ansell-Pearson, Keith, *Nietzsche contra Rousseau: A Study of Nietzsche's Moral and Political Thought* (Cambridge: Cambridge University Press, 1991).

Barry, Norman P., *An Introduction to Modern Political Theory* (Basingstoke: Macmillan, 1989).

Benhabib, Seyla, *Situating the Self: Gender, Community and Postmodernism in Contemporary Ethics* (Cambridge: Polity Press, 1990).

Bennington, Geoffrey, *Lyotard: Writing the Event* (New York: Columbia University Press, 1988).

Benton, Ted, *The Rise and Fall of Structural Marxism: Althusser and his Influence* (London: Macmillan, 1984).

Callinicos, Alex, *Althusser's Marxism* (London: Pluto Press, 1976).

Carroll, David, *Paraesthetics: Foucault, Lyotard, Derrida* (London: Methuen, 1987).

Conway, Daniel, *Nietzsche and the Political* (London: Routledge, 1997).

Dallmayr, Fred, *Twilight of Subjectivity: Contributions to a Post-Individualist Theory of Politics* (Amherst, Mass.: University of Massachusetts Press, 1981).

Dreyfus, Hubert L. and Rabinow, Paul, *Michel Foucault: Beyond Structuralism and Hermeneutics* (Brighton: Harvester, 1982).

Eagleton, Terry, *Ideology: An Introduction* (London: Verso, 1991).

Grant, Ruth W., *John Locke's Liberalism* (Chicago: University of Chicago Press, 1987).

Gray, John, *Liberalisms: Essays in Political Philosophy* (London: Routledge, 1990).

Grosz, Elizabeth, *Sexual Subversions: Three French Feminists* (London: Allen & Unwin, 1989).

Habermas, Jürgen, *The Philosophical Discourse of Modernity*, tr. Frederick Lawrence (Cambridge: Polity Press, 1987).

Jameson, Fredric, *Postmodernism, or, The Cultural Logic of Late Capitalism* (London: Verso, 1991).

Kenny, Anthony, *Wittgenstein* (London: Allen Lane, 1973).

Kymlicka, Will, *Liberalism, Community and Culture* (Oxford: Clarendon Press, 1989).

Owen, David, *Maturity and Modernity: Nietzsche, Weber, Foucault, and the Ambivalence of Reason* (London: Routledge, 1994).

Readings, Bill, *Introducing Lyotard: Art and Politics* (London: Routledge, 1991).

Sim, Stuart, *Jean-François Lyotard* (New York: Prentice Hall, 1996).

Smart, Barry, *Foucault, Marxism and Critique* (London: Routledge, 1989).

Index

CPSIA information can be obtained
at www.ICGtesting.com
Printed in the USA
BVOW01s2027211116

468547BV00002B/2/P